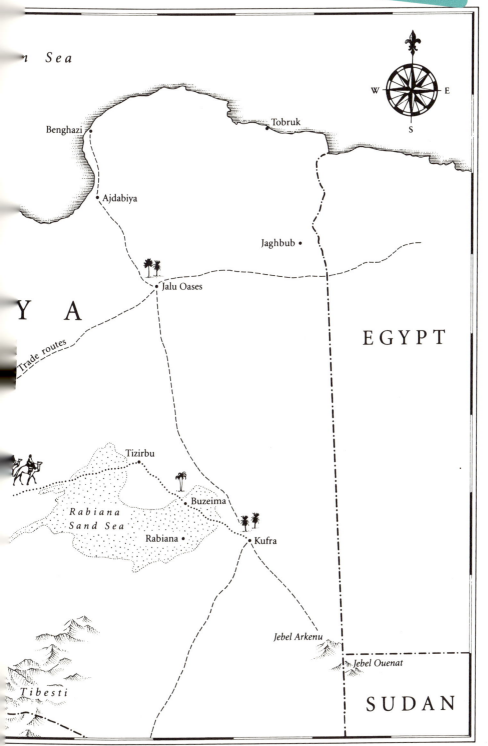

n Sea

Benghazi

Tobruk

Ajdabiya

Jaghbub

Jalu Oases

Y A

EGYPT

Trade routes

Tizirbu

Buzeima

*Rabiana Sand Sea*

Rabiana

Kufra

*Jebel Arkenu*

*Jebel Ouenat*

*Tibesti*

SUDAN

# SOUTH FROM BARBARY

2

# SOUTH FROM BARBARY

*Along the Slave Routes of
the Libyan Sahara*

JUSTIN MAROZZI

HarperCollins*Publishers*

HarperCollins*Publishers*
77–85 Fulham Palace Road,
Hammersmith, London W6 8JB

www.fireandwater.com

Published by HarperCollins*Publishers* 2001

1 3 5 7 9 8 6 4 2

Copyright © Justin Marozzi 2001

The Author asserts the moral right to
be identified as the author of this work

A catalogue record for this book
is available from the British Library

ISBN 0 00 257053 X

Set in Sabon by
Rowland Phototypesetting Limited,
Bury St Edmunds, Suffolk

Printed and bound in Great Britain by
Clays Ltd, St Ives plc

To Julia

The hour is nigh; the waning queen walks forth to rule the later night,
Crowned with the sparkle of a star, and throned on orb of ashen light:
The wolf-tail sweeps the paling East to leave a deeper gloom behind.
And dawn uprears her shining head, sighing with semblance of a wind:

The highlands catch yon Orient gleam, while purpling still the lowlands lie;
And pearly mists, the morning-pride, soar incense-like to greet the sky.
The horses neigh, the camels groan, the torches gleam, the cressets flare;
The town of canvas falls, and man with din and dint invadeth air . . .

Do what thy manhood bids thee do, from none but self expect applause,
He noblest lives and noblest dies who makes and keeps his self-made laws.
All other life is living death, a world where none but phantoms dwell,
A breath, a wind, a sound, a voice, a tinkling of the camel-bell . . .

Wend not thy way with brow serene, fear not thy humble tale to tell:—
The whispers of the Desert-wind, the tinkling of the camel's bell.

*THE KASÎDAH OF HÂJÎ ABDÛ AL-YAZDI*
SIR RICHARD BURTON

# Acknowledgements

have incurred many debts over the course of the past two years. First of all I would like to thank my parents Silvio and Rosemary Marozzi for all their support and encouragement. Few parents can contemplate their only son disappearing into the Sahara with much enthusiasm but mine were a constant source of practical advice and humour. In particular, I would like to thank my father for introducing me to the romantic world of North Africa – the Barbary that once was – when he took me to Tripoli for the first time in 1992.

I am grateful to Andrew Roberts for his early assistance when I was contemplating ending two years of tropical indolence working for the *Financial Times* in Manila and wondering what to do next. Andrew kindly introduced me to his agent, Georgina Capel, without whom I would never have been able to make the journey or publish this book. I would like to thank Georgina for all her help and enthusiasm throughout this project.

In London I owe a great deal to Shane Winser, director of the Royal Geographical Society's excellent Expedition Advisory Center. Shane put at my disposal a number of extremely useful materials, not least those relating to desert navigation and the obscure but priceless piece on how to tell a dud camel from a top of the range desert-ready thoroughbred. I am also grateful to Shane and her husband Nigel, director of the RGS, for putting me in touch with several desert explorers of various vintages. Times have changed since the heyday of exploration in the nineteenth century, when the RGS sent British expeditions to the unexplored corners of the globe, but is is thanks to people like the Winsers that the RGS remains such a mighty institution.

Before I left for North Africa I consulted a variety of sour
Anthony Cazalet gave me numerous memorable whiskies w
we pored over Michelin maps of the Sahara together and assu
my travel companion and me that we would be 'bloody cold
the desert, whatever precautions we took. He was right. Brigac
Rupert Harding-Newman and his wife, Muriel, who invited
to their home in Scotland, were generous hosts and provided ،
great deal of practical information on desert travel. Sir Wilfred
Thesiger, the last great desert explorer, was a mine of useful
advice on the two occasions I consulted him.

Mohammed al Mahdi of the School of Oriental and African
Studies in London was an enlightening, if somewhat eccentric
Arabic teacher. Although one of the expressions he recommended
for use in Libya helped put us under hotel arrest for a week
another had the benefit of saving us several hundred dollars when
procuring a desert guide in Tmissah.

My travelling companion Ned Cecil deserves special thanks
for agreeing to my foolish suggestion of crossing the Libyan
Sahara by camel. Despite a definite aversion to washing up duties,
he was a splendid companion in the desert and brave enough to
travel alone with me for almost three months.

In Tripoli I owe a particular debt to Othman, an old friend
of my father's. During my various visits to the Libyan capital over
the years, he has been unstinting in his hospitality. He provided
enormous support and guidance while we planned the expedition
from Tripoli and rolled out the red carpet again on our return
from Kufra. Dr Noel Guckian, British Consul in Tripoli and Eric
Taylor, Vice-consul, were kind hosts and provided useful reading
suggestions.

With a certain caveat I should also thank Taher Aboulgassim,
the travel agent who was one of our first ports of call in Tripoli.
If it had not been for Taher we would never have met the irre-
placeable Mohammed Ali. My gratitude to Taher is slightly tem-
pered by the fact that he still owes us several thousand pounds
for the five camels we sold him. It is of course highly unlikely
we will ever see the money again but I would like to point out

to anyone who might hire, or even purchase, five handsome camels from the Ghadames, that they still belong to Ned and me.

Mohammed Ali was heroically selfless in his efforts to help us get started from Ghadames. Without his tireless assistance, we might never have found the necessary camels or guide. He also took the time to visit us in the desert one week after we had left Ghadames to check we were all right. I am grateful to him for his friendship.

Over the course of our 1,150-mile journey by camel, we were fortunate enough to be aided by a succession of desert guides. Abd al Wahab introduced us to the rigours of an extended expedition across the Sahara with patience and courtesy. Salek Habib, a jauntier character by far, took us through the fearsome dunes of the Awbari Sand Sea in his own inimitable, some would say chaotic, way. Saleh Hassan stepped in at short notice to guide us from Germa to Murzuk. Mohammed Othman, our last and at seventy-six our oldest guide, was perhaps the most inspirational figure we met on our travels, and a walking advertisement for the benefits of a lifetime's diet of camels' milk and dates.

The hospitality of desert peoples is legendary. Throughout Libya we were overwhelmed by the friendly reception we encountered from rich and poor alike. Special thanks are due to Othman al Hashashe in Ghadames, Salek in Idri, Ahmed Sherif and his family in Murzuk, the ebullient D.I.Y. obsessive Muftah Kilani in Tmissah and Faiz Mohammed in Tizirbu. In Kufra, Abd as Salem came to our rescue shortly after we had been placed under hotel arrest. Without his intervention our stay in the Hotel Sudan would have been considerably lengthier and less comfortable. All of these men went far beyond the call of duty to make us feel welcome in their homes.

Michael Fishwick and Kate Morris at HarperCollins were patient and excellent editors, providing invaluable assistance on the maniscript. Thanks are also due to Lee Motley for her jacket design and Cecilia Amies in the publicity department. In Morocco

I would like to thank Michael Parkin for the loan of his idyllic townhouse in the Rif mountains where I spent three happy months writing this book. My historical research was helped in no small part by John Wright's three excellent histories of Libya.

Last and most important, I wish to thank Julia, the love of my life. A guardian angel during the long days and nights in the desert, she has tolerated my lengthy absences with a minimum of complaint and a maximum of understanding. I am grateful to her for the many hours she has spent helping me on the manuscript and, more than anything else, for her love. This book is dedicated to her.

# Contents

# CHAPTER I

# Desert Fever

*'Basically, you're going to be bloody cold.'*

ANTHONY CAZALET

'Help me with this camel,' said Abd al Wahab, while Ned and I were busily applying Elizabeth Arden Visible Difference Eight Hour Cream to our faces. Abd al Wahab, our guide, understood camels. They were part of his world. Moisturizer was not. Hastily we packed it away, put the finishing touches to the last camel load, and marched off into the desert. We were under way.

For six years I had longed to make the journey we were now beginning. In a way I owed it to my father, for it was he who had taken me to Libya for the first time. Together, in the warmth of February, we had walked through Tripoli as the wind streamed in from the sea; past the forbidding castle, which had seen 1,000 years of wars and intrigues between marauding corsairs, pirates, Spaniards, Italians, Englishmen, Arabs and Turks, and still stared out impassively towards the southern shores of Sicily; through the ancient Suq al Mushir and into an exotic medley of sights, sounds and smells that roused the senses and stirred the imagination. Throngs of prodigiously built matrons haggled ferociously with softly spoken gold- and silversmiths for jewellery they could not afford. Some were still dressed in the same white, sheet-like *farrashiya*s their forebears had worn hundreds of years before.

Others hid behind their gaudy *hijab*s (Islamic veils) as they sailed through the narrow alleys hunting for perfume. Deeper into the market, beneath a minaret from which the *muaddin* was calling the faithful to prayer in haunting, ululating cadences, we had found a dilapidated café, its courtyard open to the sky, and taken our places alongside men playing cards and drinking mint tea, hunched protectively over their bubbling *shisha* pipes stuffed with apple-flavoured tobacco.

My father's old friend Othman had taken us for a drive around the city in his Peugeot 504, a brave wreck of a car that had somehow survived several decades of neglect. In the squalid port area, men pored over slabs of tuna and disputed prices with the fishermen. One of these, a great hulk of a man, was tenderizing an octopus, throwing it to the ground, picking it up by its tentacles and then hurling it down again and again.

'We call Tripoli ar Roz al Bahr, the Bride of the Sea,' Othman told me as we drove past whitewashed houses along the old corniche, watched over by the palm trees that swayed in the coastal breeze. There was something unmistakably forlorn and beautiful about this city, a sense of wistfulness and a largely unspoken resentment. For centuries it had been a thriving commercial metropolis – cosmopolitan, elegant and refined. Now there was nostalgia and regret in the peeling paint of the colonial Turkish and Italian mansions that, one by one, were being targeted for demolition as vainglorious symbols of the white intruders onto African soil. Thirty years of the revolutionary regime had almost brought the city to its knees – cars fell apart, homes crumbled away, roads rotted – and now sanctions held the city in a tight and unforgiving embrace. My father knew Tripoli well. He had got caught up in the 1969 revolution and had met the young Muammar al Gaddafi just as the old order of King Idris was being consigned to oblivion, but for me it was all new and instantly, wildly, romantic.

Before we left, my father took me to one of Tripoli's few English-language bookshops, where I picked up the book that for the first time thrust the desert before me in all its guises.

Here was silence and loneliness, the glory of wide African skies, unbroken plains of sand and rock, loyalty and companionship, adventure, treachery and betrayal. It was an account of the 1818–20 expedition into the Libyan Sahara led by Joseph Ritchie, 'a gentleman of great science and ability' – a diplomat, surgeon and friend of Keats – tasked by the British government to reach and chart the River Niger from the north, one of the last remaining puzzles of African exploration. The enormity of his mission was not matched by corresponding resources and eight months after leaving Tripoli disguised as a Muslim convert, the penniless Ritchie had perished from fever in the insalubrious town of Murzuk, leaving his ebullient companion Lt George Francis Lyon to record their adventures for posterity. Back in London, reading his high-spirited tale, I felt the pull of the desert and started to dream of a similar journey by camel.

Like many ideas, it eventually faded away into a distant fantasy. Six years later, I was working in Manila for the *Financial Times*, when Ned, an old friend from school days, arrived unexpectedly. During lightning trips south to visit the jungle headquarters of the Moro Islamic Liberation Front rebels, and north to go duck shooting with a gun-toting provincial governor, we started discussing a longer expedition. I had spent almost two years in the Philippines and felt it was time to move on. Ned, a Dorset farmer, was feeling equally restless. We had travelled together several times over the years, from Hong Kong to Costa Rica, and knew and got on well enough with each other to attempt a more serious journey. Deep in the tropical jungle of Maguindanao I revived the long-dormant idea of crossing the Libyan Sahara by camel.

Ned would be the ideal companion. Solid and unflappable, with a keen sense of the absurd, he had travelled widely, was always ready for an adventure, and was practical in a way that I was not. Several years before, he had travelled across the Andes on horseback, and so was probably good with knots and would know what to do if a camel fell sick. At least, that was how I saw him. The truth was that neither of us knew the first thing

3

about desert travel, but with some research in London and a reconnaissance trip to Libya much of our ignorance could be put right. The idea appealed to Ned at once. So much so that he wanted to know whether I was really serious about the expedition. I told him I was going with or without him. He said he was coming. Perhaps he felt the same lure of the desert. His great-uncle David Stirling, founder of the SAS, had fought in the Libyan Sahara during the Second World War, taking men like Wilfred Thesiger, the great desert explorer, on daring raids behind enemy lines.

From the jungle we returned to Manila where Joseph Estrada, the flamboyant former movie star, hard-drinking womanizer and self-confessed philanderer, had just been elected president in a landslide vote. The country looked as though it was heading back to the extravagant corruption of the Marcos era. Foreign investors cringed nervously on the sidelines, wondering if the currency would fall through the floor again. One by one, the Marcos cronies were welcomed back into the fold. The stock market was plummeting. Watching the rot set in again was depressing. 'See you in Libya,' said Ned at the airport. My boss thought otherwise, but it was time to leave.

Six weeks later I was back in England planning the journey with Ned. Poring over maps of Libya in the Royal Geographical Society, we decided we would retrace the old slave-trade routes into Africa, making our way across the desert in a south-easterly direction by way of Ghadames and Murzuk, two of the three principal slave-trade centres in Libya, to the third, the fabled and inaccessible oasis of Kufra. A brief trip to Libya in September confirmed it would be wisest to start the expedition from Ghadames, an ancient and once prosperous Saharan town 300 miles south-west of Tripoli. Although camels were not as plentiful as they had been 150 years ago, when Ghadames was still a major centre of the slave trade, they would be more easily procured there than in the capital. More importantly, so would a guide who understood, as we did not, the practicalities of desert travel.

From Ghadames we would head south-east, for the most part

skirting the wastes of the Awbari Sand Sea, to the small outpost of Idri. Then it would be several days' hard going across the mountainous dunes to Germa, which several thousand years ago had been the capital of the fearsome Garamantes. This desert warrior race had once held sway over vast swathes of the Sahara between the Nile and the Atlantic and had, until its final defeat, refused to be cowed by the mighty Roman armies sent to subdue it. Next on our route was the central town of Murzuk, where in 1819 the gallant Ritchie, betrayed by avaricious tribesmen, floundering in delirium and beset by agonizing kidney pains, had succumbed to fever. After Murzuk it would be a week's march or so to the remote settlement of Tmissah, the last town for 350 miles, and from there a bleak journey to Kufra via a handful of tiny oases – Wau al Kabir, Wau an Namus, Tizirbu and Buzeima – that would test our camels' endurance to its limits. Kufra, the far-flung oasis town that lay on the most easterly, and least old, of the country's three slave-trade routes, formerly home of the fiercely ascetic Sanusi confraternity, would be our endpoint. One of the most romantic and elusive Saharan oases, it had remained unseen by Western eyes until the late nineteenth century when the pioneering German explorer Gerhard Rohlfs arrived, only to find a hostile reception from xenophobic tribesmen, from whom he narrowly escaped with his life.

The best time to start our journey would be in December, to allow us enough time to cross the desert in the cooler temperatures of winter. If we left much later than that, the weather would make travel unrealistically difficult and dangerous. The next thing to arrange was some language training. The Arabic I had picked up over the years from trips to the Middle East and North Africa would not be sufficient for a long journey in the Libyan desert with guides who do not speak English. I duly enlisted for a course in colloquial Arabic at the School of Oriental and African Studies in London.

Several days later, a small bespectacled man in a thick woollen three-piece suit (tailored in Cairo) greeted me warmly in the SOAS language centre and introduced himself as Mohammed al

Mahdi. I had told the school I would be spending several months in Libya and would prefer to learn colloquial Libyan Arabic rather than the more customary and widely spoken Egyptian. Mohammed was my man. An Egyptian who had spent five years in Tripoli in the early seventies teaching Libyan fighter pilots English, he was the only teacher in the school familiar with the dialect. His opening announcement was inauspicious. 'I felt a complete stranger in Libya for the first ten days,' he told me. 'I just couldn't decipher their dialect. It was like a completely foreign language. I didn't know what to do.' This was particularly galling because the little Arabic I knew was Egyptian.

For the next six weeks before our departure for Tripoli I put myself in Mohammed's hands. I asked him to keep the lessons as relevant as possible. In practice this meant conjuring up hypothetical desert situations and finding the appropriate expression in Arabic. Lessons alternated between translating phrases such as 'Please help me unload this camel,' and 'I am thirsty because I have been in the sun too much today,' to spontaneous asides from Mohammed on a bewildering range of subjects, some connected with Libya, others concerning the various women he had been chatting up in the coffee room. Sitting across the table from me as I waited for him to conjugate a verb, he would suddenly remove his glasses and look at me with an expression of avuncular sympathy.

'Do you know how to ride a camel?' he would ask solemnly. 'It's absolutely awful. Be very, very careful.' He might then return briefly to the verb in hand before interrupting himself again to deliver another piece of advice. For an effete urban Cairene who had hardly set foot in the desert, he was not afraid to venture strong opinions on the Sahara and its people. 'I am positive you will never have any problems in the desert,' he declared. 'It is true the people may lack polish, yes they do, but that does not mean they are dangerous or have evil intentions, so don't worry at all. You will be 100 per cent protected by the people.'

For those occasions during our travels when things were not proceeding well, Mohammed advised a particular expression. By

6

its direct appeal to the Almighty, the judicious use of '*Itaq Illeh*' (Fear God) should ensure we were not ripped off or misled by an unscrupulous merchant or guide. We would use it several times on the journey to amusing, if not entirely profitable, effect. One afternoon he suggested the stronger term '*Enta gazma*' (You are a pair of shoes) to deter any troublemakers, before deciding against it. 'No, no, no, on second thoughts you must not say this because the response will be fatal. This is considered a very big insult. Please don't use it. If anyone said that to me I would spring at his throat and kill him.'

While the Arabic lessons proceeded at this relaxed pace, we sought advice from various quarters. First we consulted Anthony Cazalet, an old friend of Ned's and the rotund veteran of several trans-Saharan expeditions by car. Apart from an apparently inexhaustible supply of smooth Scottish malts, this yielded very little. The sum of his guidance was distilled into the frequently repeated observation: 'Basically, you're going to be bloody cold.' Unfortunately, this did not lead to any practical suggestions about how we might combat such extreme temperatures. Might it be a good idea, we asked, to take down sleeping bags, or wear special fleece jackets? To which the answer was that it really didn't matter. Whatever we did, whatever equipment we took, we were going to be 'bloody cold'. This amused him greatly and he appeared to take a perverse delight in telling us how freezing we were going to be. Not knowing at this stage how accurate his forecast was, we thought little more of it, consoling ourselves with the thought that perhaps he felt the cold more than most, although his generous padding suggested otherwise. Besides, he had a certain reputation for travelling in great comfort, if not splendour. On one desert expedition he had shocked his companions by turning up with a deluxe camp-bed and, more eccentrically still, a 'thunder-box' – a portable commode. Travelling by camel, such luxuries would be beyond us.

Through the Royal Geographical Society I was put in touch with Brigadier Rupert Harding-Newman, who had been one of the first men to travel in the Libyan desert in the twenties and thirties in heavily modified Model T and Model A Fords. Well into his eighties, he was still straight-backed and sprightly and he and his wife welcomed me into their home outside Inverness with great hospitality. Over a fine chicken pie and claret, he talked with relish about those ground-breaking days of Saharan exploration and showed me an old film of improbably built Fords sliding down mountainous sand dunes before grinding to a halt and having to be dug out and started up again. As the youthful cook, quartermaster and mechanic on those expeditions from Cairo led by the desert explorer Major Ralph Bagnold, he had always taken a supply of 'fancy biscuits' to help keep up morale. He and his companions would invariably stop for elevenses and afternoon tea. We might like to do the same, he suggested. It was only later that we learnt such stops were impossible when travelling by camel. Whereas Harding-Newman and team had been racing across sand flats at speeds of up to sixty miles an hour, we would have to be content with the camel's more leisurely pace of three miles an hour. Making such ponderous progress through the desert, more often than not we could not even afford to stop for lunch. That did not stop us thinking wistfully of the Harding-Newman tea and biscuit breaks.

Our last port of call was to Britain's greatest living explorer. At eighty-eight, Sir Wilfred Thesiger, the man who had twice crossed the Empty Quarter of Arabia by camel in the late 1940s, was now marooned in a genteel retirement home in the suburbs of Surrey. He was waiting for us by the entrance, impeccably clad in a thirty-year-old three-piece suit. As we walked across to the neighbouring golf club where we were to lunch, he leant heavily on my arm, quietly reminiscing about his times in the desert.

I had been advised not to be too discouraged by this interview with Thesiger. He would almost certainly pooh-pooh the whole idea and dismiss our proposed journey as a meaningless stunt. Fortunately this was quite untrue. He was obviously cheered by our visit and honest about the difficulties we would face in trying to get an expedition like this off the ground. 'Your trouble will be that people will say why on earth go by camel,' he said. 'They'll say you can do the journey perfectly well in a car. Arab life and tradition has all changed. It used to consist of loyalty to one's travelling companion, undergoing hardship together and so on. When you had that you could count on them. They wouldn't know how to do it now. They would think it absurd.' He stopped himself for an instant. 'Oh dear, I'm being very depressing I'm afraid.'

He recommended the Royal Geographical Society for maps of Libya, in particular those that had been used by the SAS and Long Range Desert Group in the Second World War. His cold azure blue eyes glowed as he recalled the campaigns in Libya, when he had approached David Stirling to volunteer for action, saying he spoke Arabic and knew how to travel in the desert. He was taken on and subsequently fought with the SAS behind enemy lines where he 'shot up' tentfuls of soldiers in enemy camps.

As far as riding camels was concerned, he said it took some time to get used to their strange loping gait. 'The first day I rode one I found it very hard to get up the next day,' he said. 'You swing around a lot when they walk.' He had once ridden 115 miles in twenty-four hours in what is now the northern Sudanese province of Darfur, and did not know of anyone who had ridden farther in one day. Travelling long distances with a small caravan, however, it would be inadvisable for us to go faster than walking pace. The camels would not be able to sustain it. Besides, with heavy loads, trotting would be a perilous affair that risked throwing off and smashing valuable *bidoun*s of water.

After lunch, we returned to his modest room decorated with a few tokens culled from a long, nomadic life: a walking stick made from a giraffe's shinbone, a tattered Oriental rug, a black-and-white photograph of Marrakech. Burton, Conrad, Kipling, Sassoon, Buchan and Thesiger on the bookshelves.

On equipment, he was a ruthless minimalist: 'I wanted to meet the Bedouin on their own terms with no concessions,' he insisted. For an Old Etonian from Edwardian England, this meant foregoing such staples of travel as tables and chairs. He had travelled barefoot in the desert, armed always with a dagger and a gun. This might be problematic in Gaddafi's Libya. Radios, as used by Harry St John Philby, the second man ever to cross the Empty Quarter in 1932, were out. 'When Philby travelled with the Bedouin he liked having a radio to listen to the Lord's Test Match,' he growled into his strawberry and vanilla ice cream. 'To me that would have wrecked the whole thing.'

Back in London we were not having much joy with maps. We needed to get our hands on the Russian Survey maps, the most detailed and accurate maps of the Sahara, which were proving difficult to locate. Stanfords said it might take two months. We needed them in two weeks. Eventually, I tracked down a supplier on the Internet and ordered a set by email. Nothing happened. I telephoned Munich. The German voice on the other end of the telephone said the maps might arrive before we left for Libya but appeared unconcerned about whether they did. In the meantime we had to make do with the US Tactical Pilotage Charts from Stanfords, no doubt helpful if you were flying over the Libyan desert, but curiously short of detail for an expedition travelling by land.

With several days to go before our departure we paid a swift visit to Field & Trek on Baker Street to buy sleeping bags and other equipment. Sleeping bags proved easy. We lay inside three-season down bags while an assistant enthused about their many features which would make life so comfortable. Choosing walking boots involved a lengthy discourse from him on the merits of Gore-tex versus leather. Ned, easily bored by detail, started to look distracted, as though he wished he were somewhere else. His patience, always finite, was running out.

On to socks, which surely would be straightforward. Before we could pick up a pair, the assistant launched into a glowing recommendation of Coolmax, some sort of high-tech material. Coolmax socks, designed for walking in summer, apparently boasted five special features, such as reinforced heels, ability to wick away moisture from the feet, and so it went on. I wondered what Thesiger would have made of all this. When it came to discussing the best way to filter water, mutiny broke out between the assistant and his more senior colleague. The latter, spotting the chance to talk gadgetry in front of gadget neophytes, had emerged from the farthest recesses of the shop. A peevish argument broke out between them over whether we were better off using iodine treatment or taking a more expensive water filter. Ned had even less interest in this conversation than I had and headed fast upstairs for the exit, past a Field & Trek nylon washing line with four special features.

The next problem was that neither of us knew how to navigate. A Royal Geographical Society publication on desert navigation was explicit on this point. It was imperative that every expedition should include 'a meticulous, even perfectionist, navigator who worships at the altar of Truth rather than the altar of convenient results'. I had used a compass a long time ago while in the school cadet force. It was not much to go on. Ned was probably more proficient but did not appear to take much interest in the sort of equipment we would need. Sometimes he would telephone and in a curiously detached way make noises about buying a theodolite so we could navigate by the stars, but eventually nothing more was said of it. Perhaps he was waiting for me to find one.

Harding-Newman had shown me the famous Bagnold sun compass, a cleverly designed navigational device that made use of the shadows cast by the sun and was designed to be mounted on the front of a vehicle, but said it would not be of much use to us travelling by camel. Thesiger had surprised us by confessing he had never been able to navigate by the stars and nor did he know how to use a sun compass. My uncle, a retired naval officer, warned us off sextants. The Royal Navy used to run two-week courses teaching men how to use them, he said, and after two weeks they still had only the most basic knowledge of the instruments. We decided on the less romantic, small and inexpensive, battery-powered Global Positioning System devices to back up our compasses. These would pinpoint our location on the globe to within 10 metres or so.

Shortly before we left, the Royal Geographical Society sent me a recent guide on travelling with camels written by Michael Asher, the British desert explorer. It contained plenty of useful advice on how to choose camels, saddles and guides. Asher, a former SAS man, was insistent on fitness. 'Whatever country you are trekking in, travelling by camel is inevitably going to involve a great deal of walking. Cardio-vascular fitness is therefore the main area to concentrate on in preparing yourself physically for a camel-trek; jogging, long-distance walking, cycling, swimming. Loading camels usually requires a certain amount of lifting so weight training is also appropriate.'

Neither Ned nor I had ever been great fitness aficionados or taken exercise for as long as we could remember. At Ned's house in Dorset, we were quizzed closely on our preparations by a friend of his. Julian Freeman-Attwood was a mountaineer who announced rather grandly that he only climbed unclimbed peaks. We told him how we planned to get across the desert and he looked at us in amused disbelief. A veteran of many expeditions around the world, he concluded we were thoroughly unprepared.

'It's worse than an expedition planned on the back of an envelope,' he said with authority. 'You haven't even got an envelope.'

Two days later we flew to Tunis.

# CHAPTER II

# Bride of the Sea

*Properly to write the wonderful story of Tripoli, daughter of sea and desert, one must be not only an accomplished historian, a cultivated archaeologist and an expert in ethnology, but profoundly versed in Arabic and the fundamental beliefs and general practices of Mohammedanism, as well as the local customs of that great religion, coloured as it is by differing environment. If one aims to give a clear exposition of this enthralling though tragic coast of northern Africa, he must be a thorough student of political economy, too, with a world outlook on cause and effect in government.*

MABEL LOOMIS TODD, *TRIPOLI THE MYSTERIOUS*

*Happy for poor forlorn, dusky, naked Africa, had she never seen the pale visage or met the Satanic brow of the European Christian. Does any man in his senses, who believes in God and Providence, think that the wrongs of Africa will go forever unavenged? . . . And the time of us Englishmen will come next – our day of infamy! unless we show ourselves worthy of that transcendant position in which Providence has placed us, at the pinnacle of the empires of Earth, as the leaders and champions of universal freedom.*

JAMES RICHARDSON, *TRAVELS IN THE GREAT DESERT OF SAHARA IN THE YEARS OF 1845 AND 1846*

We hired a car in Tunis airport and drove to Jerba, en route to the Libyan border. In 1992, the United Nations imposed sanctions on

Libya to bring to heel the alleged culprits of the 1988 bombing of Pan Am Flight 103 over the Scottish town of Lockerbie, in which 270 people were killed. Since that date, all flights into and out of the country had been prohibited, leaving overland travel from Tunisia or a boat from Malta as the main alternatives to reach Tripoli.

For as long as I was behind the wheel Ned was a difficult passenger. Repeatedly, he told me what a poor driver I was and how unsafe he felt. Coming from a man whose entire driving career seemed to have consisted of writing off one car after another, this was especially irritating. I took exception to his comments and drove even faster. As night fell on us and the road became progressively harder to navigate, Ned's warnings became ever more insistent. I told him to shut up. Moments later, to my horror, I found I was driving straight towards a head-on collision with an enormous lorry. Ned shouted something furiously, I jerked the wheel to the right, swerved across the road and only narrowly managed to keep the car on four wheels. We skidded violently to a halt and one of the tyres burst. 'Justin, you're a complete idiot,' he said, fuming. I let him drive for the rest of the night.

We slept on Jerba, an island that was, according to the Greek geographer Strabo, 'regarded as the land of the Lotus-eaters mentioned by Homer; and certain tokens of this are pointed out – both an altar of Odysseus and the fruit itself; for the tree which is called the lotus abounds in the island and its fruit is delightful'. Herodotus also mentions the islanders, 'who live entirely on the fruit of the lotus-tree. The lotus fruit is about the size of the lentisk berry, and in sweetness resembles the date. The Lotophagi even succeeded in obtaining from it a sort of wine.'

Two hours into our taxi ride to Tripoli the next morning, we joined the languid snake of cars wriggling across the Libyan border. Our bags were searched and I was asked whether I had a camera. I was then led into a cavernous warehouse, derelict save for a rickety table that stood in an inch of dirty water, behind which sat a Libyan customs official. All around him piles of rotting debris emerged from their bed of slime and wafted up a disgusting stench. His temper appeared as foul as his surroundings. He looked me up and down, almost incredulous, as I was, that I should be referred to him for possessing a camera. Other customs officers were inspecting the boots of Mercedes saloons for contraband. I was small beer. Gruffly, he condescended to stamp my passport with the information that I was carrying photographic equipment and waved our car through. Outside, the first of many propaganda portraits of Muammar al Gaddafi welcomed us to the Great Socialist People's Libyan Arab Jamahiriya, or GSPLAJ for short. Sporting a hard hat and shades, he was presiding benignly over a scene of oil wells in the Sahara. The border area was an ugly scattering of buildings and warehouses and the heat was intense, but none of this mattered. We were a step nearer the desert.

Before preparing for the camel journey in Tripoli, we first had to visit the Roman ruins of Sabratha, forty miles west of the capital. With its more august sister city of Leptis Magna, 120 miles to the east, Sabratha is one of the Mediterranean's great Roman sites. If it had been in Tunisia, the city would have been clogged with tourists. Thanks to Libya's status as one of the world's last remaining pariah states, we had the place to ourselves.

Sabratha dates back to Phoenician times, probably between the late fourth and seventh centuries BC, when it was established as an emporium or trading post, but is an essentially Roman creation. Sabratha, Leptis Magna and Oea (as Romans knew Tripoli) together formed the *provincia Tripolitania* – province of the three cities – created by the Emperor Diocletian in AD 284. All three both grew through commerce with the Garamantes, the great warrior-traders of southern Libya, and through commercial exchange with Rome. Before the Romans set foot in North Africa, the Phoenicians had introduced agriculture to the coastline, encouraging the cultivation of olives, vines and figs. Tripolitania was, above all, a great exporter of olive oil for use in

Rome's baths and oil lamps, if not its kitchens. The Romans considered African olive oil too coarse for their palates.

After olive oil came wild animals, exported in staggering numbers to feed the bloodlust of Rome's circusgoers. Tens of thousands of elephants, flamingoes, ostriches, lions, and wild boar were shipped to their destruction. Titus marked the inauguration of the Colosseum by dispatching 9,000 animals into the arena to fight the gladiators. Augustus recorded that 3,500 African animals were killed in the twenty-six games he gave to the people, while Trajan had 2,246 large animals slaughtered in one day. On one occasion, Caesar sent 400 lions into the arena to kill or be killed by gladiators, outdone by Pompey, who sent in 600. North Africa's 'nursery of wild beasts', as noted by Strabo, could not take such wholesale decimation and its animal population never recovered.

By contrast with this northern-bound traffic, the desert trade, whose staple products would later include gold, ivory and ostrich feathers, was not yet advanced. 'Our only intercourse is the trade in the precious stone imported from Ethiopia which we call the carbuncle,' remarked Pliny in the first century AD. With abundant sources of slaves in both Asia and Europe, the Romans felt little need to tap the Sahara. Negro slaves, besides, could be procured from the North African coast without having to venture farther south.

We walked slowly through the Forum Basilica, where Claudius Maximus, Proconsul of Africa, had acquitted the Latin writer Apuleius of Madura of a fabricated charge of witchcraft in AD 157. Behind us the magnificent theatre, a warm terracotta in the fading afternoon sun, dominated the eastern part of the city. It was built in the late second century at the outset of the Severan dynasty, a time that would prove to be Roman Africa's finest hour. It is hard to imagine a more romantic or dramatic spot for a theatre: the cool blue sea is visible only yards behind the three-storey *scaenae frons* that towers 25 metres above the stage. Gracious marble reliefs on the stage front depict the three Muses, the goddess Fortuna, Mercury with the infant Dionysus, the

Judgement of Paris, Hercules, and personifications of Rome and Sabratha joining hands alongside soldiers. Intoxicated by his plans to recreate the Roman Empire, Mussolini reinaugurated the theatre in 1937, almost 1,800 years after its birth. Inside, we came across a small family of Libyans from Tripoli, the only other visitors in Sabratha that afternoon. Passing the crumbling mosaics of the seaward baths, unprotected from the elements, we headed to the easternmost part of Sabratha, to the serene Temple of Isis, smoked cigarettes and stared across at the elegant ruins of the city as a lilac sunset flooded across the sea.

Anxious to press on the next morning, we commandeered a taxi to take us the last few miles to Tripoli. Gleaming white, it rose before us, staring out across the Mediterranean as it had done for three millennia since the bold seafaring Phoenicians established a trading post here. For centuries it had been the principal terminus of the slave-trade routes of Tripolitania that penetrated across the Sahara deep into Black Africa. Today, the city steamed under a shocking noon sun, its fierce glare an unforgettable feature of arrival for as long as anyone can remember. 'When we approached, we were blinded by the brilliant whiteness of the city from which the burning rays of the sun were reflected. I was convinced that rightly is Tripoli called the "White City",' wrote the Arab traveller At Tigiani during his visit of 1307–8.

Arriving by boat from Jerba on 17 May 1845 James Richardson, the opinionated British explorer and anti-slave-trade campaigner, part of whose travels in Libya we would be following, thought it massive and imposing. He admired the slender lime-washed towers and minarets that rose towards the heavens, dazzling in the shimmering sunlight. But, he went on deflatingly, 'such is the delusion of all these sea-coast Barbary towns; at a distance and without, beauty and brilliancy, but near and within, filth and wretchedness'.

We checked in at a small hotel in Gargarsh, formerly the American part of town in the more cosmopolitan, pre-revolution times of King Idris. In those days, the streets were lined with foreign restaurants and eating out in Tripoli was a joy. If you were looking for Greek food, you could choose between Zorba, the Akropol in front of the Italian Cathedral, and the Parthenon in the Shooting and Fishing Club. If it was Italian you were after, there was Delfino, Romagna and the Riviera, while Chicken on Wheels, Black Cat and Hollywood Grill catered for the thousands of Americans in town, together with a long list of French, Tunisian and Lebanese restaurants. Now they had all gone, replaced by the occasional hamburger bar and second-rate Libyan pizza outlet. Here in Gargarsh, a rusting miniature Eiffel Tower, which once had marked the hottest nightspot in town and was now home to the local post office, was all that remained of those livelier days.

On the ground floor of the hotel were the offices of a small tourism company owned by a man called Taher Aboulgassim, whom I had met during my visit to Libya the previous September. He was a smooth, straight-talking businessman in his mid-thirties, one of the new generation of Libyan entrepreneurs, who had been intrigued by the plans I had put to him. No-one had attempted anything like this in recent years, he had informed me, but he would do everything in his power to assist us with the purchase of camels, selection of guides and so on. He had another office in his home town of Ghadames, from where we would probably set off into the desert. During the three months that I would be back in England, he would begin preparations on my behalf and would be waiting for us when we got to Tripoli. The initial encounter inspired confidence. Taher looked like a man we could do business with.

The first hint that arranging a camel trek in Libya might be more difficult than anticipated was that there was no sign of him in his office the next morning.

'Taher no come,' said Hajer, his Sudanese office assistant. He said it with some satisfaction. In a country where little was certain here was an incontrovertible fact, and he relished it.

'Where is he?' I asked.

'No problem. He will come,' he replied with the confident air of one who had inside information.

'What time will he come?'

'Maybe 12 o'clock. Maybe 5 o'clock,' came the vague reply.

'Which one?'

'He will come.'

Hajer's hairstyle, an exuberant greying Afro, suggested a man still caught in the giddiness of the seventies. On times and appointments he was consistently casual. He had heard of our plans and, like his boss Taher, heartily approved of them.

'No-one do anything like this since Second World War,' he declared. Excitable and warm by nature, he launched into a passionate recommendation that we extend our desert crossing into Sudan. 'If you are British and you have money, you can do anything in Sudan,' he promised. 'We like the British too much.'

I told him Ned was a farmer in England.

'Then you must invest in Sudan agriculture,' was the unhesitating reply. 'You will have a letter from the government and then you can do anything. ANYTHING.' His eyes grew large with enthusiasm. 'You want farm? You can buy farm. You want camels? You buy camels. No problem in Sudan. You do ANYTHING you like.' He spoke in an excited, breathless staccato, a patriotic investment adviser in overdrive. There was no stopping him. 'Sudan is VERY, VERY rich country. We have EVERYTHING in Sudan.'

For years Sudan had been one of the poorest countries in the world, crushed by civil war, famine and corrupt, xenophobic governments. None of this had dented Hajer's boundless optimism.

'You must see it. Not for one month or two months. No,' he went on emphatically, 'you must go for nine months.'

'First we must talk to Taher,' I said, trying to steer the conversation around to the present.

'The government will help you too much if you like Sudan agriculture,' he went on, looking meaningfully at Ned.

'Perhaps we can discuss this a little later,' I suggested. 'But could you tell us where Taher is. He should be expecting us.'

Hajer looked upset. He had not expected to be diverted from

his talk on Sudanese agriculture. 'He will come,' he said stubbornly.

Taher did not come. We waited several hours and still there was no sign of him.

'Do you think he's reliable?' asked Ned over lunch in a semi-derelict hotel opposite our own. Like most swimming pools in Tripoli, this one was empty and looked as though it had been for years. Ned looked bored. I was, too, but was used to waiting for appointments in Libya.

'As reliable as you can expect in Libya.'

'Well, it doesn't look like he'll come today. Shall we go to Leptis Magna?' he went on. We waited another couple of hours and returned to the office.

'Taher come tomorrow,' said Hajer, as though he had known this all along.

'Come on, let's go,' said Ned, who had waited long enough.

We called a taxi and drove to the stately ruins of Leptis Magna, Libya's most imposing Roman city.

Leptis owes its greatness to its most famous son Septimius Severus, the first African Roman emperor. He seized power in AD 193, after the murders of the emperors Commodus and Pertinax in quick succession. Elevated to greatness in Rome, Septimius never lost sight of his African origins and Leptis rose to the height of imperial grandeur, becoming one of the foremost cities of the empire. Architects and sculptors descended in droves from Rome and Asia Minor to create monuments such as the two-storey basilica, overwhelming in its sheer scale, gorgeous in its design, paved with marble and ruthlessly decadent, with soaring colonnades of Corinthian columns embellished with shafts of red Egyptian granite. Up went the Arch of Septimius Severus, built in AD 203 for the emperor's visit to his birthplace, an immense testimony to Rome's mighty sway, with marble reliefs detailing triumphal processions, naked winged Victories, captive barbarians and a united imperial family. A new forum was erected, the circus was enlarged and the port rebuilt to accommodate 1,000-ton ships guided into the harbour by a 100-foot lighthouse. Leptis had never known such glory and would never again. When Septimius died campaigning in York in AD 211, the city embarked upon a long decline from which it did not recover. Fifteen centuries later, Louis XIV had many of the city's treasures exported to Paris.

For the art historian Bernard Berenson, Leptis was unforgettable. 'We went on to the Baths, the Palestra, and the Nymphaeum,' he wrote to his wife in 1935. 'Truly imperial, even in their ruins, for one suspects that ruins suggest sublimities that the completed building may not have attained. In their present state they are evocative and romantic to a degree that it would be hard to exaggerate.' Today, we wandered along the shore and clambered undisturbed over these neglected buildings, past piles of fallen columns and discarded pedestals lying strewn under the wide African sky. The hot silence of the place was overpowering. Deep in drifts of sand and choked by spreading trees and plants, Septimius's city slept.

Through his encouragement of camel breeding on the North African littoral, the African emperor had provided a huge fillip to Saharan trade. The merchants of Leptis are thought to have been the first to benefit from the introduction of this animal. The days of the horse, used for centuries to great effect by the formidable Garamantes, were numbered. The camel offered improved performance in the desert, was economical to run, and comfortable to ride. The Romans wasted little time in increasing the numbers of this versatile beast. By AD 363, when Leptis was invaded by the Austurians, a group of tribes from the central region of Sirtica, Count Romanus, commander of Roman troops in Africa, demanded 4,000 camels from the townsmen as his price for intervening on their behalf.

We met Taher in his office the following morning. He appeared taken aback by our arrival, like a burglar caught in the act. Sheepishly he confessed that nothing had been arranged.

'I thought maybe you would not come to Libya,' he said feebly.

'But Taher, I told you exactly when we were going to arrive,' I replied, exasperated. My previous trip to Libya seemed to have been for nothing.

'We have too many problems in Libya,' he said, as though this explained everything.

'Well, it's a great start,' I said, turning to Ned. He was phlegmatic about this first upset to our plans. I should have been, too. Planning anything in advance in Libya was a lost cause. The country didn't work like that. You had to be there on the ground to get anything done.

'Now you are here I will go to talk to my friend,' Taher said more hopefully. 'Maybe you can buy your camels in Tripoli.' It seemed unlikely.

We headed into Tripoli's Old City and threaded our way through Suq al Mushir, the gateway into the *medina*, to drink tea, smoke apple-flavoured tobacco in *shisha* pipes, and mull over our situation, which did not seem particularly promising. On the outside of the old British Consulate on Shar'a al Kuwash (Baker Street) was a plaque put up by the Gaddafi regime describing the building's history. Reflecting the leader's distrust of western imperialism, it referred to the pioneering nineteenth-century missions into the Sahara that left from here as 'the so-called European geographical and explorative scientific expeditions to Africa, which were in essence and as a matter of fact intended to be colonial ones to occupy and colonize vital strategic parts of Africa'.

Built in 1744, it served first as a residence for Ahmed Pasha, founder of the great Karamanli dynasty. Turkey had administered Tripoli since 1551, when Simon Pasha overcame a small force of the Knights of the Order of the Hospital of St John of Jerusalem, who until then had been maintaining the city as 'a Christian oasis in a barbaric desert'. The Karamanlis themselves hailed from the racial mix of Turkish soldiers and administrators who had married native women.

From the second half of the eighteenth century, the building became the British Consulate, from where successive consuls kept London up to date on the Saharan slave trade, various measures to suppress it, and the continued obstruction of such measures by the Turkish authorities. Local officials tended to disregard with impunity Constantinople's imperial *firman*s (decrees) and vizirial orders outlawing the trade for the simple reason that they benefited enormously from it. Typical of the correspondence between London and Tripoli was the instruction in 1778 to the British Consul Richard Tully to provide

> an account of the Trade in Slaves carried on in the Dominions of the Bey of Tripoli, stating the numbers annually brought into them and sold, distinguishing those that are natives of Asia from those that are natives of Africa, and specifying as far as possible, from what parts of Asia and Africa the slaves so sold in the Dominions of the Bey are brought, and stating whether the male slaves are usually castrated.

Such correspondence makes grim reading. For all the British determination to stamp out this 'miserable trade', it continued apace and for more than a century after Tully's time, consuls would write to London of the Turkish authorities' 'apathy and utter indifference' to the slave trade, their 'palpable' neglect and 'flagrant infraction' of orders from Constantinople. In 1848, the sultan prohibited the Turkish governor of Tripoli and his civil servants from trading in slaves and in 1856 slave dealing itself was outlawed throughout the Ottoman empire. But in practice, the trade continued, albeit in reduced volume. In 1878, 100 years after the letter to Tully, Frank Drummond-Hay, the British Consul, was telling the Foreign Office that 'the vigilance required in watching the Slave Trade, in thwarting the devices resorted to by the local authorities in order to evade the execution of the orders for its suppression, in obtaining information on the arrival of slaves by the caravans from the Interior, of intended shipments and other numerous matters in connection with this traffic' justified a substantial increase in his salary.

On the other side of a massive wooden door was the cool marble floor of an elegant courtyard, decorated with plants, on one side of which a worn flight of steps led up to the 'general scientific library' to which the building was now devoted. This was the house in which Miss Tully, sister of the British Consul, composed her fascinating *Narrative of a Ten Years' Residence at Tripoli in Africa* between 1783–93. This doughty lady lived through the great plague of 1785 that carried off a quarter of Tripoli's inhabitants and regularly witnessed slave caravans arriving from the Sahara. One limped into town in the dreadful heat of summer in 1790. 'We were shocked at the horrible state it arrived in,' she wrote. 'For want of water many had died, and others were in so languishing a state, as to expire before any could be administered to save them from the parching thirst occasioned by the heat. The state of the animals was truly shocking; gasping and faint, they could hardly be made to crawl to their several destinations, many dying on their way.'

An intimate of the Pasha of Tripoli's family, Miss Tully heard eyewitness accounts of the assassination in 1790 of Hassan Bey, his eldest son and heir. Sidi Yousef, the Pasha's youngest son and pretender to the throne, had been feuding with his elder brother for some time before announcing he was ready for the sake of the family to effect a reconciliation in front of their mother Lilla Halluma.

> The Bey replied, 'with all his heart' that 'he was ready' upon which Sidy Useph rose quickly from his seat, and called loudly for the Koran – the word he had given to his eunuchs for his pistols, two of which were brought and put into his hands; when he instantly discharged one of them at his brother, seated by his mother's side. The pistol burst, and Lilla Halluma extending her hand to save the Bey, had her fingers shattered by the splinters of it. The ball entered the Bey in the side: he arose, however, and seizing his sabre from the window made a stroke at his brother, but only wounded him slightly in the face; upon which Sidy Useph discharged the second pistol and shot the Bey through the body.

Hassan's gruesome murder – Miss Tully informs us he was stabbed repeatedly by Sidi Yousef's black slaves as he lay dying and had eleven balls in him when he perished – plunged Tripoli into chaos. Further assassinations of leading figures followed and the Karamanli dynasty, which had ruled Tripoli since 1711, found itself under siege. Fighting broke out against the neighbouring Misratans and the rapacious Sidi Yousef prepared to attack Tripoli Castle. From its 'situation and strength', the British Consulate was regarded as the only safe asylum among the consular houses. Miss Tully braced herself for an invasion: 'The Greeks, Maltese, Moors and Jews brought all their property to the English house. The French and Venetian consuls also brought their families; every room was filled with beds; and the galleries were used for dining-rooms. The lower part of the building contained the Jewesses and the Moorish women with all their jewels and treasures.'

While the family's internecine conflict raged, on 29 July 1793 a Turkish adventurer named Ali Burghul – well acquainted with the turmoil – sailed into Tripoli harbour with a fleet of Turkish vessels claiming to have a *firman* from the Grand Signior to depose the Pasha and assume the throne. The crimson flag with the gold crescent was raised over Tripoli, Turkish guards rampaged through the city and the Tullys fled. After the failure of their initial attempt to repel the usurper, the princes Sidi Yousef and his second brother Sidi Hamet escaped to join their father who had taken refuge with the Bey of Tunis.

By 1795, the father and his two sons had made up their differences and a reunited Karamanli family expelled the Turkish impostor from Tripoli, installing Yousef as the new Pasha. His rule dovetailed neatly with growing British interest in unexplored Africa, born of the desire both to extend commercial relations with the continent and to investigate and suppress the Saharan slave trade. In 1788, in recognition of the fact that 'the map of the interior of Africa is still but a wide extended blank', the Society Instituted for the Purpose of Exploring the Interior of Africa (African Society for short) was founded in London. European knowledge of the continent and its peoples had hardly developed since the times of Herodotus, Strabo, Pliny and Pto-lemy. Arab writers and travellers of the Middle Ages such as Abu Obeid al Bekri, Ibn Khaldun and Ibn Battuta, the fabled fourteenth-century adventurer who blazed a swathe through the lands of Islam, had forged ahead. In the sixteenth century the Arabs pressed home their advantage, most notably through the travels of Ali Hassan Ibn Mohammed, or Leo Africanus (the African Lion), who crossed the Sahara to Timbuctoo in 1513. It fell to Jonathan Swift to lampoon this lamentable European ignorance.

> So Geographers in Afric-Maps
> with Savage-Pictures fill their Gaps:
> And o'er unhabitable Downs
> Place Elephants for want of Towns.

As Pasha of Tripoli, Yousef later gave assurances to the British government that he would, for a princely fee, guarantee safe conduct to any expedition to the River Niger. He held sway over parts of Fezzan, south of Tripoli – the central province to the south of Tripolitania that extended as far west as the borders with modern Algeria and, to the south, as far as the borders with present-day Niger and Chad – and claimed to be on friendly terms with the Sultans of Bornu and Sokoto in the heart of what Britons knew as 'Negroland' or 'Soudan', from where the caravans dragged their wretched human cargo across the Sahara to the Mediterranean coast. London duly dispatched the adven-ture-seeking surgeon Joseph Ritchie to Tripoli in 1818. His brief, as ambitious as it was unlikely, was to attempt an exploration from the north across the Sahara, install himself as British Vice-consul in Fezzan and chart the Niger. Like many of his assur-ances, Yousef's promise of safe conduct proved worthless – the lands he controlled extended no further south than Ghadames, not, as the British believed, as far as Timbuctoo and Bornu. But what tempted London to launch the Ritchie expedition was the fact that it offered a considerably less expensive alternative to penetrating towards the Niger from the west coast of Africa. An expedition from Sierra Leone had already been devastated by disease and would end up costing Britain £40,000. Ritchie was given £2,000.

Once landed at Tripoli, he and Lyon met the redoubtable British Consul Colonel Hanmer Warrington, who took them to an interview with the Pasha to discuss their journey into the Sahara. Warrington, a brilliant servant of the Empire and a leading figure at the Pasha's court, would watch British expeditions into the interior come and go during his residency from 1814 to 1846. Such was his influence that to many of his contemporaries, including the French Consul, it appeared that it was he, rather than the Pasha, who was running the country.

It was to the British Consulate once more that a sunburnt and bearded James Richardson headed on arriving in Tripoli in 1845. Sponsored by the British and Foreign Anti-Slavery Society, Richardson had volunteered to investigate the Saharan slave trade, which he regarded as 'the most gigantic system of wickedness the world ever saw'. His initial reception by Warrington was inauspicious. 'Ah!' said the British Consul, 'I don't believe our government cares one straw about the suppression of the slave-trade, but, Richardson, I believe in you, so let's be off to my garden.' Warrington, by now approaching the end of his marathon posting, was as superior as ever in his observations. 'Whether the extraordinary indolence of the people proceeds from the climate, or want of occupation, I know not,' the British Consul told the new arrival, 'but they are in an horizontal position twenty hours out of the twenty-four, sleeping in the open air.' Richardson and Warrington did not hit it off. With typical acuity, the supremely pragmatic British diplomat recognized Richardson as a loose cannon. 'I wish again to say your conduct and proceedings require the greatest prudence or you may lose your life or be made a slave of yourself and carried against your will into the Interior,' Warrington advised him in a letter. 'Over zeal often defeats the object but I pray for your health and success.' After waiting interminably and in vain for letters of recommendation, Richardson departed Tripoli for Ghadames 'without a single regret, having suffered much from several sources of annoyance, including both the Consulate and the Bashaw'.

Fifty years later, it was the turn of Mabel Loomis Todd, an American writer who adored Tripoli, to descend on the British Consulate, this time to observe the eclipses of 1900 and 1905. Around her, excited Tripolitans watched the heavens in awe.

> The fine Gurgeh minaret with its two balconies towering above the mosque was filled with white-robed Moslems gazing skyward. As the light failed and grew lifeless and all the visible world seemed drifting into the deathly trance which eclipses always produce, an old muezzin emerged from the topmost vantage point of the minaret, calling, calling the faithful to remember Allah and faint not. Without cessation, for over fifteen minutes he continued his exhortation, in a voice to match the engulfing somberness, weird, insistent, breathless, expectant.

Todd was also one of the few travellers to witness the final moments of the great caravan trade. The large expeditions that for centuries had carried off European arms, textiles and glassware into the desert, were no more, replaced now by much smaller and more infrequent missions into the interior. One morning, after ten months in the desert, a caravan of more than 250 camels was sighted approaching the city. Todd hurried over to watch its entrance:

> The camels stepped slowly, heavily laden with huge bales securely tied up – ivory and gold dust, skins and feathers. Wrapped in dingy drapery and carrying guns ten feet long, swarthy Bedouins led the weary camels across the sun-baked square. In the singular and silent company marched a few genuine Tuaregs, black veils strapped lightly over their faces

and enshrouded in black or dark brown wraps ... In their
opinion even the veils were hardly protection against the
impious glances of hated Christians, and with attitudes
expressive of the utmost repulsion and ferocity they turned
aside, lest a glance might be met in passing. All were ragged
beyond belief and incredibly dirty.

We left the Consulate and descended a gloomy street to
Tripoli's only Roman ruin, the four-sided triumphal arch dedicated to the emperors Marcus Aurelius and Lucius Verus in
AD 163. With innocent disregard for the city's glorious past, a
young boy was urinating on its base. We exited the *medina* and
walked around the fish market next to the port, where mountainous men were hacking tuna into pieces. Behind them rose the
ghostly water pipes commemorating Gaddafi's Great Man Made
River, at one time the largest engineering project in the world,
designed to bring fresh water up from the desert to the coast via
5,000 kilometres of pipelines. The last time I had been here, this
bizarre urban sculpture had been a working fountain. Today,
there is no sign of water. It is probably still too early to know
whether the project is an act of genius or an ecological catas-
trophe waiting to happen. Certainly, it had an inauspicious start.
When, with great fanfare, Gaddafi turned on the taps in September 1996, as part of the 27th anniversary celebrations of the
revolution, half the city's streets promptly exploded. After
decades of corrosion by salty water, the antiquated pipes could
not take the pressure. Many of the streets across the capital still
lay in rubble, monuments to the leader's madness.

Looping back into the Old City, we passed through throngs
of African immigrants selling fake Nike and Adidas T-shirts,
tracksuits and trainers, and drank more tea in a café belting out
mournful love songs from Oum Koulthoum, the late queen of
Arab music. Opposite us was the elegant Turkish Clock Tower
(all of its timepieces stuck at different times, its windowpanes
dusty and broken), given to the city in the mid-nineteenth century
by its governor Ali Riza Pasha. In Green Square, renamed by

Gaddafi as another reminder of his revolution, we went into the Castle Museum. After the open-air glories of Leptis and Sabratha, it was of less interest, except for the top floor, which was given over entirely to Gaddafi propaganda. Photos traced the leader's development as international statesman from the meeting with his then hero Nasser shortly after the 1969 revolution to later encounters with revolutionaries like Syria's President Assad and Fidel Castro (the latter being the winner of the 1998 Gaddafi Prize for Human Rights). On the walls were reality-defying slogans from Gaddafi's *Green Book*.

'Representation is a falsification of democracy'
'Committees everywhere'
'Arab unity'
'Forming parties splits societies'

We picked up a copy in a hotel. It was marked 1.5 dinars but the man behind the counter (who thought we were lunatics) let us have it for nothing. Libyans have to live with the grinding follies of their leader on a daily basis. 'The thinker Muammar Gaddafi does not present his thought for simple amusement or pleasure,' the dustcover proclaimed. 'Nor is it for those who regard ideas as puzzles for the entertainment of empty-minded people standing on the margin of life. Gaddafi's ideas interpret life as it erupts from the heart of the tormented, the oppressed, the deprived and the grief-stricken. It flows from the ever-developing and conflicting reality in search of whatever is best and most beautiful.' *The Green Book* rejects both atheistic communism and materialistic capitalism in favour of the Third Universal Theory. Libyans have yet to work out what it all means.

There is an unmistakable whiff, then, of Orwell's *1984* about Tripoli, an Oceania on the shores of the Mediterranean, a city whose people just about get by. The wonderful climate is deceptive. The first-time visitor sees a handsome, whitewashed city basking in the sun. A refreshing breeze blows along the boulevards lined with palm trees and grand stuccoed buildings from the Turkish and Italian era. In the square to the south of the castle, water dances in the Italian fountain. Here and there are cafés, filled with men smoking *shisha* pipes, playing chess and backgammon. Women bustle along, window-shopping in the brightly lit gold boutiques. Bride of the Sea and gateway to the desert, Tripoli is an elegant place.

But these are only first impressions. When he looks more closely, the visitor finds that much of this handsome city is falling apart. Even the charm of the *medina*, with its colonial-era architecture, shaded streets and small, labyrinthine *suq* is one of decay. Its graceful Turkish and Italian buildings, once the finest homes in the city, are crumbling away. The visitor finds, too, that the men are smoking pipes and playing chess in the cafés because they have no jobs to go to. And the women waddling through the *suq* are window-shopping because they can only afford the bare necessities.

Nonetheless, children of senior government officials, chic in designer clothes, chat into mobile phones and congregate in the new fast-food outlets springing up around the town. Together with high-ranking military personnel, they hurtle along the roads in black Mercedes and BMW saloons with tinted windows, past less favoured government employees rattling along in ancient Peugeot 404s held together with string, while African immigrants from Nigeria, Chad, Niger and Sudan sit by the roadside, waiting for construction and painting jobs that may never come.

Back at the hotel there was no sign of Taher in his office.

'It might be a good sign,' I said to Ned. 'Perhaps he's still talking to his friend about buying camels.' I didn't really believe a word of it. Ned looked equally unconvinced. Fearing the worst, I checked in with Hajer to see if he could shed some light on Taher's prolonged disappearance.

'Taher go to Tunisia,' he said matter-of-factly. 'He go to meet new tourists.'

This was testing our patience excessively. It was all very well waiting in the hope of something happening, but Taher was obviously over-stretched and doing nothing on our behalf. There was no point delaying any further in Tripoli. We had to get on with looking for camels ourselves. Hajer looked uncomfortable, as though he feared the worst from his boss should he let us leave during Taher's absence. He implored us to stay. We shook our heads. He changed tactics.

'Taher very angry you go Ghadames.'

'Well, we're very angry he went off to Tunisia without even telling us,' I replied.

'No, you stay in Tripoli,' said Hajer. 'Taher go to Tunisia.'

'We go to Ghadames,' we responded firmly.

CHAPTER III

# 'Really We Are in Bad Condition'

*Libya is – as the others show, and indeed as Cnaeus Piso, who was once the prefect of that country, told me – like a leopard's skin; for it is spotted with inhabited places that are surrounded by waterless and desert land. The Egyptians call such inhabited places 'auases'.*

STRABO, *THE GEOGRAPHY*

*The details of the [slave] traffic are really curious. A slave is heard of one day, talked about the next, reflections next day, price fixed next, goods offered next, squabblings next, bargain upset next, new disputes next, goods assorted next, final arrangement next, goods delivered and exchanged next, etc., etc., and the whole of this melancholy exhibition of a wrangling cupidity over the sale of human beings is wound up by the present of a few parched peas, a few Barbary almonds, and a little tobacco being given to the Soudanese merchants, the parties separating with as much self-complacency, as if they had arranged the mercantile affairs of all Africa.*

JAMES RICHARDSON, *TRAVELS IN THE GREAT DESERT OF SAHARA IN THE YEARS OF 1845 AND 1846*

Outside Tripoli, we got out of our taxi and stopped in a roadside restaurant for a hasty supper. The news bulletin was just beginning. Until recently, the opening sequence had showed Libya and the Arab world as a solitary block of green in a black world. In the heavens hung a copy of *The Green Book*, growing steadily brighter as a ray of light beamed up towards it from Tripoli. Then, like a satellite sending out signals, the book started zapping countries one by one until the whole world had succumbed to Gaddafi's malevolent genius and turned green itself. All this was until 1998, when invitations were sent to Arab leaders to join the celebrations in Tripoli for the 29th anniversary of the revolution. Not one turned up. Several premiers, including Hosni Mubarak of Egypt, had arrived several days earlier and made a discreet exit before the ceremonies began. Foreign heads of state were limited to a handful of African leaders. Stung by this snub from his Arab brethren, the man who had spent three decades in power campaigning for a single Arab nation, declared that henceforth Libya was an African, not an Arab, nation. The news no longer showed the outline of the Arab nations. Libya beamed out green light to the black continent of Africa instead.

The main item tonight was the meeting in Libya between the All African Students Union, an African president and Gaddafi. The African leader sat in impressively colourful costume, nodding off periodically during a long ranting speech from his host. Flanking the Libyan head of state was Louis Farrakhan, the American Muslim firebrand, who had probably been given a handsome stipend to lend revolutionary Islamic chic to an otherwise tedious function. Dutifully, he praised his Libyan host. 'We admire your great moral stature in international affairs and your fight against the imperialist policies of colonialism,' he droned on sycophantically. 'You are one of Islam's great revolutionary leaders. We salute you for your work around the world in support of our Muslim brothers.' The next item reported claims made by the renegade MI5 officer David Shayler that Britain had plotted to assassinate Gaddafi. 'It was a pity they didn't kill him,' muttered a driver on the neighbouring table.

We sank into the seats of our Peugeot taxi and sped through flat, barren country, listening to French rap, soft Arab rock and

All Saints. All that broke the emptiness of the evening landscape were occasional car scrapyards, unsightly heaps of abandoned Peugeot hulks next to squat Portakabins, and thick bands of rubbish on the roadside, mostly car tyres, food packets, and empty tins and bottles. And then darkness fell. At three in the morning, we nosed into the black mass of Ghadames and drove to the house of Othman al Hashashe, where I had stayed the last time I was here. Othman, a gangling twenty-six-year-old accountant and devoted Manchester United fan resplendent in Nike leisure suit, rubbed the sleep from his eyes wonderingly, recognized me and let us in. It was a bitterly cold night inside the house, a harbinger of things to come.

Richardson reached this oasis on 24 August 1845, after an uncomfortable two weeks on camel. He had been preceded by a letter announcing him somewhat disingenuously as the 'English Consul of Ghadames'. Initially, he was ecstatic. By his own account he was only the second European ever to set foot in this holy trading city. Another Briton, Major Alexander Gordon Laing, had passed through twenty years before en route to becoming the first European to reach Timbuctoo, but had been murdered shortly afterwards. Back in 1818, Ritchie and Lyon had intended to travel to this far-flung town but had been discouraged by Yousef Karamanli 'on account of the alledged dangers of the road'.

'I now fancied I had discovered a new world, or had seen Timbuctoo, or followed the whole course of the Niger, or had done something very extraordinary,' Richardson gushed. 'But the illusion soon vanished, as vanish all the vain hopes and foolish aspirations of man. I found afterwards that I had only made one step, or laid one stone, in raising for myself a monument of fame in the annals of African discovery!' For the time being, the great mission to investigate and help eradicate the slave trade had been forgotten. Richardson's personal ambitions as an African explorer were proving more immediately compelling.

I awoke next morning to a familiar booming voice. Mohammed Ali, who had acted as guide and interpreter for me during my last visit, was breakfasting with Othman. I joined them and was instantly bombarded with a barrage of greetings from Mohammed.

'Mr Justin, *kaif halek* (how are you)? Fine? Really, I have missed you, believe me. I thought maybe you were not coming to Libya. How are you? Fine? How is your family? Now I am happy to see you, *alhamdulillah* (praise God). Believe me, I am too shocked now you come to Ghadames. *Alleye berrik feik* (God bless you). How is your father? How are you? Fine?' The exchange of greetings lasted some time. Libyans are an exceedingly courteous people. It reminded me of Lyon's first impressions of Tripolines in 1818, when he observed:

> Very intimate acquaintances mutually lift their joined right hand, repeating with the greatest rapidity, 'How are you? Well, how are you? Thank God, how are you? God bless you, how are you?' which compliments in a well bred man never last less than ten minutes; and whatever may be the occasion afterwards, it is a mark of great good breeding occasionally to interrupt it, bowing solemnly and asking, 'How are you?' though an answer to the question is by no means considered necessary, as he who asks it is perhaps looking another way, and thinking of something else.

Mohammed was small and stodgily built, bordering on the portly, with a hurrying ramshackle gait and a baritone laugh. A man of constant good humour, he had a lazy right eye, so it was often difficult to know if he was addressing you or someone else. On the basis of my brief time in Ghadames the previous September I was now considered an old friend. Throughout our stay in Libya, Mohammed would behave like an old friend too – unstintingly helpful and loyal. Without our asking for assistance, he had taken today off from his job as one of Ghadames's three air traffic controllers to show us the Old City and help us look for camels. With an average of one incoming flight every month or so, it was not a demanding job. Before the 1992 embargo, there had been three flights a week to Tripoli and two to Sebha, the capital of Fezzan. Mohammed owed his staccato command of English to a nine-month course at the Anglo-Continental Educational Group of Bournemouth. This was our first experience of the Libyan Dorset connection that would resurface bizarrely during our time in the Sahara. Trained at Herne airport in Dorset in 1978, Mohammed was an ardent Anglophile, though this probably owed more to his extracurricular activities than to any great love of air charts. He spoke fondly of his time in Badger's and Tiffany's nightclubs, where he had spent many happy hours slow dancing ('Oh, my God, really very slowly, believe me') with the belles of Bournemouth and a girlfriend called Anne.

'Now we go to Taher's office,' he said reassuringly. 'Believe me, soon you will have camels and then you will leave Ghadames.' Ned and I exchanged glances – would it be so easy? – and followed Mohammed to the office, a whitewashed hole in the wall run by Taher's younger brother Ibrahim. He could hardly have looked less like his brother in Tripoli. Where Taher was slim, well-dressed, alert and enjoyed handsome, aquiline features, Ibrahim was a dozy mountain of a man, shambolically clad in a voluminous *jalabiya* which hung off him like a tent. Overweight and unhurried, he contemplated his surroundings with a lazy air of equanimity. Everything about him took place in slow motion. He was as laid-back as you needed to be in the sleepy town of Ghadames, where nothing much happened these days. If it had been a mistake to count on Taher to get things done, the prospect of definite assistance from Ibrahim seemed infinitely remote.

We discussed the first leg of our journey from Ghadames with him and asked if he could find a guide to take us to Idri, a little less than 300 miles south-east of Ghadames. Ned and I had already agreed that it would be better to look for the camels ourselves, rather than go through a middleman who would doubtless receive some sort of commission and force up the price. Ibrahim considered our request for a couple of minutes, talking intermittently to Mohammed Ali as he did so, and then turned back to us.

'I find you good guide,' he said slowly. He knew someone suitable to escort us to Idri and would talk to him later that afternoon. 'No problem,' he continued, 'I arrange everything for you.'

Perhaps we looked unconvinced. Mohammed, as unswerving in his optimism as Hajer in Tripoli, was quick to reassure us all would be well.

'Believe me,' he confided sotto voce, 'Ibrahim is very good man. My God, he will help you. Really, he will do everything for you. Don't worry about a thing. Mohammed is also praying for you.'

We left Ibrahim to it and set off with Mohammed to explore the old city of Ghadames, one of the most evocative oases in the Sahara. From the searing noon heat and light that bleached everything in sight a painful white we stepped into the deep shade and delicious cool of its covered streets. The contrast was intense. We plunged into a labyrinth of streets and *zinqa*s (alleys), through gloom penetrated every few metres by strong shafts of sunlight shining through the openings between houses. In and out of the light we walked, sometimes emerging into the open air alongside gardens of date palms and vegetables. We climbed up on to one of the roofs and looked down on the tattered maze of paths running between walls of dried mud that sliced through this lush growth. To the south the mosque of Sidi Bedri loomed above the shadowy streets.

The columns and capitals of its interior are thought to have been removed from the Byzantine basilica that stood here during the time of Justinian, the sixth-century Roman emperor, when Ghadames was an episcopal see. A deathlike stillness lingered over the place, broken occasionally by the bleating of sheep and goats and the hum of a few small farmers tending their plots of land. Against the drab beige desert that pressed in on all sides, Ghadames was a bright emerald splash of life.

Until recently, these whitewashed rooftops had been the entire world of the women of Ghadames. Only on three occasions in the year – including the birthday of the Prophet Mohammed – were they allowed to descend to the streets and make their way to one of the town's seven squares to celebrate their return to earth. The rest of their lives they led in airy seclusion on the interconnected roof terraces of the town, surrounded by date palms, passing from one housetop to another to gossip, exchange presents or buy goods such as scarves, silk sandals, brooches and coloured leather slippers from their neighbours.

'It is a very old city – 2,000 years old or 5,000 or 12,000,' Mohammed said definitely, as we surveyed Ghadames from this lofty vantage point. Ten thousand years seemed to be a wide enough range to cover all the options. 'I have been on government tourist course,' he went on. 'This is what they told us to tell the tourists – 2,000, 5,000 or 12,000 years – but believe me, it is very old city.' And, then, as an afterthought, he added: 'There are only six guides in Ghadames but only Mohammed Ali can speak English.'

Richardson met with little more success in his attempts to establish the exact age of Ghadames when he visited the town in the mid-nineteenth century. Rais Mustapha, the Turkish governor, told him then it was 4,000 years old. 'The people of the town, I suppose, have told him so,' the Englishman wrote sceptically, 'but where is their authority?'

We know from Pliny the town is at least 2,000 years old. In 19 BC, with war breaking out along Rome's southern frontier, Cornelius Balbus, the Cadiz-born Proconsul of Africa, set out to conquer the Garamantes, the trouble-making confederation of tribes which then held sway over much of the Sahara. He marched first from the coast to Cydamus (as Romans knew Ghadames), one of their most vital trading centres, and made it an allied city. Two centuries later, it was garrisoned by a detachment of the Legio III Augusta, the celebrated force that for 400 years was the sole Roman legion permanently garrisoned in north-west Africa. From Ghadames, Balbus marched his soldiers almost 350 miles south-east to Garama (now Germa), his enemy's capital in the

Wadi al Ajal. The rout did not stop there. According to Pliny, apart from Ghadames and Garama, Balbus went on to subdue an area containing a further twenty-five tribes, villages, mountains and rivers. It is likely these military successes were exaggerated to emphasize the Roman triumph, but Balbus' achievements in moving his army across such vast distances in the desert and imposing the *pax Romana* on a powerful enemy were prodigious. The Garamantes, who had previously enjoyed a trading monopoly far and wide through the Sahara, were soon reduced to the ignominious role of escorting Roman caravans. Balbus was given citizen rights and a triumph, 'the only foreigner ever so honoured,' says Pliny.

When the French traveller Henri Duveyrier visited Ghadames in 1862 he came across a bas-relief that he judged could only be ancient Egyptian in style. Ghadamsis told him then that the town dated back to the time of Abraham. Duveyrier concluded Ghadames was a sister community to the early settlements on the Nile.

The town's precise age may never be known, but Ghadamsis tell a popular tale of how it was founded. Long ago, a group of travellers heading south stopped in the area for lunch one day before continuing their journey. One of them forgot to take his iron plate with him when he left, the loss of which he only discovered the following morning. Returning to the spot, he wandered about searching until he found it. As he did, his horse kicked the ground and out burst a fountain of water. And so the town took its name from the place where the travellers had eaten lunch (*gheda*) yesterday (*ams*).

Another legend has it that Oqba bin Naf'a, the seventh-century Arabian conqueror who wiped out the last vestiges of the Garamantes' empire in Fezzan, arrived in Ghadames after a gruelling journey. He searched in vain for water to quench his burning thirst. Like the travellers before him, his mare then stamped her hoof, and a spring was found. It was named 'Ain el Fars (Mare's Spring) and, until recently, was the city's main water supply.

Water, the most valuable resource deep in the desert, had always been measured and distributed with the greatest care in

Ghadames. After collecting in the large rectangular basin at 'Ain el Fars on the fringes of the *medina*, it passed beneath ground level to a vaulted grotto in which sat the *gaddas*, the man responsible for measuring the quantity of water passing through the canal into the town's gardens via a network of narrow channels. The gauge was a small copper bucket with a hole in the bottom, through which the water flowed in a certain number of minutes. For each bucket emptied the *gaddas* tied a knot in a cord of palm leaves, before refilling the bucket and continuing his thankless job. There were three such men in charge of the water supply, employed day and night on rota. They were not paid for their pains but received a ration of barley, fruit and dates from the town.

Mohammed took us into Mulberry Square, formerly the market for male slaves. Women were purchased in nearby Little Mulberry Square. Traces of its miserable past were still evident when an English traveller visited Ghadames in pre-war Libya. 'Where once human flesh was exposed for sale the walls are slimy and foul: the thousands of slaves have left their mark,' he wrote. Today, there are no such signs and the square was empty. The last time I had been here, I met two refugees from Sierra Leone whitewashing the walls in preparation for the annual tourist festival.

We padded along empty alleys, kicking up veils of dust that glittered in the stabbing sunlight, past stone benches built out from the walls of houses where the town's old men had once sat and gossiped together, past abandoned house after abandoned house, their massive doors made of date palm trunks tightly closed to the world. Some were still decorated with scraps of coloured rags that showed the owner of the house had performed the haj (pilgrimage) to Mecca. The old Turkish school, built in 1835 and later used by the Italians, burnt uselessly under the sun, its roof caved in, its stairs falling ruinously apart.

This was the sad silence of decline and fall. For centuries Ghadames had been a great trading city whose fame and influence stretched thousands of miles across the Sahara. From Bornu to

Timbuctoo, Ghadamsis had held sway commercially and had their own affluent quarters in far-flung southern cities like Jenne and Kano, now northern Nigeria. The Ghadamsi quarter of Timbuctoo was the most flourishing of the entire city, a visitor noted in 1591. Not so long ago, the streets of Ghadames had been filled with the hubbub of commerce, the cries of slaves and slave-buyers, children reciting their lessons in school and the *muaddin*'s mellifluous call to prayer. Now, all that had gone. The houses were empty. No-one lived here anymore, and the city sat in the heavy stupor of the desert.

Of the half dozen historic trade routes running from the Mediterranean coast across the Sahara, three were in what is now Libya, and Ghadames had sat astride the richest. Caravans from Tripoli, southern Tunis and Algeria assembled here before taking their goods farther south in three separate directions. Some went south-west via Tuat to Timbuctoo, others south to Ghat and Kano, and a third group travelled south-east through Murzuk to Bornu. For hundreds of years, until the mid-nineteenth century at least, the caravan trade was the bedrock of the town's economy and most of the trading enterprises, bankers and wholesalers operating in the interior were head-quartered here.

In the twelfth century, Venetians were bringing arms, textiles, glassware and exotic products like Arabian spices, Indian gems and Chinese silks to Tripoli, carried off by local merchants into the desert. By Leo Africanus's time, four centuries later, European cloth was still a staple of the Saharan caravan trade. Together with clothes, brass vessels, horses and books, it was exchanged for gold, slaves and *zebed* (civet). This olfactory delight was procured from civet cats, which were kept in cages and periodically harangued and taunted until through intense perspiration they secreted a perfume from glands beneath the tail. They were then secured, the goo was scraped from their nether regions, preserved in small boxes of hide and sold at great expense as a scent-fixer for perfumes (did Victorian women know what they were dabbing onto their necks?). 'A savage old cat will produce ten or twelve dollars' worth in three heats,' noted Lyon in 1819 (at the ripe age of twenty-two and without consulting anyone he had promoted himself from lieutenant to ensure a more respectful reception from the natives). 'Their price is enormous, some being sold for three or four slaves.'

Lyon provided one of the most comprehensive accounts of the goods traded along Libya's second trade route running south from Tripoli to Murzuk, Bilma and Kukawa, west of Lake Chad. It gives an idea of what the caravans were trading with Ghadames at the same time. From the coast came horses, beads, coral, needles ('four of which purchase a fine fowl'), silks, copper pots and kettles, looking-glasses, swords ('very long, straight and double edged; bought greedily by the Tuarick'), guns, carpets from Tripoli, Venetian glass, muslins and woollen cloaks. Among goods brought up from the south, slaves still predominated, accompanied by civet, cottons, gold in dust and small bars or rings, leather, ostrich skins and feathers, ornamental sandals, *gerba*s (water skins made of goats' hides), honey, pepper, elephants' teeth and *gooroo* nuts, a luxury that went at the rate of four to the Spanish dollar. 'It is said, that in certain years when the nut has been scarce, people in Soudan have given a slave for one of them,' the indefatigable Lyon reported. Ghadamsi merchants meanwhile brought swords, guns, powder, flints, lead, ironware and clothing to Murzuk for the annual spring market.

By the time Richardson arrived, Ghadames had passed its apogee. Turkish rule, with its capricious system of extortion, was hurting. During the Karamanli dynasty, the city had paid an annual tribute of 850 mahboubs to Tripoli. Richardson learnt that when the Turks took control of the city after their reconquest of Tripoli in 1835, they had demanded a forced contribution of 50,000 mahboubs, stripped women of their gold and silver, ransacked houses, and instituted an annual tribute of 10,000 mahboubs from the city. To make matters worse, Tripoli had just demanded an extraordinary levy of 3,200 mahboubs, which the beleaguered merchants said they were unable to pay.

Richardson, who was soon on friendly terms with the Turkish governor, listened to him explaining the essence of Ottoman colonial policy in the territory. 'You know Arabs to be very devils,' he told the Englishman.

> There are two ways to consider Arabs, but whichever way they are robbers and assassins. When they are famished, they plunder in order to eat; when their bellies are full, they plunder because they kick and are insolent. Now we (Turks) keep them upon a low diet in The Mountains; they have little, and always a little food. This is the Sultan's *tareek* (government) to manage them. Their spirits are kept down and they are submissive.

Having mulled over his own ambitions as an explorer, Richardson now rediscovered his 'humane mission on the behalf of unhappy weak Africans, doomed by men calling themselves Christians, to the curse of slavery', and set about his investigation of the trade. It did not take him long to realize the scale of the challenge facing the abolitionists: 'Slave-dealing is so completely engendered in the minds of the Ghadamsee merchants, that they cannot conceive how it can be wrong. They are greatly astonished that slavery is not permitted among us.'

One day, he watched a caravan of forty slaves arrive from Bornu. 'They were as much like merchandize as they could be, or human beings could be made to resemble it,' he recorded. 'They were entirely naked, with the exception of a strip of tanned skin tied round the loins. All were nearly alike, as so many goods packed up of the same quality. They were very thin, and almost skeletons, about the age of from ten to fifteen years, with the round Bornouse features strongly marked upon their countenances.' As the Turks had taxed Ghadamsis with such ferocity, there were few merchants in the town who could afford to purchase the slaves, and Richardson had to fend off repeated attempts by the Touareg and Tubbu slave owners to get him to buy these hapless creatures himself. The merchants had hoped to sell them for forty to fifty Spanish dollars a head, but were reduced to disposing of them for twenty, of which half went to the government in duty.

Later, he encountered another slave caravan and was deeply moved by the misery of these

> poor little children – child-slaves – crawling over the ground, scarcely able to move. Oh, what a curse is slavery! How full of hard-heartedness and cruelty! As soon as the poor slaves arrived, they set to work and made a fire. Some of them were laden with wood when they came up. The fire was their only protection from the cold, the raw bitter cold of the night, for they were nearly naked. I require as much as three ordinary greatcoats, besides the usual clothing of the day, to keep me warm in the night; these poor things, the chilly children of the tropics, have only a rag to cover them, and a bit of fire to warm them. I shall never forget the sparkling eyes of delight of one of the poor little boys, as he sat down and looked into the crackling glaring fire of desert scrub.

Since the slave drivers were paid per capita to deliver their charges to their destination, they saved expenses by giving them as little food as possible. As a result, they were kept on survival rations consisting of barley meal mixed with water. Richardson's attendant, he noted, ate more for dinner than a slave's entire daily ration. By the time they got to their destination, they would be no more than 'living-skeletons'.

Richardson stayed in Ghadames for three months, spending much of his time dispensing medicine to treat the most common illnesses – ophthalmia (inflammation of the eye), diarrhoea, dropsy, smallpox and syphilis – telling his unsuspecting patients it came from the Queen of England, 'which, I have observed, heightens its value in their eyes'. He was something of a chameleon, at one moment the impassioned liberal, the next a Christian bigot, sometimes a patriotic British imperialist, at others the vitriolic anti-slave trade campaigner. But whatever his mood, he was a consistently – perhaps unintentionally – entertaining observer of his surroundings. The discovery that some men wore *kohl* to blacken their eyelids, for instance, completely threw him. 'I confessed I was surprised at this monstrous effeminacy,' he fumed.

More importantly, his investigations led him to conclude that two merchants under British protection were providing credit to slave-traders. He promptly wrote a letter to that effect to Colonel Warrington in Tripoli, asking him not to publicize this information until he himself was safely out of the desert, for fear of reprisals. The correspondence must have made Warrington squirm:

> We may expect one of these days to see some American President coming forward in the Congress of the United States, as the late Mr Slaveholder Tigler, or some French Deputy in the Chamber with a statement to the following effect: 'that whilst the British Consuls of Barbary, and the agents of the British and Foreign Anti-Slavery Society are labouring for the suppression of the Slave Trade in Northern and Central Africa, the traffic in Slaves between Soudan and Tripoli is principally carried on by the means of British capital'.

Worse still was the news that Richardson had tactlessly conveyed his allegation ('I do not believe one word of it,' Warrington wrote London) to the Anti-Slavery Society in England, thereby undermining the British Consul's own position. The diplomat's response was equally direct. A public notice was put up announcing 'the strictest inquiry' into the affair and threatening a tribunal. Richardson, meanwhile, was pressed by Warrington to provide evidence to support his controversial claims, 'or I apprehend you will be subject to an action'. Furious with the British Consul for revealing his allegation and jeopardizing his safety in Ghadames, and unable, he claimed, to procure hard evidence, Richardson retreated to his journal and vented his spleen there instead.

The whole affair, which was still occupying Warrington seven months later when Richardson returned to the coast, caused a great scandal both in Tripoli and Ghadames and was illustrative of the changing climate. From the mid-nineteenth century, the combination of the official prohibition of slave-dealing and mounting international opposition made life increasingly difficult for the illegal traffickers in human flesh. By the turn of the century, new economic realities had added to the slavers' troubles. Transportation costs from Black Africa to Europe had been reduced with the advent of a train link from Kano to Lagos and the introduction of steamers from the African coast to Liverpool. It cost £3 to transport one ton of goods from Liverpool to Kano in 1905 and more than double that just to send the same consignment from Tripoli to Kano. The Saharan caravan trade was under threat as never before.

For Ghadames, the accelerating demise of the slave trade, on whose back the city had grown so prosperous, was the first calamitous setback. With fewer and fewer slaves available to irrigate the gardens and keep back the ever-encroaching sands, the city started shrinking, and emigration started apace. After the middle of the nineteenth century, the decline proved irreversible, but Ghadames lived on, propped up by the Italian Fascists in the early twentieth century through improvements to the water supply. It was in 1986, however, that Gaddafi's government dealt the age-old *medina* a potentially fatal blow. All the inhabitants were ordered to vacate the Old City and move into newly constructed houses outside the city walls, equipped with the usual modern conveniences. These houses, unimaginative squares of cheap concrete, are already deteriorating fast. Those inside the *medina*, though they did not have such luxuries as running hot water, had lasted hundreds of years. Since this forced relocation, the Old City, quite unlike anything else the length and breadth of the Sahara, has been crumbling away steadily. If its oldest houses remain empty, Ghadames's days are surely numbered.

We still needed camels. That afternoon, we mounted Moham-med's battered Peugeot 404 pick-up, a clattering veteran of eighteen years of erratic driving, and drove off to see Haj Jiblani, an elderly Touareg who several months before had taken me for an introductory ten-mile camel ride. We sat on the ground and chatted above a depression in which his two white Mehari camels were being fed. Next to the old man, two young boys amused themselves by piling large stones on a tiny helpless puppy. They were toying with the animal as though it was the most normal recreation in the world.

In 1995, at the age of seventy, Jiblani had performed his haj by camel, from Soloum – on the Libyan border with Egypt – to Mecca. We asked if he was interested in selling us his camels and accompanying us as guide on the first leg to Idri. He replied softly, from beneath the shroud of white cloth that covered most of his head and face, that these camels were all he had so he could not part with them. As for guiding us, he would have liked to but could not leave Ghadames because he had a sick relative in the hospital. We should find someone younger and fitter. I had already spoken to another local Touareg called Okra, a man whose main claim to fame was that he had played Sophia Loren's youthful lover in a film shot around Ghadames many years ago. He had said he was not fit enough for the journey. We did not seem to be making much progress. Even Mohammed, the most optimistic of our trio, seemed to agree.

'Really we are in bad condition,' he lamented. A selfless man, he was entering whole-heartedly into the spirit of our quest for camels and guide. 'You will be the first to do this trip for 1,000 years,' he enthused with a questionable degree of historical accuracy. 'Really, we are not used to this. Everyone in Ghadames is surprised by you.'

For most of Gaddafi's three decades at the helm tourism has not fitted comfortably within the regime's broadly anti-imperialist mindset and a foreign policy that has led inexorably to isolation. It was only in the early nineties that a faltering programme of encouraging tourists to the country began and tourist visas were issued in greater earnest. For many Libyans we met, the whole notion of a long camel trek by foreign travellers was simply incomprehensible.

Mohammed suggested what was beginning to appear inevitable: 'I think you must go to the Mehari Club of Ghadames.' This was an organization that owned several riding camels and hired them out for special occasions.

'If we do, it's not going to be cheap,' I said to Ned.

Abu Amama, its head, had previously offered to sell me five camels at a rate that seemed murderously excessive. We were a captive market in a nine-camel town. The collapse of the slave trade, followed decades later by the arrival of the motor car, meant that the town, through which countless caravans had passed over the centuries, now struggled to equip a tiny party like our own with five camels. Bracing ourselves for a financial showdown, we arranged through Mohammed to have an inspection of the animals the next day.

'We must look as though we know what we're doing,' said Ned firmly when we were both back in Othman's house. He was in serious mode now. Most of the time he was not, so it was sometimes difficult to adjust.

'We haven't got a clue,' I replied.

'Yes, but you mustn't let them see that.'

'I'm sure you're right, but I can't see us pulling it off for long,' I said doubtfully. Somehow I could not see us fooling the assorted officers of the camel club that we were anything but neophytes as far as camels were concerned.

The next morning, taking another day off from monitoring Ghadames's untroubled airspace, Mohammed collected us from Othman's house. We squeezed into the front seat of his pick-up and he tried unsuccessfully to hotwire the ignition. 'Really, this car is in bad condition,' he boomed blithely, bustling about beneath the bonnet and tinkering with the engine. This was an understatement. Most of the basic components of a vehicle – such as seats, windows and dashboard – had disappeared long ago and if you looked down between your feet, there was more road than car. It said much both for Peugeot engineering and Ghadamsi mechanics that the car was still, albeit precariously, on the road. After several more attempts, it rattled reluctantly to life and we howled off several kilometres out of town to see the animals, clutching our paper from the Royal Geographical Society on how to choose camels.

'Judging a camel's age and condition takes experience and a novice will need the help of a local,' it warned,

> However, certain facts can be ascertained by examining the animal closely. First, make the camel kneel and inspect its back and withers. Any open galls or wounds immediately rule it out as a mount: on a long desert trek it can mean death. Let the animal stand again and look for obvious defects like crooked legs, in-growing nails, a hobbling pace, excessive fat on the legs. Check the inside of the front legs where they meet the chest: if you find evidence of rubbing there, the camel will be weak and slow. Generally, look for an animal that is well covered: no ribs showing, a fairly robust hump, bright eyes, well formed long legs and an erect carriage of the head. Finally, have someone saddle and ride the camel: note whether it snaps, bolts or roars at its handler; lead it around and see that it walks freely; make it kneel and stand up several times.

We thought we could manage that. Abd an Nibbi, who was deputizing for Abu Amama during the latter's absence in the southern town of Ghat, welcomed us to a makeshift camel enclosure on a patch of wasteland. He looked faintly amused, and at the same time – was it our imagination? – crafty. There were seven Mehari camels inside, of which it took no expertise to see that two were clearly unsuitable for a long journey. They were puny youngsters, half the size of the others. It did not leave much room for choice. We needed five.

At close quarters, they looked terrifying. Huge hulks of beasts with mighty, towering legs, together they formed a striking picture of grace and power. The first Mehari camel Richardson had seen walking into the *medina* of Ghadames had had a similar effect on him. 'It amazed me by its stupendous height. A person of average size might have walked under its belly.' An Arab philologist suggested to him the word Mehari derived from Mahra, the Arabian province on the south-east coast adjoining Oman, from where the animal was supposed to have originated. 'This remarkable camel, which is like the greyhound amongst dogs for swiftness and agility, and even shape, they train for war and riding like the horse,' he wrote. The Touareg warriors of Ghadames sitting astride their Meharis looked 'splendid and savage' to him.

Massive, disdainful and apparently in no mood to be paraded around for our convenience, these Meharis roared terribly, jerked from one side to another and lashed out at the handlers with their legs to show their displeasure. Not a man to be cowed by mere animals, Abd an Nibbi entered the fray. Masterfully he subdued them, throwing a rope around their heads, pulling down their necks and grabbing their nose-rings with supreme assurance. Once he had hold of the nose-rings he tugged at them vigorously until the camels were completely cowed. Within seconds they had been transformed from proud, dangerous-looking beasts into the meekest creatures conceivable. Abd an Nibbi shot us a knowing look, as if to make sure we had witnessed this demonstration of camel skills. I remembered Ned's advice of the night before and thought ruefully of what amateurs we were. There was no going back now. We had to look convincing. One by one, Abd an Nibbi brought the five camels in front of us.

I looked across at Ned, who had begun to scribble notes with what I imagined was the practised calm of a professional camel-buyer. He looked every bit the part. It was time to join the act. Together, we walked slowly around each one, trying to look as though it was the most normal thing in the world. We bought camels all the time, of course. We nodded sagely, conferred and shook our heads regretfully (we did not want to look over-eager), checked their legs (all of which to our untrained eyes looked crooked), stared into their eyes, slapped their flanks with what we hoped was the air of connoisseurs, and pondered carefully. Ned continued to take notes throughout the inspection. Mohammed Ali pottered about here and there, pausing occasionally to admire a particular animal. 'Ohhh, really, these are good camels, Mr Justin. They are in good condition.'

At this initial viewing, three of the camels appeared particularly impressive. Cream in colour, they exuded a definite aristocratic hauteur and swaggered about with the greatest nonchalance. They paid us little attention beyond a certain sneering look before continuing their perambulations. Another, a barrel-chested brown, did not seem to be on good terms with the whites, but looked a robust mount. A handsome and effeminate beige, slighter than the others but with the demeanour of a lively thoroughbred, completed the party.

Ned looked up from his notes for a second. 'Get them to trot,' he said to me, as though addressing his camel boy. All that training on horseback in the Andes had not been for nothing. He was warming to the task. I looked at the tall beast beside me and wondered how I could get it to do anything, let alone trot. Then I remembered it was essential to show no fear in front of a camel. Grabbing the rope that was attached to its nose-ring, I ran off with the first. Disturbed from an otherwise peaceful afternoon munching hay, the camel appeared to think this was the greatest impudence but within seconds broke into a light trot behind me. At last. I was in control.

'That's good,' said Ned, with the same air of authority. 'Keep going.'

We took it in turns to take them trotting and got them to kneel down and stand up again repeatedly. Whether we presented a convincing picture to the Ghadamsis around us was a moot point. Judging by his face, Abd an Nibbi was struggling hard not to laugh.

Undaunted, Ned continued taking notes. I saw them several days later. They went something like this:

(1) 13 years old. Wound on front left leg. Slightly knock-kneed.

(2) 12 years old.

(3) White. Bobbles on nose.

(4) 'V' on neck. Good temperament.

(5) Brown.

All were for sale, Abd an Nibbi told us with a confident expression that indicated he knew something we did not. We started discussing prices, at which point he pulled out his own paperwork. It consisted of a letter from Abu Amama saying on no account were the camels to be sold for a dinar less than the figure he had quoted me on my last trip. In other words, they were going for £800 each. We could take it or leave it. There was to be no haggling.

We returned to Othman's house to think it over.

'What do you think?' asked Ned.

'It's a lot of money,' I replied, 'and I don't like the way there's no haggling.'

It was too much money, certainly. Our problem was that Abu Amama was not even particularly keen on selling the camels. He would have preferred to hire them to us, he had said before, since if he sold them he would then have to make a long journey south to Niger to replace them. Meharis were relatively rare in Libya, he had explained, freely admitting that this was why they were so expensive. More importantly, if we were determined, as we were, to buy our camels here, we had little alternative, and everyone in Ghadames knew it.

'What do you think are our options?' Ned went on.

Short of having a look for camels down in Ghat or, less practically, Kufra (a little under 900 miles away as the crow flies, much more by road), there appeared to be no alternative. Besides, we would lose valuable time leaving Ghadames and would still have to pay the transportation costs to bring the camels back to our starting-point. I didn't think there was much we could do but pay the exorbitant sum demanded.

'You know what Anthony Cazalet would say in this sort of situation?' Ned said.

'Something about being bloody cold no doubt.'

'No, he'd say it's time to throw money at the problem.'

It was. There seemed nothing else for it. We returned to our lodgings and, after holding off an attempt by Abd an Nibbi to dispute the black market exchange rate, handed over several thousand dollars. Everyone was smiles. The transaction was complete. The camels were ours. Now we needed a guide. The next morning Mohammed Ali arrived with a message from Ibrahim saying one had been found. 'You see, Mr Justin, really we are in good condition. I tell you Ibrahim help with everything, *alhamdulillah*.'

Things were looking up. We trooped back into the hole in the wall to find a fat man with two lazy eyes waiting for us. With him and Mohammed Ali in one room, it was almost impossible to know who was speaking to whom. He shook hands without warmth and was introduced to us as Mohammed Ramadan from Awbari. There was something unpleasant about his manner. He did not seem at all interested in getting to know the people with whom he was volunteering to travel several hundred miles across the Sahara. This was a simple business transaction, no more, no less. In a bullying tone, he told us he knew the area between Ghadames and Idri intimately and was ready to go with us. We started to discuss the route in more detail and asked him how he travelled in the desert. Things went rapidly downhill from there and his manner became ever more aggressive and confrontational. He would only travel by camel if we had a car as back-up, he insisted. It would carry food and water supplies for us and the camels. Each day his sidekick would drive ahead of us for thirty miles or so and in the evening we would rejoin the car for dinner. Mohammed Ali looked embarrassed. He knew this was not what we wanted to do.

Having talked over the route together and ascertained there were several wells en route to Idri, we asked Mohammed Ramadan why he needed a car. We were happy to go without one. It seemed an unnecessary, profoundly unromantic and expensive means of travel. He took this as an attack on his desert skills and pounded his fist on the table.

'The journey is very difficult and dangerous,' he insisted. 'There is no food or water for the camels for many days.'

'But you've just said there are several wells along the route, so how can it be so dangerous?' I asked.

'I go with a car or I don't go at all,' he spluttered aggressively. He banged the table with his fist again and his pudgy face wobbled with the impact.

I thought of the RGS notes again.

> Choosing a guide or companion is very much more difficult than choosing a camel. As the Arabs say, 'you cannot know a man until you have been in the desert with him' . . . Many who present themselves as desert guides may have only a rudimentary knowledge of camels. Even those who are official desert guides may have become so used to travelling in motor vehicles that they have grown lax. Do not fall for the 'Wise old Arab' syndrome.

A heated exchange followed between Ibrahim and Mohammed Ramadan about taking the car. The latter repeated his conditions, pounding the table at intervals to drive home his point. The meeting was over. This was not the man we wanted to travel in the desert with and it appeared the feeling was mutual.

'So much for that,' I said to Ned as we returned in low spirits to Othman's house.

'Look on the bright side. He was too fat for the job,' came the phlegmatic reply. Never one to moan about our bad luck, Ned was adept at making light of such failures.

Mohammed, too, had his own style. 'Really, I am sorry for you,' he mourned sympathetically. 'Now we are in bad condition. I am embarrassed about this, really I feel shy.'

I asked him if he knew anyone else in Ghadames who might agree to come with us.

'Really, I don't know, Mr Justin, because you are the first to do this,' he replied sombrely. 'Oh my God, you like camels too much. Other people go by car. But I am also wanting you to go by camel now. Maybe tomorrow we will find good guide for you, *inshallah* (God willing).' From the tone of his voice, it was clear he thought our chances of success extremely limited. And then, in a gesture that took both Ned and me by surprise, he suddenly raised his hands to the heavens in the most theatrical supplication to the Almighty. 'Please God, help us so they can do the journey without a car!' he implored. Would He listen?

The next day, Ibrahim confessed he no longer held out great hopes of finding another guide prepared to travel from Ghadames to Idri by camel. He had lost the urge, never very great in the first place, to look for one. Mohammed Ali, a more enterprising character altogether, said he would talk to some of the people from the Mehari Club. Buying camels in one of the ancient centres of the caravan trade had been difficult but manageable. We now wondered whether finding a guide prepared to exchange the comforts of travel by Toyota Landcruiser for the hardships of a camel trek would prove too much in late-twentieth-century Ghadames.

While we waited to hear the results of Mohammed's efforts, we visited the museum, a very basic series of rooms in the old fort containing traditional Ghadamsi costumes, utensils, folkloric medicines, a Touareg tent and the usual Gaddafi propaganda. In one room lay a few stones with barely legible Roman inscriptions. In another was a rope above a sign saying 'It used for climbing tree' and a photograph of a man delicately balanced with a rope tied around his waist and the date palm, resting his feet on the trunk. Mohammed Ali's uncle had fallen to his death several years ago while collecting dates from a tree. The museum did not do justice to Ghadames' past, but after those of Tripoli, Leptis and Sabratha there was something to be said for brevity. A tour took about ten minutes.

Outside Ibrahim's office, an elderly Land Rover with two *gerba*s (waterskins) attached to the wings had arrived. Two languid Frenchmen came to say hello. They were looking for another vehicle with which to make a convoy down to Ghat. We said we could not help, but there seemed to be a fair amount of tourist traffic heading that way if they waited around. Moments later, a monstrous Mercedes Unimog desert vehicle pulled in. Emblazoned on the sides in lurid colours was a romanticized desert scene and the hideous caption ETHNOGRAPHISCHE EXPEDITIONEN. Its German occupants spilled out. They too were en route to Ghat. 'Ja, ve make documentary about ze Touareg und little bit about ze Sahara,' they told us. Ned and I retired to one side. The Frenchmen, whose faces had fallen when they saw this brute of a vehicle arrive, approached the Germans reluctantly. It was obvious they would rather not have gone with them but had no alternative. We British sat apart from the Continental throng. 'A microcosm of Europe,' said Ned.

Mohammed reappeared later that afternoon in a state of excitement. 'Now really we are in good condition!' he bellowed. 'I have found someone who will go with you. His name is Abd al Wahab and he is very good guide.' He had spent several hours talking to the Touareg of the Mehari Club. 'Now you can go without car, *inshallah*. Believe me, this will be good for you. I know you are liking the camels!' He would bring the man to see us in the evening.

Ruminating over this apparent change in our fortunes, we were interrupted by the unannounced arrival of Taher Ibrahim, an oleaginous Ghadamsi travel agent I had bumped into on my last visit. He spoke fluent English with a Cockney accent, unexpected in someone whose contact with England had been limited to two years in Colchester.

'You speak excellent English,' said Ned.

'Yes, I know, best in Ghadames,' he replied smugly. He started prying. How much were we paying for the camels? How much was the guide going to cost? Where were we going? How long would we be in Ghadames? To the last we replied shortly: 'As long as it takes.' This expression reminded him of an encounter with a prostitute on London's Gloucester Road. Captivated – as he seemed to think we were too – by the recollections of his sexual triumph, he launched into an account of the episode.

'I asked her how much. She said £20 or something like that. How long do I get with you, I asked? As long as it takes, she said.' He burst into laughter.

We met Abd al Wahab for the first time that evening. A handsome Touareg possessed of the silent *gravitas* of the desert nomad, he had a dignified bearing, benevolent eyes that peered out from his clean white *tagilmus* (the veil worn by all Touareg men), and a large slug of a moustache that crawled greedily across his upper lip and would have reached the bottom of his sideburns if he had worn any. He was smartly dressed in a black woollen *burnous* and his manner was calm and retiring, a welcome contrast to the aggressive hectoring tone of Mohammed Ramadan. When he spoke – and he did so rarely – it was in a soft assured voice. We discussed the journey and his terms for accompanying us around a dinner table on a dais in Othman's house. I repeated to Abd al Wahab what Mohammed Ramadan had told us about the great dangers of the route. He shook his head.

'It is not so dangerous,' he replied quietly. We would reach our first well after three days, the second after another three and thereafter they would appear regularly, so we need not be concerned about water for the camels. 'Also, it is winter now, and the camels can go longer than that without water,' he went on. 'Of course, we do not need to take a car.' Everything about him inspired confidence.

This was our man. We shook hands with him, delighted at having overcome our first serious difficulty, and arranged to go the next day but one. Leaving, he did not look where he was going, stepped down from the dais onto a bed below and was promptly trampolined into the air, before returning to the floor in a confused heap of white cotton and black wool. He laughed at himself good-humouredly, if somewhat sheepishly, and excused himself. He looked as though he would be far happier in the desert than surrounded by these trappings of modern civilization.

The next morning was a flurry of shopping. We descended on the town's market to buy ten- and twenty-litre plastic water *bidoun*s, cooking pots, buckets, a tarpaulin and blankets to cover the riding saddles that we were buying from the club. Neither of us had ever provisioned for a journey of two weeks, so it was a hit-and-miss affair. Mohammed Ali totted up our bill while we both raided the shop shelves. We thought it best to err on the side of generosity, and tin after tin of tuna fish duly flew into cardboard boxes, joining a plethora of pasta, tomato puree, tea, coffee, sugar, bread, biscuits, tinned fruit, olive oil, garlic, onions and oranges. These complemented our scanty supplies from England. I had brought packet soups, packet sauces and a pot of Marmite. Ned, more of a minimalist, had half a dozen bottles of Encona West Indian Hot Pepper Sauce to enliven the pasta. Having heard that arguments with guides over food were notorious in the desert, we took pains to ensure Abd al Wahab liked everything we were buying. Ned picked up a tin of beans. Here was a chance to practise the Arabic he had been learning on his Linguaphone course.

'Are you a *fasulya* bean?' he asked him, in flawless classical Arabic.

Abd al Wahab smiled and nodded.

The last things we needed from the market were some suitable clothes for the desert. I suggested to Ned we buy a couple of cotton *jalabiya*s, the free-flowing garment worn throughout the Arab world, as well as a *shish*, a five-metre length of cotton to protect our heads from the desert sun. As Michael Asher had written,

> it seems to me that the West has devised no better dress
> for travelling than that worn by desert people. The long,
> loose-fitting shirt allows a layer of cool insulating air to
> circulate beneath it. The baggy trousers or loin-cloths worn
> by most desert tribes are extremely comfortable for riding.
> The turban or headcloth, with its many layers not only keeps
> the head cool but can also be used in a number of other
> ways, including veiling the face in a sand storm.

Ned, resolutely English, was initially unconvinced and took some persuading of the advantages of going native. While he hesitated I bought the last large cotton *jalabiya* in the shop. All that was left in his size was one in diarrhoea-coloured polyester.

Hearing of our imminent departure, Othman had kindly arranged an interview for us with his uncle, Abd as Salam, the chief government official of Ghadames. Minders showed us into his office where he welcomed us graciously. He sat behind a desk sporting a pair of glasses with lenses so thick they distorted his eyes into a demonic grimace. Despite the daytime heat, he wore a heavy beige cardigan, two jumpers, a shirt and thermal vest. This was midwinter for Ghadamsis.

The town dated back to 895 BC, he told us, and had long been an important transit point for goods going north and south across the desert. 'I tell you something else you do not know,' he said, with an air of mystery. 'Ghadames was first city in world to have passports, post office, free market and water gauge.' 'Passports' had once been necessary, he explained, to cross from one half of Ghadames into the other. The system of gates dividing the town into two sections – one each for the predominant but mutually hostile Bani Walid and Bani Wazit tribes – dated back more than 2,000 years. When a man from one tribe wanted to visit someone from the other, he had to have a certain paper, like a passport, that enabled him to pass through the gateway into the neighbouring quarter. Richardson called these two long-feuding tribes 'the Whigs and Tories of Ghadames'. On asking his guide about the history of their conflict he was told: 'The Ben Weleed and the Ben Wezeet are people of Ghadames, who have quarrelled from time immemorial: it was the will of God they should be divided, and who shall resist his will?' These strict tribal divisions no longer existed and intermarrying was increasingly common, Abd as Salam informed us.

The postal service consisted of a small box, into which people would place letters to various destinations across the Sahara. Anyone setting out by caravan to Tripoli, for example, first had to see if there were any letters bound for that area. 'If he do not

look in box before he go, he make big mistake,' Abd as Salam
said. 'He will be in big trouble with the people.' The world's first
free market consisted of a square with mosques on two sides.
Both the Bani Walid and Bani Wazit were at liberty to meet here
and conduct business.

Abd as Salam told us the removal of the town's population
from the Old City had started in 1972, when Gaddafi authorized
the construction of new houses. We asked him about the solitary
inhabitant of the ancient *medina*. One old lady, whose house we
had seen, had refused to move. 'She is still in love with her
husband,' he replied. 'He died several years ago. She does not
want to leave because it was his house and she has memories of
him there.' What of the rest of the *medina*, we wondered? 'There
will be big programme to increase tourists,' he replied optimistic-
ally. 'We will have fairs and festivals, new hotels, cafés, and
handicraft shops. We will not forget Old Ghadames.'

That evening, we revisited the camels, tried out the saddles,
and packed up the bags ready for a morning start. At last we
were ready to set off into the desert. 'Really, I am happy now
because you are leaving,' boomed Mohammed, staring up at the
evening sky with his lazy eye. 'Believe me, before we had too
much problems. Now you have camels, you have Abd al Wahab
and you can go into the desert and we are all in good condition,
*alhamdulillah*.'

We returned to Othman's house, made final preparations for
the journey, and retired to sleep after thanking our host for all
his kindness and hospitality. He had been good natured throughout our stay, despite the constant invasions of his house by parties
of unknown Touareg men and daily interruptions from the high-
spirited Mohammed Ali.

This was our last night in civilization, and it was another
freezing one, but neither Ned nor I really noticed it. Submerged
under heavy blankets, my mind was racing, already dreaming of
the desert and its open spaces, of unbroken horizons and long
nights beneath the stars with our small caravan of five camels
and Abd al Wahab. Tomorrow it would all begin.

CHAPTER IV

# The Journey Begins

*The transition from camel to car is under way; it cannot be checked. But the passing of a romantic tradition is certainly sad. We can but console ourselves with the thought that it has all happened before – that Roman travellers must have felt the same sense of sacrilege when the hideous camel was introduced to penetrate the sanctity of mysterious desert fastnesses, destroying all the romance of donkey journeys.*

RALPH A. BAGNOLD, *LIBYAN SANDS*

*Though your mouth glows, and your skin is parched, yet you feel no languor, the effect of humid heat; your lungs are lightened, your sight brightens, your memory recovers its tone, and your spirits become exuberant; your fancy and imagination are powerfully aroused, and the wildness and sublimity of the scenes around you stir up all the energies of your soul – whether for exertion, danger or strife. Your morale improves; you become frank and cordial, hospitable and single-minded: the hypocritical politeness and the slavery of civilisation are left behind you in the city. Your senses are quickened: they require no stimulants but air and exercise . . . There is a keen enjoyment in mere animal existence. The sharp appetite disposes of the most indigestible food; the sand is softer than a bed of down, and the purity of the air suddenly puts to flight a dire cohort of diseases. Hence it is that both sexes, and every age, the most material as well as the most imaginative of minds, the tamest citizen, the parson, the old maid, the peaceful student, the spoiled child of civilisation, all feel their hearts dilate, and*

62

*their pulses beat strong, as they look down from their dromedaries upon the glorious Desert. Where do we hear of a traveller being disappointed by it?*

SIR RICHARD BURTON, *PERSONAL NARRATIVE OF A PILGRIMAGE TO AL-MADINAH AND MECCAH*

We left Ghadames on 4 December, making our way through a series of farewells that began at the camel pen and carried on right into the desert. Looking less crafty than usual, Abd an Nibbi and his friend Billal came to wish us well, joined by Ibrahim and our host Othman. Mohammed Ali pulled up alongside in a minibus as we left the road.

'Really, I am going to miss you, believe me,' he bellowed across the plain. 'I am too sorry you are leaving now but I am happy also because you are in good condition. You must be very careful now because the desert is too dangerous. Maybe I will come to see you after one week, *inshallah*.'

One by one they left and the silence of the desert began to enfold us. It was a still day and the heat bore down on us steadily as we marched away from the diminishing smudge of green that was Ghadames. The noises of the town receded into nothing. None of us spoke. Only the rhythmic padding of the camels and our own footsteps broke the quiet. There was something mesmerizing about these first steps into the desert, a sense of wonder that increased as we left behind the familiar comforts of civilization.

In front, the vastness of the Hamada al Hamra (Red Plain) unfurled before us. It was golden and supremely monotonous, stretching out as far as the eye could see and disrupted only at its extremities by the distant bosoms of hills, discernible as sloping summits floating above the ground, their bases lost to sight in the vaporous shimmering light that rolled over the horizon like a pool of mercury. It was impossible to estimate their distance from us on a plain like this. The light played too many tricks. They could have been three or four hours away or a whole day's march. Even Abd al Wahab, a man who had grown up in the desert, confessed he did not know how far off they were.

At last we were under way. The desert expedition, which I had longed to make for six years, was beginning. Behind us were all the delays, negotiations and hitches which had felt so interminable, although it had taken us only three days from our arrival in Ghadames to get started. By the standards of nine-teenth-century travellers in Libya, we had not tarried unduly. Ritchie had arrived in Tripoli in October 1818, joined by Lyon a month later. Beset by difficulties in arranging the expedition and receiving permission to visit the interior, they did not set off until the end of the following March. Their plans to reach the Niger from the north were subsequently ruined, first by the exhaustion of their limited funds and then, on 20 November 1819, by the pitiful death of Ritchie from bilious fever in Murzuk. Three decades later, Richardson, who had also intended to pene-trate farther south, this time to Kano, found himself marooned in Ghadames for three months while waiting for a caravan to Ghat. There, in failing health and running out of medicines, he was forced to abort his plans to continue and diverted north-east to Murzuk instead.

Abd al Wahab walked at the head of the caravan, leading the five camels roped together. I brought up the rear, watching the five great bottoms – three white, one brown, one beige – swaying regularly beneath their awkward-looking loads. Ned wore a Moroccan porkpie hat that cut quite a dash but completely failed to protect either his face or neck from the mid-morning glare. When his nose had been burnt red, he exchanged the hat for the more practical cotton *shish*, the best protection against the desert sun. Abd al Wahab was already wearing his *tagilmus*. For the next two weeks he would rarely be seen without it, day or night.

For centuries, his ancestors had derived their living from escorting caravans through the desert. Merchants had been 'encouraged' to retain guides or armed guards for the journey through areas under Touareg control. Charges were based on the estimated value of the goods in transit and the supposed wealth of the owners. Those caravans which did not co-operate ran the very real risk of being plundered by the same men who had offered themselves as escorts. This payment might be in addition to the fees levied by tribal chiefs mentioned by Leo Africanus, the sixteenth-century traveller and diplomat from Granada. 'If any carouan or multitude of merchants will passe those deserts, they are bound to pay certaine custome vnto the prince of the said people, namely, for euery camels load a peece of cloth woorth a ducate,' he noted. The Touareg supplemented these earnings by raiding neighbouring territories for booty, live-stock and slaves, trading salt with merchants from the north, and maintaining herds of camels, sheep and goats.

Richardson, who was among the first Europeans to come into contact with the Azger Touareg, or 'Touarick' as he called them, was not impressed by their manners. They showed, he thought, 'an excessive arrogance in their manners. They look upon the Ghadamsee people with great disdain, considering them as so many sheep which they are to protect from the wolves of The Sahara.' What struck Lyon most about the Touareg was what he regarded as their extraordinary lack of personal hygiene. 'No people have more aversion to washing than the Tuarick generally have,' he sniffed.

> Many attempts were made by us to discover the reason why they kept themselves in such a dirty state; but to all our inquiries we obtained the same answers: 'God never intended that man should injure his health, if he could avoid it: water having been given to man to drink, and cook with, it does not agree with the skin of a Tuarick, who always falls sick after much washing.'

Richardson's attempts to establish their historical origins met with little success. One Ghadamsi told him the Touareg were 'formerly demons', another that they 'sprang out from the ground'. He cited one scholarly opinion that they formed one portion of the tribes expelled from Palestine by Joshua. After their first rendezvous at Oujlah, near the Egyptian oasis of Siwa, they then dispersed south and west to people these arid regions.

The Azger Touareg, who have long enjoyed a reputation for courage and derring-do, are regarded by some scholars as the purest of the Touareg. They were known to Leo as the Lemta, one of the four divisions of the *Muleththemin* (People of the veil), and occupied the desert and steppe between Air and Tibesti, from Ouargla and Ghadames in the north to Kano in the south, an area that encompassed Ghat and western Fezzan in modern Libya. Over the centuries the Touareg drifted south-west under pressure, first from the east and later, with the European scramble for Africa in the late nineteenth century, the north. The southern portion of Lemta territory, which reached Lake Chad, as well as the Kawar road and the steppe north of Chad, was lost to the Azger Touareg as the Kanuri and Tubbu tribes swept across from the east. This ethnic pressure on their eastern borders forced the Touareg to look elsewhere for their expansion. Some moved to Air, others to Tademekka.

The exact origin of the Touareg is probably unfathomable. It may be, as one historian surmised, that their claim to have reached Africa during the Himyaritic migration from the east coast of the Red Sea, is no more than an attempt to root them-selves firmly in the history of Arabia and thereby strengthen their links with the Prophet. This might be compared with the scattered evidence that the Touareg were once Christian. The symbol of the cross features widely among Touareg accessories. Swords, shields, spoons and ornamental strips around doors all bear the cross, as does the Touareg saddle. The latter, in particular, is worth comment since it patently has no practical use. Watching Abd al Wahab swing his legs awkwardly over the crucifix-like fork protruding from the saddle in his flowing *jalabiya*, while twisting his camel's upper lip to ensure it remained kneeling as he mounted, confirmed that. Certain words in the Touareg's Temajegh language also suggest a contact with Christianity. *Mesi* for God; *anjelous* for angel; *arora* for dawn (from the Latin *aurora*). The German traveller Dr Henry Barth, who accompanied Richardson on the latter's second expedition to the African interior in 1849, thought the word Touareg came from the Arabic *tereku dinihum*, meaning 'they changed their religion'.

The Touareg's use of the veil has also baffled scholars for years. The confusion stems from the curious anomaly that the classical authors never referred to the veil when writing about the ancestors of the Touareg. It has to wait until the Arab writers for recognition. 'They that will seeme to be accounted of the better sort, couer their heads ... with a peece of blacke cloth,' wrote Leo, 'part whereof, like a vizard or maske, reacheth downe ouer their faces, couering all their countenance except their eies; and this is their daily kinde of attire.'

Sociologists and historians have agonized over its significance. If, for example, it is simply to protect against the sun, why is it then that only the men wear the *tagilmus* and Touareg women remain unveiled? Whatever the answer, the veil has remained a defining, some would say romanticizing, symbol of the Touareg. 'Almost all Tuareg, unless they have become denationalised, would as soon walk unveiled as an Englishman would walk down Bond Street with his trousers falling down,' observed Francis Rodd, author of *People of the Veil*, the seminal study of the Touareg, in 1926. The slit left for the eyes and part of the nose was no wider than an inch, Rodd observed, and sometimes less. To judge by Abd al Wahab, such strict sartorial standards have slipped somewhat and it is no longer the heinous offence it once was for a Touareg to let another man see his mouth. The Touareg used to lift up the lower part of the veil to eat but would cover their mouth with their hand as they did so. Abd al Wahab, a gentle and well-mannered man in his early forties, was not so prudish.

We had walked for three or four hours on our first day when Abd al Wahab suggested we stop for lunch. Here, in a small patch of pasturage, we received our first ominous insight into what a camel trek involved. All five camels first had to be couched and unloaded, a slow and awkward process for the inexperienced. To prevent them escaping, they then had to be hobbled. To us, this looked a formidably difficult and dangerous undertaking. With one hand holding the head-rope, Abd al Wahab crouched down alongside the two colossal forelegs and plaited an already doubled length of rope about a foot and a half long around the ankles. A large knot in one end fitted neatly through a loop at the other, and the hobble was complete. He then loosened the knot that kept the mouth-rope firmly attached, the camel happily lowering his head to help get rid of this undignified halter. With a firm slap on the rump the animal was encouraged to go off to feed, a stimulus that was rarely necessary. He was already making a beeline for the nearest morsel of unappetizing-looking scrub. Trailing thick twines of frothy saliva, the head-rope was thrown to the ground and the whole process repeated on the next camel. Hobbling the camels enabled them to move about grazing without, in theory, wandering too far. The scope for disaster – such as a swift hoof in the head – seemed huge. Not the least of the difficulties was getting the camel to stand still while the hobble was tied. Every time Ned or I approached one, he would shy away with a flustered flick of the head. Abd al Wahab would not let us attempt it for now. 'The camels do not know you yet and they are frightened,' he said. 'They have to become familiar with you first. You must wait for a few days.'

The sun was fierce and the shade elusive as we fell upon our first lunch of tuna fish sandwiches. I watched the camels receding in the distance, moving ever onwards to the next patch of food. I began to think we had bought fine specimens, for in no way were they ugly animals, as many people suppose camels to be. Perhaps ours was an unusually vain caravan, but together they formed an extremely handsome group. When not hobbled they walked proudly with carefully placed steps, always minutely aware of the slightest obstruction on the ground. Even the darkest and least elegant of the five had a certain dignity of bearing. His svelte, confidently planted legs suggested a long-legged French-woman striding prettily into a brasserie. In due time he would be christened Gobber, due to his habit of spraying anything or anyone around him with generous quantities of saliva.

The hobble reduced the camels to an amusingly inelegant gait. Unable to stretch out their forelegs to anything like their full extent, they shuffled forward instead with tiny steps, an awkward mince that was an absurd contrast to the great length of their limbs. When they wanted to cover ground more quickly while hobbled – whether from fear or having spotted food – they lurched forward with both forelegs together in a rude canter. Their lower lips fell down and quivered each time their padded hoofs landed with a jolt.

By the time we were ready to move on again, lunch had lasted more than two hours. This was far too long. Travelling by camel was already a slow business without holding it up further. We came to the reluctant conclusion that having a lunch stop and covering a respectable distance in a day were mutually exclusive. Having seen us fumble around uselessly while attempting to repack and load the baggage on to the camels, Abd al Wahab, who was never a great eater anyway, thought the same, and we never unloaded the camels again for a lunch break.

The absence of this midday meal was the 'first inconvenience' suffered by Frederick Horneman, the explorer who in 1796 was commissioned by the African Society to explore the continent from Cairo. He had had a difficult start to his expedition. The French fleet had landed at the coast and the invasion of Egypt was under way. Initially imprisoned, he was later presented to Napoleon himself, who offered the traveller his protection for the onward journey. 'Young, robust, and, in point of constitution and health, suited to a struggle with different climates and fatigues,' Horneman nevertheless was a man who liked his food. 'We had travelled from day-break till noon, and no indication appeared of halt or refreshment,' he groaned, 'when I observed the principal and richest merchants gnawing a dry biscuit and some onions, as they went on; and was then, for the first time, informed, that it was not customary to unload the camels for regular repast, or to stop during the day-time, but in cases of urgent necessity.'

Our first and last lunch break ended as soon as Abd al Wahab had retrieved the camels, who had wandered off several hundred yards. A camel is an intelligent and stubborn animal. He understands life is more comfortable without a heavy load on his back so can hardly be blamed for trying to put as much distance as possible between himself and the deposited baggage whenever the occasion presents itself. Besides, there is always the siren call to freedom across the desert. It has always been like this. Richardson's camels were no different. 'The camels are terrible things for straying,' he complained. 'If they are surrounded with immense patches of the most choice herbage, even which is their delicium, they still keep on straying the more of it over miles and miles.' In this respect, Gobber was the worst culprit. Whatever time of day we stopped, he would always make a doomed bid for freedom, invariably heading for his beloved Ghadames with unerring accuracy. The other four, buoyed by his confident departure for better things, would soon follow his lead. Sometimes they would wander maddeningly far.

The first week passed in an aching, weary blur. A little dazed and more often than not exhausted, I did not manage to keep a diary. Part of the problem was a lack of fitness. I had never walked more than twenty miles a day, day in, day out and now wished I had paid a little more attention to Asher's exhortations on pre-departure fitness. It was also a question of acclimatization, learning the routine of desert travel – the early nights and the waking at dawn – and becoming used to the meagre quantities of food, which seemed to consist almost entirely of tuna fish in various guises. We existed in a condition of permanent ravenousness. By the end of each day bones were groaning, stomachs were rumbling and feet were in shock. There never seemed to be a free moment. We were either walking or riding, cooking or washing up, packing or unpacking the camels, hobbling the camels one minute, rounding them up and removing the hobbles the next, adjusting loads or repairing saddles. The only time when there was nothing to do we slept.

The days of hungry monotony marching across unrelieved plains were enlivened periodically by the sight of Ned filing his nails carefully on the back of Gobber, who became his favourite mount during this early stage. At other times I would look across to see a figure striding away from the caravan at some arbitrary tangent, lost in P. G. Wodehouse's *Life at Blandings*, his scruffily arranged *shish* flapping hopelessly behind him in the wind, tufts of hair sprouting between the gaps. Occasionally, he would look up to see where he was, check his course abruptly, and then wander off again.

For the first two mornings, getting started was frustratingly slow. Too tired at night to pack away the opened boxes of food, we woke late to find a confused mess of loads strewn across the camp. Abd al Wahab, an exemplar of quiet efficiency, had removed the five hobbles tied around the camels' knees (in addition to those around the ankles) to prevent them escaping at night, and set them off grazing. Too polite to wake us, he had already lit a fire and was preparing tea. With breakfast over, the camels had to be rounded up, hobbled at the knee again, and loaded. Abd al Wahab and Abd an Nibbi had prepared several camel bags for us. The design was simple but ingenious. A rope was tied around a stone inside the top of each side of the bag and made into a loop. The two loops were then passed over the camel's back, slipped into corresponding loops from a bag on the camel's other side, and held in place by two pieces of wood inserted at right angles. Water *bidoun*s, tied together in specially sewn bags, were similarly loaded.

'What time is it?' asked Abd al Wahab as we set off after our first night in the desert. Embarrassed, I told him it was 11 a.m. He looked mortified. We needed kicking into shape. 'This is not good. We must leave at 8.30 or 9,' he admonished. Earlier than that, it was too cold to start, he added. He told us we had to repack the bags at night and make sure the things we needed for dinner – such as food, teapot, mess tins, saucepan and plates – were in one readily accessible bag and not buried at the bottom of different sacks. We should also get up much earlier in the morning, he said pointedly.

We had only been walking an hour after this inauspicious start when a smart Land Rover in British Racing Green appeared on the plain. It was Abd an Nibbi and Billal coming to check up on us and deliver fresh bread and a large bag of oranges. They teased Abd al Wahab for the extremely modest distance we had covered in the past twenty-four hours – thirteen miles that had felt like fifty. 'My God, you are slow!' said Abd an Nibbi.

Demonstrating great and undeserved loyalty to his new travelling companions, Abd al Wahab rebuffed their comments. He told them we were doing well and our camel skills, still next to nonexistent, were improving. It was kind of them to come but we hoped this was not going to be a daily event. We had not come to the desert to see cars.

We settled into a certain routine, continuing across the plains, already yearning for a change of scenery and what we then fondly considered the romance of sand dunes. Instead, we traversed an unending, rolling mass of flinty grey and wondered why this expanse was called the Red Plain. In the daytime the desert sun sucked all colour out of the landscape, leaving a dazzling blandness in its place. It was only at dawn and dusk that it came to life with the richest lilacs, mauves, navy blues, pinks, reds and ambers flooding across the horizon to chase off this searing austerity.

Moving up a *wadi* (dried riverbed) filled with scrub we reached our first well on the fourth day. A trough made of rough pieces of stone ran next to the well itself, which was covered with a sheet of metal, complete with rope and rubber vessel. Seeing the water being drawn up by Abd al Wahab splashing into the trough, the camels registered a flicker of interest and walked over to see what all the fuss was about. An effete bunch of young men – all were geldings – they quickly arranged themselves to best effect, the three whites flanked by the dark mass of Gobber on one side and Asfar, my beige, on the other. In unison, they lowered their heads gracefully, sucked up a formidable quantity of water and walked off with a look of supreme indifference, spraying us with their dripping muzzles as they tossed their heads from side to side.

From an aesthetic perspective alone, it was difficult not to be won over by Asfar. Tall and slender, with his head held high, he walked with the dignified gait and self-confident bearing of a thoroughbred. His coat was the colour of honey, his black eyelashes were of an excessive, dandified length and he had the tuftiest ears imaginable. He was a handsome fellow and knew it. A good-natured beast with gentle manners, he was also the swiftest of our small caravan and walked with a quick, light step. Where Gobber thundered and Bobbles (named after the three protuberances on his nose) whined, Asfar simply purred. The other camels seemed to be fond of him, too.

In an unhappy display of camel racism, the three whites generally refused to have anything to do with dark brown Gobber. Interaction between him and this group was generally restricted to provocative attacks – usually bites to his rump – by Bobbles. It was Asfar who bridged this divide, getting on equally well with both camps, and maintaining camel morale with discreet diplomacy. Ned had chosen Gobber as his mount, perhaps out of sympathy, and evidently felt obliged to defend him at all costs, both against my jokes and the regular sallies from Bobbles. Riding Gobber was a perverse decision, though. However good-natured and stoic a camel, he was also unquestionably the slowest. A plodding, barrel-chested animal, if he had been a cricketer he would have been the village blacksmith batting at number eleven.

The next day, with laborious, stuttering steps we climbed a pass east of the ridge of Qa'rat Wallamad and arrived at another bleak plateau at about 2,000 feet above sea level. On the ground were small stones arranged in a definite outline, the size of a small house in circumference, with a marked recess in one side. Next to them was a rectangular mound of stones the length of a man. We stopped for a minute and looked at these strange features.

'This is an old mosque where travellers in the desert could pray,' explained Abd al Wahab. 'Now people do not use it because they do not travel by camel anymore.' The recess was the *qiblah*, which indicated the direction in which the faithful should pray to face Mecca. 'And this,' he said, pointing to the smaller outline, 'is the grave of a traveller who died in the desert.' It was as remote a spot as you could find.

Later that afternoon, two tiny puppies, one a grubby white, the other black and white, suddenly appeared and began to trot beside us, gaining in confidence until they were almost at our heels. We thought they might have been abandoned by their owners because we had discovered them next to car tracks. Their chances of survival seemed slim.

'No, they will be fine. They belong to farmers over there,' said the unsentimental Abd al Wahab, pointing vaguely to a line of raised ground in the distance. They looked desperate things, squeaking pathetically and looking exhausted from their efforts to keep up with the massive camels. I felt the same. That evening, after twenty-seven miles – our most productive day yet – my feet were screaming in my stiff new walking boots as we limped across a rambling pasture of rough scrub. In front of us, his profile uncertain in the dreamy glow of sunset, a young Touareg from Dirj, the oasis eighty miles east of Ghadames, was tending a flock of sheep and goats, perhaps 200 of them. The sun was strong but sinking, brightening and blurring the clumps of vegetation into a steaming amber haze as we made a weary camp. Ned and I flopped to the ground with aching legs that felt like iron rods. Abd al Wahab, as unmoved as ever by our exertions that day, walked off purposefully to hunt for firewood. Nothing seemed to tire the man.

Nights were freezing. On this higher plain, as we trudged along the Wadi Qa'rat al Handua, the temperature dipped sharply. Mornings found a pretty covering of frost on our mauve sleeping bags, from which cosiness there was little incentive to depart. I woke each day to the soft cadences of Abd al Wahab beginning his prayers with 'Allahu akbar' (God is great). From my sleeping bag he was an undefined silhouette in the darkness. Listening to the steady flow of his prayers and watching his shadowy figure perform the acts of devotion, rising up, kneeling down, bowing down again, his head touching the ground, was a marvellous way to begin the day. You could sense him shivering in the hostile chill as his modulated voice rushed through this first prayer of the day. I lay on my back watching the bruised sky slowly lighten to dawn and listened to this whispered poetry of praise, one of the most beautiful and evocative aspects of Islam.

'In the desert, prayers are no mere blind obedience to religious dogma, but an instinctive expression of one's inmost self,' wrote Ahmed Hassanein Bey, the Egyptian diplomat who in 1923 travelled 2,200 miles by camel and discovered the 'lost oases' of Jebel Arkenu and Jebel Ouenat, south-east of Kufra. 'The prayers at night bring serenity and peace. At dawn, when new life has suddenly taken possession of the body, one eagerly turns to the Creator to offer humble homage for all the beauty of the world and of life, and to seek guidance for the coming day. One prays then, not because one ought, but because one must.' Richardson, a robust Christian of Victorian England, regarded Muslims as 'superstitious pharisees'. But he, too, was moved by the religious devotion of his travelling companions.

> It was a refreshing, though at the same time a saddening sight, to see the poor Arab camel-drivers pray so devoutly, laying their naked foreheads upon the sharp stones and sand of The Desert. People who had literally so few of the bounties of Providence, many of them scarcely any thing to eat – and yet these travel-worn, famished men supplicated the Eternal God with great and earnest devotion! What a lesson for the fat, over-fed Christian!

Emerging slowly and with the greatest conceivable reluctance from our cocoons each morning, we were met by the instant smash of cold. It numbed limbs and made fingers useless when they were needed to tie and untie knots during the loading of the camels. Unlike any cold I had felt before it seemed to dig deep into my bones. Swathed in blankets and woolly hats, we cut ridiculous figures, panting vigorously, shivering and trying to revive frozen hands around the morning fire. At least we were not alone in feeling the chill. It was just less excusable because we had warmer clothes than Abd al Wahab and down sleeping bags rather than a few woollen blankets to keep us warm at night. Shrouded beneath the erect, pointed hood of his woollen *jalabiya*, Abd al Wahab looked like a character from the mythical world of Tolkien. He beat his hands together, muttered, '*Sugga wajid*,' (It's very cold), and then disappeared to bring in the camels, something for which we were not yet considered ready.

One of the most miserable tasks of the morning (after getting up) was washing up, usually done while Abd al Wahab was fetching the camels. The saucepan, mess tin, spoons, forks and plates were all encrusted with the remnants of the tuna fish pasta from the previous night, the glasses sticky from the heavily sugared tea. With no water to spare, we filled them up with freezing sand and scoured them with bare hands. For the first few times, there was at least a certain novelty about washing up. After that, Ned and I both loathed it equally. If there was ever an opportunity of escaping washing up duty – such as walking off to bring the camels in ourselves – we took it unashamedly. Ned seemed to be particularly skilled at evading the job. Sometimes, usually when I was feeling irritated and therefore petty, it led to arguments. They went like this:

> Justin: 'How come you never do the washing up?'
> Ned (heading away from the camp in the direction of the camels): 'Don't be ridiculous, Justin.'
> Justin: 'Well, you're doing it tomorrow. I'm fed up with doing it every morning.'
> Ned: 'Oh, shut up.'

Long (by our standards) walking days ended around dusk when we had found pasturage for the camels and fuel for our fire. In this part of the western desert it was common enough. Later, the grazing would be perilously scarce. Evenings, too, had their own routine. On stopping for the day, the camels were immediately unloaded and hobbled. They pottered off into the thickening darkness while we set about the most important ritual of the day. The first glass of tea in the evening was always a much longed for treat. In England we would have considered it unpalatably sweet, but after a day tramping across this empty wilderness, it was perfect. Hassanein Bey was initially shocked by the sweetness of the tea prepared by his Bedouin. 'The result would have driven a housewife of the West almost insane,' he wrote, 'but it is a wonderful stimulant after a hard day's trek in the desert, and a glorious revival of one's energies and spirits.'

For Abd al Wahab, a man whose emotional repertoire did not include excitement, preparing tea was something of a sacred rite. It was unthinkable that either Ned or I could make it. With great care he would extract a small amount of tea leaves from a bag, fill his beaten-up teapot with water and put it into the fire to boil from cold, raking the embers around it. Within a few minutes tea was bubbling from the spout, hissing onto the fire below. It was not strong enough yet for Abd al Wahab so was left to brew noisily. At intervals he would remove the lid, inspect the tea knowingly and put the pot back on to boil. Sugar – enough to make a diabetic tremble – was then added to the pot. There was no such thing as stirring. It was dissolved instead by pouring out a glassful, returning it back to the pot, pouring out another and so on. This last process sometimes continued to what seemed to us – tired and thirsty as we were – unnecessary lengths, frequently until the tea was no longer hot but merely warm.

When Abd al Wahab finally deemed it ready (having tasted it first), the tea was then poured out with great ceremony. The spout was initially held close to the rim of the glass, steadily rising up a foot or so until it required definite skill to aim the sputtering stream. The height to which the teapot was raised depended on how flamboyant he was feeling or whether he was in good spirits. The tea came from China, as did the teapot, but the end product was regarded as definitively Touareg.

After this glass or two of tea, the blackness of the night was complete, intensified by the golden light of the fire. It was a little awe-inspiring to watch Abd al Wahab dissolve into the darkness to collect the camels. Twenty minutes later – it varied according to how far they had roamed – a sound of shuffling announced their return. They were still invisible. One by one they were made to kneel down. 'They knelt without noise: and I timed it in my memory,' wrote T. E. Lawrence in *Seven Pillars of Wisdom*.

> First the hesitation, as the camels, looking down, felt the soil with one foot for a soft place; then the muffled thud and the sudden loosening of breath as they dropped on their fore-legs, since this party had come far and were tired; then the shuffle as the hind legs were folded in, and the rocking as they tossed from side to side thrusting outward with their knees to bury them in the cooler subsoil below the burning flints . . .

At night, hobbled upon the ground close together, they were a wonderful sight, great beached ships of the desert irregularly illuminated by the jumping flames of our fire, sniffing the air and searching the ground about them for tufts of grass or other delicacies. Sleeping looked a less romantic affair. The camel would begin in the light doze position, which consisted of craning out his neck to its full extent and lowering it until only the underside of the jaw was resting on the ground. The rest of the neck slanted stiffly aloft. With the whole weight of the beast's great neck resting on the chin, it looked comically uncomfortable. Later, the eyes would close and the neck progressively relax until all of it was resting on the ground, at which point the camel had an air of gentle helplessness. However well secured at night, if they had a mind to move they did, and mornings would often find them thirty or forty yards away. Sometimes they went farther.

Rejoining us after settling the camels, Abd al Wahab would dip his huge hands near the fire to burn off the cold that set in briskly after sunset. He would cast an expert eye on its structure and, without a word, rearrange any branches we might have added in his absence.

'What are we having for dinner?' he would ask either Ned or me, as though addressing his wife.

'Tuna fish pasta,' was invariably the reply.

Rightly, he did not appear to rate our culinary skills highly. A packet soup – perhaps chicken and cumin or, more exotically, Stilton, cauliflower and potato – would be followed by endless variations of this meal. One night, in a crude attempt to vary our diet, I threw together a stew of lentils, potatoes, tomato puree, garlic, onions and tuna. It was revolting. Ned obviously felt the same but, ever polite, murmured something about it being 'interesting'. Abd al Wahab dutifully pushed a spoon around his bowl for a few minutes and then retired to bed earlier than usual. I looked for it the next morning, thinking it might do for a quick lunch on the move. Abd al Wahab had emptied it into the sands.

The country continued remorselessly flat, stony and grey. The horizons were unchanging. The sense of limitless space, of being a tiny, insignificant party moving through a timeless continuum, was affecting. We felt a great freedom, contemplating the surrounding wilderness that was purged of modern life, slipping into a more natural state of eating when hungry, sleeping when tired, waking with dawn, and forming a strengthening bond with the five camels without whom we could not get across this bland, burning expanse.

But it was difficult to concentrate on the landscape for long. More often than not it was too monotonous: there were too few features of interest to break the flint-strewn emptiness. Dwelling on it for too long made you realize how slowly the caravan was travelling and what a vast distance still lay ahead. Sometimes we talked to while away the time, bringing the camels alongside each other as we smoked cigarettes, sometimes we drifted several hundred yards apart and lost ourselves in our own thoughts.

The country was so flat and lifeless that the slightest shape in the distance aroused great excitement. 'What's that black thing over there?' one of us would shout. Twenty minutes later we would be inspecting a discarded oil barrel or wandering through debris from an old army camp – junked machines, water tanks, rusting equipment. We kicked through piles of flints despondently and asked ourselves how long this sort of country would last.

On the seventh day, it changed gloriously. In a fulgor of sunshine we arrived at the top of a steep, boulder-strewn pass that looked out over an immeasurable plain flanked on the south by the outer shores of the Awbari Sand Sea and on the north by an unbroken ridge of ruddy sandstone, cropped off to a level height. We split the camels into smaller groups and picked our way down, obsessed with sand and impatient to put the boredom of flint behind us. The camels did not share our enthusiasm. After a week on the flat, the gradient was an affront. They descended in lurching jolts with heavily planted steps and terror in their eyes. Only Gobber was unruffled. As ever, thick creamy cords of saliva poured from his mouth: walking within thirty feet of him in a rasping wind was a hazardous affair. Sometimes, when I was lost in a deep daytime reverie, Gobber's billowing streams of spit, spangling attractively in the sunlight, splashed across my face and I came to with a start.

We skidded the final yards on to the plain. Our first sight of sand dunes was unforgettable. They started several miles away across the flats, piled high, row after row of them massed together like troops ready for battle, an unconquerable army whose rearguard reached deep into the horizon. The first few rows were clearly delineated and the smooth curves of their outlines were distinct, now stretching towards the sky, now plunging sharply into deep troughs, blown into elegant shapes by the invisible wind. As you looked farther into the distance, their contours started to fade under the blaze of sun, merging into each other until all that remained was a mass of eye-dazzling sand bearing only the faintest trace of shape or slope.

On the plain it felt as though we were entering a no-man's land between two ancient foes of sand and rock. To the south, among the first soothing waves of the incandescent sand sea, hulks of dark rock stood like advance scouts behind enemy lines, a rallying point for the next attack. It was a hopeless conflict that neither side would ever win.

We passed a couple of acacia trees – the first we had come across – and Abd al Wahab said this was Nahiyah, an area in which we would reach another well that evening. In late afternoon we sighted a broad band of green that marked the watering point. There seemed to be signs of life among the blur of scrub, but from this distance it was impossible to say what they were. Gradually, as we approached, they became clearer, until we could make out three tiny silhouettes, immobile on a shoulder of elevated ground above the plain. They faced us directly across the plain and there seemed to be an open challenge in their manner. Was this a Touareg reception committee? A fearless party of desert raiders? Or were they hostile tribesmen guarding their well against the hated infidel?

With each step we took towards them, the figures grew larger. One was a tall, lithe figure, an elegant man wearing a *jalabiya*. Around his head, the ruffled outline of the *tagilmus* was clearly visible. There was, even from this distance, a marked nobility and self-assurance about him. The figure next to him could hardly have been more different. His profile was enormous. Part Sumo wrestler, part urban Arab, he wore a dark anorak over a voluminous *jalabiya*, making the latter look like a clownish flowing skirt. This comic trio was completed by a much smaller figure, dwarfed by his two companions, in army jacket, purple trousers, and shades worn over a khaki attempt at a *shish* that looked like a bandanna gone wrong. He seemed full of nervous energy. While his companions stood stock still, he was bustling about, growing more animated as we drew nearer. When we were yards away, this mad figure hurried forward at us. It was Mohammed Ali. He had said he might drive out to see us in a week.

'Ohhhhhh,' (this in a tone of prodigious satisfaction), 'Mr Jesten and Mr Nid, really I am happy to see you!' he shouted into the bloody sunset. 'God bless you. How are you? Fine? As soon as you left Ghadames I was worrying about you and wondering if you were OK. I thought maybe you died from no water or something. Now I see you, I am in good condition. How are you? Fine?'

It was like meeting up with a long-lost friend. He was a bouncy ball of enthusiasm, rebounding between patches of scrub, amassing a towering pile of firewood, and repeating at intervals his delight at seeing us ('I am too happy now, believe me!'). Ibrahim, a man whose figure suggested a heavy and lifelong involvement with food, smiled and suggested a dinner of tuna fish pasta. The most unobtrusive newcomer was Ali, Abd al Wahab's elder brother.

Mohammed Ali, our air traffic control expert, produced a roaring beacon of a fire that could have been seen for miles around. While Ibrahim attended to the cooking, Abd al Wahab and Ali set about dividing a fifty-kilogram sack of *sha'eer* (barley) among the camels. The scattered pasturage we had come across every day had been decent enough feeding for them. This was an added luxury. Eagerly, they hustled forwards on their knees to the troughs made from empty oil barrels sliced in two, and pounced on the grain.

It had taken the party from Ghadames ten hours to cover what we had travelled in a week. Mohammed Ali was anxious to know how it had been.

'How is the desert? How are the camels? Fine? Are you too tired now? Have you been cold at night? How are your sleeping bags?'

'Everything has been fine, *alhamdulillah*,' we replied.

'How are you? Fine? Are the camels thirsty now? How is Abd al Wahab as a guide?'

'Abd al Wahab has been an excellent guide.'

Ali nodded wisely. 'Yes, he is a good guide, but he is still learning.' It would have been unseemly for an elder brother to praise his younger sibling too effusively. This would have upset the pecking order.

'How is your health? Fine?' added Mohammed.

As the oldest man among us, Ali was the master of ceremonies that night. Preparing the tea was thus his prerogative. He went through the familiar process but finished with a new flourish, pouring out the tea from such a height that each glass had a layer of froth on the top. We were not sure what the point of all this was (after all these exertions the tea was disappointingly warm), but it looked pretty.

Abd al Wahab ate heartily for once. I asked Mohammed Ali to find out what our guide thought of our cooking.

'He says everything is all right,' Mohammed Ali replied quickly.

'No, but ask him what he really thinks of it. Tell him he doesn't have to be polite,' I persisted.

'Abd al Wahab says when you are in the desert you must eat whatever you are given,' came the reply.

The cold was seizing. Mohammed Ali disappeared on several occasions during dinner, reappearing each time with a new layer of clothing. On retiring for the night he looked like a bizarrely muffled Michelin man wearing three pairs of socks, four pairs of trousers, seven shirts and jumpers. With so many clothes on, he could move about only with difficulty. His walk, shambolic at the best of times, was reduced to a teetering stagger. Every time he stood up he looked as though he would fall over. In hysterics, his Ghadamsi friends teased him mercilessly. He fought back gamely, with a few well-placed remarks about Ibrahim's obesity. His British Army sleeping bag also attracted several wry comments. But Mohammed Ali had the last laugh. He, at least, was not cold that night.

In the morning we watered the camels at the well and met a distinguished-looking man called Saleh Omar, a wealthy farmer who had come to inspect his camels, which were being cared for in the desert by two camel boys. On learning that his old friend Ali was with us, he joined him for a lengthy exchange of greetings and several glasses of tea. We remained at the well, and watched as about 150 camels streamed in from behind the dunes. Most were brown dromedaries: a dark shifting mass with a handful of bright specks that were the taller white Meharis. Our own caravan, whose aesthetic qualities we had much admired for the past week, suddenly looked of little consequence.

'Saleh is a very rich man,' observed Mohammed reverentially. 'Maybe he has 200 camels.' Owning a large herd of camels denotes considerable wealth by rural Libyan standards. It was doubly true in the sixteenth century, when the traveller Leo Africanus visited North Africa. 'The Arabians esteeme [their camels] to be their principall possessions and riches,' he reported. 'So that speaking of the wealth of any of their princes or governors, he hath (say they) so many thousand camels, and not so manie thousand ducates.'

Goodbyes were protracted that morning. This would be the last time we would see Mohammed Ali. 'Really, I will miss you too much now,' he thundered in his staccato English. 'I am too sad because you are leaving. Believe me, you must be careful in the desert, but you will have a very good journey with Abd al Wahab.' Before he left, he gave Abd al Wahab a pair of fake Adidas trainers. It was a timely present. The thin pair of leather sandals our guide had been wearing offered no support for the ankles and for the past two or three days he had been walking heavily (and uncomplainingly) on a swollen ankle the size of a pear. He exchanged the sandals for the trainers and thanked Mohammed Ali in his customary quiet and understated style.

Full of tuna and with camels fed and watered, we left the three Ghadamsis packing up their vintage Toyota Landcruiser (regulation royal blue in Libya). Ned and Abd al Wahab stayed on the plain. Childishly keen to climb my first dune, I headed for the nearest one, a giant caramel blancmange, and grunted my way up slowly. On its steeper inclines close to the summit, it was thankless going. For each yard climbed up, half a yard was lost as the sand gave way beneath my feet and I sank in to just below the knee. The twenty-minute ascent (smoker's lungs screaming all the way) purged me of my romantic ideas about sand seas. Ethereally beautiful things to look at, they are hellish to scale.

The summit wave commanded a view over many miles. To

Italian fountain in Green Square, Tripoli.

Propaganda portraits in Tripoli: Gaddafi as desert falcon and (below) jetset, sanctions-busting Arab leader.

قائد الثورة .. قائد القارة الشعبية الاسلامية العالمية

The late-second-century theatre at Sabratha, built at the outset of Rome's Severan dynasty.

Ned strikes a pose in Sabratha.

Mohammed Ali in Ghadames, an ancient centre of the Saharan slave trade.

A slave caravan in the Libyan Sahara, drawn by Captain George Francis Lyon in 1819. 'These poor oppressed beings were… so exhausted as to be scarcely able to walk,' he wrote. 'Many of their inhuman masters rode on camels, with the dreaded whip suspended from their wrists, with which they… enforced obedience from these wretched captives'.

The Big White

Lebead

Gobber

Bobbles

Asfar

Ready to leave Ghadames. From left to right: Ned, Billal, the author, Othman, Mohammed Ali, Abd al Wahab.

Abd al Wahab and The Big White. Note the crucifix-shaped front of the saddle, which some historians believe provides evidence that the Touareg were once Christian.

Nahiyah: the beginnings of the Awbari Sand Sea.

Refreshment: our first well outside Ghadames. 'Nothing is more important in trekking than the condition of your camels,' wrote the Egyptian desert explorer Hassanein Bey in 1925. 'Not only must they be fat and well nourished at the start, but they must be allowed to drink their fill with deliberation and permitted to rest after the drinking.'

Abd al Wahab leads the caravan as we approach Idri.

Traversing the Awbari Sand Sea.

Salek and the caravan.

Salek pours tea in the evening. Hassanein Bey found tea 'a wonderful stimulant after a hard day's trek in the desert, and a glorious revival of one's energies and spirits'.

the south, beyond the patches of scrub where we had camped the night before, were lines of rocky outcrops dribbled over with sand, like cakes sprinkled with sugar. Here and there, silent kingdoms of sand were piled up independently among them, in greater and greater numbers until the rocks were no more and the dunes were one sweeping mass hurrying towards the horizon. To the north were the matchstick figures of Ned and Abd al Wahab leading the camels away from the splash of blue Toyota and beyond them the neat ridge of sandstone, mile after mile of it, like a smudged crayon dashed across the sky.

We moved on towards Idri, covering 20–25 miles a day. Most of the time we walked. Abd al Wahab, who gave the impression of being completely indefatigable, rarely asked us whether we wanted to ride and we were too proud to suggest it ourselves. It was always a joy, then, to hear him ask '*Tibbi tirkub?*' (Do you want to ride?). Ned and I would consult each other first, so as not to look overeager – the result of the conference was always a foregone conclusion – and roar '*Nirkubu!*' (Let's ride!). The camels would then be halted and made to kneel down.

To mount from the camel's left flank, you first grabbed his upper lip, a sensitive part of his anatomy that he was very keen not to have interfered with. Coquettishly, he would duck and swish his head away until, after several attempts, you managed to grab it. Twisting it a little in your hand for maximum control over the animal, you then pulled his head round towards his left side, enabling you to stand with all your weight on your left foot on the camel's reclined left foreleg. Keeping your outstretched left hand on his lip – if you did not, he might throw you off vengefully for the indignity and discomfort of it all – you then swung your right leg over the pommel of the saddle. As soon as your bottom touched the saddle, he would lurch up violently, first the rear legs, which catapulted you forwards, then his forelegs, which would throw you backwards.

We reached the top of another pass that towered over a frazzling cauldron of a plain, whose farthest reaches rippled into the glimmering horizon. It was broken land, hemmed in to the north by dark, chopped mountains. Scattered across the plain were large indistinct shapes, fragments of some great geological upheaval from time immemorial. It was the wildest, most lifeless and least hospitable country yet. Nothing stirred.

Slipping and sinking down a steep sandy corridor the wobbly camels wore an expression of prim defiance, but with the leading camel being led by the nose and the four others by the mouth, there was little they could do to halt our progress. It took an entire day to cross this giant's playground. In places he had hurled rocks the size of tower blocks into the middle of the plain, upending them for his amusement here, smashing them into pieces the size of large houses there. In less violent moods he had arranged a series of graceful Art Deco sculptures for our pleasure: warm curves of sandstone that singed beneath the afternoon sun. The single ridge that had flanked us to the north stuttered into smaller sections several hundred metres long, row after row of them. Some stretches were breaking up altogether, leaving only a few metres of vertical rock presiding over a frozen avalanche of fragments.

It was the scale of the place, unlike anything before, that was most affecting. We scurried through like puny insects. I thought of Lawrence's first sight of the fabled Valley of Rumm in Jordan when he was subdued into silence by the unearthly grandeur of 'this processional way greater than imagination. The Arab armies would have been lost in the length and breadth of it, and within the walls a squadron of aeroplanes could have wheeled in formation. Our little caravan grew self-conscious, and fell dead quiet, afraid and ashamed to flaunt its smallness in the presence of the stupendous hills.'

Forty miles from Idri, we were padding through dreary sand flats when a pick-up carrying four Touareg men forced itself into view. They descended sharply to greet us, shocked and amused to see two foreigners riding camels. After a brief exchange of greetings, Abd al Wahab told us he had heard of the family of one of these Touareg from Idri. We had asked him to help us find a guide for the next leg to Murzuk via Germa. This we were keen to do without Taher's assistance, to avoid unnecessary expense for something we could easily arrange ourselves. We were not sure Taher would see it that way. Having arranged our Libyan visas, he had told us in Tripoli he was now 'responsible' for us (whatever that meant) while we stayed in the country. Abd al Wahab quickly established that one of these men had a brother who might be able to accompany us from Idri to Murzuk. Like almost every other desert guide in Libya, he usually travelled by four-wheel drive but was probably well versed in camel expeditions too. There was something about the way Abd al Wahab said 'probably' that did not inspire great confidence.

The next night, the last before Idri, was the coldest yet. At sunset there was no sight either of any scrub for the camels or fuel for us. Pulling on our woolly hats and fleece jackets we pressed on into a snarling wind that smacked faces and deadened limbs. Fumbling about in the dusk, we roamed from shadow to shadow, mistaking changes of light for patches of choice herbage. Imagination took hold as the light rolled off the horizon. We seized greedily on the slightest alteration to the thickening grey of the plain, veering off our path again and again only to find yet another cascade of dark boulders. At last, in low spirits, we gave in and prepared sullenly for a chilly night.

This was the moment for my kerosene camping stove to make its triumphant Saharan début. It had last been used on a trekking expedition in Pakistan's North West Frontier Province and had worked brilliantly. That was in 1991, however, and it had spent the intervening seven years untested on a garage shelf. I had not checked it back in England, but it had seemed to show signs of life in Ghadames. We would still have a fine dinner and hot tea, I told Abd al Wahab and Ned confidently, hauling out the machine from a dirty sack filled, like most of our bags, with sand.

There was no joy to be had. Pathetic flickers of flames pulsed forth occasionally and then would choke away into an evil little hiss before retiring altogether. Abd al Wahab looked on unmoved by Western technology. Pasta was out of the question. We would never manage to get anything hot enough. It had to be Babylac, baby breakfast food from Ghadames, a mush of porridge in two flavours – banana and mixed fruit. It proved impossible to heat it beyond the tepid but Ned and I, ever hungry, thought it delicious. Abd al Wahab, who disagreed emphatically, was unusually taciturn, pulled his blankets over his head and went to sleep.

Ned tuned his shortwave radio to the BBC World Service. The last time we had listened to the radio there had been an item reporting that President Omar Bongo of Gabon was about to hold elections. The scattered opposition was crying foul and accusing the long-standing leader – thirty-two years at the helm – of rigging the vote. In strident language the ebullient president had dismissed them as silly children with no experience of politics. In the stiff silence of the desert it smacked more of bizarre comedy than the predictable grind of African corruption. Tonight, the incongruous juxtaposition continued with a thirty-minute documentary about the fraught church–state relationship in the Philippines. I could hardly believe what I was listening to. This was a documentary produced by a friend of mine from the BBC World Service several months previously. He had flown into Manila to make the programme and I had arranged a series of interviews for him. Suddenly Kitty Go, one of my Filipina friends, burst onto the airwaves. In forthright language she was denouncing Cardinal Sin, the conservative Archbishop of Manila, who had played a leading role in the downfall of Ferdinand Marcos in 1986 and still enjoyed meddling in politics, as one of the worst things to happen to the Philippines since Imelda Marcos. It was one of the surreal moments of the journey. Thesiger surely would have disapproved.

Fifteen days after we had left Ghadames, and after innumerable are-we-nearly-theres to Abd al Wahab, we sighted the needle outline of a radio mast at the end of a slim plain sandwiched between inconsequential hills to the north and the patient sand dunes to our south.

Every ten minutes or so, a pick-up truck glided soundlessly

past us on a road far to our left. All were loaded precariously with bonfire size piles of firewood, that most precious commodity in a small oasis town.

We edged the camels onto the road and the next pick-up stopped alongside us. Its elderly driver looked mystified at our arrival but would not leave until we had relieved him of two fresh sticks of bread. There were no hotels in town, he informed us, rapidly killing off our fond dreams of a luxurious stopover and celebration of Ned's birthday that evening. More outlines appeared. The red and white stripes of the radio mast grew bolder; square white buildings jostled for space within a distant sludge of green that revealed itself as a battalion of date palms; a pencil line of a minaret gradually emerged, an elegant contrast to the crouching ugliness of a grey concrete water tower.

Contemplating these signs of life in a state of mounting excitement, we were interrupted by another Toyota pick-up driving at rather than towards us. Its front seat was a mass of white *tagilmus*es and black moustaches. We dismounted to see who they were. There was little preamble.

'Get into the car and come with us,' said one, in remarkably good English. His name was Khalil. He was tall, immaculately dressed and of middle age. Judging by his tone and demeanour, he worked for the government. Perhaps he was from the Libyan secret service.

We did not like his tone.

'You speak excellent English,' I ventured neutrally.

'I think so too. Now you come with us. Leave your camels with this man,' he replied, pointing to the youngest of his three companions. His manner was hectoring and aggressive.

'Who are you?' I asked.

'Get into the car.'

'No thank you. We're walking to Idri. We're not travelling by car.'

He looked annoyed, as though unaccustomed to contradiction.

'You will see me later then,' he said haughtily. 'Yes,' he continued, staring at us unpleasantly, 'I will see you in Idri.'

He threw his navy blue *burnous* over his shoulder in disdain, got into the Toyota and drove off, leaving a lanky stick of a man called Salek, and Mubarak, a jaunty black teenager, to lead us into town. Salek, it emerged, was the guide Abd al Wahab had in mind to accompany us to Germa and Murzuk. His father, Haj Habib, whom Salek told us had died in the desert two months previously, had been a well-known figure in these parts. 'He comes from a good family,' said Abd al Wahab. 'I think he will be a very good guide for you.' Ned and I were not so sure. He looked an unlikely, waif-like character, but appearances could be deceptive.

Sunset wafted us into Idri, throwing a golden veil over the salt flats that lay outside the town centre. In the dying light they looked like recently ploughed fields hoary from a January frost. And then traces of life started to intrude on this picturesque evening. Beautiful as it was, the light was not able to soften the sudden ugliness of the mountains of detritus that came at us thick and fast: rusting, burnt-out car hulks; old shoes and trainers; tons of discarded tins of corn oil and tomato purée; cigarette packs by the thousand; school text books; plastic bottles; egg containers; garlands of burnt car tyres; ruined carpets under wrangling coils of wire; haphazard piles of clothes and rags; heaps of rubble where houses had once stood. Idri was a rubbish dump on a grand scale. The camels ripped hungrily at whatever greenery they could lay their teeth on. Children in bright, ragged clothes screamed past us at speed. Women in gaudy *farrashiya*s moved at a more leisurely pace, wiggling along beneath buckets or large parcels on their heads.

The path petered out into a broad wasteland over which more derelict houses were thinly scattered. Some of them had been converted into makeshift animal enclosures for goats, sheep and camels. Several miles away to the south were the mild shades and slopes of the Awbari Sand Sea, across which we must go to reach Germa, en route to Murzuk. This was where we could leave our animals, said Salek. The camels were quickly unloaded and hobbled. Khalil, the man who had accosted us abruptly before we reached Idri, reappeared like a bad smell. For the next forty-eight hours he was ubiquitous. With great care, he reclined on a mat and without lifting a finger started barking out instructions and pieces of advice concerning the camels, most of them nonsense, all of them unwelcome.

'No, you must not undo the bag like that. You're doing it wrong.'

'Thank you for your suggestions but we can manage on our own,' I replied. There was no stopping him.

'No, no, no (watching me hobble a camel). NO! Don't do it like that.'

'Would you like to do it instead?'

A rare silence. Khalil stayed put on his mat, waving his hand at me like an indolent sultan. 'No, not like that (as I carried on with the job).'

The temptation to punch him, already compelling, was growing all the time. By the time we left Idri, his only contribution had been to procure us a fifty-kilogram sack of barley and then overcharge us for it.

Gobber had other thoughts on his mind. While the other camels stood about, he hastened over to a pen in which a tatty she-camel was rubbing herself against a post. Once there, he set about sniffing this unlikely seductress with great passion. With a hobble between his forelegs and missing two balls between his rear legs, it was a courting mission condemned to failure.

Salek invited us to stay at his house and have dinner with him. We accepted gladly, praying only that Khalil would not be coming.

'I am coming with you,' said Khalil. He forced his way unceremoniously into the front seat of Salek's Toyota. 'I have many questions to ask you.'

# CHAPTER V

# Onwards with Salek

*I wonder what the people of Europe will say when I tell them that The Desert – pictured in such frightful colours by the ancients, as teeming with monsters and wild beasts, and every unearthly and uncouth thing and being, not forgetting the dragons, salamanders, vampyres, cockatrices and fiery-flying serpents, and as such believed in these our enlightened days – is a very harmless place, its menagerie being reduced to a few small crows, and now and then a stray butterfly, and a few common house and cheese-and-bacon and fruit flies!*

JAMES RICHARDSON, *TRAVELS IN THE GREAT DESERT OF SAHARA IN THE YEARS OF 1845 AND 1846*

*I am rather afraid that Europeans often make camels stupid by their own foolish treatment of them, whereas I was wont to treat this noble animal, which had carried myself or the heaviest of my things all the way from Tripoli, as a sensible companion, giving it in the beginning the peel of the oranges I was eating, of which it was particularly fond, or a few of my dates (for which it did not fail to turn round its beautiful neck), or granting it a little extra feed of Negro millet, which it ate like a horse . . . Its fidelity will ever remain in my memory as one of the pleasantest recollections of my journey.*

HENRY BARTH, *TRAVELS AND DISCOVERIES IN NORTH AND CENTRAL AFRICA*

Salek's house was a squat bungalow prefab of the type favoured by Gaddafi's town planners. It was falling apart. Doors and locks were broken. There was no bath or shower. Taps leaked. Pipes were rusting. Ants and flies jostled for space in the murky hole in the ground that was the lavatory. Damp walls looked down on this dereliction in despair and were decomposing fast in sympathy. It was the squalor of Orwell's *1984* spiced with the chaos of Black Africa. Discerning London squatters would have turned up their noses at it.

Its main room, into which we were introduced, was bordered by long foam cushions with faded floral covers. Sitting-room flies, a cut above their lavatory cousins, meandered distractedly across the stripes of an ancient carpet festooned with age-old crumbs and other debris. The television occupied pride of place. Clustered around it, fixated on an Arabic news programme, were half a dozen Touareg, each man battening down his *burnous* against the shrill chill of December that raced through the thin walls. They were waiting for the evening call to prayer that signalled it was time to eat. It was day one of Ramadan, the great Muslim fasting month, one of the five pillars or religious obligations of Islam.

We took our place in this bijou cinema. Satellite television, newly arrived in Idri, was considered the ultimate entertainment. Thinking we would like it, one of the men graciously switched to CNN on our behalf. The United States was at that time engrossed by the just released Starr report on President Clinton's affair with Monica Lewinsky. We listened to Henry Hyde, the Republican chairman of the House Judiciary Committee, advising his fellow representatives on how to proceed with this unprecedented account of carnal misdemeanours in the White House. 'Follow your conscience and you will serve your country,' he concluded to a standing ovation. 'May God bless this Congress,' slurped Richard Gephardt, the House Democratic Leader. The Touareg nodded gravely, unable to understand a word of what was happening in the land of the Great Satan. Someone switched back to the Arabic news channel and we watched Allied bombs raining down on Iraq in the latest confrontation with Saddam Hussein. This time the Touareg were entirely clear what was happening and they shook their heads in dismay. After the silence and emptiness of the desert, it was bizarre to sit in front of live news coverage from the US in this small oasis town, and both Ned and I would have rather gone without it. Having stepped out of modern life for the time being, we did not want to dip back into it yet. Abd al Wahab showed no interest in it whatsoever.

We waited hopefully for dinner. At first, the deep comfort of the cushions was all we cared for. After the mean thinness of our rollmats they enfolded us like the finest feather bed, but pangs of hunger began to steal up on us, fended away for the time being by endless cigarettes. Tobacco was indispensable on a journey like this. The epicurean Hassanein Bey had also been an enthusiastic smoker during his camel expeditions. 'A stock of Egyptian cigarettes and tobacco afforded me constant pleasure and comfort throughout the journey,' he recorded with satisfaction. We had a kilogram of Dutch rolling tobacco.

The phone rang. It was Taher. Somehow he had traced us to Salek's house in Idri. He wanted to talk to us, said our host. This was the last thing we felt like doing. The three of us had been travelling for two weeks and after a trek of a little less than 300 miles were filthy, hungry and completely exhausted. All we wanted to do was sprawl out on the cushions, rest and wait for dinner. A late-night chat with a travel agent was not high on our priorities – he would have to wait. We would talk to him tomorrow. Several minutes later, the phone rang again. It was Taher. Abd al Wahab said he would talk to him this time and returned moments later with the surprising news that Taher was about to set off on an overnight journey from Tripoli to Idri. He would meet us in the morning. Salek's friend Khalil, who had been following these developments with increasing interest, pushed into the conversation.

'Why does Taher want to see you?' was his opening gambit. He was becoming an unwelcome busybody.

'I have no idea,' I replied irritably.

'I think there must be something between you and Taher.'

'If there is, it's none of your business.'

'What is it?'

'Perhaps he wants to wish me happy birthday,' said Ned pointedly.

'No, I don't think so. He would not come all the way from Tripoli for that,' replied Khalil, a stranger to irony. 'No, that is not it. But I will find out what business you have with him.'

It was approaching eleven o'clock. Dinner had not happened. Nor were there were any drifting smells that might hint at its imminent arrival.

'Tell me,' Khalil continued haughtily, 'what is the difference between tonight and last night?' He probably expected me to contrast the discomforts of the desert with the unceasing bounty of Idri.

'Last night we had dinner,' I replied, venting my anger on him and forgetting for a moment we were in Salek's house. Hunger was having the better of me. Ned looked shocked. Khalil, too, was initially taken aback, then proceeded to translate my tactless remark with obvious satisfaction. Salek looked mortified and flew out to the kitchen.

A minute later, he returned bearing a circular tray the size of a small paddling pool. In a similarly gargantuan bowl it appeared that half a sheep had been massacred. There was barely room for the pieces of pasta that filled the spaces between chunks of meat that might have doubled up as cricket bats. Next to this hearty fare was a platter of fried camel cubes. I had requested this delicacy earlier in honour of Ned's birthday. For pampered Western palates the mutton was a tough uphill climb, huge blocks of stringy meat, fat and unknown parts of a sheep's anatomy that neither Ned nor I was particularly keen to discover. The camel meat, however, oozing in rich bovine juices, was tender and delicious.

For as long as these luckless beasts have existed, camels have been eaten with much delight. 'The slaughtering of a camel affords a feast to the camel drivers and slaves,' reported the foodie traveller Frederick Horneman in 1798. 'The friends of the owner of the beast have a preference in the purchase; and after dividing the carcase, every slave comes in for a share: no part of the animal capable of being gnawed by human tooth, is suffered to be lost; the very bones pass through various hands and mouths, before they are thrown away.' Foreign travellers vary considerably in their opinions of this fine dish. Richardson, perhaps discouraged at having seen a sickly camel, unappetizingly ridden with fly-covered abscesses, slaughtered for the table, was not a fan. 'Today I ate camel's flesh for the first time, but did not like it much,' he wrote. Ensconced in the British Consulate in Tripoli, Miss Tully, so intrepid in most respects, declined to try it at all, contenting herself with the observation that, 'the flesh is eaten by the Moors, and they say it is extremely good'.

The youthful Captain Lyon, travelling under the assumed name of Said ben Abdallah, spent the equivalent of 6s. 8d. on a strapping Mehari weighing 600lb for his caravan. The enthusiasm as he plunges the knife into the camel's jugular whistles off the page.

> I killed it, and made every one merry, as it was sufficiently large to afford, for freemen and slaves, each two days' allowance . . . The hungry Arabs had many quarrels cutting it up; and I sometimes feared there would be mischief amongst them; but the altercations ended, like other quarrels amongst these people, in great noise, and biting tongues at each other.

Limited for the most part to a diet of bread and water while they blew up Turkish railway lines in the Hejaz desert in 1917–18, Lawrence and his men fell lustily on camel meat whenever an animal died or had to be slaughtered. Growing fonder of our five every day, we wondered whether we could ever do the same. In any case, we had more food than Lawrence. And we had Babylac, our fruit-flavoured baby porridge.

Exhausted and full of camel, we retired to the cushions

and stretched out to sleep, fending off more questions from Khalil, who was loath to leave us even at this late hour. He had made no progress in his quest to find out what business we had with Taher and was aggrieved on this account. Eventually, the sight of three men flat out on makeshift beds proved too boring for him and he left, assuring us he would be back the next day.

The next morning, after a breakfast of tuna sandwiches, hard-boiled eggs and tea, we said goodbye to Abd al Wahab. It was a quiet farewell, more moving for the few words spoken. As our first guide in the Sahara he had been masterful throughout, teaching us a whole range of desert skills, from riding, hobbling and loading the camels, to tying knots and identifying suitable fodder for the camels and fuel for the evening fire. Despite our slow progress, he had never shown any impatience or the slightest irritation. He was a quiet, simple, God-fearing man and we would miss him for the rest of our time in the Sahara.

He wished us well for our onward journey and repeated his assurance that we were in safe hands with Salek. In return, we thanked him for all his instruction and encouragement. Flushed with dollars, and resplendent in clean *jalabiya*, he slipped into a gleaming white four-wheel drive and left for Ghadames. We were on our own again. It was time to find Abd al Wahab's successor. Negotiations began with Salek. He started from the premise that the journey from Idri to Murzuk – about 120 miles as the crow flies – would take about two weeks. We reckoned it would take half that. He shook his head, hamming up an expression of great melancholy.

'Much *ramla* (sand),' he explained, pointing to the swathe of gold on our Michelin map that denoted the Awbari Sand Sea.

'Yes, but only for three or four days,' we replied, 'and then another three or four on the plain to Murzuk. There's no way it will take two weeks.'

'The camels have to go slowly in the dunes,' Salek countered. 'Abd al Wahab said they have not been in sand before.' This may or may not have been true.

'Even if we go very slowly, it will never take that long.'

'*Meshahallah* (it is the work of God),' said Salek with resignation.

There was no use arguing with the Almighty but we repeated our estimation of the time it would take to reach Murzuk. Salek shook his head wearily.

'Too much *ramla*. Also it is Ramadan. I am holy man. It will be difficult for me not to fast.'

This last observation was a little disingenuous. Apart from the fact that he seemed anything but holy, Islam itself did not require Salek to fast. In recognition of the tough physical challenge of Ramadan, the Koran explicitly excuses long-distance travellers, the elderly, the young and the sick from the burden of fasting. The Touareg's attitudes to Ramadan had evidently changed since Richardson's time. During his stay in Ghadames, the Englishman had found them less meticulous than the Arabs about fasting. 'Come, consul, let's have a drink of the pipe,' one suggested to him. 'These people who fast all day are asses.'

Having outlined the reasons why this was such a difficult journey for him, Salek then suggested a fee that was clearly exorbitant. In our eagerness to start, we had already paid over the odds for the first leg of our journey from Ghadames to Idri. We did not want to do so again. Stubbornly but with good humour, Salek refused to budge either on his estimation of how long the journey would take, or on his fee for guiding us to Murzuk. 'Justin, we're wasting our time,' said Ned, whose patience was exhausted. 'Let's go alone.' He could see the negotiations were going nowhere.

I pictured the two of us meandering confusedly across this fearsome sand sea and remembered a line from the RGS notes on desert navigation. It was imperative to have 'a meticulous, even perfectionist, navigator who worships at the altar of Truth rather than the altar of convenient results' when travelling in the desert. Neither of us remotely fitted the bill. We had not even compiled a dead reckoning chart on the last leg. Instead we had relied entirely on our guide and GPS equipment throughout. We could, of course, navigate by GPS, compasses and maps, but it seemed to me that travelling with a local man who knew this part of the country intimately would always be preferable to going alone.

'I don't want to go without a guide,' I said, feeling like a spoilsport ruining an adventure.

'We don't need a guide to take us 120 miles,' Ned replied. 'We've got everything we need to do it ourselves.'

'We've never travelled through dunes before, not even with a guide. We can do that later, once we're more experienced with the camels. What's the rush to go alone?'

Ned looked exasperated. 'He's ripping us off,' he said. 'If you really want to go with a guide, I'll leave you to negotiate with Salek. I'm going to water the camels.'

He was having nothing more to do with it. He left the room and I pressed on with Salek. If he would not suggest a realistic price, we would look elsewhere or do it alone, which I did not want to do. Ned was quite happy to leave Idri without a guide, so it was in Salek's interests to make me a sensible offer, I told him. He replied with an insincere profession of Touareg hospitality. Since we were his guests, he said, he was already obliged to act as our guide. 'You are staying in my house now and I have told Abd al Wahab I will go with you. Even if you have no money I must go with you. This is our custom.' He followed this remark with a price only marginally less extortionate than the first. I began to think Ned was right.

The two of us haggled on doggedly. A gangling, gormless waif of a man, who looked as though a stiff breeze might snap him in two, Salek wore a moustache that hung precariously to his upper lip beneath a long beak of a nose. Unlike the neatly groomed Abd al Wahab, his hair was matted together in an unruly shock. His eyes were like bright white Ping-Pong balls and wore a permanent expression of wonderment. The overall impression was of a benevolent urchin. He spoke with a syrupy lisp, which was exaggerated by a whistling gap between two front teeth that sloped crazily apart from each other. Many others were either dark, rotting fragments or had fallen out altogether, victims of three decades of sweet tea.

The lisped 'alhamdulillah' was his favourite expression, modified when discussing times and distances to 'inshallah'. Before eating, he would look longingly heavenwards and fire off a theatrical 'bismillah' (in the name of God). If a register of surprise were called for, a pert 'wallahi' (oh my God) sufficed. During our negotiations, he had no compunction in invoking divine authority to justify his inflexibility with a solemn but defiant 'meshahallah'. When burping, which he did frequently, he turned to 'astaghfarallah' (excuse me, Lord).

Richardson, a God-fearing Christian, was upset by this constant invocation of God among the Arabs and the Touareg. 'No people in the world use the name of God more vainly than the Mussulmans, nor swear more than they, the greater part of the words being different epithets of the Divine Nature,' he harrumphed. 'I confess I was greatly shocked on hearing these most awful words used in such a way.'

At thirty-one, Salek was much closer in age to us than Abd al Wahab. Whereas the latter was a serious man of the desert and inspired complete confidence, Salek appeared to be a goodnatured joker who laughed inanely and at great volume. Perhaps he knew as little about the desert as we did. But even if not entirely practical, he would, at the very least, make an entertaining companion for a week. Besides, I was determined to take a guide for this stretch of the journey and, having stayed in his house, it would have been awkward to seek another guide elsewhere.

After several more glasses of tea, we finally agreed a price and in better spirits we joined Ned at the well. There was neither a bucket nor a rope to hand, and since the well was deep, he had dug out our length of parachute cord and tied it to a leaky one-litre oil tin. By the time he had hauled the line up thirty metres or so from the bottom, the container was almost empty. As a result, he was not in a good mood. The camels, who by now had decided they were in need of a serious drink after their exertions of the past fortnight, looked equally fed up. Despairing of Ned's antics with the oil tin, Gobber had given up the ghost entirely and returned to his interrupted inspection of the ropy she-camel's nether regions. It was fortunate that Khalil – for once – was not on hand to observe the scene. It could have led to blows.

Salek went off to fetch a bucket and I told Ned I had fixed a price for the guide. We were all set to leave the following day if he was happy with the arrangements. Although it was not his preferred choice, he went along with it, pleased at least that we would soon be on our way again.

While we were talking, a sleek white minibus bumped over to the well and deposited Taher, haggard from the first day of fasting and a twelve-hour drive from Tripoli. We shook hands and small-talked awkwardly. He was still peeved that we had left Tripoli so suddenly without informing him first. Back at Salek's house, things became more amiable. I paid him for the Libyan visas he had arranged for us and he said he would take our passports back with him to Tripoli to insert new ones. Ours were about to expire. Travelling across Libya without a passport seemed inadvisable, but he promised us it was not a problem. Khalil lingered, but with less confidence than usual. A translator by profession, he was daunted by Taher's formidable command of English.

After Taher had gone, the desert town slipped into a heavy afternoon stupor. With the mounting heat and the inactivity of Ramadan, it was a lifeless place. Even the flies were still. Salek retired to his bedroom and advised us to do the same. 'Sleep good,' he lisped with a manic grin. 'Too hot now.' We disregarded this sound advice in order to explore the ruins of Idri before we left for the desert. Sweating heavily and panting in the afternoon blaze, we climbed the hill that rose above this unlovely town. The immediate view hardly justified our exertions. There was next to nothing left of the old castle that had once formed part of this large outcrop above the plain. Its ancient walls, truncated by time, were fast merging with the soil around them.

No-one had seen fit to maintain this historical building, and soon there would be nothing left of it. Clustered around the base of the hill were the pathetic remnants of Idri's *medina*: small houses rotted away, deep in grime, their palm-frond roofs long collapsed. In the narrow alleys between them, children played among the heaps of fallen walls mingled with piles of fetid rubbish. The rebounding stench of sun-baked urine and coiled faeces, together with the brooding heat, was unendurable. Idri was a Godforsaken place. We cut short our excursion and headed into a long line of palm trees presiding over a thick slice of agricultural land. After a few games of cards and several packets of wafer biscuits, consumed discreetly in the shade of a date palm so as not to offend those men and women who were fasting, we returned to Salek's house.

Before we left for Jerma, Salek was anxious for us to check in with the local police. We were keen to have as little to do with them as possible. 'If you go to desert, you must see police, or Salek in trouble,' he explained. We set off in first gear and remained stuck in first gear for the several kilometres to the police station. A group of officers was sitting round a table in the sun playing cards, each man immaculately dressed in navy blue uniform with white flashes. It seemed a shame to disturb this scene. Salek told the senior officer about our plans.

'Where are your passports?' he asked shortly.

'They're in Tripoli with a travel agent,' I replied. 'We were advised to leave them with him.'

'You cannot leave Idri until you show me your passports,' the policeman continued.

'That's not possible. They've just been taken to Tripoli,' I repeated, thinking dark thoughts of Taher.

'Then you cannot go.' He was admirably direct.

Salek remonstrated with him. The officer looked over to the game of cards he was missing and weighed the two alternatives. Take the foreigners to task for this breach of protocol – which would doubtless prove tedious – or get on with the game and pretend he had never seen us. He gave us to understand he had chosen the latter option and saved face by not waving goodbye to us as we shot off in first gear.

All that remained for us to do was fill the water *bidoun*s and stock up on more tins of tuna fish and any other supplies we could get our hands on. In the 'market', which consisted of three or four poorly stocked general grocery stores, hardly more than holes in the wall, the shopkeepers, who had heard of our trip on the Idri grapevine, were ready with a myriad questions.

'Why are you travelling by camel?'

'Where are you from?'

'Do you like Libya?'

'Where are you going?'

'Do you like camels?'

'Do you have a desert in Britain?'

'How much did your camels cost?'

Initial disbelief was their first reaction (was this due to our choice of guide?), followed soon after by a chorus of '*wallahi*' and '*alhamdulillah*'. It was good to travel in the Sahara, they said. It was the most beautiful place on earth. We struggled through our shopping under this good-natured inquisition. Tuna fish, perhaps unsurprisingly, proved easy to find, as were Sando chocolate bars (made in Egypt), later to become one of our most cherished staples. Garlic and onions, however, proved elusive.

Back at Salek's house, I snatched a quick makeshift shower from a bucket inside a filthy cubicle that served as the family bathroom. Peering out of the prison cell window I was met with a nose and a pair of flashing eyes. It was Khalil, staring in with undimmed curiosity.

'What are you doing in there?' he asked imperiously.

'Bugger off,' I replied.

There was no escaping this infuriating man. Wherever we went, he was always only a few steps behind, prying into what-ever it was we were doing. He would accompany us into shops, follow us from room to room in Salek's house, ask what we were doing, recommend alternatives, upset the camels by handling them too roughly and generally get in the way.

'Can't you get rid of him, Salek?' I asked. 'We don't need a translator.'

'Don't get angry Mr Justin,' he grinned. 'He is not a bad man. He just has nothing to do.'

Inside the main room, where we had eaten and slept the night before, two of Salek's friends were elbow-deep inside the rubbish bin, fighting over the surplus items we had thrown away. One of Ned's Elizabeth Arden moisturizers was pounced on greedily. Even empty Biro refills aroused great interest among these frantic scavengers. Having seen the bare shelves of Idri's shops, I could understand their enthusiasm. The things we were discarding to reduce the weight of our packs were not available here and therefore had enormous novelty value. There was very little doing in Idri: we were the only action in town.

Over by the camels, a swelling crowd had gathered to watch us load the caravan. Salek's saddle, borrowed from a friend, looked impossibly tiny. There was no way he could ride on it. It perched ridiculously on his camel's hump, slipping forward so that the cross-shaped pommel was targeted above the animal's head like a primitive missile launcher. It had been left out in the rain one night, apparently, and had shrunk badly.

'Saddle no good,' Salek grinned.

'Can you find another one?' I asked.

'No problem. Salek walk.' He burst into laughter at this. I wondered if he would feel so blasé when we were deep in the dunes.

Inevitably, Khalil was on hand to advise on the loading of the caravan, once again from a recumbent position several yards away. He hissed out various instructions.

'Move the rope to the other side.'

'No! Listen to me. You don't know what you're doing. I know camels.'

'Tsk. Not like that. No, that's wrong.'

'You don't understand how to load the camels.'

'You see, I told you.'

Ned and I turned towards him, glowering.

'SHUT UP!'

For a few moments he fell silent. Then, when we were attaching the head-ropes, he could no longer resist the urge to interfere again.

'No, don't tie the rope to the mouth. Use the nose.'

It was too much even for his friend Salek.

'That's enough!' he shouted. 'Shut up.' Khalil retreated, muttering something under his breath, and we finished packing up the camels without further ado.

A lisped 'bismillah' from our new guide and we were off in the late afternoon, the sunlight dancing in the looming dunes. The flamboyant Mubarak, who had been showing off earlier, trotting about on one of the whites, started to accompany us. He was very keen to come to Germa too. I thanked him, but said we only needed one guide. Crestfallen, he said goodbye and turned back. Life in Idri must have been dull.

Tantalizingly close to the dunes, we marched parallel to them for an hour or so, crossing more crispy salt flats, and stepped into them under a magnificent slanting sunset. There is nothing like the beginning or the end of a day in the desert. First, there is a wonderful purity about the light, intensified by the loneliness of the plains and the dunes that engulf the traveller. For several minutes, the magic monotony of sky and sand is broken and the creeping light at last suggests a challenge to the pitiless glare of day or the oozing dark of night. At dusk, the sun drops into the parched horizon, dragging with it long-lingering fingers of radiance until they too slip from sight and the darkness is complete. Tonight, we were bathed in lilac, ruffling through a filter of clouds that poured in towards the sinking orb. In the evening fire, the light played over the rolling slopes of the dunes, brushing some with veils of amber, draping others in the darkest shadows. A mess of green – patches of scrub and the occasional date palm – appeared through the gloaming and we called stop for the day. Salek, who had been fasting, was looking forward to a drink.

Briskly, we unloaded the camels. Salek reached for a *bidoun* and took a huge slug. His face contorted instantly and he spat and spluttered viciously. It was kerosene, a disastrous way to end his daily fast. I picked up another *bidoun* quickly and started pouring him a cup of water. Trembling uncontrollably with laughter, I succeeded only in spilling it over his outstretched arm. For the rest of the evening he spat and burped in disgust, interrupting these noisy bodily exertions with regular '*astaghfa-rallah*'s.

After tea and tuna fish pasta, we settled down to listen to Salek extolling the many merits of fat women. He was not married yet, but had a generously proportioned girlfriend of twenty whom he intended to marry later in the year, *inshallah*. Slim women he would not entertain for a moment as potential brides. 'My girl-friend is very, very fat, *alhamdulillah*,' he rejoiced. 'Thin women no good.' This predilection for well-covered women, by Touareg and Arab alike, goes back a long way in Libya.

In the sixteenth century, Leo Africanus noted both the chunki-ness and the dangerous sensuality of North African women:

> The women of this nation be grosse, corpulent and of a swart complexion. They are fattest vpon their brest and paps, but slender about the girdle-stead. Very ciuill they are, after their manner, both in speech and gestures: sometimes they will accept of a kisse; but whoso tempteth them farther, putteth his owne life in hazard. For by reason of iealousie you may see them daily one to be the death and destruction of another, and that in such sauage and brutish manner, that in this case they will shew no compassion at all.

In a letter of 1783, Miss Tully wrote of certain 'ladies in Tripoli who think if they are not too fat to move without help, they cannot be strictly handsome, and to arrive at this, they actually force themselves, after a plentiful meal, to eat a fine small wheaten loaf soaked in cold water'. In 1819, Lyon and Ritchie met a woman at Benioleed, south-east of Tripoli, called Lilla Fatma. The famously Falstaffian wife of a Sheikh Barood, she was described by a boy from Tripoli as 'the most beautiful creature he had ever seen, and so fat that she could scarcely walk'. She asked to be introduced to the English travellers. 'I must say I never before beheld such a monstrous mass of human flesh,' Lyon marvelled on setting eyes on her.

> One of her legs, of enormous size, was uncovered as high as the calf, and every one pressed it, admiring its solidity, and praising God for blessing them with such a sight. I was received most graciously, and invited to sit close to her, when one of the first questions she asked me was, if in my country the ladies were as fat and handsome as herself? For the plumpness of my countrywomen, I owned, with shame, that I had never seen one possessed of half such an admirable rotundity, which she took as a great compliment; but I did not attempt to carry the comparison farther.

Richardson, of course, was another sharp observer of the lavish dimensions of Muslim women. 'The embonpoint of Mooresses is well known, and beauty among them is literally by the weight,' he wrote. Once, Arabian poets like Havivi and Montannibi had idealized women's figures more modestly, the Englishman went on: 'Her person should be slender like the bending rush, or tapper lance of Yemen.' All that had changed. 'The taste of the Arabs has been greatly vitiated, and the slight, spare, "bending rush" is often rejected for the bridal beauty who requires a camel to carry her to the house of her husband.' The Moors in Ghat had their negresses fattened up especially to fetch higher prices at the slave markets, Richardson learnt.

Eventually, we moved away from the subject of weighty women. On learning Ned was a farmer, Salek christened him 'Mr Fellah' (peasant), which became his nickname for the rest of the journey to Germa. Turning to Gobber, whom he greatly admired, Salek said he had probably been castrated much later than the other four. 'He understands women, this camel. You saw him with the she-camel in Idri. He still remembers what to do, but now he cannot do anything because he has no balls. It's too bad.'

The night was rounded off by a conversation about the Lockerbie bombing of 1988. Britain and America had long demanded the surrender of the two Libyan suspects – Abd al Basset Ali Mohammed al Megrahi and Al Amin Khalifah Fhimah. The official Libyan news media had propagated the idea, embraced by most Libyans, that there could be no resolution of Lockerbie between London, Washington and Tripoli until the Western imperialists first attended to what Gaddafi referred to (in a bad pun) as Locker-A. This was the American bombing of Tripoli and Benghazi in 1986, when then President Ronald Reagan decided to punish the 'mad dog' Gaddafi for his acts of international terrorism. Apart from the airport and Aziziya army barracks, residential areas were also hit and the French Embassy was badly damaged. A poster on the outside of the Al Kabir Hotel in Tripoli still showed a crying child superimposed above a montage of the wreckage caused by the attack. Beneath was the caption: 'Reagan and Thatcher have vanished and the Libyan people will remain forever with his [sic] everlasting doctrine and principles.' Salek was adamant Libya should not hand over the two Lockerbie suspects (both since surrendered for trial) until America had first handed over those responsible for this 'terrorist' bombing of Tripoli.

The next two days went like clockwork. Every quarter of an hour, something would fall from one of the camels. It tended to be Salek's camel, invariably unburdening himself of his master's cumbersome and poorly packed bedding. Tied behind his swaying saddle, his mass of blankets was the size of a carpet in which Cleopatra could have hidden herself, an unwieldy contrast to the minimalist chic of Abd al Wahab. No matter how tightly Salek tied it back on, within minutes it was sloping off the camel's rump again, and the saddle was cascading down the camel's neck, bringing with it a ten-litre *bidoun* of water. For the camel, it looked uncomfortable to say the least. For us, initially it was amusing, then embarrassing, and later still increasingly irritating. The first few times, Salek giggled good-naturedly while we stopped and helped him reload. Then, when it happened again, he began muttering to himself and was soon cursing the saddle with gusto. 'Come on, we're never going to get anywhere,' said Ned, taking charge, and trying a new arrangement of the bedding. We continued until the next thud of something falling into the sand.

Bobbles, one of the whites, was particularly effective at this. He was named after the row of three protruding lobes, several inches apart, which ran along the ridge of his nose. This is an old Touareg tradition to distinguish the offspring of a famous camel. When the animal is still young, three folds of skin are pinched up and a leather thong is tied tightly around their base.

After a certain time these are cut away and the bobbles remain aloft, 'a kind of hallmark of outstanding quality', according to one anthropologist of Saharan tribes. In Bobbles' case, the seal of approval was perhaps misplaced. Although a strapping beast, without fail he protested vigorously on being loaded each morning, letting out a terrible high-pitched whine that might have been mistaken for a young child being murdered. He was the most temperamental member of the caravan.

The obstreperousness of camels has long been a feature of travel in the desert. 'They invariably grumble and growl, sometimes most piteously, when they are being loaded, as if deprecating the heavy burden about to be placed upon them, and appealing to the mercy of their masters,' Richardson observed.

H. C. Seppings Wright, the English war correspondent who reported on the Italian invasion of Turkish-held Libya in 1911, met a similar reaction from his caravan:

> This so-called beast of burden seems to have every note of complaint in his vocabulary, and the predominant note seems to be ever one of lamentation. He grumbles when lying down, protests whilst he is being loaded, and when he is at last relieved of his burden, you may not stand in front of him, neither may you pass him by, without the calling forth of the most venomous animal curses ever given vent to.

We tried reducing Bobbles' load, thinking that the eighty litres of water he was carrying might have been excessive. To no avail. It soon became clear his objections were based not so much on the specific weight of his own load as the general principle of being obliged to carry anything at all. It was not difficult to sympathize with him. A camel's lot is not an especially happy one. In his foulest moods, he would wait until he had been fully loaded (emitting all the time the same plaintive moan) before maliciously shaking the entire saddle off his back so that we had to reload him from scratch. Sympathy and patience wore thin on such occasions.

As well as being high-spirited, Bobbles was also the most nervous of our camels. One afternoon, I was riding at the head of the caravan in the dunes while Ned and Salek walked alongside. The plastic sheet on which we fed the camels barley started detaching itself from Bobbles' rear, caught the wind and started flapping noisily. The other camels thought little of it. Bobbles, however, was petrified and started bucking wildly and roaring before launching into a panic-stricken, full-blooded trot. By now, the alarm had spread to the other four, who joined the trot – roped together, they had little option but to follow – and started dashing around in a circle, as the plastic sheet, steadily slipping off with all the jolting, grew larger and larger. Through the careering blur I could see Salek standing helplessly, arms aloft, with a look of frozen shock on his face. Only Ned was doing something about it, lunging about until he had got hold of the lead camel and calmed the caravan. If you were worried about accidents in the desert, Salek was not the safest pair of hands around. 'I have never travelled by camel before,' he lisped by way of explanation. Ned looked at him in disbelief. Perhaps he could have told us this before. 'With tourists,' Salek added hastily.

He was an unlikely desert guide, wearing his *tagilmus* with a messy nonchalance that made Ned look dapper. Over his *jalabiya* he wore a thick black felt jacket that must have been murderously hot in the daytime. The ensemble was completed with a pair of fake Nike basketball boots with shoelaces undone. Unlike our first guide, Salek was definitely not Old School Touareg. Abd al Wahab had possessed a natural grace and nobility that was completely lacking in Salek, but the younger man compensated for it with a generous nature and an exuberant sense of humour. Whatever he did wrong, and there was no shortage of mistakes, it was impossible to hold it against him.

My navigational fears about crossing the Awbari Sand Sea without a guide were misplaced, although Ned was too polite to mention it. Salek did not navigate by the stars – we always stopped well before they appeared – and his skills at taking our direction from the position of the sun were also erratic (at best) when compared with the compasses. His preferred method was the less romantic pursuit of car tracks from Idri to Germa, which we had not known existed before setting out. Sometimes they sliced directly across the dunes. When confronted with the larger ones, towers of sliding sand that rose above us like frozen tidal waves, they snaked around in languorous 's' shapes until the gradient was more manageable. Camel prints, though evident in places, had given way to the tyre tracks of Toyota Landcruisers.

The distances we marched each day with Salek were the lowest of the whole journey. This was due both to the endless stops caused by loads falling off camels as well as the more difficult progress through the monumental dunes. Abd al Wahab had been a strict and serious taskmaster, and there had been little doubt about who was in charge. He hated unnecessary delays, got up early, lit the fires, packed his camel alone, helped us with the others, and always made sure we left in good time for a long day's march.

Travelling with Salek was more like looking after an absent-minded schoolboy who didn't know what he was doing. Where Abd al Wahab had taught us how to load and unload the camels, more often than not we found ourselves in the role of teacher with Salek, time after time helping him repack his unfortunate animal. The ill-fitting saddle did not help matters.

Climbing the dunes was an arduous, trudging affair. Descents were painstakingly slow. Never keen on steep downhill inclines, the camels tiptoed daintily, stopping periodically to review the situation. At the crests of dunes they considered unacceptably steep, they dug in in disgust and refused to budge. If yanking on the ropes failed to bring them forward, we traversed the knife-edge ridges until the gradient softened. Bobbles and the other two whites were the most squeamish about this. It was left to the uncomplaining stalwart Gobber and my prettier, more effeminate, Asfar to show the way.

The camels had also come to their own judgement about Salek. As far as they were concerned, he was not the right man to lead them through this difficult country. While he walked up and down the slopes quite jauntily, he hardly gave them a second thought and rarely looked behind him to check the caravan was intact. On the way up, this was not a problem. The camels were unlikely to lose their footing.

But walking too quickly downhill was lethal. Suddenly, the desert stillness would be shattered by a series of thumps, bangs and crashes, often accompanied by a chorus of roaring from the camels. Looking across, you would see all five hurtling wildly downhill, bumping up and down and spilling pans, clothes, barley and almost anything else we carried, liberally across the sand. Salek would turn around when it was too late, discover the problem, stop and look sheepish. The camels would look upset by the accident and Bobbles would be completely distraught. No matter how many times we told him, Salek never seemed to remember the need to adjust his pace.

'Salek, you must go more slowly,' one of us would say. 'Look what's happened to the camels again.'

'Salek is good guide. No worry,' he would reply and then slow down for a few minutes until the next collapse of the caravan on another steep dune.

Our modest progress through the Awbari Sand Sea was also explained by Salek's more relaxed approach to travel (which itself was infectious). One afternoon, two days before Germa, we were etching our way through hillocks covered with *rassu*, an excellent shrub both for fires and camel fodder. Sand and wind had blown the countryside into a fantastic mass of giant molehills dug up among the bare dunes, while the roots of the shrubs had been exposed by countless years of swirling erosion and sat on the slopes like oversized black snakes and lizards.

'Mr Justin and Mr Ned, we should stop here,' Salek said abruptly. It took us completely by surprise. We looked at our watches. It was barely five o'clock and we had travelled a measly twelve miles. 'No more food for camels and no more wood over there,' he said unconvincingly, gesturing towards the horizon.

'What do you think?' I asked Ned. Neither of us wanted to be the first to suggest stopping.

'I don't know. We haven't gone very far,' he said. There was a slight pause.

'I suppose it would be quite nice to stop and have some time to read or do nothing,' he added.

That was enough for me. The prospect of leisure, however brief, was irresistible. Up to now we had never had any time just to laze about and rest. There was always some task to attend to when we stopped for the day.

'OK Salek, that's enough for today,' I said.

We unpacked joyfully, let the camels wander off to browse among the shrubs, climbed several hillocks to rip out some wood for the fire, and read greedily as the sun dipped towards the dunes. Indulging his taste for nineteenth-century politics, Ned was engrossed in Trollope's *The Prime Minister*. I had Lawrence, whose stirring adventures in Arabia made our own journey in the desert seem rather inconsequential. Salek lay down and chain-smoked contentedly on his back.

'Mr Fellah, do you grow dates on your farm?' he asked.

'Actually, we don't,' replied Ned, more interested in the Duke of Omnium's political career than introducing a new fruit to south-west England.

Salek looked extremely disappointed. 'Oh, Mr Fellah, you must have dates. They are the best food in the desert. Dates and tea, *alhamdulillah*.'

His mood had improved since the nadir of swallowing a mouthful of kerosene, from which time he had no longer been fasting. While Salek cooked our dinner, a gregarious beige jerboa that looked like a shrunken gerbil shot around between the food bags looking for his own nourishment. It was one of the few traces of wildlife we saw. A bold animal, he scampered across our faces throughout the night, having consumed the few scraps of pasta we had thrown his way. The next day, we sighted a crow drifting gracefully on the thermals. In the sheer noon sunlight it melted from black into white as it hovered and circled over us. We had to squint to make it out against the bleached dunes before it turned black again. Now, we moved into the most lifeless stretch of the sand sea yet.

Sometimes, standing on the crest of one of these giant dunes, our spirits soared in contemplation of the wild rippling beauty that stretched all around, as far as the eye could see. Nothing could touch these matchless wastes. It was exhilarating to be so removed from any signs of life, and to feel a liberating solitude, deep in this terrible expanse. The stillness was compelling. The only thing that stirred was the wind. It hissed across the summits of the rollercoaster dunes, showering us with grainy missiles, cascading dark veils of sand that disappeared as fast as they arose, and swept imperiously across the wide slopes, repainting the dunes a new sheen of gold that lasted only until the next encroaching blast of air. Wind alone had shaped this dreadful expanse, gouging out strange and beautiful patterns in the sand. With a sense of wonderment, we drifted through this hypnotic landscape.

At other moments, when tiredness and lethargy stole up on us and robbed us of the pleasures of this primeval land, a sense of futility would set in. Then, we asked ourselves glumly why we were here and what we were doing. We felt profound boredom too, exaggerated by the endless drudge of hauling our caravan up and down, dune after dune. We slogged up slopes, hoping for a change of scenery or some new aspect on the horizon to provide a diversion. Instead, the summit would reveal yet another dune ahead and an infinity of glimmering sand beyond. The sight of Salek with camels careering into chaos behind him brought smiles and frowns alike.

Our last night before Germa, like our last night with Abd al Wahab outside Idri, was cold and barren. We crouched in a cavernous depression at the foot of a vertiginous dune and mourned the lack of firewood. Morale was lower than usual as we unpacked the camels and prepared camp. Without giving it much thought, I hobbled Asfar where he stood.

'Do you mind if I say something really annoying?' said Ned. 'You can't leave him there in the middle of all the food bags. He'll be able to get into them during the night.' Normally, we hobbled the camels some distance away from the luggage. The haughtiest and most confident member of the caravan, christened The Big White by Ned, occasionally tried to steal into the bags in the middle of the night, for extra rations. Ned was right, but I was far too tired, and irritated by his schoolmasterly tone, to agree. I looked over to see Asfar, of whom I had grown inordinately fond, chewing the cud in memory of more bountiful times. He was surrounded on all sides by the camel bags and appeared perfectly happy and unthreatening. As always, he looked splendid and his long eyelashes blinked innocently.

'You can move him if you want to,' I replied shortly, 'but don't expect me to help.' Ned, who tended to contain his irritation far better than me, took exception to this comment and refused to have anything to do with me or Salek that evening. He took to his sleeping bag almost immediately and, despite repeated invitations, declined joining us for an unusually good dinner of tuna fish pasta and Sando chocolate bars.

It was the tiniest of disagreements and one of those exchanges that are only comprehensible in the rarefied solitude of the desert when trifles become issues of great moment and the natural tensions of travelling day in, day out with one other person burst out. Salek, a man of unfailing good humour, looked uncomfortable and asked why Ned was angry.

'It's nothing serious,' I told him. I spoke too early.

'Justin, you're being a complete shit,' came a shout from the recumbent Ned. 'We've got to talk about this tomorrow.' I said we would and turned back to Salek, who by now looked slightly nervous. When expressed, which was rarely, Ned's temper was undoubtedly impressive and our guide was troubled by this note of discord. From this point on, he started complaining of a painful foot. Ned was not given over to sulking. Once sweetened by the olive branch offering of a Sando bar the next morning and my apologies for the comments of the night before, he joked about how we would divide the camels if one of us should ever want to separate from the other.

'I'd take Gobber and then we'd race you to Kufra,' he said.

'I'd have Asfar, and there'd be no contest,' I replied.

Whether from loyalty to Gobber or jealousy that he was my camel, Ned had never shown great interest in Asfar and referred to him as Bambi, in recognition of his slightly feminine traits. He was certainly the most fleet-footed of the five and, in my eyes at least, by far the most elegant mount. While acknowledging Gobber's many strengths, I had question marks over his temperament and speed. He (like Ned) could be pigheadedly obstinate at times and, although he moved steadily, his stately progress was no match for Asfar's trotting. The whites we would divide by drawing lots, the whining Bobbles being the wooden spoon.

The dunes gathered themselves together in a final show of force the next day. They rolled and climbed to new heights, dwarfing our diminutive caravan before falling away abruptly into yawning troughs. It was delicate going in places, but we pressed on, keen to celebrate Christmas in some sort of comfort in Germa rather than spend another day eating tuna in this unforgiving country. Today was Christmas Eve. Gobber obligingly presented me with an early gift, a sharp swinging kick in the knee that knocked me to the ground. Back in Tripoli, I had already opened the Christmas present my mother had given me in England. It was a New Testament in which she had inscribed a verse from Deuteronomy 2: 'The Lord your God has blessed you in all the work of your hands. He has watched over your journey through this vast desert.'

In the early afternoon, Salek said we were approaching the southernmost shores of the sand sea and would soon see a mountain range. I scaled a ridge and sweated along it for a view of the land ahead. For an hour or so, there was no trace of the dunes giving up their hold. Then, a thick ruddy band appeared above them. It was the southern edge of Wadi al Ajal, the long valley in which lay the town of Germa. The ridge appeared to run parallel to the dunes, guarding a fertile belt several kilometres wide that ran between them. This flourish of green, which sprouted at the bottom of the mass of striated rock, was blissful to see after several days of uninterrupted dunes. There was no sign of Germa, or any other habitation, but the chain of oases looked thick enough to hide several reasonably sized towns. The camels snorted over the remaining pikes of sand, stacked together at great height as if for dramatic effect, before sliding precipitately into the *wadi* below.

At the bottom of the last dune, we paused on the stone-strewn plain to regroup and celebrate the end of the sand sea. Salek insisted we head straight towards the oasis. Ned checked his GPS to see exactly where we were in relation to Jerma and discovered we were at least twenty kilometres away. Our hearts sank. The celebrations had been premature. There was still a long way to go. Salek looked horrified and started blabbering. 'Salek say Germa this way,' he said defiantly, pointing straight ahead, 'No good GPS.'

We checked again and got the same answer. The town was twenty kilometres away. The problem was that since Germa was not marked on our large-scale maps the GPS could be wrong. Salek asked how far away Awbari was according to the GPS and then calculated we were on course after all, a discovery that removed all traces of horror and replaced them with great guffawing and a rare note of triumphalism. 'GPS no good,' he lisped accusingly. With the index finger of his right hand he tapped his head. He considered it a beacon of navigational excellence. 'Touareg GPS good. Salek find Germa no problem. Oh yes.'

Trusting Salek's instinct, we marched on in the direction he suggested. Birds wheeled overhead, escorting us towards the furry shades of green that grew at the foot of the terracotta curtain of rock behind the town. In the steaming sunset we zigzagged past farmers' plots, some dull and untended, others oozing fields of verdant grass. Different families of date palms converged on the hinterland. There were the familiar clusters of trunks that rose like slim, swaying minarets, casting lancelike shadows across our way. The evening chorus was in full swing from these heights. Beside them, their less elegant cousins looked squat and bushy. Hares hiding in these leafy homes took fright at our approach and hotfooted it out of sight, a kicking blur of legs and dust.

As we walked through the outer reaches of Germa, Salek muttered a remark about not coming to Murzuk with us. He repeated his unease at not fasting during Ramadan, and referred to his sore foot – thanks to his shrunken saddle, he had walked all the way from Idri, whereas we had ridden for much of the journey – and the argument Ned and I had had the previous night. Ever since that brief disagreement between the two of us, Salek had been acting out of character.

He was no longer the amiable, exuberant young man. Instead, he had become subdued and serious, as if preparing for a fateful decision. I tried to dissuade him from backing out now and reminded him he had agreed to go with us as far as Murzuk. He looked ashamed and said he might start fasting again while we were in Germa and then see how he felt. Otherwise, he was sorry, but he would arrange for another guide to take us on from Germa.

The track we were following wound through a twisted mass of decapitated palms. It was difficult to know what had happened here. It might have been an incomplete attempt to clear the area by cutting down and burning the palms. Whatever it was, the appearance was startling. Palm trunks sloped from the ground at improbable angles, as though ranks of archers had unleashed a flight of giant arrows into the soft underbelly of the desert. Some had been cut down entirely and lay lifeless among the stump-littered patches of grass. Most had been burnt while still standing; the charred black spikes were arranged as though in some chaotic defence of the town. There was something sinister about these jagged silhouettes. In the evening light, it was like a battlefield smouldering hours after a massive napalm attack, a quagmire of destruction that made you think of Vietnam.

Hemmed in by dilapidated fencing and overgrown with palms, the ancient *kasbah* (castle) had long lost its own battle against gravity and neglect alongside a girdle of equally ruined, smaller settlements. This was prehistoric Garama, home of the Garamantes, the desert race that had endured for more than 2,000 years, one of the greatest groups of tribes ever to rule the Sahara and the most formidable challenge to Rome's sway in North Africa.

It was night as we slipped into Germa itself, a grid of unremarkable square houses and naked light bulbs. The town had retired for the night and the streets were almost bare. The camels moved twitchily along the tarmac road, nervous in our new surroundings after the sweeping width of the dunes. Salek greeted a solitary young man wearing a black bomber jacket and asked him where we could stay. The man gave a fulsome recommendation of the Germa Tourist Hotel – it was by far the most comfortable place in town, he said – and we started dreaming of saunas and swimming pools, room service and minibars, the sort of illusions so easy to come by after days of austerity. Instead, we checked into a fairly shabby little place with a weary receptionist who did not take kindly to the combination of two British tourists with five camels and no passports. Grudgingly, he said we could stable them in the garden in front of the hotel, a small oblong of grass studded with date palms. They settled happily in this urban oasis, nosing the ground for food and stripping the trees of bark and leaves with unrestrained glee, watched by a growing reception committee of hotel hangers-on. All were eager to know where we had come from, where we were going, why we were travelling by camel and, most pressingly, how much the animals had cost. We answered them one by one and pretended not to understand the last question.

After what felt like endless days of tuna fish pasta, Christmas Eve dinner was an unspeakable luxury of bean soup, mutton stew, fried chicken, chips and salad prepared by the hotel chef Mukhtar, a pleasant middle-aged Mauritanian. We asked him if he could cook us a special Christmas dinner the following day. He said he would be happy to oblige. Though less important to Muslims than Christians, Christmas Day, as the birthday of the prophet Jesus, is still an important date in the Islamic calendar.

After dinner, Ned repaired to the hotel bath (the first since Tripoli) with Trollope. While he was away, Salek repeated his determination to call it a day in Germa. This time there was no talking him out of it. His manner, so positive and carefree before, was now despondent and embarrassed. He knew he was letting us down but his feet were too sore to go on, he said. He was very sorry for the inconvenience, but wanted to return home to his family to continue the fast. There was no point arguing any more. It would be no good travelling across the desert with a reluctant guide. Salek had had enough.

# CHAPTER VI

# Christmas in Germa

*Their [Touareg] manner of riding is most ridiculous. For sometimes they lay their legs acrosse vpon the camels neck; and sometimes againe (hauing no knowledge nor regard of stirrops) they rest their feete vpon a rope, which is cast ouer his shoulders. In stead of spurres they use a truncheon of a cubites length, hauing at the one end thereof a goad, wherewith they pricke onely the shoulders of their camels.*

JOHANNES LEO, *A GEOGRAPHICAL*
*HISTORIE OF AFRICA*

I woke with a burgundy sock in my face.

'Happy Christmas,' said Ned.

He had made me a stocking. With childish excitement and shame (I had not bought him anything), I delved into it. First there was something called the Pro-Yo III, the world's longest fixed axle yo-yo ('as used by World Pro-Yo Master Yo-Hans'), next Ned's well-worn copy of P. G. Wodehouse's *Life at Blandings*. There followed a Rubik's cube and lots of chocolate and sweets, rounded off with a blood orange in the toes.

I left the hotel quickly to scout the shops for something for Ned. The combination of Friday (Islam's holy day), Ramadan and Christmas Day was not auspicious. Only one shopkeeper could be persuaded to open up, and I duly purchased a carton of 200 Marlboro cigarettes, assorted lollies and other sweets, a couple of chicken stock cubes and a dubious-looking aftershave called Black Silk. The cigarettes went down particularly well.

We breakfasted handsomely on fresh bread, La Vache Qui Rit cheese, jam, cappuccino and orangeade. After hearing us speak English, an effeminate Libyan driver called Mohammed Adib, who was also staying in the hotel, joined us. He worked for an Anglo-German oil company and was en route to Tripoli from the desert.

'You know, I like England too much,' he began politely. Suddenly, the mysterious Dorset connection resurfaced. 'I lived in Bournemouth one year,' he continued. 'My landlady, she have four cars. Every Sunday, she give me newest one and I collect her daughter from Poole.' Like Mohammed Ali, he was a connoisseur of Bournemouth's hottest night-spots, but preferred Tiffany's to Badger's. 'Oh yes,' he purred fondly, casting his mind back to happier times, 'the men there were very nice.'

Salek reappeared in a clean *jalabiya*, having stayed overnight with a friend in Awbari. Now that he had opted out of the journey from Germa to Murzuk, his morale had improved – he was fasting once again, he told us later – and the old spring in his step had returned. There did not seem to be much wrong with his 'sore' foot.

A loud, exuberant greeting. 'Happy Christmas, Mr *Fellah*, Mr Justin! How are you?' He had only been gone a night but already it was good to see him again. We asked if he had made any progress in finding a replacement guide. 'Don't worry. Very soon, Salek find you good guide, just like me,' he assured us, and went off, promising to return later with more news.

Leaving Ned immersed in Trollope, I went off to explore Germa. In the town centre, a woman in a brightly coloured *farrashiya* ambled along the dusty street, carrying a heap of palm fronds and other firewood. Surreptitiously, another peeped out from behind a metal gate. On the road out of town, half a dozen cars formed a queue by the solitary petrol pump. (No matter that Libya was one of the world's top oil producers. Filling up your car was still hard work.) Children ran between the houses. Their favourite toys were 'cars' consisting of flattened oil tins with four or six wheels made from the ends of tin cans attached by wire. The whole contraption was raced noisily along with a stick, throwing up clouds of dust amid the boys' shrieking catcalls.

It was a cleaner town than Idri but still wore the familiar detritus of empty corn oil tins, cigarette packs and the occasional burnt-out car skeleton. More care had been taken with the houses here. Most were painted, an improvement on the unfinished ugliness of the grey breeze blocks that had dominated Idri, but many were in various stages of decay. A medley of coloured clothes and blankets hung from cracked balconies and broken windows. Across the main road – Germa was little more than a one-street town – thirty Touareg workers from Niger were digging foundations for a new school. Each man stood in his own hole in the ground, toiling through the pink, orange and white layers of soil in the slick midday heat like a medieval serf. Grander houses were being constructed nearby. An elaborately decorated green and beige minaret dominated the skyline.

Farther on were two derelict Nissen huts that were once the offices of the Libyan Red Crescent and Jerma Youth Club ('Lorghing and Accomodation') respectively. The roofs had long since collapsed and the walls were daubed in graffiti. Pages from Russian newspapers had been glued to the inside of broken windows. Behind the buildings was a swimming pool with a broken diving board, half filled with a treacly black mire teeming with rubbish. The interminable Gaddafi propaganda – 'Revolution Forever' – seemed a fitting epitaph for this pathetic scene of squalor.

In the town itself there was little to suggest Germa's former greatness. If the museum in Ghadames required ten minutes from start to finish, that in Jerma demanded little more than a quarter of an hour to see its dull collection of pottery, assorted photographs and random bric-a-brac. This had been the ancient capital of the Garamantes, the Rome of the Sahara, headquarters of a prehistoric trading empire that had stretched for thousands of miles across the desert, yet today you would hardly know it.

Apart from the tombs that survived along the *wadi* and the scattered evidence of rock art in the area, there was nothing other than this half-baked municipal museum to honour a once great civilization. From this town for centuries the Garamantes had terrorized vast swathes of the Sahara, infuriating successive emperors across the Mediterranean with their repeated refusals to buckle down under the *pax Romana*. To all intents and purposes, we were following in the footsteps of eighteenth- and nineteenth-century explorers and campaigners against the slave trade, but it was the Garamantes who far earlier had mastered this hostile territory and forged ahead as pioneers of a desert trade that would continue virtually unchanged in its essentials until the twentieth century.

The Garamantes were a loose confederation of Libyan tribes dating to *c.* 1000 BC. What we know about this enigmatic warlike race is patchy, due to the passage of time, but accounts begin with the classical authors. Herodotus, who visited Libya around 450 BC, was greatly taken by their distinctive cattle, 'which as they graze, walk backwards. This they do because their horns curve far outwards in front of their heads, so that it is not possible for them when grazing to move forwards, since in that case their horns would become fixed in the ground'. The Greek geographer Strabo paid tribute to the Garamantes' skills at horse breeding (100,000 colts were born every year, he said), which helped explain their prodigious success in the desert.

Horses were to the Garamantes as camels later were to the other tribes of the Sahara. As warriors they were marvellously ahead of their time with four-horse chariots 'in which they chase the Troglodyte Ethiopians, who of all the nations whereof any account has reached our ears are by far the swiftest of foot,' wrote Herodotus. The troglodytes were the forerunners of the Tubbu tribe of Tibesti. Here in Jerma, we were on the easternmost fringes of Touareg country. As we moved on towards the south-eastern oasis of Kufra, assuming Salek found us a guide, we would be crossing into territory that had once belonged to their age-old foe, the Tubbu.

Herodotus contradicted himself in the same section of his *Histories* by saying the Garamantes 'avoid all society or intercourse with their fellow-men, have no weapon of war, and do not know how to defend themselves'. This was inaccurate. Their familiarity with the desert was a powerful advantage in resisting invaders, as the Romans repeatedly discovered to their cost. Five centuries later, Pliny complained that it was 'impossible to open up the road to the Garamantes country, because brigands of that race fill up the wells with sand'. Whatever their defensive skills, few were in doubt about their offensive strengths. The Garamantes did nothing if not look beyond the 100-mile chain of oases linking Wadi al Ajal to Wadi ash Shati and Wadi Barjuj. As traders they dominated from the Atlantic to the Nile and from the steppes of Sudan, possibly as far south as Lake Chad, to the Mediterranean coast. Introverted and retiring the Garamantes were not.

Long before the Romans arrived, they were trading in precious stones (the carbuncles later mentioned by Pliny) with the Phoenicians and Greeks on the coast, as well as in slaves and gold, those old staples of Saharan commerce. Goods from the Mediterranean were taken south into Black Africa and exchanged for other commodities like silver, tin, dates, and ostrich feathers, which would continue to be traded into the twentieth century.

It was the Romans who shattered the lucrative existence of these early Saharan monopolists. The rout suffered by the Garamantes at the hands of Cornelius Balbus in 19 BC was a defining moment. Their unchallenged ascendancy in the Sahara was over: never again would they hold such wealth and military power. Their appetite for war and booty had still not been sated, however, and they continued to raid Roman territory sporadically, prompting two new campaigns against them, the first five years after Balbus, the second in AD 6.

In AD 68–9 the Garamantes made what proved to be their greatest mistake. After Oea (Tripoli) had offered them payment for military support in its war with Leptis Magna over control of coastal and Saharan trade, the horsemen surged north and laid waste the country around Leptis. A large force under Valerius

Festus came to Leptis' aid, peace was restored between the two Tripolitanian cities, and the Garamantes were punished again, this time by a defeat so comprehensive it led to outright pacification.

We next hear of them several years later in their reduced role as allies of Rome, when their subdual had opened the door to renewed Roman exploration of the continent. An expedition led by Julius Maternus at the turn of the century left Garama escorted by the King of the Garamantes and 'arrived in four months at Agisymba [probably Air] a district or province of the Aethiopians where rhinoceroses congregate', according to Ptolemy of Alexandria. From the descriptions of the expedition it seems likely that Maternus penetrated as far south as Lake Chad, an astounding venture that would go unmatched until the nineteenth century. Men like Horneman, Lyon, Ritchie, Laing, Richardson, Barth and the great German traveller Gerhard Rohlfs saw themselves as pioneering African explorers, but they had in fact been preceded in most of their discoveries by 1,800 years.

After the disappointments of the museum, we returned to the Germa Tourist Hotel, where Mukhtar was putting the finishing touches to our Christmas Dinner. It bore an uncanny resemblance to the dinner of the previous night as well as the lunch we had eaten that day. The only difference, to mark the birthday of Christ, was a flourish of two congealed fried eggs. Our celebrations were further improved when a convivial Italian family at the next table kindly presented us with some excellent *panettone*. The reconstituted meat stew, however, was lethal stuff and I spent the next forty-eight hours in an uncomfortable head-spinning blur, marked at two-hourly intervals by voluble vomiting. I lay in my sleeping bag, marvelling at Mukhtar's power to wreak havoc with my innards, and read Lawrence in a daze. Stokes, an English sergeant brought in to teach the Arabs how to use trench-mortars, had just been laid low by dysentery. 'So few Englishmen seemed to have been endowed by their upbringing with any organic resistance to disease,' Lawrence observed tartly. Fortified by Trollope or simply possessed of a more robust constitution, Ned did not succumb. Instead he struck up a conversation with a Frenchman staying in the hotel, who had written a book on prehistoric rock art and was in Germa to research another. He and his wife gave us copies of the detailed Russian Survey maps of Libya that had never arrived from Germany.

Mubarak, Salek's excitable friend from Idri, called in on us one afternoon to find out how we were. Travelling in a four-wheel drive, it had taken him two and a half hours to get here. We had spent a little over four days on the same journey. He greeted us with a flurry of kisses and hugs and for several minutes would not let go of our hands. Once he did, he could not stop patting us, pinching our cheeks, and putting his arms around our shoulders.

Undaunted by our refusal to employ him as guide from Idri, Mubarak now suggested joining us in this capacity from Germa. 'I must come with you,' he insisted, claiming expert knowledge of the terrain for hundreds of miles around. 'I take you anywhere. You want Murzuk? Easy, no problem. I take you Murzuk. You want Kufra? I take you Kufra. I know desert too much.'

As a companion he would probably have been great fun to travel with. But he talked too much, appeared to know even less about the desert than Salek, and would not stop touching us. We declined as politely as possible and waited in the hotel for Salek, who had already promised to find us a guide. He arrived that evening with a taciturn Touareg of apparently advanced age. It was difficult to tell. A black *tagilmus* hid most of his face, revealing only a pair of lifeless eyes and a flicker of snowy stubble. A tatty black *burnous* covered the rest of his frame against a frosty December night. His name was Saleh Hassan Suleiman, a sixty-three-year-old former policeman who now worked as a farmer. He knew this area extremely well and was happy – his manner suggested otherwise – to guide us to Murzuk, Salek said. It would take us three to four days. Once we arrived in Murzuk, *inshallah*, Salek would then pay Saleh from the fee we had originally agreed for the whole leg from Idri to Murzuk. That was to be arranged between the two of them. I remembered Salek's original estimate of two weeks for this journey and wondered how much he would pay the new guide for this remaining stretch. He was bound to take a commission but we did not begrudge him it. He had been too good a companion for that. Besides, with the recent death of his father he was now the main provider for a large family.

Before we left Germa, we made a brief excursion to Gabraoun by four-wheel drive. The former desert settlement, the most remote we had yet encountered, was surrounded on all sides by a golden mantle of dunes, towering cathedrals of sand that fell sharply to ground level. Set like a bright jewel among a thousand square miles of the Dawwada Sand Sea, its most startling feature was a shimmering lake that reflected the dazzling blaze of the sun, perhaps 300 metres wide and more than a hundred across, bordered by a thick forest of reeds and bright green date palms that swayed in the slight wind. The Winzrik Tourism Services company had established a forlorn attempt to persuade the few tourists who visited Gabraoun to spend a night in this lovely spot. A dozen collapsing palm huts, each containing filthy mattresses, were presided over by a circumspect young Nigerian, who had recently emigrated to Libya in search of a better life. His washing hung out on one of the lodges, burning in the sun. Once a thriving if isolated small village, Gabraoun was now a mass of derelict houses covered in graffiti, another example of modern Libya's quixotic relocation schemes.

The English traveller Dr Walter Oudney, who later died of consumption south-east of Lake Chad, was the first European to visit Lake Gabraoun in 1822. Like Ritchie before him, Oudney had been appointed a vice-consul, charged with investigating opportunities for British business and making the country's name generally known in the African interior. There were few openings, it seemed, in Gabraoun. Oudney found the oasis inhabited by a strange population called the Dawwada (worm-eaters), which referred to the brine shrimp that lived in the lake. Women fished for them and exchanged their catch for goods such as tobacco, cotton and olive oil from passing Touareg caravans. The inhabitants of the oasis also cultivated dates, apples, figs, apricots, pomegranates, peaches, almonds, tomatoes and onions.

By the time we returned to the hotel, we were growing restless to leave Germa. The manager of the hotel, increasingly grieved while we prolonged our stay to watch his front garden disappear down the camels' mouths, felt the same.

'You must go now,' he said tetchily.

'Yes, we'll be leaving tomorrow,' I replied.

'You must leave hotel. Your camels no good. They eat my trees,' he continued accusingly, pointing to half a dozen thread-bare skeletons that only three days ago had been flourishing symphonies of green. What grass there had been was now trodden into a quagmire of camel faeces mixed with the hay, barley and water we had given them. The five camels themselves, rested and well-fed, looked on this unhappy scene blithely and with undisguised contentment, basking in the admiration of a couple of Italian children who stroked them with awe.

We left Jerma on 28 December, bracing ourselves for New Year's Eve celebrations in Murzuk. It was a revitalized caravan. We had recruited a couple of unemployed Niger Touareg to make some much-needed repairs to our creaking saddles. Although they had relieved me of my Swiss Army knife in the process, they had also done some good work sewing together the water *bidoun*s, which now looked less precarious than usual.

Saleh was a squat man, half sergeant-major, half small-town tramp. Apart from the ubiquitous *tagilmus*, he wore an old black anorak, faded mauve *jalabiya* and holed desert boots. Deep lines railroaded across his forehead and he looked older than his years, an impression to which his generally morose nature must surely have contributed. He marched briskly, his head tucked into the wind, and always carried a stick that he took to the camels with more gusto than we liked. Whether he was beating a camel or merely grumbling bitterly about the many inconveniences of travelling in the desert, there was a coarse brutality about him that made you wonder how it would have felt to have been interrogated by him in his time as a policeman. By day he was invariably moody. The contrast with the self-containment and quiet efficiency of Abd al Wahab was obvious as he grunted orders while we packed the camels, hurrying around to undo and retie our knots with stormy mutterings and great shakings of the head. Abd al Wahab had taught us one way of loading the animals. Saleh had his and, as far as he was concerned, it was the only way to do it.

The Royal Geographical Society notes sprang to mind again: 'However good your guide or companion, there will inevitably be conflict sooner or later [very soon in our case] and this will tend to revolve around the age-old question of "who is boss?" Desert guides tend to be dominant characters and, however experienced you may be, they will inevitably regard you as a stranger in a strange land.'

His favourite expressions were *mishkilla* (problem) and *mishkilla kabira* (big problem). He used them liberally. If, for example, the length of rope separating one camel from another was a trifle too short or too long, he would stop with a look of disgusted disbelief at our incompetence and reel off a round of *mishkilla*s. When, as was sometimes the case, wood was either scarce or non-existent where we camped, Saleh invoked the dread power of the *mishkilla* again. When there was no grazing for the camels, it was a venomous *mishkilla kabira*. Admittedly, this was a more serious problem, but the camels had been well looked after in Germa and this was only a short stretch. They were, as Mohammed Ali might have said, still 'in good condition'. Saleh was an expert at discovering problems where none existed. We wondered whether he was surly by disposition or merely resentful at having to work as a guide for two young travellers at the age of sixty-three.

His only redeeming aspect on this first day was his admiration of Asfar, my light-footed mount. 'He is an excellent camel,' he said approvingly, 'the best of the five.' He spoiled it, however, by following with some contemptuous remarks about Gobber and did not endear himself to Ned on this account.

'That one is nothing,' he said dismissively, pointing to the blameless Gobber. He started highlighting Gobber's weaknesses, the gravest apparently being the diminutive size of his hump.

'God, he's irritating,' Ned said to me, as the list of Gobber's failings went on. Loyally, he stood by his favourite mount, pointing to Gobber and saying pointedly to Saleh, 'good camel, good camel'.

An uncouth man when challenged, Saleh tut-tutted loudly.

'You're a very rude man,' said Ned in English.

Saleh muttered darkly to himself and walked away with an unpleasant sneer on his face.

Sandwiched between two cliffs of dynamited sandstone, perhaps thirty metres high, we climbed the road leading south from Germa on to the Hamada Murzuk (Murzuk plateau). A maze of clouds hid the sun above us. The wind fizzed stingingly off the parched plain below into our faces – it was penetratingly cold in the morning, relentlessly hot as the day wore on. We soon left the road for the direct approach to Murzuk across another featureless grey expanse reminiscent of the country outside Ghadames. After the four-day sedentary stopover in Germa, it was blissful to march once more through these unchanging horizons.

We sat around our first camp fire that night and Saleh revealed himself to us more fully. The change, as he sat drinking tea, was visible. The bullying sergeant-major and petty policeman melted in front of the fire, mellowing into a contented, talkative companion. The moodiness of the day was undone by the irresistible combination of a thriving fire and a glass of tea. He talked of his days as a policeman in various towns across Libya. In Benghazi he had been part of King Idris's security team and thought highly of the deposed monarch, as he did of his successor Gaddafi. A Touareg by birth, he had lived a nomadic life outside the desert and shared the respect, so common to the elderly Arab, of the strongman leader.

A full moon rose above us in the clear night. There were no clouds to obscure the bleached light that streamed down from the luminous disc, but strangely it appeared partly veiled and threw off a ghostly halo of light around it. Saleh saw us watching this unusual light display in the heavens. 'When the moon looks like this, it means the Sultan is travelling in the desert,' he said. 'This is our saying.' Attributing certain powers or meanings to the moon has a long history in Libya. 'They sacrifice to the Sun and Moon, but not to any other god,' wrote Herodotus. 'This worship is common to all Libyans.'

Beside us, the camels were dining on the *tholh* tree (*acacia gummifera*), the hardiest tree of the desert, mentioned in the Koran as one of the trees of paradise. To look at, it appeared forbidding fodder. The thin twisted needles of its branches were heavily guarded by a bristling detachment of thorns. It was uncomfortable enough to wrench off branches for the fire. Eating it seemed the height of self-sacrifice. Saleh watched the camels closely as they dealt with their imposing dinner. First, they carefully nipped a branch with their teeth, detaching it partially or wholly from the tree to minimize contact with the other thorns. Having isolated it like this, they then cut their losses and started crunching away on the branch quite happily.

'These camels are very clever,' said Saleh, becoming more expansive with each glass of tea and the prospect of tuna fish pasta for dinner. Gone the *mishkilla*s and *mishkilla kabira*s. 'Most camels do not know how to eat this tree, but it is very good food for them. I can see your camels have eaten the *tholh* tree before. When you are travelling on a long journey like this it is important they know how to eat it because you find it in many places where there is no other food.'

Richardson was equally impressed by the sight of his own camels tackling this improbable tree. 'The camels browse on it always, and when hungry crop with avidity a great number of the prickles and thorns, and thorny leaves. It is a mystery to me how the camel can chew such thorns in its delicate mouth.' The mystery is probably best explained by the simple fact of hunger outweighing the pain caused by the thorns. The next morning the muzzles of all five were spattered with blood.

In this more fertile stretch of the desert there were increased signs of wildlife. In the half-light of dawn on our first morning out of Jerma we woke to the eerie sound of jackals howling nearby. Sitting by the fire eating the remnants of last night's dinner, we watched a falcon swoop over the scrub to our south. Later we saw it rise magnificently with a songbird between its claws. The occasional hare belted out from its form and kicked for cover as we marched through.

For much of these four days we marched to the north of a bright strip of green. This was Maknoussa, one of Gaddafi's more successful agricultural projects, initially started in 1978 under American supervision with sixty circles of cereal crops, each covering 40 hectares. Saleh spoke highly of the scheme and praised Gaddafi for his efforts to green the desert. I attached Asfar to the caravan and walked half a mile to the fringes of this surreal desert farm. Some sort of frame had been erected above the field. From afar, it looked as though a giant crouching insect was devouring this smooth carpet of grass. It was a prodigiously sized mobile irrigation unit, spraying a fine mist that sparkled in the sun. Gaddafi has long stressed the need for Libya to achieve self-sufficiency in food production, railing against the foreign imports that he despises but Libyans flock to buy. Products from America are particularly unwelcome, but the Great Satan also has its uses. The irrigation equipment was manufactured in Nebraska, USA.

The village of Maknoussa was a haphazard scattering of houses bordered with animal pens. We skirted the place several hundred yards to our left. Many of the houses were unfinished and the skyline was thick with metal uprights protruding from roofs waiting for building to resume. Animals were more prominent than people. Behind fences made from dried palm fronds neatly criss-crossed together, came the sounds of goats and sheep. In the distance, camels were visible as fat, coiled 's' shapes lolling lazily or standing with that poise, so remarkable to the camel, of total immobility. A shepherdess wearing gaudy rags led her flock past us. Behind her a dog barked defensively. Saleh said most of the town's inhabitants worked on the government farm. He pointed out a far-off petrol station on the outskirts of town to show us this was no mere desert hamlet. Modern technology had reached Maknoussa.

Tentatively, we started riding our camels apart from the caravan. It was time to master the art of riding. Abd al Wahab, so busy teaching us everything from loading camels and repairing saddles to stopping up opened tins of olive oil with melted dates, had not been keen to show us how to ride independently. He probably thought, quite correctly, it would delay our progress. In any case, the pack saddles we had bought were so designed that it was next to impossible to sit sufficiently forward on the camel's back so as to be able to place our feet in the hollow of his neck, the most effective way to control the animal. So it was that while Abd al Wahab had looked splendid astride his distinctive Touareg saddle on the swaggering Big White (now ridden by Ned, who had grown bored with Gobber) we rode humbly behind on camels roped to the rest of the caravan. With Salek, we had ridden less in the Awbari Sand Sea to avoid wasting time by continually mounting and dismounting among the mountainous dunes.

On The Big White, Ned was at a disadvantage. He was, by a considerable margin, the most arrogant and independent-minded camel in the caravan. Too loyal to acknowledge Gobber's limitations explicitly, Ned had nevertheless determined to have a new mount. Unlike Asfar, who was good-natured to the point of spirited meekness, The Big White was a camel with something to prove. Ridden by Abd al Wahab on a Touareg saddle, he had been subdued. Now, with a less experienced rider on his back, it was time to show his mettle. He made life difficult for Ned before he had even mounted, roaring defiantly and lunging at him with an open mouth poised to take a chunk out of his arm. His bark was more impressive than his bite, but it was still an alarming prospect. Once Ned was aboard, The Big White would stop, turn his neck round imperiously until he was facing him and then snap at his thigh, the force of the bite varying according to his mood. It could be anything from a playful nip to a teeth-sinking declaration of carnivorous intent, and made riding problematic.

The best way to deal with this rebellion might have been to take a stick or rope to the camel, thereby conveying what was acceptable behaviour and what was not. With Asfar, this was neither necessary nor advisable. On the rare occasions I hit him, he invariably responded by launching into a panicky but graceful trot. The Big White seemed to relish the confrontation, however. Struggling to keep up with Saleh, who was riding the third, somewhat anonymous white – known simply as Lebead (white) as he had been called in Ghadames – I looked round occasionally on hearing an indignant roar from The Big White. With book in one hand, Ned was encouraging him to proceed.

'Walk on, walk on,' he urged. The camel contemptuously bit him, before agreeing, as though it constituted a marvellous concession on his part, to move on again at his own speed.

'*Mishkilla kabira*,' snarled Saleh, who had reverted to his customary daytime mood. 'It is not good to travel like this.'

'What's the problem?' I asked, preparing myself for another litany of complaints.

'It is very dangerous,' he replied. 'Your friend is too far away. If he travels like this, he may get lost in the desert.'

This was nonsense. Although gradually losing ground, Ned was only a hundred metres behind, deeply engrossed in Oscar Wilde's short stories. He had discovered before me the joys of reading while riding. Between us we had a copy of the Koran, some P. G. Wodehouse, T. E. Lawrence, Trollope, the complete works of Shakespeare, a volume of poetry, Homer's *Odyssey* and an Arabic language book.

'An European who has to traverse these Saharan solitudes might supply himself with a few entertaining books, in large type, and while away many lonely and tedious hours, when riding on the camel's back,' Richardson had suggested 150 years ago. It was good advice, although he failed to point out that the camel tends to strike a reciprocal pose of leisure and relax his pace accordingly. Never a bookish man, Saleh failed to see the point of reading.

'Keep your camel next to mine!' he thundered. 'Otherwise my

camel will only go slowly.' This was true. Lebead, the most nondescript of the five with no distinguishing characteristic that could be labelled anything except steady, was plodding forward listlessly. With a companion on one side, however, he would keep a smarter pace. '*Mishkilla kabira*,' Saleh repeated angrily, as I slipped back again. I left him to it, let him pull ahead and settled into P. G. Wodehouse.

We continued across a sandy plain strewn with rock and shingle. The rock was of a dark hue, stained with layers of burgundy and mustard. Several hours later, a thin black line appeared on the horizon, indicating a suitable camp. Having exhausted his complaints about Ned, The Big White and me, Saleh started on a more general critique of our baggage. He cast a doubtful look over the camels and predicted that several of our bags were about to split. This he had repeated several times since leaving Germa, but the disaster still had not materialized. Then it was on to the lack of firewood ahead.

'*Mishkilla*,' he spat. 'We will be very cold tonight and there won't be any tea.'

I pointed out the long line of trees we were marching towards, but he was not mollified.

'That's all green wood,' he replied morosely. 'No good for the fire.' There was no consoling him.

Minutes later, the three of us were sitting around an extravagant fire that burned greedily, like a small funeral pyre. Saleh's grumbling petered out, his grievances were forgotten and he gave way to satisfaction at a pot of tea and our daily chocolate ration. Always open to alternatives to tuna fish pasta, Ned experimented with frying up some chips. They turned out to be more like crisps and were delicious. Before he went to sleep, Saleh rubbed his face, feet and hands with the used corn oil to keep warm. Every guide had his own idiosyncrasies.

On our third and last night with Saleh, having passed electricity pylons and farmsteads, some deserted, others showing a few traces of life, we camped eight miles from Murzuk in a pleasant dell of stocky clumps of date palms. The camels fed busily together, all except Gobber who, as always, ate separately. Sometimes he would approach the other four to join them for dinner, only to be turned on and repelled by Bobbles, his implacable nemesis. Tonight, after another rebuff, he took himself off and started mincing slowly towards Ghadames. The three whites looked on, completely unmoved by Gobber's cheerless plight.

Asfar was generally more sympathetic but still preferred eating with the whites, who seemed to adore him.

'He's a naughty camel, that one,' said Saleh almost affectionately, looking over to the departing Gobber. 'All he thinks about is returning to Ghadames. If you set him free now, he would find his way home.'

A score of clouds thrust in on the sinking sun and turned slowly pink and then red. Crickets hummed. Gobber gave up his brief quest for freedom and sat down heavily, framing himself against the sunset, a solitary silhouette staring out sadly across the plain towards Ghadames.

# CHAPTER VII

# Murzuk

---

*'Thy chains are broken, Africa, be free!'*
*Thus saith the island-empress of the sea;*
*Thus saith Britannia. – O ye winds and waves!*
*Waft the glad tidings to the land of slaves;*
*Proclaim on Guinea's coast, by Gambia's side,*
*And far as Niger rolls his eastern tide*
*Through radiant realms beneath the burning zone,*
*Where Europe's curse is felt, her name unknown,*
*Thus saith Britannia, empress of the sea,*
*'Thy chains are broken, Africa, be free!'*

JAMES MONTGOMERY, *POEMS ON THE*
*ABOLITION OF THE SLAVE TRADE*

Frederick Horneman entered Murzuk in some style on 17 February 1798, seventy-four days after leaving Cairo with a caravan of pilgrims returning from Mecca. They were received by Mohammed ibn Sultan Mansur, the Sultan of Fezzan, who sat on a throne on raised ground outside the town 'attended by a numerous court, and a multitude of his subjects'. The sultan wore the Tripolitan vest beneath a shirt embroidered with silver. On either side stood white Mamelukes and Negro slaves with drawn sabres. Behind them were six banners and half-naked slaves holding lances and halberds 'of a fashion as old, perhaps, as the times of Saladin'. One by one, the most distinguished members of the caravan removed their slippers and approached the sultan bare-foot to kiss his hand before filing behind the throne. The pilgrims chanted praises to God for delivering them to Murzuk in safety and continued until the Sultan dismissed their sheikh (the leader of the caravan) with a promise to provide dates and meat for every tent. 'This ceremony of audience being over, the Sultan remounted his horse and rode back to the city of Mourzouk, preceded by kettle-drums and banners, and amidst his lance-men and halberdiers; whilst his courtiers, joined by the Arabs of our caravan, pranced and curvetted their horses on each flank of the procession.' During his stay in Murzuk, Horneman was much taken by the licentiousness and 'wanton manners' of the women, the number of prostitutes and the prevalence of venereal disease. Haemorrhoids, too, were a common ailment, he observed, 'no doubt greatly increased by the immoderate use of red pepper'.

Two decades later, Ritchie and Lyon were also received with great fanfare when they reached Murzuk on 4 May 1819, thirty-nine days after leaving Tripoli. They had travelled through the desert with Mohammed al Mukni, the Bey of Fezzan who was returning from a visit to the Pasha of Tripoli. Murzuk was his home town and, as the most powerful and feared man in the interior, he required a suitably grand welcome. A large body of horse and foot advanced to meet the party with six silk flags. Dancers, drummers and pipers joined the throng. Two men on each side of the bey warded off flies with fans made of ostrich feathers. When they had passed through the gate into town, two six-pounder guns saluted them from the castle.

The spectacle over, Ritchie and Lyon were escorted to their lodgings. Mukni, who had promised them every favour in his gift, did not invite them to stay in the castle, where his courtiers, his harem of fifty Negresses and other guests were lodged. Instead they were led to a large windowless house with mud walls. They were in dire straits. Their funds were almost exhausted and, as Lyon would shortly discover, the goods Ritchie had brought to use or trade in the interior – 600lb of lead, a camel load of corks, two loads of brown paper, and two chests of arsenic – were worthless in Murzuk. The prospect of making progress seemed remote.

Apart from the mission's main objective – to reach and chart the River Niger from the north – Ritchie and Lyon had also been appointed Vice-consuls of Murzuk, in which capacity they were to further Britain's commercial interests and seek ways to end the slave trade. While waiting for Mukni in Tripoli, Ritchie had written letters to Lord Bathurst, Secretary of State for Colonial Affairs, outlining plans to put 'a total stop to the ravages of the Slave Trade'. He gathered from his inquiries that Tripoli exported 3,000–4,000 slaves annually, with another 1,000 leaving from Benghazi, principally to Constantinople. If the Pasha of Tripoli were provided 'pecuniary compensation' for the abolition of the trade, Ritchie felt the chances of success were high. 'I am . . . convinced from the whole tenor of His Highness' conduct that in the present commanding position of Great Britain, he will easily accede to any proposition from your Lordship,' he wrote. As for Mukni himself, if he were given a large present, doubtless he would also become an advocate of abolition. The letter concludes naively with Ritchie announcing his intention to write to the King of Bornu, ruler of the territory to the south of Fezzan, among the most prolific sources of slaves, to learn his views on outlawing the traffic.

The assumption that the slave trade could so easily be suppressed was unrealistic in the extreme. By nature a greedy and deceitful man, Yusuf Karamanli, Pasha of Tripoli, pretended to go along with this objective to Colonel Hanmer Warrington, the British Consul, but had no intention whatsoever of doing anything about it. He himself profited handsomely from the trade. In the smaller town of Murzuk, abolishing it was equally unthinkable. The bey was one of the greatest slave-hunters and carried off 4,000–5,000 slaves a year. For each slave entering his kingdom, he received two Spanish dollars, and a further one and a half dollars for each one sold. When Lyon first met him in Tripoli, he had just returned from a successful slave-gathering expedition in Kanem 'and was, in consequence, in the highest favour with the Bashaw [of Tripoli]', to whom he paid an annual tribute of 15,000 dollars.

In any case, these high-minded intentions on the part of the two British explorers were rapidly overtaken by the dreaded bilious fever. Ritchie, the less robust of the two, was laid up in bed for three months, deep in delirium and racked by severe back and kidney pains. Reduced to borrowing pathetically small amounts of money from the pitiless Mukni to stay afloat, they went six weeks without eating meat. (Rather cavalierly, Ritchie had spent the bulk of the £2,000 allocated to him on instruments of astronomy and other equipment before even reaching Tripoli.) Finally, on 21 November, he perished, stoic to the last. 'At night he became delirious at times. He was averse to all kinds of nourishment,' Lyon wrote to Lord Bathurst. 'To every inquiry, answered "that he felt better" ... On the day of his death he slept much but appeared to breathe with difficulty. To the last I had hopes for his recovery ... At 10 his breathing became apparently easier and I thought he slept – but on turning him in his bed I found him lifeless.'

Within an hour of burying Ritchie, Lyon received a letter announcing an extra £1,000 allowance from the British government, redeemable only in Tripoli. It had arrived too late. 'He [Ritchie] had been looking forward with much eagerness to the arrival of a letter which would authorize him to draw for money as we have been for two or three months living in a very precarious way,' Lyon continued. 'I fear the want of money, in this very dear place, weighed heavily upon him.' No one in Murzuk was prepared to advance Lyon the sum and he had to content himself with a month's reconnoitring south of Murzuk before returning to Tripoli exactly a year after leaving for the interior.

Besieged by local difficulties from start to finish, and dogged by ill health, it was hardly surprising that Ritchie and Lyon had failed either to reach the Niger or make meaningful progress against the slave trade. Whatever the reasons, the mission had not covered itself in glory. Nevertheless, Lyon still expected a hero's welcome, or at least a promotion for his efforts, when he returned to England in 1820. Instead, the government promptly refused to promote him to the rank of commander. Profoundly aggrieved by this treatment, he retaliated by refusing to return to Africa and the government was forced to look elsewhere for a successor (Lyon later joined Sir William Parry's expedition to the North West Passage, worked in various positions in Mexico and Brazil and died at sea in 1832 on his way to seek medical treatment in England for the ophthalmia he had contracted in the Sahara). The result was the vastly more successful 1822–5 expedition of Lt Dixon Denham, Lt Hugh Clapperton and Dr Walter Oudney, which charted the shores of Lake Chad, explored the oasis of Ghat, and brought back a wealth of political, commercial and ethnographical information.

Like Ritchie and Lyon before him, Richardson was also in low spirits on reaching Murzuk on 22 February 1846. The man who had come to North Africa with the object of 'exciting an abhorrence of the Slave-Trade in the hearts of my fellow countrymen and countrywomen' was developing an increasingly powerful ambition to become a celebrated African explorer. 'What I want to do is, to effect some real discovery, or do something great in Africa,' he confessed. 'Ghadames is not enough, nor even Bornu; it is, must be, Timbuctoo.' Alas, Timbuctoo was not to be. Running out of both money and medicines after reaching the southern city of Ghat, with the greatest reluctance he abandoned plans to push farther south. The diversion to Murzuk, by now well known to Britain, did not constitute 'something great' and Richardson knew it.

Having enjoyed the stunned reaction to his unexpected arrival ('Englishmen arrive here once in half a century, or rather never ... The consul was as astonished to see me as his servant. He stared at me as if I had just been dropped from the clouds.'), Richardson noted down his first impressions of the town. They were predictably acerbic. 'The appearance of Mourzuk was not very pleasing to me, the major part of its dwellings being miserable hovels,' he complained. 'Mourzuk is but a miserable dirty place, and would kill with ennui, if fever were wanting, some score of English Vice-Consuls.' It was known by the Arabs as Balad al Hemah, the country of fever. Other common diseases were consumption, syphilis, ophthalmia and rheumatism. 'Thus Mourzuk is not quite one of those oases, or Hesperian gardens, where the happy residents quaff the elixir of immortal health and virtue. Contrarily, it is a sink of vice and disease within, and a sere foliage of palms and vegetation without, overhung with an ever forbidding sky, of dull red haziness.' Taking in the atmosphere, Richardson soon felt feverish himself and rushed off to his dwindling supply of medicines.

Gustav Nachtigal, the German doctor who reached Murzuk on 27 March 1869 – one month into a five-and-a-half-year, 6,000-mile African odyssey – was similarly struck by Murzuk's unhealthy aspect. 'The folly of the founders of the town in choosing to settle it in an area of extensive salt marshes will always remain incomprehensible,' he observed. 'The desert in general enjoys such a high level of salubrity that it must have required deliberate consideration to discover the most unfavourable, the most unhealthy locality, the poisonous exhalations from which have since deprived so many men of their health and their lives.' According to Henri Duveyrier, the French traveller who visited Libya in 1862, every Turkish governor of Murzuk had perished from bilious fever.

By contrast with our eighteenth- and nineteenth-century predecessors, our arrival at the outskirts of Murzuk lacked the faintest whiff of pomp. There was no body of horse to greet us, no Bey or Sultan of Fezzan to welcome us to his kingdom and feast us on meat, no sign even of dancers, drummers, pipers or courtiers to celebrate our arrival. Instead we made our way along an empty cracked road, bordered with swathes of rubbish. The litter was of a higher quality here, with more varieties of soft drinks, fruit juices and washing up powder on display. After a while, a pick-up slowed down alongside us, hooting insistently, until eventually it pulled over in front of us. The driver, a fat man swaddled in the Touareg *tagilmus* and a tent-like *jalabiya*, eased himself out of the vehicle with great effort. After the customary exchange of greetings, he launched forth on an impromptu sales pitch.

'You want camel saddles?' he began. As a matter of fact we did. We only had four of our own and had always relied on our guide to provide his own. In Salek's case it had been a disaster.

'Can we have a look at them?' I asked.

'I have good saddles, maybe best in Murzuk,' he replied.

'I don't doubt it for a minute, but we'd like to see them first.'

'Saddles in Murzuk. Later I bring you look.' And with that he was off, already sensing a windfall profit. Here, in the wastes of the Libyan Sahara, the caravan trade was no more, but man's indomitable entrepreneurial spirit still flourished.

A mile or so out of Murzuk, a grey Nissan saloon coming from the opposite direction slowed down on noticing our caravan. A strange figure hung his head out of the window and started screaming at us.

'Mr Fellah! Mr Justin! How are you? How is Saleh? Now you come to Murzuk, *alhamdulillah*!' It was Salek. Baring his sloping fangs in a full-blooded smile, and with his *tagilmus* unwinding in the breeze, he looked like a lunatic. The driver stopped the car and Salek got out. One by one, he shook our hands.

'Welcome to Murzuk, Mr Fellah!' he said to Ned. 'Salek very happy to see you.'

'Very good to see you again,' Ned replied.

Salek was his old self again, all smiles and lisps and nervous energy. He inspected the camels approvingly and was obviously delighted we had arrived safely in Murzuk with the guide he had chosen for us. Apart from being genuinely pleased to see us, he also had about him the excitement of a man who is about to receive a lot of money. A few minutes later, once the initial exuberance had calmed down, he said he would meet us in town. 'Salek go to Murzuk now. Hurry up, you come to town after me. Now you have arrived, *alhamdulillah*!'

The car moved off and Salek leaned out of the window again, departing in a final flurry of thanks to the Almighty for bringing us safely to Murzuk. We carried on along the road into the fringes of town and before we knew it our caravan too was making a distinctive, late-twentieth-century entrance to Murzuk. All activity seemed to come to a standstill as we walked by. Drivers stopped their vehicles in the road to look at the unlikely sight of two foreigners, five camels and a Touareg guide. Shop-keepers hurried to the front of their stores, shouting out questions and greetings of welcome, mechanics downed their tools and children cheered and shouted, trotting along behind us, delighted with the new arrivals. Reaching Murzuk by camel was something of an oddity.

It was not long before we had our own moment of drama. There was no hotel in town, we soon discovered, and Salek and Saleh were trying to find us somewhere to stay. A young, smartly turned out man called Ahmed Sherif invited us to stay in his house, a clean whitewashed bungalow opposite a new mosque. 'You may keep your camels in my garden,' he said in immaculate English, anticipating our next question. We accepted gladly and started unloading the camels, watched by a swelling crowd of children and other hangers-on. The children in particular were fascinated by the camels, half entranced, half petrified by the size of these disdainful giants.

The problem was how to get the camels into the garden. A narrow trench, where pipes were being laid, had to be crossed first and there was no bridge. We hunted around for something suitable and with some difficulty heaved two large metal doors across the gap. Asfar, the first to go, stepped across briskly. Gobber, the next in line, was unimpressed by the makeshift bridge. He was not having any of it and held back while Saleh yanked with increasing ferocity on his nose-ring. At last, when you thought his nostril would have to give way, he surrendered, took one uncertain step onto the door, wobbled for a moment, missed the door with his next step, and fell off, landing on his back, tightly wedged in the trench. The crowd gasped in shock.

It was a sickening sight. With terror in his eyes, Gobber lay upside down, his four legs helplessly kicking the air while the walls of the trench steadily caved in around him, burying him beneath a thick carpet of dust. The hangers-on, delirious with excitement, started shouting like ringside spectators at a prize bout. Some screamed advice, others started whooping madly, thrilled by the spectacle. Salek stood next to the trench not moving, apparently hypnotized by the accident and powerless to help. I yelled at him to send for some men to help pull Gobber out.

'We must be quick,' he replied, coming to. 'If he stays like that for a few more minutes he will die.' I looked around, filled with dread. There was no sign of Saleh, the man who had led Gobber across the bridge.

'We've got to make a cradle with the ropes or we'll never lift him out,' said Ned. He rushed inside the house, where our bags had been unloaded, and started making one. Moments later, he returned to the scene, the crowd growing ever denser around this live burial. The sense of helplessness was increasing in proportion with the swelling number of spectators. It was pandemonium. 'Justin, they need a general,' Ned roared. 'Someone's got to take charge, or we'll lose him.'

We were losing him with every second. Gobber's large eyes, filled with fear only a few moments before, were now dull and listless. Every few seconds, another deluge of dust would fall into his open mouth as the walls continued collapsing. The legs that had kicked so violently were now still save for an occasional desperate convulsion. There was a pathetic resignation to his fate that was awful to watch.

A dozen Nigerian men suddenly arrived. I jumped into the trench with the cradle and tried to get the rope underneath the huge bulk of the trapped camel, beginning with his head and neck. The men, who had split into two noticeably unequal groups on either side of the trench, pulled before the cradle was ready. Gobber's head rose momentarily, then the rope slipped over his head and he fell back again with a heavy thud. I shouted at them to balance their numbers on each side. For several minutes I scrambled in the dust, the Nigerians pulled again and Gobber rose once more. With his head now aloft, he was wedged upright in an unnatural sitting position but still unable to kick himself up. The only chance left was to get the rope beneath his tail if it could be reached. After several frantic and unsuccessful attempts, I groped deeper in the trench, grabbed a piece of his tail and passed the rope underneath. The Nigerians tugged again and Gobber started to move, no doubt prompted by the pain and indignity of having a coarse rope pulled hard across his backside. He rose with a great roar, forelegs wildly treadmilling the air, shaking off thick clouds of dust as he found his feet, like an angry god rising from the depths. Terrified, the crowd rushed for cover. Standing on four legs at last, he shook himself again and surveyed the onlookers imperiously with an expression that said, 'Well, what are you looking at? Go away and mind your own business.'

Furious, I asked Salek where Saleh had been during the commotion. Noticeably absent from the fray once Gobber had fallen, he had reappeared only at the end. 'Please don't be angry with him,' he replied. 'He is an old man and did not want to see the camel die. He loves camels. I know how old men are.' Salek walked off with Gobber to see if he had broken anything. He had a nasty cut on his right foreleg but was otherwise gloriously unruffled. Having righted Gobber, we discovered we still had nowhere to stay. While we were struggling with the camel, Murzuk officialdom had silently intervened and Ahmed Sherif had been told he was not allowed to have us stay with him. A polite and hospitable man, he was embarrassed at this poor reception.

'I am very sorry for this,' he apologized. 'But we have another house a mile away where you can stay with your camels.' He and Ned went off to have a look at it while I stayed and watered the camels. Four of them slurped from the plastic basin while Gobber, streaked in dust, stood aloof from the fray, shaking himself occasionally and recovering from the trauma. A few seconds longer trapped on his back and he would have died. I always felt a particular fondness for him after this near-fatal accident. He was a robust, dependable animal. There was none of The Big White's arrogance or aggression, none of Bobbles's pathetic whining, no trace of Asfar's pretty posing. He was an honest, good-natured and uncomplaining beast. Ned later reminded me he had championed Gobber from the start.

The saddle salesman we had met a couple of hours ago on the road arrived with several sturdy saddles to choose from and a deal was struck after several rounds of haggling. Ned and Ahmed then returned and we were about to set off for the new house when the invisible Murzuk authorities struck again and declared that this was not allowed either. Confronted with the unusual phenomenon of two British travellers and five camels arriving in their town, they had reacted as only Libyan officials knew how. Someone in the small crowd of men watching us evidently did not want us to stay in Murzuk. 'Really, this is ridiculous,' stormed Ahmed, who had wanted to take us under his wing. 'This is very bad for you. I am very sorry.'

He told us we were required to stay on a government youth farm a couple of miles out of town. It was not going to be a particularly festive New Year, after all. Was this another example of Gaddafi's paranoid Big Brother state at work, or was this sort of reception peculiar to Murzuk, perhaps? This town had once been a major slave market and an important trading centre of the Sahara. Caravans had streamed through it for hundreds of years and yet today it was unable even to accommodate three travellers and five camels.

Even Richardson, a man less prone to praise than indignant criticism, acknowledged that the town's hospitality had improved markedly since the time of Ritchie and Lyon's visit in 1819. The British explorers Lt Denham and Lt Clapperton had not even been allowed to reside in the town, Richardson noted, but had been kept in the castle under the Bey's special protection from the people. In our case, it was not clear who was protecting whom or why.

It was time to settle up and say goodbye to Salek and Saleh. The older man was more withdrawn than usual, still embarrassed by the incident with Gobber. With a pocketful of dollars, how-ever, Salek was in high spirits. He handed over some of them to

Saleh with the air of a wealthy businessman tipping a lowly porter. Looking morose, the older man inspected his share of the takings and immediately started disputing his fee vigorously. Voices were raised.

'No problem for Salek,' Salek said airily, getting into a taxi with Saleh. Inside the car the argument continued. We left them to it. This was private business. 'Good luck Mr Fellah, Mr Justin,' Salek said, leaning out of the window. 'I wish you good journey in the desert.'

Saleh muttered thanks and looked away. We shook hands, thanked them both again and said goodbye. The car moved off in a cloud of dust and Ned and I were alone again.

After an abortive telephone call to Tripoli to ask Taher to send our passports to Murzuk, we headed off towards the farm, passing the old Italian fort on the way. On 11 January 1941, it had been attacked by the Long Range Desert Group, offspring of the Light Car Patrols of the First World War and, later, the Bagnold expeditions into the Libyan desert that had begun with Model T Fords in the 1920s. Murzuk had long lost its importance as a great Saharan trading centre but was still an important Italian garrison town and road junction. The airfield and its guard of twenty Italian soldiers were first to surrender to the Anglo-French attack. Three Colonial bombers were doused in petrol and set alight, the hangar was torched and bombs and other ammunition exploded. The fort appeared to be on the verge of surrender but the officer in charge decided it was time to cut short this foray behind enemy lines. As they left, they came across the Italian commander returning from lunch with a woman and child. 'One shell from the Guards Bofors put an end to them,' recorded William Shaw in his history of the LRDG in 1945. 'It was unfortunate about the woman and the child but people should arrange their lunch parties more carefully.'

The walk to the farm was notable only for the piles of rubbish we passed on the roadside. The ubiquitous empty tins of corn oil sat alongside discarded tractor tyres. A doll's leg perched incongruously on plastic bags filled with rotting food. Flies moved around in force. Perhaps nervous after the near disaster with Gobber, which he had witnessed, Asfar, with Lebead behind him, refused to walk behind me and instead kept swerving in front, repeatedly stepping heavily on my feet. After being stamped on several times, and having completely failed to calm him down, I lost my cool, swung round in anger and landed a right hook on his neck. He roared in terror, panicking and moving forward on the rope again so that I could not move forward.

'Can you give me a hand?' I shouted across to Ned, who was already leading three of the five camels.

'You look like you're having a good time,' he observed on joining us. 'Is Bambi playing up again?'

'Well, I didn't help things much. I've just punched him in the neck.'

'You see, you can never trust these thoroughbreds,' he joked. 'They're too highly strung.'

He fastened Lebead on to his caravan and left me with Asfar. I walked on, the camel dutifully following behind, feeling guilty about having hit him. Striking a camel is never advisable, as the Egyptian explorer Hassanein Bey observed.

> If you ill-treat a camel he will never forget it, but he will not attack you on the spot. He will wait, and if you repeat the offence again and again, he makes up his mind to get his revenge. Not, however, when there are many people about. Here he behaves in a most human way. He watches his chance until you and he are alone and then he goes for you; either by snatching at you with his mouth and throwing you to the ground, or by kicking you and then trampling upon you.

Asfar looked at me reproachfully but revenge did not seem to be on his mind yet. The road wound on across the plain, terminating at the gates of the farm where we were greeted by three shambolic smiling figures. Omar, a Sudanese worker of thirty, had been here for four years. Ali and Daoud, Chadians in their early twenties, had arrived more recently. All three lived in one half of a grim-looking Portakabin. Watching the camels with a certain awe, they led us to our accommodation. This was where all tourists who visited Murzuk had to stay, they told us.

It marked a change from Othman's house in Ghadames and the Germa Tourist Hotel. First, it was more alfresco, a large circular building fifteen metres in diameter with a wall that was two metres high. Supported by a central steel post, the roof of dried palm fronds was five metres at its highest and sloped down towards the wall, which it did not reach. It was a draughty place. The wind hurled through ravenously, sweeping in a fine carpet of sand. The builders had constructed two doorways on opposite sides of the circle, but had not bothered to fit doors. As if to compensate for this small oversight, they had installed a comprehensive lighting system. Two dozen strip lights beamed down forensically on the old carpet that covered part of the concrete floor, helping to identify an impressive collection of insect life crawling across a faded pattern of roses. Many species appeared to be represented. Cold showers were available in a separate building a hundred metres away.

Having hoped for a more luxurious stopover in Murzuk and still exhausted after Gobber's accident, I felt slightly flat. Ned, who understood the need to maintain morale on a long journey like this, was more enthusiastic. 'Fantastic place!' he grinned. 'It's going to be a wild New Year.'

Omar then led us to a small paddock bordered by firs and a small orchard of orange trees where we hobbled the camels and said goodnight to them. Surrounded by long grass, they sat down to dinner like five giant trenchermen.

By the time we returned to our lodgings, Ahmed Sherif was waiting for us. He had driven out from Murzuk. A model of courtesy and generosity, he gave us a ten-kilogram bag of rice for our travels and would not hear of being reimbursed. Earlier, we had joked with him about the monotony of tuna fish pasta dinners in the desert. He was a medical student living in Tripoli, spoke good English with a slightly fastidious accent and enjoyed using long words like 'manifestation'. As a sophisticated young urbanite, he was disappointed we had been made to stay in such primitive rural surroundings. Wanting to make us feel at home he started enthusing about the circular shelter.

'You know, you can use this building for anything at all, for cooking, playing, discussion, anything you like,' he said, sounding like an unconvincing estate agent. His expression changed to one of deadly seriousness. 'For discussion this place is OK. But you must not sleep here. There will be too much wind and sand coming in.' Barely overcoming his evident distaste for it, he recommended we sleep in the Portakabin with our hosts. He wished us goodnight and drove back into town.

We celebrated New Year's Eve with a few hands of gin rummy. Ned taught our three hosts how to play. They caught on very quickly, aided by an astounding ability to cheat with impunity. Without much subtlety they hid cards in their sleeves or sat on them and would invariably pick up more cards than allowed. It was all done in raucous good humour. Libya being a fiercely dry country, we saw in the New Year with bottles of Coke and ate our way through a pack of two dozen Sando bars.

The next morning I woke to a shout from Ned: 'Justin, the camels have gone!'

They had. All five had disappeared from the paddock. A few ropes lay scattered across the grass. I had never been entirely confident in my knots. The fact that those hobbles tied by Ned and Omar had also been thrown off was little consolation. Ruefully, I remembered the RGS notes that lay in the bottom of one of the bags. 'Take great care to secure your camels. No matter how well you have looked after them, they may be inclined to abscond: "Never trust a camel," the Arabs say . . . Many, including Western travellers and hardy nomads, have died because their camels disappeared in the desert: it pays to keep watch on them all the time.' There had been a vigorous sandstorm in the night, part of which we had felt inside our dubious shelter. The camels would have felt its full force and, not unreasonably, had decided to relocate.

It was a cold, white morning wrapped in clouds. The silence of the desert was complete, the light wan and ghostly. There was nothing visible on the horizon and there were no signs of camel tracks. We were already some way off from the farm. Then, walking over a rise, we came across the solitary Lebead, moored on the ground with his hobble still in place. Camels are independent-minded animals but are also governed by a strong herd instinct. Seeing his friends make their most purposeful bid for freedom yet, he had been desperate to follow, but had not been able to shed his hobble. As a result he had been left far behind and sat stupidly on the ground looking bewildered. Far ahead of him, perhaps half a mile from the farm, the other four were standing around in an early morning conference. All of them were facing away from us, standing stock-still. Without moving the rest of their bodies, they craned their necks right round to observe us as we approached. All appeared unrepentant but returned to the farm without a fuss.

We walked into town at noon to explore Murzuk and stock up on supplies. It was warmer, though the sun had still not shaken off the dense covering of clouds, and flies flocked to greet us as we threaded through the piles of stinking litter. On the right of the road, there was a rectangular expanse of what looked like outsize dolls' houses or rabbit hutches, laid out with military precision – each building looked big enough to house only one or two men. These were the old Italian barracks. The neatness of their arrangement on the plain contrasted with their ramshackle decay: all were roofless and many of them had been requisitioned as animal pens. From within came the familiar plaintive cries of sheep and goats, and a man wandered between the buildings carrying a heap of firewood.

Beneath the overcast sky, Murzuk was a slope of dull white houses, presided over by the occasional minaret. A somnolent hush had fallen over the town, as though the entire population had overindulged heavily the previous night to welcome in the New Year. Outside a decrepit factory, a janitor lay sleeping on a large table. He woke as we passed, mumbled a greeting and slumped back again. In front of the fort, now occupied by the Libyan military, a guard with an elderly machine gun around his neck looked at us without interest. A woman with a young daughter was washing clothes on the roadside.

Compared with this trance-like quiet, the market place, framed by date palms, was a square of dense activity. Traders were hanging up clothes, blankets and towels next to tables covered with household goods. A man sat at the foot of a tree repairing shoes. Another strode through, holding a chicken by its wings. Toothless old women sat down in front of their few goods for sale. One of the most popular items was a perfume called Bint As Sudan (Sudan Girl). The label showed the handsome torso of a black woman and the small letters MADE IN NIGERIA. ROBB, another favourite, was a camphor gel in tiny red, white and blue tins for colds and muscular aches, also made in Nigeria. Some women sold copper and brass bracelets neatly arranged on coloured strips of cloth. One side of the market was given over to well-stocked fruit and vegetable stalls, where pyramids of oranges and lemons towered over trays of potatoes, dates, cucumbers and peppers. On the far side, women wrapped in *farrashiya*s squatted on the ground, a florid patchwork of colour against the white shroud of sky and the dull grey breeze blocks of a neighbouring building. Bold royal blue and white stripes sat next to loud pink and black gingham checks. The dumpy shapes were hunched over straw baskets filled with the lush green leaves of carrots, onions, garlic, lettuces, cabbages, parsley and radishes. Its days as a great slave-trading centre were over, but Murzuk still drew in streams of immigrants from the south. Many of these women were from Chad, Niger and Sudan.

It was Ramadan, but we were both thirsty and hungry. Restaurants were closed, as were most of the shops. We found one store manned by a cheerful youth and won his favour by purchasing twenty tins of tuna fish and some biscuits. Under the pretence of sampling a range of chocolate bars, we ate our fill and the shopkeeper was happy to serve us cold drinks. It was always a delicate business. In Ghadames several days before the beginning of Ramadan, Richardson declared he was 'afraid I shall find them all ill-natured during the fast. Besides, they can't stomach seeing Infidels eat, whilst they the Faithful fast.' Shortly after this, a woman caught sight of him drinking during the day and screamed at him, asking why he was not fasting. A straight-talking man for whom tact was always elusive, he replied shortly, 'because you are a Mussulman and I'm a Christian'.

Ned returned to the farm and I called in on Ahmed, who was passing the day with his elder brother Mohammed, a heavily built man who worked as an urban planner in Murzuk. They were one of several local families of Sherifs, they said, and claimed to be able to trace their family back to the Prophet. Both insisted I drink tea, although they were fasting, and brought in a tray stacked with sweet cakes. To make me feel welcome (like the group of Touareg in Idri), they switched the television to CNN, which was carrying reports of the launch that day – 1 January – of the new European currency, the Euro. Why was the United Kingdom not joining this splendid scheme, they asked? I tried to explain that many people in Britain felt uneasy about handing over monetary and fiscal sovereignty to Frankfurt and Brussels. Mohammed was having none of it. 'I believe the United Kingdom is afraid of Europe,' he concluded solemnly.

The two brothers then began an off-the-cuff history lesson. Both the castle and the first government of Murzuk dated back to the early fourteenth century with the arrival of Sherif Aulad Mohammed from Morocco, they said. (Almost 500 years later, Nachtigal had met one of the Sherif's descendants in Murzuk, 'a very kind, superstitious man, whose intellectual powers, originally already not very extensive, he had still further diminished by his passion for opium'.)

'Murzuk was the best city in the south,' said Ahmed. 'Why? I will explain.' He spoke of the city's importance as a trading entrepôt and the capital of Fezzan, a cosmopolitan metropolis of Africans, Arabs, Tubbu and Touareg. 'Murzuk was like London,' he said grandly. Neither had studied history but both were keen students of the city's past, quoting figures from Herodotus to Oqba bin Naf'a and Ibn Battuta, talking above each other in a competitive, friendly tussle for my attention.

I asked them what was left of Murzuk's old city. Apart from a cluster of crumbling mud houses around the castle there seemed to be little evidence of the *medina*. This was the province of Mohammed, the urban planner. 'Apart from the *qalah* (castle), all the old city was demolished in 1977,' he answered. 'They wanted to make space for the new town, for schools and mosques and modern houses.' History does not occupy a valued place in Gaddafi's Libya. For the revolutionary leader, the history of Libya is merely that of a long line of hated colonial invaders from Phoenicians, Greeks and Romans to Arabs, Turks, Italians, Germans, French and British. Even with independence, won in 1951, the country still bowed unacceptably to the West, according to revolutionary orthodoxy. Only with Gaddafi's revolution of 1969 did the Libyan people finally realize their aspirations for freedom. This jaundiced view of the past has had destructive physical effects on the fabric of the country. In Tripoli, a fine Italian building fronting the harbour was recently demolished on a whim of the leader. Why was that, I asked a friend? 'Gaddafi said it was Italian,' was the simple answer, delivered with that fatalistic shrug of the shoulders that is so common in modern-day Libya. Excavations at Leptis Magna and Sabratha, once pursued with great energy by Italian archaeologists, have dwindled pitifully since their expulsion. In Ghadames, history had been swept aside by the forced evacuation of houses. In Murzuk, it had been bulldozed away in the name of progress.

Ahmed and his brother were familiar with Ritchie's expedition of 1818–20. I asked whether his grave was still here. Ned and I both wanted to pay our respects, as Richardson had done before us. He had described the bleak burial site, 200 metres away from the Moorish cemetery in which rags and rubbish hung from palm trees, with Christian distaste. 'I was glad to see the grave of Ritchie lying apart from this, though in its infidel isolation. There lies our poor countryman, alone in The Sahara. . . . But, though without a stone or monument to mark the desert spot,' he added in a patriotic aside, 'still it is a memorial of the genius and enterprise of Englishmen for travel and research in the wildest, remotest regions of the globe.' That cemetery was no more, Mohammed said. It had disappeared with the demolition of the *medina*.

We drove across to the castle that had once been the terminus of the town's single street running south-east to north-west. Four weary arches framed the entrance across the road. In the open space beyond them was an unusually stout minaret, swollen and misshapen. Its girth was such that it resembled a shrunken light-house. Layer upon layer of whitewash, cracked and yellow in the sun, was flaking off like parchment. Behind its wobbly vertical lines, the neat horizontal profile of the castle battlements with triangular crenellations that zigzagged across the top of the walls was crisp against a blue sky brushed with clouds. Deep cracks in the walls stretched towards the ground, and the old steps leading up to the main gate had been worn down into an indeter-minate ramp of mud, dust and stone. It was Friday and the castle was closed.

In Ritchie's time, with walls thirty metres high and twenty metres thick at their base, the castle had loomed over the small desert oasis of 2,500 inhabitants even more impressively than it did today. It no longer dominated a town whose population had grown to 18,000. Ritchie admired it greatly, as did Nachtigal, who thought it 'splendid'. Originally, it had housed the Sultan of Fezzan and his harem of forty slaves, and later the Turkish governor with his garrison of 500 men. The Turkish governor Halim Bey vacated the castle in 1866, ostensibly because of the evil *jinn* (spirits) in the building, but more likely, thought Nachti-gal, because it was exceedingly draughty. Richardson, perhaps inevitably, found fault with it. He thought it dirty and tumbling down. G. B. Gagliuffi, the British Vice-consul of Murzuk from 1843–55, told him he was trying his utmost to improve the look of the city and had received a promise from the Turkish Pasha to whitewash its walls.

Richardson arrived four years after the Turks had taken over

Murzuk. Abd al Jalil, the Bey of Fezzan, had held the castle until 1842, when he was decapitated by the Turks, who subsequently assumed control over his territories. According to Richardson, the news of this triumph was met with jubilation in Tripoli, where the Turkish Pasha Asker Ali celebrated by insulting the British Consul and boasting that God would now deliver into his hands his two other enemies, the British Consul himself and the Vice-consul of Murzuk. London threatened Constantinople that if Ali was not recalled, Britain would send a squadron to depose him. Ali was duly recalled, and left North Africa in tears.

Murzuk's government had changed at a time when international opposition to the 'infernal [slave] trade', led by Britain, France and the United States, was loud and clear. Only three years earlier, in 1839, the British and Foreign Anti-Slavery Society, which sponsored Richardson's first mission to Africa, had been inaugurated. Buoyed by public support, it mounted a high-profile campaign calling on Lord Palmerston, the British foreign secretary, to press for the abolition of slavery and the slave trade in the Ottoman empire. By the mid-nineteenth century, the traffic in slaves was under attack like never before.

It had taken a long time for these forces to emerge. In Europe, pressure for abolition had been growing since the Enlightenment. In France, the voices of Rousseau, Montesquieu, Diderot and Marivaux had risen against the iniquities of the trade in the latter half of the eighteenth century. They were joined in England by men like Dr Johnson and Adam Smith, author of *The Wealth of Nations*, published in 1776. In 1787, the Committee for Effecting the Abolition of the Slave Trade was founded in London by a group of Quakers. The Prime Minister William Pitt the Younger spoke in favour of abolition and Edmund Burke and Charles James Fox, a future Foreign Secretary, joined the chorus. But it was William Wilberforce, the young Member of Parliament known as 'the nightingale of the House of Commons' for the sweetness of his voice, who emerged as the political champion of abolition.

Speaking in the House of Commons in 1789, he launched a scathing attack on the apologists for the slave trade.

By their conduct they had placed the inhabitants of Africa in a worse state than that of the most barbarous and savage nation. They had destroyed what ought to be the bond of union and safety; they had rendered the whole country one general scene of discord and anarchy; they had set kings against their subjects; had set subjects against each other; had rendered every private family miserable, and created one general scene of disunion and despair.

Wilberforce presented the House with twelve propositions for abolition. Perhaps the most important was the fourth. It called for the establishment of 'an extensive commerce' with Africa in a range of commodities unique to that continent as a substitute for the trade in human flesh. Together with the geographical quest to chart the Niger, this was the propelling force behind many of the nineteenth-century British expeditions to penetrate the unknown continent from the Mediterranean coast.

It took another two decades for British legislators to make their move. In 1807, in the same month as the United States Congress undertook a similar measure, the then British Prime Minister Lord Grenville introduced a bill for abolition in the House of Lords. Amid uproar from the vociferous defendants of the slave trade – a number of peers and Members of Parliament owed their fortunes to it – the bill was passed by 283 votes to 16. Wilberforce received a standing ovation for his brilliant oratory. The slave trade was illegal from 1 May 1807.

There was a difference, however, between theory and practice. Laws in London meant little to slave-dealers in Tripoli, Ghadames, Murzuk, Kufra and Benghazi. In 1819, Lyon rode out to meet a large caravan of 1,400 slaves arriving in Murzuk, whipped across the Sahara from Bornu by Arab, Tripoline and Tubbu slave-dealers.

These poor oppressed beings were, many of them, so exhausted as to be scarcely able to walk. Their legs and feet were much swelled, and by their enormous size, formed a striking

contrast with their emaciated bodies. They were all borne
down with loads of fire-wood; and even poor little children,
worn to skeletons by fatigue and hardships, were obliged to
bear their burthen, while many of their inhuman masters
rode on camels, with the dreaded whip suspended from their
wrists, with which they, from time to time, enforced obedience from these wretched captives.

The slaves were unable to continue in this condition, so the
caravan had to halt in Murzuk to fatten them up for the onward
journey to Tripoli, Benghazi and Egypt. Seized from their homes
in Bornu, the slaves had to walk a death-defying 1,600–1,800
miles across the Sahara before embarking on a life of servitude.
The Tubbu exchanged their slaves for horses from Tripoli, Lyon
noted. A fine horse sold for ten to fifteen Negresses, each of
which was worth 80–150 dollars on the Mediterranean coast.

The 'island-empress of the sea' had outlawed the trade, but in
a town like Murzuk relied on one man for her attempts to end
it. The post of British Vice-consul in Murzuk was established
primarily for this purpose and also to improve the treatment of
the slaves dragged across the desert on the forty-day journey
from Bornu and Sudan. Records compiled by the irrepressible
Gagliuffi reveal the scale of the challenge.

In 1843, 2,200 slaves passed through Murzuk. A year later,
the figure had fallen to 1,194, of which 618 had been taken from
Bornu and 576 from Sudan. 'The mortality of those brought
from Tibus was great, owing to maltreatment and want of food,'
wrote Gagliuffi. Males sold for 20–35 dollars and were in great
demand in the Levant. Females, more highly prized, went for 35–
75 dollars. 'Both males and females were forwarded to Tripoli,
Benghazi, Egypt and Tuat [now in southern Algeria], where they
are sent to Morocco and some ones to Algeria.' In 1845, the
number of slaves fell to 1,105, and Gagliuffi estimated the mortality rate did not exceed ten per cent. The total number of slaves
arriving in Murzuk in 1844 and 1845 together was less than the
year of 1843, he reported hopefully, noting that imports of ivory,

senna, wax, feathers, gum and gold were on the rise, while British exports were also increasing. The slave trade through Fezzan and Murzuk was, in fact, on a gentle decline from the mid-nineteenth century, but this owed more to the rise of the most easterly trade route (from Wadai to the Mediterranean coast via Kufra and Jalo), as well as the increasing prominence of Ghat, another trading town to the west, than from direct efforts to suppress it altogether. Merchants were increasingly loath to chance the trade route from Murzuk to Bornu. As Barth noted in 1850, it was no longer safe from attacks by bandits and had degenerated to 'such a precarious state, that the merchant who selects it must convey his merchandise on his own camels and at his own risk'.

Of course, this did not mean that the slave trade had simply ceased to exist in Fezzan. Travelling from Ghat to Murzuk with the 'usually humane' slave-dealer Haj Ibrahim, Richardson found no signs of its imminent demise. Instead, it was business as usual. One day, he noticed an eleven-year-old slave girl being viciously beaten by her master: 'I heard the noise of whipping, and turning round to my great surprise, I saw the Haj beating her not very mercifully. He had a whip of bull's hide with which he gave her several lashes.' The girl died soon after this brutal treatment. 'If Haj Ibrahim, who is a good master, can treat his slaves thus, what may we not expect from others less humane?' Richardson wondered. 'There is no doubt but that the whipping of this poor creature hastened her death. She was, indeed, whipped at the point of death.'

Disgruntled by the premature termination of his first mission, in 1849 Richardson was commissioned by Lord Palmerston to make a

> more extensive expedition through the Northern Parts of Africa to the Great Desert of Sahara and further south if possible to Lake Chad, in order that a more intimate knowledge may thus be obtained of the state of those Countries, their Production, and commercial Resources and also with a view to substitute legitimate Commerce for the Traffic in

Slaves in the Interior of Africa, by encouraging an exchange of the Productions of those Countries for the Production of Europe.

This was the Central African Expedition of 1849–55, which would result in the great discoveries of Henry Barth.

It has been estimated that slaves represented one half of the value of all northbound trade across the Sahara in the mid-nineteenth century and that of the 10,000 slaves who survived the crossing each year, one half came through Turkish Libya. In Murzuk, Richardson was appalled by what he found. 'The Tibboos cannot bring a female child over The Desert of the tender age of six or seven, without deflowering her,' he claimed. Many Tubbu slave-dealers engaged in the trade purely for this purpose: 'A slave-dealer will convey a score or two of female slaves from Mourzuk to Tripoli, and change the unhappy objects of his brutal lust every night. This is, he considers, the *summum bonum* of human existence, and to obtain it, he will continue this nefarious trade, without the smallest gain, or prospect of gain, and die a beggar when his vile passions become extinct.'

At the end of his first African mission, Richardson returned from Murzuk to Tripoli with a slave-dealer called Essnoussee, witnessing once again the sort of treatment that could be meted out to a defenceless charge by a cruel master:

I then saw Essnoussee bringing up a slave girl about a dozen years of age, pulling her violently along. When he got her up to the camel, he took a small cord and began tying it round her neck. Afterwards, bethinking himself of something, he tied the cord round the wrist of her right arm. This done, Essnoussee drove the camel on. In a few minutes she fell down, and the slave-master, seeing her fallen down, and a man attempting to raise her up, cried out, 'Let her alone, cursed be your father! You dog.' The wretched girl was then dragged on the ground over the sharp stones, being fastened by her wrist, but she never cried or uttered a word of com-

plaint. Her legs now becoming lacerated and bleeding pro-
fusely, she was lifted up by Essnoussee's Arabs. Thus she
was dragged, limping and tumbling down, and crippled all
the day, which was a very long day's journey.

Richardson gave his hard-won blessing to Gagliuffi's work and
thought the establishment of British Consuls and Vice-consuls
throughout the desert and African interior would be 'an immense
benefit to humanity' as well as a great fillip to British and international commerce. It was all very well making representations
to the Pasha in Tripoli, where the caravans brought their human
cargo for sale and onward shipment, but without a check on
the sources of supply, such efforts to suppress the trade would
inevitably be in vain. In Murzuk, Gagliuffi, a man of considerable
enterprise, was encouraging the population to diversify away
from the slave trade and collect gum from trees to sell to Tripoli,
Richardson noted with approval. It was a short-lived hope.
British interest in North Africa, at its apogee during the tenure
of Colonel Hanmer Warrington as Consul in Tripoli between
1814–46, was waning fast. With Algeria under their belt, the
French were taking over. In 1860, the British Vice-consulates of
both Murzuk and Ghadames were closed.

Even though it was declining, the slave trade was still active
by the time Nachtigal reached Murzuk in 1869, sixty-two years
after it had been 'abolished' in London. 'No merchant, to be
sure, can any longer enter the towns and visit their markets with
hundreds of slaves,' he wrote. 'But the smaller slave troops of
the minor merchants can easily be accommodated in the gardens
of the towns, whether in Murzuq or Tripoli, and in the neighbouring villages, and disposed of clandestinely.' He estimated the
number of slaves passing through Fezzan annually at 1,700–
2,700 at most. Although local government officials were frequently directed by Tripoli to stop the trade, such orders were
more for foreign than domestic consumption. Besides, the poorly
paid officials were easy targets for bribes from slave-dealers.
Nachtigal's account of the trade differed from Richardson's

chronicle of cruelty and stressed the 'mild administration of the institution of slavery', which the German believed derived both from the precepts of Islam and the good-natured character of Fezzaners. 'Slaves are treated quite as members of the family and have nothing to complain of,' he concluded blithely.

If the implicit objective of Turkish colonial policy in Libya was, as the governor of Ghadames had told Richardson, to keep the Arabs poor and submissive, the explicit aim of officials was to get rich as quickly as possible. After all, their foreign postings were only temporary. The slave trade was simply the most bountiful cash cow, to be milked for all it was worth. If town officials were too assiduous in their activities against the trade, they merely deprived the local government, and themselves, of the tax levied on slaves. While Nachtigal was staying in Murzuk, an ordinance against the slave trade was renewed and made more stringent. Because a slave caravan was due any day, however, officials merely waited until it had arrived and they had received the tax on the slaves, before making the ordinance public.

So pervasive was the slave trade that there were rumours that Gagliuffi himself was involved through capital he lent to a man named Mohammed as Sfaqesi, his agent in Bornu: a merchant could not trade with the south without being connected in one way or another. Gagliuffi found it profitable to remain in Murzuk long after the British Vice-consulate had been closed. In the late 1870s, by now well into his eighties, he was still active as Belgian Consul.

As for the final collapse of the traffic in slaves, it was a long time before Africans could share the joy of the poet James Montgomery, who had not been able to resist a patriotic celebration of Britain's 1807 legislation declaring the slave trade illegal. Africa's chains were not yet broken, she was not yet free, and there were few 'glad tidings' to waft to 'the land of slaves'. The last known slave consignment in Murzuk arrived 122 years later, in 1929.

After we had returned from the castle, Ahmed invited Ned and me to dinner at his elder brother Salem's house. He was a gentlemanly host with bright eyes and a face alternately smiling and grave. He wore the immaculate suit of *bedla a'rabiya*, an embroidered blue cotton waistcoat worn over a long shirt that reached below his knees and baggy *ziboun*, matching embroidered trousers. He showed us into a large rectangular room bordered on three sides by the customary cushion pads on the floor and against the wall. A large mock wood cabinet at the far end of the room was bright with china, books and a prayer rug. Its centrepiece was a television that occupied Ahmed's undivided attention. Like a child with a new toy, he was waving the remote control at it, flicking through dozens of Arabic satellite channels as though this was the greatest pleasure known to mankind. 'This is Saudi, this is Dubai, this is Egypt, this is Lebanon, this is Sudan,' he chirped as he surfed through the channels, oblivious to the fact that no one was listening. 'Now the world is only a small village. In Murzuk we can know what is happening in Britain and the United States now.' Salem smiled. He treated Ahmed like an indulgent father.

We had arrived half an hour before sunset and sat down with the brothers to await the call to prayer that marked the end of the day's fast. Another brother, Omar Abd al Kader, introduced himself to us. He was a pharmacologist in Murzuk. The Sherifs were a family of professionals. Salem, the oldest sibling, was one of the most senior government officials in Murzuk, but was reticent when replying to our questions about what he actually did. He mumbled something about approving budgets and quickly changed the subject to camels.

'*Allahu akbar. Allahu akbar.*' The call of the *muaddin* from a nearby mosque rose above the drone of a Saudi television channel showing prayers at Mecca. Ahmed stopped talking and disappeared into the kitchen. As the youngest brother, he was the uncomplaining gofer in the house. None of the others lifted a finger. He returned with a tray bearing a bowl of sticky dates and two cold drinks. The first, *qasib*, was a thick cereal drink, something like liquefied porridge. The other was *ruweina*, a mixture of wheat, sugar and water. Both were commonly served in the evenings during Ramadan, Salem said, and were deliciously refreshing after a hot day walking about town. We joined the four brothers sitting around the tray on their knees, embarrassed at how thirsty and hungry we felt without having fasted. 'In this weather, fasting is not a problem, *alhamdulillah*,' remarked Salem. 'It is much more difficult when Ramadan falls in summer.'

The conversation bounced from subject to subject. Mohammed spoke of a new private consultancy business he had started in addition to his full-time post. His urban planning job in Murzuk was for the government and the work was necessarily limited and limiting. He said he had visited Prague and Berlin as a student to learn about European architecture, which he wanted to introduce to Murzuk. Depending on how his new business progressed, he intended to move to Tripoli, where he would be able to exercise his professional skills on a larger field. 'You see, there is not much urban planning we can do in Murzuk,' he said. From a practical point of view at least, Murzuk was a success. The basic infrastructure, while not advanced, worked. Water flowed from taps, the roads were good, the houses had electricity and some had telephones. From an aesthetic perspective, however, the whole place was a Saharan carbuncle and would have to be rebuilt from scratch.

More plates followed, and the feast began. Salem took more interest in talking us through the bewildering assortment of dishes than in eating himself. There were bowls of *shirba Libiya*, Libyan soup mildly spiced with beans, rice and vegetables, *felfel ma'shi*, bulging peppers stuffed with rice and meat, and a saucer of *felafel*, small balls of fried chickpeas. Next came *boreik*, thin potato slices stuffed with fish, *kofta* meatballs, a plate of home-made mini-pizzas, a cucumber, onion and tomato salad and half a dozen discuses of *bazin*, the unleavened bread we had eaten in the desert with Abd al Wahab.

Having exhausted the discussion of what a wonderful invention satellite television was, Ahmed began on his medical studies in Tripoli. 'You know, I could tell you many things you do not know,' he said gravely. 'I could tell you about colostomies, kidneys and other things. You would not know these words even.'

Operations and ailments brought him onto his own condition and he assumed an air of dignified suffering.

'You know, I have irritable bowel syndrome,' he announced sadly, as Ned and I shovelled down mouthfuls of *kofta*. We made no reply. 'You know what irritable bowel syndrome is?' he continued remorselessly.

'I'm very sorry to hear it,' said Ned, hoping he would change the subject.

'Yes, I am sorry too,' Ahmed went on. 'I have had irritable bowel syndrome for too long.' I struggled not to laugh. 'My God, irritable bowel syndrome is a problem. What can I do?' He ended with a dramatic rhetorical flourish, as if to say he could not possibly expect to be understood with such a medically undistinguished audience.

There seemed to be no end to dinner. A bowl of huge blood oranges arrived, quickly followed by *mahalabiya*, a custard dessert sprinkled with coconut, raisins and chocolate. We marvelled at the succession of plates, trays and bowls coming in and thanked Salem for our finest meal in Libya. He smiled appreciatively and ordered a tray of red tea, green tea, coffee and biscuits. We departed sluggishly, our shrunken stomachs heavy with food.

'I wish you good luck with the rest of your expedition,' said Salem, standing on his doorstep beneath the blue cloak of night. The moon cast a pale light over the town and the stars glistened. 'You are having a very interesting journey and you will see many things in our great desert. Remember, you are always welcome here in Murzuk.' He shook hands and instructed Ahmed to drive us back to the farm.

The next morning I left Ned with the camels and walked into town. We wanted to depart that day but first needed to contact the elusive Taher, who still had our passports in Tripoli. In Idri he had promised to return them to us in Germa or Murzuk. Phone calls to anywhere outside Murzuk could only be made from the post office, a small and shabby building in which a forlorn bunch of men were waiting to be connected. Nigerians, Sudanese, Chadians, Egyptians and Libyans sat patiently on a bench opposite two operators in a grimy glass booth. Above them was a poster-size postal stamp depicting Gaddafi with raised revolutionary fist towering over an enthusiastic crowd. Behind the leader were the massed ranks of the Libyan army, above him fighter aircraft, warships and tanks. With all this technology, you wondered why it was necessary to go to a post office to place a telephone call.

An Iraqi teacher sat next to me, waiting stoically. He worked in a school twenty miles outside Murzuk and for several days had been coming into town to try telephoning Iraq to check that his family in Baghdad was safe after the recent Allied bombing of the capital. Three other Iraqis, teachers and engineers, had also been coming in, with no more success. After waiting for two hours he gave up and left with a sad shrug of the shoulders. Gaddafi and Saddam had brought their countries many things. An effective telecommunications system was not one of them. Eventually, after repeated attempts, I was connected to Tripoli on a line fuzzy with static. Hajer's voice boomed away, remote but unmistakable.

'Oh, Mr Justin, how are you? I am VERY, VERY pleased to talk to you.'

'We're very well, thanks. Is Taher there, please?' I asked, dreading the reply.

'How are you, Mr Justin?' he continued. 'How is Mr Ned? How is the desert? How are the camels? How are your guides?'

'Hajer, I need to speak to Taher.'

'Taher no here now.'

'What time will he be in the office?'

'Maybe he come later.'

It was useless. Wearily, and with the feeling that it would be futile – Hajer might never pass on the message, and even if he did Taher would probably do nothing about it – I asked for someone to bring us our passports. Perhaps they could meet us at Tmissah, the small oasis 125 miles east of Murzuk.

'Someone come to see you in Tmissah,' said Hajer bullishly. 'No problem, Mr Justin. Maybe Taher come, maybe Hajer.' We would see.

Before leaving, I walked over to the castle. At the gate, a man asked for my passport. 'I haven't got it with me,' I replied. 'I'm only going to look around the castle.' Gruffly, he waved me through. There were more than twenty rooms inside. Many were empty. In others there were feeble displays of old tools and locks, straw mats, leather bags, a few clay pots and an old camel saddle. The view from the ramparts was more absorbing. Several miles distant to the south and west, were the beginnings of the Murzuk Sand Sea, 15,000 square miles of burning dunes whose southern-most edges reached Libya's borders with Niger and Algeria, its rippling waves blurred in the refraction of the glaring light. The oasis town stretched out before me to the north and east, a mass of date palms, whitewashed rectangles of houses, several water towers and the pencil-like minarets that gleamed brilliantly beneath the sun. Clustered on one side of the castle several hundred metres away were the crumbling remnants of the old city, a picturesque scattering of mud houses occupied by the poorest Chadian and Tubbu families.

On my way out, the man at the entrance stopped me again, more insistent and hostile this time, and said he wanted to see my passport. I repeated that I did not have it with me, said goodbye and tried to leave. He blocked my exit.

'I am from Murzuk tourist police,' he said firmly. 'You must come with me. I want to see your papers.'

'You're very welcome to accompany me but first I have some important shopping to do,' I replied. He shouted to a colleague to fetch a car and descended the castle steps with me.

As both men appeared determined not to let me out of their sight, I thought it best to get the most out of them and their car while they were here and asked to be driven to somewhere I could buy water *bidoun*s and some lengths of rope. This done, we drove back to the farm, where Ned was preparing some bags for the camels. He did not like the look of my new friends, either. After we had shown them photocopies of our passports and explained, once again, that the originals were with a travel agent in Tripoli, the officers appeared partly pacified. To regain the initiative they then asked where were our entry stamps proving we had entered Libya from the Tunisian border at Ras al Jadir. They had us here. 'How can we show you the entry stamps when our passports are in Tripoli?' I asked. Ned was beginning to grow impatient. Being policemen, they insisted on making a report, for which my presence would be required at the police station. Ned, whose concept of the inalienable personal freedom of an Englishman did not square with their own, started getting shirty. 'Ned, I'll go into town with them and be back in a few minutes,' I said, before the argument escalated. He said he would prepare the camels for our departure. As soon as I returned, we would leave. We had outstayed our welcome in Murzuk.

On the way to the station the officers asked me why we were travelling by camel, where we were going and where we had been. On the basis of this information they compiled a report while I sat in the car outside their office. They returned me to the camp, delivered a final lecture on the unacceptability of travelling in Libya without a passport, and prepared to depart. In an effort to leave on good terms, I asked them where they were going. They were returning to Sebha, the capital of Fezzan.

'How long will it take you?' I asked.

'Sebha is 180 kilometres from Murzuk,' he replied. 'I can drive there in an hour.' I made a quick calculation.

'That would take us four days by camel.'

He looked at me with an expression of unutterable scorn. 'You are crazy Englishman.'

# CHAPTER VIII

# The Hunt for Mohammed
# Othman

*By day the hot sun fermented us; and we were dizzied by the beating
wind. At night we were stained by dew, and shamed into pettiness by
the innumerable silences of stars.*

T. E. LAWRENCE, *SEVEN PILLARS OF WISDOM*

*We tourists of The Desert acquire a peculiar affection for the melancholy
animal, whose slow but faithful step carries us through the hideous
wastes of sand and stone, where all life is extinct, and where, if left
a moment behind the camel's track, certain death follows.*

JAMES RICHARDSON, *TRAVELS IN THE GREAT DESERT OF
SAHARA IN THE YEARS OF 1845 AND 1846*

From Murzuk to Kufra is a little over 600 miles as the crow flies.
It is the most barren stretch of the Libyan Sahara, culminating
in the fiery wastes of the Rabiana Sand Sea, with no oasis or
other settlements approaching the size of either town. Finding
sufficient grazing and water for the camels would be our greatest
difficulty here, so it was essential to break down this portion of
the journey into more manageable legs. From maps and conversations in Germa and Murzuk, it seemed advisable first to follow
a fertile *wadi* 125 miles east to the small town of Tmissah. There

we would need to find a man who knew the surrounding country well to discuss the best route onwards to Kufra. The leg from Tmissah to Kufra, 500 miles with only the most isolated of oases at Wau al Kabir, Wau an Namus, Tizirbu and Rabiana, would test the camels' endurance to its limits. In the meantime, we could continue alone.

After the slight brush with the authorities, we were keen to depart Murzuk as quickly as possible. For as long as we were travelling without proper documents there was always the worry that Libyan officialdom might interfere with the expedition again, this time with more serious consequences. As the farm was located east of Murzuk we did not have to walk back into town, attracting fresh attention with the camels. Omar helped us finish packing them and we strode off in mid-afternoon on 2 January across a sandy plain marked by the occasional patch of scrub. To the south, a car drifted noiselessly across the horizon on the road to Tmissah.

We both felt a thrill to be travelling alone across the desert for the first time, to be in charge of our own caravan and fending for ourselves. Up to now we had been spoilt. If ever there was a serious problem, we could rely on our guide, with the possible exception of Salek, to help us. Now we had the opportunity to test the desert skills we had learnt from Abd al Wahab and, to a much lesser extent, from Salek and Saleh. If anything went wrong, and there was no shortage of accidents waiting to happen, we would have to manage alone. Doubtless, progress would be much slower with two men, rather than three – we still had five camels to look after, load and unload, hobble and feed – but we walked out into the desert fired with optimism and a sense of increased adventure.

There was the added bonus, too, of having a reprieve from the constant discipline of the guide (Salek being the exception again). At last, there was no one to tell us what to do. Knots could be tied without a snort of disgust from a guide who promptly retied them, fires lit without a grunt to indicate they should be made elsewhere, and camels ridden without a constant barrage of complaints that we were falling behind. Perhaps most luxuriously of all, we could stop and start whenever we liked without a gruff voice commanding us to wake up or announce our halt for the night. For the next week, at least, we were our own bosses.

It was difficult to tell whether the camels shared this enthusiasm. Celebrating our new-found independence, Ned threw himself on to The Big White. The saddle immediately slipped to one side and he was thrown to the ground. Undaunted by this slight to his *amour propre*, he remounted. This time the saddle fell on to the camel's neck and he was hurled to the ground again. The Big White looked at him scornfully. We walked for the rest of the afternoon.

Sunset threw a misty haze over the groves of date palms that stood like swaying sentinels over the bleached landscape. Grouped together among sandy hillocks, they formed a forest of elegant, slender fingers clutching at the sky. Birds flew overhead, circling and swooping in the darkening light. After the noise of Murzuk and the conviviality of Omar and the Chadians at the farm, we returned with glee to the thick stillness of the Sahara. All travellers in the desert are struck by the completeness of its silence. There is nothing like it. 'The quiet of the desert is something wonderful,' wrote General Gordon, who rode 7,500 miles by camel as Governor-General of Sudan from 1876–9. 'You never hear a sound; the camel's cushioned foot makes no noise and the air is perfectly pure.' All that disturbed it this evening was the wind gently flicking through the palms and the hypnotic sound of water sloshing about in the *bidoun*s. Ned and I walked only yards apart but neither of us spoke. The camels padded along quietly, lost, as were we, in the weary rhythm of the caravan.

After our late start, we camped six miles outside Murzuk in a small dell surrounded by date palms. The camels affixed themselves to the trees with their usual gusto and in customary formation, Gobber eating alone from one tree while The Big White, Asfar, Lebead and Bobbles grouped together on a separate clump for a more companionable dinner. We hobbled them around the trees, wondering aloud at how much longer things took without a third man and settled down to our own dinner of tuna fish pasta. After a break of only two days, it tasted delicious.

The next morning, after the daily cry of *bismillah*, we made a leisurely start at 11 a.m. – with no guide to hustle us out of our sleeping bags at dawn we lapsed into laziness – and continued alongside the wavy line of palms that marked the northernmost fringes of the Murzuk Sand Sea. Starting this late, the sun was already hot and high. Tramping across this flat wilderness towards a constantly unfolding and unattainable horizon, it was easy to sink into an intense reverie. To Ned's dismay, my daydreams invariably drifted towards food, putting together imaginary lunches or dinners in which my mother's superb toad-in-the-hole featured prominently. The scarcity of meat on our travels led to cruel dreams of steak frites, roast beef and shepherd's pie. I thought wistfully of puddings (now limited to a once weekly portion of tinned fruit) and was haunted by memories of spotted dick and custard, apple pie, jam roly-poly, apricot crumble and ice cream.

In the freezing mornings, crouched over a dirty saucepan containing cold tuna fish pasta from the night before, my thoughts turned longingly to a full English breakfast of bacon, eggs, sausages, black pudding, fried bread, mushrooms, tomatoes, and bubble and squeak, all luxuriating in fat. Failing that, eggs Benedict would also have been welcome. In the afternoons, drawn into the conversation against his will, Ned would usually plump for a steak, having first pondered the merits of a cheeseburger. And then, in the middle of this paean to red meat, he would stop suddenly, struck both by the impossibility of such a lunch or dinner and the imminence of yet another tuna fish pasta.

'Stop talking about food, Justin. You're impossible,' he would say, irritably.

The Egyptian traveller Hassanein Bey, though a man of grander tastes, also sought imaginary satisfaction for the hunger that is such a feature of travelling by camel in the desert. It usually affected him most at noon. 'As I stride along I imagine myself in Shepherd's Grill Room in Cairo and I order Crevettes à l'Américaine with that subtle variation of Riz à l'Orientale which is a speciality of the house,' he slavered. 'Or I am at Prunier's in Paris ordering Marennes Vertes d'Ostende, followed by a steak and soufflé. Perhaps it is the Cova at Milan and a succulent dish of Risotto alla Milanese; maybe Strawberries Melba at the Ritz in London.'

Such dreams vanished with the arrival of a man bringing him a handful of dates. The languid Egyptian even fitted out one camel with a tent in which to eat and rest out of the heat of the sun. It came to be known as 'the Club'. To the question where was the master came the reply: 'The Bey is lunching at the Club today!' The point about hunger in the desert was that by the end of the day we were so ravenous that anything, including the stubbornly repetitive tuna fish pasta, tasted good. And if morale was low, something like a Stilton and cauliflower packet soup restored our spirits immediately.

Towards sunset the next day, having walked across plains, past the occasional postage stamp of bright green that denoted a farm – the only trace of colour in this burnished landscape – we split into two groups to investigate the grazing situation. As Ned and his four camels receded into the distance, Asfar became increasingly edgy, swinging round his head every few seconds to keep an eye on his departing friends and roaring desperately. I marched towards what looked like a deserted farmstead in the middle of a slight depression. The other caravan grew steadily smaller and then was lost to sight. Asfar stared hard in the direction it had disappeared. On discovering that his friends had vanished, he swung round on his head-rope in front of me, now roaring in a mad panic. I tried calming him to no effect. However tightly he was reined in on his rope, he pirouetted wildly around on it, lunging in front of me and refusing to walk on. When I went ahead, he swung round in front again, this time kicking out at me with his forelegs, butting me with his chest and roaring ferociously. Suddenly, there was nothing effeminate about him.

He was completely out of control. The squeaky falsetto had gone. This was a rich baritone and indicated wild terror.

Lawrence described something similar when he turned his she-camel around 180 degrees from his caravan to look for a man who had gone missing.

> From calfhood they were accustomed to live in droves, and some grew too conventional to march alone: while none would leave their habitual party without loud grief and unwillingness, such as mine was showing. She turned her head back on her long neck, lowing to the rest, and walked very slowly, and bouncingly. It needed careful guidance to hold her on the road, and a tap from my stick at every pace to keep her moving.

As Asfar was intent on going no farther, I stopped too. From here I could see the farmstead would make a good camp. There was grazing for the camels and plenty of wood. The place looked abandoned. I shouted across towards Ned and in a few minutes he reappeared. Asfar was scanning the horizon intently, desperate to catch sight of his Ghadamsi friends. With each step they came nearer, he grew calmer, his expression changing from one of blind panic to studied displeasure with me. By the time the two parties were reunited, his roars had subsided and with the other four he started eyeing the pasturage nearby with interest.

'That's what you get with trophy camels,' said Ned, amused at the tantrums he had seen from afar. 'You'd never catch Gobber behaving like that.' We ripped away at a derelict wooden shed, lit a fire and settled for the night.

We found our own relaxed pace for the rest of the journey, covering 20–25 miles a day and never emerging from our sleeping bags before sunrise. One evening we came across a small settlement consisting of several farmsteads, most of them long deserted to judge by the state of the dilapidated fences of palm fronds that surrounded the unkempt fields. One appeared in superior condition to the others, with small oblongs of green neatly separated by irrigation channels and a simple house behind a mud wall. A dog started to bark insistently. The camels, who had been about to tuck into masses of *dumran*, a feathery plant that was one of their favourite foods, were rattled and rushed away together to form a petrified committee. The idea of these majestic beasts being frightened by a small, yapping mongrel seemed absurd, but they refused to come back to graze. We turned to our own dinner instead.

When it was pitch black, two lights suddenly loomed out of the darkness. At first they looked as though they would pass us by. Then they changed course and started to bear down on us steadily, blinding us with their brightness. There was something unsettling about this. Who was so keen to discover us? The lights grew brighter until the flames of the fire revealed an old Peugeot 504 pulling up in front of us. A middle-aged man stepped out and began to question us. As soon as he saw we were foreigners with camels, he became extremely affable, complimenting us on the quality of our (hardly visible) animals and running through a list of basic supplies we might need, offering to bring anything we were lacking from his neighbouring farm. We thanked him for his offer and said we were fully equipped. Such was the hospitality of the desert that he seemed disappointed we did not even want some bread.

During the next two days we moved up the *wadi* into less fertile country, now skirting the sand dunes that lay to the south and east, now dipping into them to cut corners where they had been swept into our path. We walked parallel to a continuous low ridge that marked the far side of the *wadi* several miles to the north. The ground underfoot changed from gravelly plain to an expanse of salt flats that stretched ahead for miles. From afar they looked like a freshly ploughed field laced with frost, similar to those we had seen in Idri but on a much grander scale. Huge swollen cliffs of mud teetered over deep channels. Walking through them, you fell constantly through the thin crust with the crisp noise of walking on hardened snow. For the camels it was treacherous footing – they found it impossible to judge whether the next step would hold or crash through to below knee level. They proceeded with care, astonished that camels of such pedigree should have to go through such an ordeal. We led them on to a small path that wound laboriously around the edges of the salt flats. A narrow track studded on both sides with low clumps of date palms, it also upset the camels for some reason. Every few minutes, one of them would spot a date palm that aroused particular dread and pull up abruptly. Only the judicious use of a whip to the rump succeeded in getting them to move on. The usually unflappable Gobber and the steadfast Lebead proved the most recalcitrant. With the camels in this mood, what little order there had been in our caravan was quickly lost. When Abd al Wahab and Saleh had ridden at the head of the caravan, the others had followed behind in a neat single file. When Ned or I took the lead, they moved up alongside the lead camel, bunching awkwardly and occasionally knocking off a load in the clash. Moving among the camels to adjust the ropes and repack the bags after such an incident had to be done with great care. If you happened to stray behind Gobber, he would lash out powerfully with a catapult of a kick that could break your leg.

The country opened up again. Flanking us on our left as far as the eye could see, a slight embankment of sand slanted gently towards the sky. Among the slopes nearest us, small patches of date palms congregated independently like mini-oases. Several hundred metres across from the dunes the ground rose almost imperceptibly, enough to give the sense of an endless corridor without constricting the impression of infinite space. Looking along this wand of sand towards the horizon, the trees grew smaller and smaller until they appeared as tiny as grains of black pepper in a landscape suffused with a weak white light. The day was petering out, waiting for sunset to rouse the sky to life. Steadily, the luminous sun sank into the sand, throwing into relief two distant hills standing opposite the dunes and lengthening the shadows of the nearest palms. These dark shapes shot across the dunes like black needles, pointing to a distant hamlet behind us in which a handful of lights sparkled in the dusk. For half an hour we walked on, the countryside unchanging, the elusive horizon almost indistinguishable between sand and sky, and watched streaks of gold splash out from the sun. Gradually they paled and the sky darkened, as the thick cloak of night, punctured only by the first ranks of stars, settled into place. We veered into the dunes and camped in a small dell overlooking this magnificent country.

Trudging across the plain the next afternoon, we caught sight of a small town in the distance. White squares of houses jostled between bright green fields and the competing shades of date palms; a minaret rose slimly towards a comfortable fleece of clouds that presided over the town. There was something idyllic about the place. If a church tower had been substituted for the minaret it could have been a sleepy English hamlet. The brilliance of the green was an alluring contrast to the scorched brown of the desert. The distant hum of human life drifted over on the wind.

We sat down with the camels and foraged for a bar of chocolate and some water.

'God, I'm completely knackered,' I said. My limbs felt heavy and my knees and hips had taken a pounding. 'I could do with a break.'

'You could say it's getting a bit boring,' said Ned, who felt the same.

Boredom and exhaustion were nothing unusual of themselves. It was only today, however, just over a month into the camel trek, that we both confessed to having anything other than positive feelings about the journey. Since they turned out to be shared sentiments, there was a sense of cathartic release as, slumped on the ground, we compared notes on how wearily monotonous the journey had become. To keep our spirits up it was always imperative to have something to look forward to, whether a distant speck on the horizon (another empty oil drum) or the next town or village towards which we were heading. Sometimes, when we were riding the camels, we sang to while away the time, an imperfectly remembered 'Marseillaise' being one of our favourites. Recently, Ned had also started dipping into a collection of poems and was learning Coleridge's 'Kubla Khan' by heart.

'Do you feel like making a slight detour into town?' I suggested, thinking he might disapprove. 'We could get some more sweets and chocolate for a start.' From our maps the small town to our north appeared to be Zuweila, once the capital of Fezzan. It was not directly on our route to Tmissah but nor was it a great distance off it. To my relief, Ned felt like a diversion too.

'Let's do it,' he said. He was just as keen as me on the Egyptian Sando bars.

We roused the camels from their short-lived siesta and walked towards the widening expanse of green. Following the deep grooves of a winding car track, we approached Zuweila through thickets of date palms. The camels perked up at the proximity of food at this unexpected hour, slowing their step to tear off long fronds that protruded comically from either side of their mouths as they walked on, chewing with an air of pleasant distraction. Occasional cars slowed down alongside our caravan and drivers leaned out of windows to shout questions and greetings at us.

At closer quarters, the town was less picturesque than it had appeared from afar. The outskirts were decorated with the familiar litany of rubbish in which corn oil tins played the leading role. The houses, although constructed on a more impressive scale than those of Germa or Idri, were still squat and square. Some had been embellished with coloured metal doors and gates. Others aspired to grandeur with porches or carelessly built, unpainted concrete balconies. We passed through a small estate of single-storey houses in disrepair. Some of the roofs had fallen in and were propped up haphazardly. Young men loitered on the corners of broken roads. Most of the shops were closed behind metal shutters. Some had abandoned hope altogether and were scrappily boarded up. This was no pastoral idyll. It looked more like an inner-city ghetto.

The camels were on edge again. The concrete roads, an unfamiliar urban landscape, and the noises of a small desert town had all unsettled them. In the empty wastes of the Sahara there was hardly anything to disturb the quiet. Here they looked bewildered and nervous. A swelling crowd of children, intrigued by the spectacle of this unexpected caravan led by two foreigners, made matters worse, trotting behind it, screaming questions and abuse at us, running across the camels' path, and throwing pebbles at them. Some of the bolder ones rushed up and slapped the animals on their rumps. The camels, who had not been in a town since Murzuk, took fright at this assault and broke into a panic-stricken trot. The ropes that attached them together became jumbled, bags started unfastening themselves from the camels' backs with all the jolting, and disaster seemed imminent.

'We've got to get out of here,' said Ned. Our *séjour* in Zuweila was over. It was a pity because the town looked worth exploring. Several hundred metres from where we were standing, an immense fort rose above the rest of the buildings, looking down on what seemed to be the remnants of the old city. Like everything else here, the castle was apparently abandoned, but nevertheless exuded a powerful resilience. It had taken several hundred years for it to decay. The modern houses of Zuweila might have been only thirty years old but were already falling apart.

'You keep the camels, I'll get the chocolate,' I said, leaving Ned holding the restless camels. I dashed into a small hole in the wall that served as a general store and quickly amassed seventy-two bars of chocolate, several packets of English Custard Creams (made in Egypt) and – an unexpected luxury – a packet of processed cheese slices. While I was paying, a small man with a grizzled face and scruffy civilian clothes peered at me from behind lenses the thickness of reinforced windowpanes. Peremptorily and without any introduction, he demanded to see my passport.

'No, you can't,' I replied, in a hurry to return to the camels. 'Do you think you're a policeman or something?'

'I am a policeman.'

'Well, you can't see our passports because they're in Tripoli.

And our papers are somewhere over there among those bags on the camels.' I pointed to the caravan of agitated animals outside.

'Show me your papers.'

'I'm very sorry but our camels are frightened so we've got to leave now.'

'I want to see your papers.'

'We're not staying in Zuweila. Goodbye.'

There was a persistence about the man that was both admirable and detestable. He had the bit between his teeth and evidently did not share my opinion that our conversation was finished.

It was something of a contrast to the courteous welcome the German traveller Frederick Horneman received when he arrived in Zuweila – known as 'Belled el Shereef' (town of the Sherifs) – in 1798. Sherif Hindy, the principal man of the town, rode out to meet the caravan with a large entourage, celebrating the pilgrims' arrival 'with huzzas and discharge of muskets'. Although many were inevitably curious to catch sight of their first foreigner, 'all behaved with the greatest decorum and regularity,' Horneman recorded. 'But the family of the *Shereef* was distinguished by its particular complacency and politeness of manners.'

Lyon, too, was graciously received in Zuweila during his whistlestop tour of the region around Murzuk after Ritchie had died in late 1819. The white *sherifs*, who formed the majority of the town's population and prided themselves on their descent from Mohammed, he thought particularly good natured. 'They are certainly the most respectable, hospitable, and quiet people in Fezzan,' Lyon wrote, 'and their whole appearance (for they are handsome and neatly dressed) bespeaks something superior to the other whites.'

The policeman who appeared so interested in our caravan was neither hospitable nor neatly dressed. A shabby man who looked old but was probably not much more than fifty, he followed me out of the shop and summoned a colleague, also in plain clothes. Fortunately, the latter was a man of greater charm and better disposed towards us. He understood why we did not wish to delay in town.

'Don't worry, I have seven camels,' he said sympathetically, 'I know what it's like. Just give me your passport numbers.' He lacked a piece of paper on which to write them down and, after showing us the best way out of town, disappeared in his car to fetch some. The hangers-on melted away and we walked off in the direction he had indicated. Several minutes later he reappeared, and drove alongside us at camel's pace while we dictated the relevant details, the animals looking at the man sniffily as he scribbled away. Once he had finished taking notes, the officer waved a hand towards the plain visible in the distance between some houses and told us Tmissah was about fifty miles away. He wished us well, said goodbye and departed.

Half a mile or so beyond the easternmost edge of town, we came across six domed buildings, ruddy in the declining sun of late afternoon. Each was about ten metres high and seven across, with two windows, one above the other, on their front. All six were arranged in a line and separated from each other by little more than a metre. Five had been restored and were built of stone. The sixth, constructed of sun-dried bricks and clay, had been fiercely eroded by the elements and was losing its outline. Lyon believed these buildings, (when he visited there were five rather than six) were the tombs of the *sherifs* who settled in Zuweila sometime around the fourteenth century. He was told that the inscriptions on the top of the walls had been written by Christians 'soon after the time of Lord Noah', but on further investigation saw the characters were in fact Arabic. 'They immediately saw the resemblance, but said, that having fancied them to be of Christian origin, they had taken it for granted, and never troubled their heads about decyphering them,' he crowed. Today, the site is known as the cemetery of As Sahaba and, to judge by the brand new supermarket-size car park, was destined to be Zuweila's prime tourist attraction. All that was missing were the tourists.

We struck out across the desert, passing the last vestiges of green and entering another forlorn and lifeless plain. Something fell from Bobbles' back and he flew into a panic, bucking like a bronco and roaring in distress. The slightest mishap played havoc with his nerves. Half an hour after this smallest of incidents he was still trembling. The more pressing concern for the camels, however, was food. The grazing had been regular but not plentiful for the past few days. For the mountainous Gobber, who seemed to feel the hunger more keenly than the others, it appeared to have been little better than a light snack. He gazed at us sadly while we opened tins of tuna, and at the first rustle of a bag he knew to contain food shuffled towards it on his knees, excitement in his eyes.

The next day, the last before Tmissah, the light was a snowy white beneath a thick bed of clouds. The afternoon wore on heavily, the plain varying only in a series of light undulations. Each one we crossed revealed another bare expanse devoid of scrub or other pasturage. It was a bleak prospect for the camels and the warm glow of sunset was dimming all the time. Deceptively, the deepening shadows of the rolling contours appeared to be welcome pastures, only to melt away into the darkness on our arrival. For the first time we pressed on after sunset and the camels kept a smarter pace in the evening cool. It was exhilarating to be marching beneath the bright bustle of stars in the cold half-light of the moon, undisturbed in this stretching solitude. The wind, so constant during the day, dropped and played around our ankles as we scuffed through the light dusting of shingle, sprinkled over the desert like castor sugar.

For the past week travelling together, there had always been a certain pride in not being the first to suggest halting for the night. When we travelled with a guide, it was invariably he who decided when to stop. After an hour or so, I hinted at calling it a day.

'You know, we've still got some of that Malaysian chicken soup,' I said. 'That wouldn't be bad for dinner.'

'Isn't it fantastic walking under the stars?' Ned replied, ignoring the suggestion completely. 'We should have done it more often.' I resolved to say no more on the subject and carried on walking. When it came a quarter of an hour later, his suggestion was ingenious.

'Do you feel like stopping here?' he began. Before I could reply, he gave the question added urgency by observing that, 'If we go on in the dark the camels might cut themselves on broken glass on the outskirts of town.'

As Tmissah was twelve miles distant, this seemed neither a great nor imminent danger, but the offer was too good to decline. After another late start at 11 a.m., we had covered twenty-six miles, a laughably small distance by Lawrence's standards, but we were in no rush and, with a small caravan, could only travel at walking pace. Besides, we were not fighting a war.

We joined the camels in a somewhat dejected camp. Morale was not high. There was no food for the camels, not much for ourselves, and no wood to burn. It was the absence of a fire that always made you realize how much you needed one. Despite perspiring under the choking sun for most of the day, within minutes of sunset the cold reached into your bones. Without fuel for a fire, we had to rely once more on my kerosene stove to cook something hot. Soup, or anything else for that matter, proved impossible. The stove, suffocated by sand, spluttered away dismally for a few seconds and then gave up the fight altogether. Dinner would have to be cold. In the end, it consisted of an old tin of olives, a few shards of bread, brittle with staleness, and a joyless tin of Libyan baked beans. 'It's enough to make you feel like tuna fish pasta,' said Ned.

The next morning, six days after leaving Murzuk, we woke to the creeping feeling of damp. Sodden with dew, the down sleeping bags had to be hung on the camels' backs to dry for the rest of the morning. Gobber, the great gourmand of the caravan, looked ravenous. He had picked up a discarded cardboard box in his mouth, now waving it in the air, now tearing at it on the ground with his teeth, as if by this constant motion it might transform itself into something more succulent. The other camels looked on impassively before hoovering up the ancient remnants of bread.

The sun rose: it was another burning day and the dry wind rushed at us as we passed onto slightly lower ground bordered on our right by the easternmost slopes of the Murzuk Sand Sea. We came across the well-worn grooves of camel tracks zigzagging irregularly across the plain like the traces of drunken snails (camels are no more capable of walking in a straight line than the men who lead them). Riding east of the Dead Sea in 1918, Lawrence passed similar traces of camel caravans, a 'multitude of desert paths which led only to the abandoned camps of last year, or of the last thousand or ten thousand years: for a road, once trodden into such flint and limestone, marked the face of the desert for so long as the desert lasted'. Here, on the hardened sand of the Libyan Sahara, these personal and romantic testimonies of travel would soon fade away forever.

In the full glare of early afternoon, the tip of a radio mast jutting out of the lake of molten silver stretching across the horizon announced Tmissah. We felt a rush of relief and satisfaction, as we had on reaching Idri, Germa and Murzuk before, only more pronounced this time because we were travelling without a guide. The prospect of putting our feet up for a few days was also dazzling. Dipping in and out of small depressions as we approached the town, we watched the customary signs of life unfurl in the boiling haze: first the radio mast, its red and white stripes steadily rising out of the sand, then the line of electricity pylons snaking into town, next the dark mass of distant trees crouching in tight ranks. Nearer still, minarets appeared, standing against the backdrop of mountain ridges that hovered patchily in the pulsing light before disappearing altogether and re-emerging in altered formations. The wind dropped, the heat grew more intense, and Tmissah remained stubbornly out of range. The apparent proximity of the town was deceptive. As Richardson discovered, 'on the plains of Africa bounded by mountain ranges, one is as much at a loss to measure distances as the landman at sea, when measuring the distance from his ship to the rocks bounding the shore'. It was not until after two o'clock that we drew alongside a dense quadrangle of trees, which were guarding the approach to Tmissah like some impregnable fortress. For several minutes we searched for an opening and then plunged in, threading through a series of deserted farms with small tumbledown shacks, scattered breeze blocks and the charred hulks of Peugeot estate cars and Toyota Landcruisers.

Sensing that their enforced diet was over, the camels snatched impetuously at tree branches overhead. Bobbles, affixed at the back of the caravan on a short length of rope, found it impossible to manoeuvre his head in such a way that he could grab a piece of foliage without incurring a sharp pull on his nose-ring as the caravan walked on. It was doubly frustrating for him to watch the four camels in front all making such an agreeable lunch. Out of pity, we fed him by hand.

Signs of life were plentiful but the town's inhabitants proved surprisingly elusive. Occasional voices rose above mud walls, and sheep and goats trilled at random, but it was only on reaching the main road in town that we came upon the first people. Three men walking down the road in animated conversation stopped and looked at us as though we were an apparition. After the usual flurry of *kaif haleks*, we asked what sort of accommodation was available.

'No hotel in Tmissah,' one of the three replied simply.

'Do you know where we can stay and is there somewhere we can keep our camels?'

He looked at me blankly. 'No hotel in Tmissah.'

There was a large camel logo on a building on the other side of the road that looked familiar. In Idri, Taher had said something about having a sister company in Tmissah. The man who was sure there was no hotel in Tmissah followed my gaze.

'Yes, you must talk to Muftah Kilani,' he suggested.

'Who is Muftah Kilani?'

'Yes, Muftah Kilani.'

A new tack was called for. 'Where is Muftah Kilani?'

'Yes, Muftah Kilani will help you.'

Seeing we were not getting anywhere, his friend explained that Muftah Kilani ran a small tourism company in town. If we waited outside the building, he would come in due course. After thanking them for their help, we hobbled the camels and sat down to wait in the shadeless fire of the sun. The three men padded off softly and disappeared. There were no more signs of activity around us. It was the fourth week of Ramadan and the stupor of an oasis town weighed heavily in the blaze of mid-afternoon. Flies hummed about lazily. Shop shutters were all pulled down. There was no-one on the streets, no children playing, no sound of cars or any other machinery you would expect to hear in a town, not even the familiar bleating of sheep and goats. It was a lifeless place and the silence was overpowering.

Only one shop appeared to be open. Above its door hung a tatty Coca-Cola sign. Ned went off to investigate and returned with two bottles of chilled Coke and mineral water, which we guzzled down manically, out of sight behind the camels. After half an hour, a well-covered man of medium height arrived. He greeted us with friendly eyes and a certain solicitude. Under a large nose with flared nostrils, his tousled moustache and the rough stubble on his chin were flecked with grey. Tufts of hair gathered messily on the sides of his head, looking up towards the steady advance of the male balding process in dismay. A black *burnous* was thrown casually about his shoulders, worn over a pristine white *jalabiya*. The appearance was that of a jaunty man of consequence. This was Muftah Kilani.

We conversed in Muftah's halting English and my more halting Arabic.

'Welcome to Tmissah. I know you coming. I speak to Hajer in Tripoli before,' he began. We had left a message with Hajer for Taher to bring our long-lost passports to Tmissah.

'Is Taher here?'

'Taher not come.' It was an uncanny echo of Hajer.

'Is Hajer here then?'

'Hajer not come also.'

'Can we telephone Taher?'

'Tmissah have no telephones,' he replied cheerily, before explaining that although many houses had phones, none of them actually worked. The telecommunications revolution had not reached the middle of the Libyan Sahara. If you wanted to make a telephone call here, you had to drive back fifty miles or so to Zuweila.

'Don't worry. No problem,' he reassured us. Whereas the creed of our last guide Saleh centred around the various negative uses of the word *mishkilla*, Muftah was a man of more positive inclinations. His favourite expression was *mafish mishkilla* (no problem).

He confirmed there was no hotel in Tmissah and invited us to stay in his house. The first floor was rented out to occasional visitors, mostly tourists on four-wheel-drive expeditions in Libya. The camels could be kept outside. We walked the several hundred metres to his house, Muftah shooing away the excitable gaggle of children that thronged on all sides. They fired volleys of questions at us, each one shouting above the other. Where did we come from, where was our car, were these our camels, and did we know of the Libyan independence hero Omar Mukhtar? We were the first tourists Muftah knew of to arrive in Tmissah by camel, he explained. Despite a certain air of absentmindedness, he was quick to arrange the priorities: water and a fifty-kilogram sack of barley for the camels (bought at a fraction of the cost of the bag Khalil had sold us in Idri), for us, the long-forgotten joy of a high-pressure hot shower, followed by a tray of soup, chicken, rice, salad, tea and coffee. It was an auspicious start.

Horneman arrived in Tmissah in November 1798. He considered it 'a place of little importance', as it remained today, 'containing not more than forty men bearing arms'. Decay had set in long ago and the dilapidated walls around the town offered scant protection against attack. The houses were even worse, he sniffed, 'scarcely so comfortable as our sheds for cattle in Europe'. He lost little time in this desolate desert outpost. After overnighting in Tmissah, he hastened on to Zuweila. We were in less of a hurry. The camels had to be rested and refuelled and we were not averse to some mindless relaxation ourselves. Besides, we needed to find a guide, and that would take time.

The camels had been hobbled around their ankles and were taking in their new surroundings at leisure. There were patches of scrub scattered across the open ground outside Muftah's house, to which they were devoting their energies. Bobbles had installed himself in goal at one end of a dusty football pitch and was waiting pathetically for the other four to join him in a kick-around. None of the others was interested. Asfar stood at the other end of the pitch, scratching himself languidly against one of the uprights.

In the evening, we brought out the barley and started pouring it over the large plastic sheet we carried. Hearing the rustle, all five stopped grazing at once and lurched towards us. Asfar, perhaps forgetting the pecking order – in which he played second fiddle to The Big White while ranking above Gobber, Bobbles and Lebead – knelt down quickly and threw himself onto the middle of the sheet, burying his nose and mouth in the fast diminishing pile of grain. After a reminder from The Big White about proper decorum, he withdrew but continued to devour the barley with unaccustomed purpose. Gobber for once joined the throng. He was too hungry to be detained, and too large to be shoved aside by the others. The camels' feast continued with four bales of hay that Muftah had procured.

Watching the camels eat always gave us pleasure. Abu Amama and his colleagues in the Mehari Club of Ghadames had assured us these camels were fine animals and would not break down on the expedition we proposed, but second-hand car dealers say the same sort of thing and we were always concerned that they were as well looked after as the journey allowed. After travelling with them for more than a month, we had grown attached to them and they were serving us admirably. Richardson, too, enjoyed seeing his camels feed: 'My chief occupation in riding is watching them browse, and observing the epicurean fancies of these reflective, sober-thinking Brutes of The Desert. I observe also as a happy trait in the Arab, that nothing delights him more than watching his own faithful camel graze.' Although he had not travelled with us, Muftah seemed to share this enthusiasm.

Inside the house, he divided his time between the kitchen, where his invisible wife prepared meals and drinks for us, and the first floor, to which he came every quarter of an hour on various pretexts. His real interest lay in looking at our equipment. An inveterate fiddler, he derived enormous pleasure from inspecting our gadgets. He would have been in his element in Field & Trek, the Baker Street shop where we had bought many of them. GPS he was familiar with. Compasses were a less certain business. He asked me to show him how to take a bearing on a map, one of the few navigational skills I possessed. My compass, which had luminous plastic markings to enable night-time navigation, fascinated him. He took to shrouding himself beneath his black *burnous* with it, a fantastic figure exclaiming enthusiastically as he found north or calculated the bearing from Tmissah to the oasis of Wau al Kabir. Books were of less interest, although the photos of camels and other desert scenes in Lawrence's *Seven Pillars of Wisdom* engrossed him for several minutes. Our American pilotage charts, sleeping bags, shortwave radios, cameras and walking boots were other favourites.

His son Kilani, a thirteen-year-old magpie of a boy, was forever coming up and down the stairs, begging for chocolate bars and pens or fiddling incessantly with whatever he found on the floor. When he was not scrounging from us, he played the jealous custodian of the camels in front of the house, using his father's position as our host to ward off other curious children who had been attracted by the new arrivals. He executed this role with gusto, hurling stones the size of small bricks at those he considered had come too close to his charges or rapping them across the legs with a long stick. There was nothing gentle about Kilani. He was a bully. Sometimes we found him beating the camels or yanking them by the nose-ring for no apparent reason other than that he seemed to enjoy it. Perhaps it also contributed to his prestige among Tmissah's younger generation of heavies. Muftah, a generous-hearted man, was indulgent of his son's pranks. We found them less amusing and told him to treat the animals properly.

It was difficult, unless you happened to be a compass with luminous markings, to keep Muftah's attention for long. We steered the conversation towards our need for a guide by unfolding one of the pilotage charts of southern Libya. After he had calculated several bearings, all of them incorrect, he turned to the matter at hand. 'Don't worry, *mafish mishkilla*, we will find guide to take you to Kufra. Muftah also guide.' Like Caesar (and Salek), he spoke about himself in the third person. If Muftah did not take us himself, and it was clear he wanted to go, despite a problem with his leg, he would make some inquiries on our behalf, he said, and turned back to the compass. I went for a late-night stroll around town.

The *muaddin* began his call to prayer, one of the most melodious I had ever heard, sung in a firm but mournful tone, his voice rising and falling in the dark night, lingering with the echo of the loudspeakers. Children played in the streets, silhouetted like small phantoms in the misty, dust-filled glare of car headlights, yelling loudly, playing war games and laying about each other with their sticks. They ran up to me with the usual questions about our camels and Omar Mukhtar. Women walked along together, well wrapped up against the drifting sand blown in by the wind. Shopkeepers sat in the pools of light in front of their small boutiques, selling cigarettes and soft drinks. There was a slightly forlorn feeling to this remote desert outpost, the last town of any size before Tizirbu, almost 350 miles to the east. It was not much of an oasis but it was all there was. From Tmissah, our journey would take us across the most forbidding stretch of the desert so far. Empty plains and lifeless sand dunes were all we could expect for most of the way and the camels had to be well fed and rested here before we could move on. Once we left Tmissah, a weak camel would have little chance of surviving the expedition.

Muftah took us on a tour of the old city the next day. We stepped inside the skeleton remains of a once pretty mosque. The interior arches and the *qiblah* facing Mecca were still intact but the roof had caved in, leaving the beams of sliced date palm trunks open to the sky. Graffiti was daubed across the walls and palm fronds lay in heaps over the rubble of collapsed mud and stones. Bright needles of sunlight stole through the windows, cutting through the moist gloom. You could still make out the area in which worshippers had washed their hands and feet before praying. Muftah took us into his old family home, a generously sized place that was in better condition than most of its peers. Bags of grain lay deep in dust in a small storeroom. In the coldest winter nights, the family had gathered around a fire in one of the smallest rooms. It was a Saharan snug. A tiny aperture had been cut into the palm-frond roof to allow smoke to escape but the rest of the ceiling was still charred black. Outside, the old *zinqa*s wormed their way between deeply scarred mud walls that were either tottering towards destruction or had collapsed entirely. We walked through them, past the debris of ancient houses stacked together, past a shop in which the old shelf fixings remained in place, and reached another mosque, whose decapitated minaret presided over this mess of roofless houses that looked like a war scene from Afghanistan. Beyond them, stood the date palms, minarets and water tower of the new town, and farther still lay the barren plains of the desert.

It was easy to romanticize about what life had once been like here. The noises and the smells, the bustle and overcrowding, had all vanished now. The story was a familiar one. The old city had been vacated only fifteen years ago, Muftah told us, when its inhabitants relocated to the new town. Already, it was a relic. If the buildings and walls continued to decay at this rate, there would be nothing left in thirty years. Take people out of a town and things fall apart. Thinking about Mohammed Ali's regret at being forced to leave the old city of Ghadames, I asked Muftah if he missed the family home in which he had grown up. 'No, it is better we moved,' he replied. 'Now we have hot water and electricity in the new town, *alhamdulillah*.' Unlike Mohammed Ali, he was an unsentimental believer in progress and technology and regarded my interest in history as meaningless nostalgia. After all, the new ways were more comfortable.

That evening we were introduced to a putative guide. He was

a slim, smiling man called Ahmed Sassi, one of Tmissah's trio of desert guides (Muftah himself being the latest and most junior addition to their ranks), but travelled by four wheels rather than camel. He knew southern Libya well and had been from Tmissah to Kufra many times, he told us. We unfolded a map and started discussing possible routes. Muftah perked up at once and started to take bearings. Ahmed Sassi was amused by the idea of our journey onwards from Tmissah, but doubtful about its chances of success. 'By camel it is too difficult,' he replied, shaking his head emphatically. 'It is a very long journey and there is not enough food for them.'

My heart sank. Up to now, we had always managed to find a guide prepared to travel with us. But the journey from Tmissah to Kufra, 500 miles as the crow flies, was unlike anything we had attempted before. It was of a completely different scale and Ahmed was adamant that it would prove beyond our camels. Not because they were too weak for the journey, but simply because there was not enough water or grazing for them on the way. He took us through the route step by step, outlining the difficulties we really did not want to hear.

'First, when you leave this town there is no grazing along the Wadi Marzuq until you reach Wau al Kabir,' 100 miles south-east of Tmissah, he said. 'Maybe you will find a tree or a plant, but probably not. And there is no water. After Wau al Kabir, there is nothing before Wau an Namus,' the volcanic oasis another 100 miles away.

'In Wau an Namus there are some date palms and the camels can graze on the leaves and some dates, but the water is not sweet here. They cannot drink it. After you leave Wau an Namus, it is even worse. You will find nothing travelling across the Wadi Ma'raf, no food, no water, nothing at all [for the last 220 miles to Tizirbu]. After Tizirbu you will be OK. From here to Kufra is no problem. But I tell you, your camels will never make it to Tizirbu.'

He sat back against the wall after his animated speech, leaving us to digest the importance of what he had just said. His caution

194

reminded me of the stark advice a rich Zwaya merchant in Kufra had given Hassanein Bey about the Egyptian's plans to reach the lost oases of Jebel Arkenu and Jebel Uweinat. 'This journey you propose to make is through territory where no Beduin has passed before,' he was warned. 'The *daffa* [long waterless trek] between Ouenat and Erdi is a long and hazardous one. God be merciful to the caravan in such heat. Your camels will drop like birds before the hot south winds.'

The scarcity of food for the camels was a serious problem, but we could relieve it in part by reducing our personal equipment to a minimum and carrying quantities of dates and barley. Water would be the greater difficulty. The Italian army had completed a similar journey in this part of the desert in 1930, when it was mopping up the last vestiges of resistance to colonial rule led by the Sanusi religious fraternity under Omar Mukhtar. The attack on Kufra, the final Sanusi stronghold, was one of its boldest moves. Certainly, it defied traditional logistics by requiring that troops cross 250 miles of waterless desert from the nearest oases of Jalo and Wau al Kabir, both already occupied by the Italians. A pincer movement was made on Kufra, with one column of camel corps marching from Wau al Kabir via Tizirbu. True, they had been accompanied by a supply column of motorized transport for much of the way, but if they could do it, there was no reason why we should not, too.

Would Ahmed be interested, despite his reservations, in attempting the journey with us, we asked? He was obviously tempted. It appealed to his love of the desert, but at the same time threatened to be considerably less comfortable than his usual expeditions by car. Just then, as he was weighing up the offer, the call to prayer interrupted us. It was time to eat and drink. Discussions were over. He would think about our proposal and let us know his decision the following morning.

We waited the next day in a state of growing tension. Would he or wouldn't he? Neither Ned nor I wanted to attempt this long, final leg to Kufra without a guide, but the search for one was turning into the quest for the Holy Grail. By two o'clock, there was still no sign of Ahmed and impatience got the better of us. We had to know his decision quickly, since if he said no, we had to begin the search again from scratch. 'He told Muftah he come this morning,' said Muftah unhelpfully. In fact, we found Ahmed in his house, freshly showered, neatly groomed and clad in a clean blue *jalabiya*, the picture of unruffled contentment. He knew why we had come and was quick to put an end to our uncertainty.

'I am sorry. I cannot come with you,' he said solemnly. His wife was firmly against the journey, he admitted, and he did not want to be away from his family for a month. 'But if you want to go by car, no problem.'

Even Muftah, an optimist by nature, now expressed some doubts about finding a guide.

'What about you, Muftah?' asked Ned. 'Can you come with us?' He had expressed an interest in guiding us several times. Now, he shook his head.

'I want to go with you but my father says I cannot. He says the journey to Kufra is too dangerous for a man with a family.' We were running out of options fast.

Our last port of call was to the most elderly of Tmissah's three guides. We went to see him accompanied by Muftah, who was entering the spirit of our quest for a guide as enthusiastically as Mohammed Ali had in Ghadames. Abd al Kader was a dignified, slightly stooped man with a gentle voice and kind eyes. I had met him looking at, and admiring, our camels that morning. We got down to business and explained what we hoped to do. He spoke to us with quiet assurance, beginning by confirming, though less dramatically than Ahmed Sassi, the lack of decent grazing for the camels between Tmissah and Kufra. This did not make the journey impossible, however. We followed what he said closely, knowing the fate of our expedition was in the balance. 'You must give each camel one kilogram of dates every day,' he advised. 'And you should also carry barley and some water for them for the journey from Wau an Namus to Tizirbu. That will be the most difficult part of your journey.' He, too, was attracted by the expedition. A desert guide for years, he had returned only recently from a trip to Kufra. But that was by car and it had been a long time since he had ridden a camel any great distance, he told us.

'I would like to come with you very much and I know the route to Kufra,' he said. This was it, I thought. We had found our man. Our search was over. After a long pause, he continued. 'Unfortunately, I have a heart condition and high blood pressure, so I cannot do this journey. Besides, I am too old now. You need to find a younger man. Your problem is that no-one here knows how to travel by camel. These days the guides only travel in the desert by car.'

We groaned inwardly. This was our last chance. We had exhausted all the options – Ahmed Sassi, Muftah and now Abd al Kader. There were no more guides in Tmissah. The old man then conferred with Muftah for several minutes. 'I know what you should do,' he said at last. 'You must see Mohammed Othman in Zuweila. If he is not in the desert with his camels, he will go with you. He is the only man around here who knows how to travel by camel. He is your last chance. If he cannot take you, no-one can.'

Muftah said he would take us to Zuweila for fifty dollars in his Toyota. Like almost every other Landcruiser we had seen in Libya, his had seen far better days. Various parts of the engine were strewn across the back seat and the petrol tank lay on the ground. 'Mafish mishkilla,' he said, reading our thoughts, 'Muftah is good mechanic.' In minutes he had deftly reassembled the car and hotwired it to life. We set off in a state of nervous anticipation. One way or another, our fate would be settled.

The road was a grey ribbon tidily pasted across the dull plain. To our south ran a line of pylons tightly laced together. Beyond them lay the dunes, bare for the most part and only occasionally decorated with date palms. To the north it was an unrelieved wasteland. Just beneath the horizon, the road glistened in the still-strong sun, grey one moment, flashing silver the next as the contours of the road unfurled before us. We chatted above the flat roar of the engine and the wind that streamed through the open windows. 'Mohammed Othman is very good man,' Muftah bellowed. 'He will go with you, *inshallah*.' If he did not, we would be on our own.

We pulled off the main road several miles outside Zuweila and sped in jolts across the rough plain, engraving new tracks in its crust and throwing up a thick cloud of dust behind us. Mohammed Othman was a Tubbu farmer who owned a large herd of camels that was kept in the desert and moved around according to the state of the pastures, Muftah explained. His home, isolated for several miles around, was temporary, consisting of half a dozen shacks made from palm fronds and tree trunks. They varied in size, the main living area being two of the larger ones encircled by a high fence made from the same materials. A small girl said Mohammed Othman was not at home and suggested half-heartedly that he might be in Zuweila. We headed into town and drove past the formidable castle that towered over the labyrinthine Tubbu quarter.

With its mighty walls and crumbled battlements, this was all that remained of the town's illustrious past. Once, more than a thousand years ago, Zuweila had been the seat of power in Fezzan. Al Idrisi, the twelfth-century Spanish Arab historian who prepared a geographical compendium for King Roger II of Sicily, stated that the town was founded by Abdallah ibn al Khattab of the Hawara tribe in the beginning of the tenth century and made the capital of Fezzan. The seventh-century Arabian conqueror Oqba bin Naf'a had swept through the region before him and conquered a town of the same name. By al Khattab's time, old Zuweila may no longer have existed.

In the latter decades of the twelfth century, according to the German traveller Nachtigal, the Turkish adventurer Sherfeddin Karakosh invaded Fezzan from Egypt and put an end to the Bani Khattab dynasty. He held sway for several decades, before being killed by one of his brothers in arms in nearby Waddan. His son later made a bid for power but was soon squashed by the kings of Kanem who were extending their southern kingdom north over the lands of Fezzan. Somewhere around this time, Zuweila ceased to be the capital of Fezzan, retreating from the stage of history and making way for the town of Traghen, thirty miles to the east of Murzuk.

Today, to judge by the state of its buildings, the area around the castle was the poorest in town. There was something both feudal and exotic about this crazy jumble of mud houses, wire netting and concrete breeze blocks. Roofs and walls bulged and slanted in haphazard shapes and angles. In the dark maze of alleys, chickens vied with children for supremacy in numbers. A toddler in bright yellow dungarees stared at us in astonishment. Matching her expression, her hair was shocked up in the electrified style of the American boxing promoter Don King. Her face and those of the other children were streaked with dust. All looked at us with wild surprise or excitement. After the hushed emptiness of Ghadames or the entire destruction of Murzuk's *medina*, it was a joy just to see an old city that was still inhabited in Libya. The vitality of the place was astounding.

There was no sign of Mohammed Othman, however, nor did anyone here know where he might be. Outside the mosque a dozen men were hunched in the dust over a round of *derba*, a game played with stones. They, too, were unable to help. Muftah recognized a desert guide from Zuweila and mentioned our plan to him. It was out of the question, he replied. No-one would come with us. Like all the other local guides, he only travelled by car. We hopped about town, asking the same question over and over. There was nothing doing. Eventually, we decided to sit it out and wait back at Mohammed Othman's home.

A threadbare camel was standing, as these animals frequently do at leisure, in an ungainly posture with rear legs splayed wide apart. He was chewing a green mush of hay that spilled out of his mouth in large, frothy chunks. The sun set through a thin veil of clouds, sucking up a trail of pink vapours before scattering them across the plain, darkening the slim silhouettes of date palms that stood in the distance. The call to prayer drifted across on the wind from Zuweila. Jumma, Mohammed Othman's teenage grandson, brought us a rice drink, some tea, orange and, most delicious of all, our first bowl of *zamita*, a golden paste of ground barley mixed with water, oil and sugar. Sunset ushered in the cold as the stars gathered to decorate the fading blue sky. Still no Mohammed Othman.

Muftah suggested a last trawl of Zuweila. Wearily, we returned to town and were directed to a new house, far bigger than anything in the Tubbu quarter. The street was straight, the residences imposing. It was the Belgravia of Zuweila. Outside lights shone hazily above the entrances, small patches of white in the night. A swaggering monster of a man stood inside the dimly lit courtyard, his arms steeped in blood. Around his ankles, arranged in mountainous piles, was the huge hacked carcass of a recently slaughtered camel. His face glowed demon-like among the shadows. He still had about him the excitement of the kill. Next to him, quietly surveying his friend's butchering expertise, stood a small old man wrapped against the chill in a black *burnous*.

'This is Mohammed Othman,' announced Muftah, indicating the latter with evident relief. The larger man removed his eyes from the scene of carnal destruction, stepped over a mound of flesh and a couple of hoofs, and offered us his blood-encrusted wrist – in lieu of his bloodier hand – in greeting. His name was Ali Beshir al Mahdi.

'Mohammed, these are two British travellers,' Muftah continued, turning towards the older man. 'They are looking for a guide to take them to Kufra. They are travelling by camel.' The smaller man met this last word with an intake of breath followed immediately by a high-pitched giggle. He said nothing but appeared delighted at the suggestion. The butcher, the more talkative of the two, was quick off the mark. He conferred with his older colleague, who nodded repeatedly in between giggles.

'All right, Mohammed Othman will go with you,' he announced. 'How much money will you give him?' This was blunt talking.

'We must talk about it,' I said.

'OK, talk,' replied the butcher.

'It's not good to talk about this standing here,' I said, trying to hide my delight. If Mohammed Othman was really prepared to go with us, we would need to discuss the journey with him in detail and then negotiate his fee. 'Can we discuss it inside over some tea?' He seemed to welcome this recognition of his duties as host and softened his tone.

'Come in,' he said, leading us into a long oblong room bordered with cushions on the carpet. Imperiously, he dispatched some minions to bring tea and cakes. Then he disappeared.

Minutes later, hard on the heels of a tray bearing green tea, red tea and several saucers of cakes and biscuits, he reappeared in fresh clothes. Gone the coarse butcher in T-shirt and jeans, enter the soigné seigneur of Zuweila, gorgeously arrayed in pristine *bedla a'rabiya*. He sported an immaculate brown embroidered waistcoat over a long white *jalabiya* and matching *ziboun*. Capping this sartorial metamorphosis was a natty burgundy *fes* with luxurious black tassel. This was power dressing Saharan style. Ali Beshir al Mahdi was ready to talk business.

'So how much will you give Mohammed to take you to Kufra?' he repeated. With Mohammed Othman's tacit consent, he had appointed himself the older man's spokesman and agent. Mohammed Othman himself, evidently still taken by the novelty of our arrival and the unlikely request for his services, sat back against a cushion and contented himself with more giggles as the conversation continued. Ned and I conferred in turn and suggested a figure.

'Not enough,' replied Ali Beshir al Mahdi immediately, without referring the offer to our would-be guide. He then suggested an exorbitant daily rate. Up to now, we had avoided this method of calculating fees because it left open the possibility of deliberate delays. The guide, if he felt like it, could try spinning out the journey under various pretexts, to make more money. We wanted to pay a flat rate, based on the distance between Tmissah and Kufra and the likely time it would take us to complete it. This way, whether we arrived early or late, the fee would remain as agreed. The negotiation grew interminable. The butcher suggested another fearsomely expensive figure. It was time for the stock phrase learnt from Mohammed al Mahdi, my Egyptian Arabic teacher in London.

'*Ittaq Illeh*' (Fear God),' I said gravely.

There was a pause of astonishment and then laughter. The remark broke the ice and we inched towards agreement. Before concluding the negotiations, we wanted first to discuss the route to Kufra and hear how Mohammed Othman proposed arranging food and water for the camels for this testing journey. Our first oasis, as expected, would be Wau al Kabir, he said. We should leave Tmissah with 100 kilograms of dates to compensate for the bleak pasturage. After crossing the largely lifeless Wadi Ma'raf, we would, *inshallah*, reach Wau an Namus where, contrary to what we had been told previously, we would find sweet drinking water as well as the brackish water of the lakes that surround the volcano. Having rested the camels there, and bagged up more dates and green leaves for them, we would continue for about 220 miles (Mohammed Othman, a man for whom maps were incomprehensible, claimed it was twice this distance) across the toughest part of this leg to Tizirbu. From this small oasis town, it was 105 miles to Rabiana, the closest source of drinking water west of Kufra. Another seventy-five miles would see us in Libya's most south-easterly town. Allowing for stops and delays, the journey from Tmissah would take forty days, Ali Beshir al Mahdi insisted. This seemed excessive. We haggled it down to thirty-five days, still on the generous side, from which he refused to budge. After several more minutes, we agreed a price and shook hands, delighted to be back in business again. Mohammed Othman would come to Muftah's house, accompanied by his butcher companion and one of his sons, in two days. We drank our way through another round of tea and departed in high spirits. The hunt for a guide had been a close-run thing.

Muftah, a handyman by inclination, set about repairing our kerosene stove the next morning, having witnessed our failed attempts to resurrect it with some amusement. '*Mafish mishkilla* for Muftah,' he boomed, taking the thing to pieces with the air of a skilled mechanic. We busied ourselves sewing up split bags, washing equipment, paring our kit down to a minimum, and experimenting with new innovations such as transferring our supply of pasta into a plastic *bidoun*. This might help improve the taste. Carrying it in plastic bags tended to invite a gritty seasoning of sand. After reassembling the stove several times without success, Muftah managed to restore it to health. 'You see, Muftah good engineer,' he declared, brandishing the machine in the air.

This triumph prompted him to take Ned on an impromptu guided tour of his handiwork throughout the house. I escaped upstairs to read, but was soon disturbed by two voices shouting for me to descend. They were both crammed into the bathroom, a dark and damp cubicle from which an indefinite thicket of pipes protruded. Some ended in mid-air, others wound around the room as if there was nothing better to do. '*Koul* (all) Muftah!' he assured us proudly, sweeping his hand across the scene with pride. To demonstrate his plumbing genius he turned the basin tap on. For several seconds nothing happened. Then, after a loud shudder, water shot across the room from another, unfinished pipe at head height on the opposite wall. Muftah hurried us out of the room.

'Excellent!' we said approvingly, wiping water from our eyes.

Next stop was the staircase, whose patterned iron banisters Muftah had erected some time ago. '*Koul* Muftah!' On to the roof, where the satellite dish, brilliant beneath the sun, sat atop a confused mass of wiring. '*Koul* Muftah,' he went on proudly, 'Muftah plumber, Muftah engineer, Muftah carpenter, Muftah electrician!' Into the garage, where a primitive welding apparatus had been installed. 'Muftah, Muftah, Muftah, *koul* Muftah!' he said, pointing out, one by one, various pieces of equipment, a series of half-finished sheets of metal and a misshapen metal dustbin. There was no end to his talents.

'I'm a little tired now, but my friend is very interested in home improvements and would love to see everything else you have done,' said Ned after a while. I felt like kicking him and smiled weakly at Muftah. He looked ecstatic. He had never had such a captive audience to admire his handiwork. I cursed Ned as he beamed back at me, looking unusually pleased with himself, and took his leave of us. All I felt like doing was going upstairs to sleep through the furnace-like heat of the day.

Instead, we finished the tour of Muftah's mind-boggling DIY achievements – bedrooms, bathrooms and kitchens – and then left his house to inspect a small farmstead several hundred yards away. He showed me pomegranates, lettuces, peppers, aubergines, potatoes, mint, maize, strawberries, cabbage, rocket, clover, bullrushes, tomatoes, onions and grape vines. The fertility of the place was a triumph of man over his surroundings.

Mohammed Othman and entourage cruised in on time the next morning, comfortably housed in a brand new Honda Civic. Ali Beshir al Mahdi, who had the demeanour of a leader of men, was handsomely dressed again. Mohammed Othman had brought two of his sons with him, one of whom was a hyperactive and meddlesome man in his early twenties. His eyes burnt with furious energy and he sought to impose himself on us at the first opportunity. His chance came as we started arranging the saddles. Without first asking us, he commandeered Asfar and started loading him with Mohammed Othman's bags.

'This is my camel,' I interposed.

'My father wants this camel,' he replied fierily.

'He can ride one of the others. This is my camel.'

He stared at me, weighing up the strength of his adversary.

'My father is an old man. He needs a good camel and he wants this one. You are just a young man.' Mohammed Othman had indicated a preference for Asfar but did not appear to be nearly as resolute on the matter as his son.

'The others are all good camels,' I said. 'He can choose whichever one he likes.' The argument continued for several minutes.

'He can have The Big White if he likes,' said Ned. 'I'm completely relaxed about which one I ride.'

There was something distasteful about disregarding the preference of an old man – Mohammed Othman was seventy-six – but

I judged it better to put my foot down now and demonstrate who was working for whom rather than be overruled on this, our first disagreement, before the journey had even begun. Besides, all five were fine animals. It was not as though the other four – with the possible exception of sluggish Gobber – were wooden spoons in the camel riding stakes. Eventually, we came to a compromise in which I rode Asfar but gave Mohammed Othman my saddle in return for an inferior one that did not fit properly. From the size and number of his bags, it appeared Mohammed Othman did not travel light.

Promising to send him a compass with a luminous dial, we said goodbye to Muftah, who had failed to charge us a single dinar for all his help in procuring us a guide while charging an historically high price for 100 kilograms of decrepit-looking dates. Like Mohammed Ali, he had been a loyal friend to us and we said goodbye, sorry we would never see him again.

Ali Beshir al Mahdi and Mohammed Othman's son mounted Asfar and Gobber respectively and insisted on accompanying us to the edge of town. We stopped on the fringes of the dunes and the swaggering Ali demanded a final photo-session before dismounting. We shook hands again and set off into the desert.

A beetle scrambled desperately across our path, just in time to escape twenty camels' hoofs kicking through the sand. Behind us, winding in and out of the palm-lined dunes, a golden-coloured mongrel appeared, padding along behind the caravan. Perhaps she had had enough of Tmissah and was ready for an adventure in the desert. Maybe she was just ready to relocate. Whatever her motives, there was a grittiness in her expression that suggested she had determined on a long journey. We shouted our last goodbyes to the receding farewell committee and left Tmissah in the blaze of noon.

# CHAPTER IX

# Tuna Joins the Caravan

*Journeys in the desert make men serious and reflective; the Tuareg and the Tubu, the most genuine sons of the desert, who spend their whole lives in this lonely struggle against the wide desert spaces, have an almost sinister air, with which no innocent cheerfulness seems any longer to harmonise.*

GUSTAV NACHTIGAL, *SAHARA AND SUDAN*

We trudged across dunes for the rest of the afternoon, pausing occasionally to throw stones at the mongrel to deter her from joining the expedition. Dogs are not designed for long waterless treks across the desert and we did not want to share our limited supplies with a new companion. In spite of this discouragement she refused to abandon us, scampering away each time we threw something at her, only to reappear several moments later at the tail of the caravan. The camels, who seemed to think even less of the latest addition to our party, lost their nerve and shied away in panic each time she approached. Mohammed did not appear to regard the dog highly either, and lobbed a stone at her from time to time. 'Maybe she has had enough of Tmissah now and wants to go to a new town,' he suggested. 'She's a stray. Perhaps she will come with us into the desert.'

Wearing a black *shish* around his head and an old army shirt over a loose-fitting white *jalabiya*, he walked with a natural fluidity of movement that was marvellous to watch. Age had not wearied him, nor had it brought the faintest signs of stooping. A lithe Tubbu tribesman with handsome features and a snowy beard and moustache, he marched with shoulders pinned back in a firm, composed bearing. Despite his seventy-six years and his diminutive stature – perhaps 5'6" – he kept a brisk pace throughout the day and into the evening that humbled our own efforts. It was difficult to keep up.

Since ancient times, the Tubbu have been admired above all for their fleetness of foot. Their ancestors are believed to be the 'Troglodyte Ethiopians' referred to by Herodotus, 'who of all the nations whereof any account has reached our ears are by far the swiftest of foot'. These cave-dwelling people, he went on, 'feed on serpents, lizards, and other similar reptiles. Their language is unlike that of any other people; it sounds like the screeching of bats.'

From the time of Herodotus to the present day, the Tubbu have made only the lightest and most tantalizing impressions on the pages of history. A stateless desert people thinly spread across an area of one million square miles that includes Libya, Chad, Niger, Sudan and Nigeria, the Tubbu loom mysteriously out of the Sahara. 'Having never founded a state, having never fought great battles, having never kept chronicles and archives, the Tebu place their historiography ... before a disquieting void,' wrote the former French Camel Corps officer Jean Chapelle in 1958. Their ability to survive in the harshest and most remote desert environments (which themselves discouraged invaders), their great mobility through trading and raiding, and their renowned ferocity against enemies, all contributed to the survival of the Tubbu from the Saharan Neolithic to today. For most of their history, the natural barriers of the desert, in particular the Tibesti massif, which runs from southern Libya into northern Chad, insulated them from destructive outside forces. Kufra and Tizirbu, their north-eastern limits, only fell to the Arabs in the eighteenth century and it was not until the beginning of the twentieth that the Turks attempted a military conquest of Tibesti. There was something fitting about travelling towards Kufra with our own Tubbu guide.

The parallels between the Tubbu and the Touareg are striking. In many respects the Tubbu were their eastern mirror image. They too once derived a living from running their own caravans – trading especially in slaves – attacking neighbouring territories, and extorting 'protection' fees from other caravans. For centuries they were renowned as raiders, from the Nile valley to the Niger Bend, across the sweep of the eastern central desert extending far south into what is today Sudan. Lyon and, three decades later, Richardson found the Tubbu and Touareg still engaged in *razzia*s (raids) on each other's territory, stealing camels and slaves, killing only when resistance was offered and never taking prisoners. Such booty supplemented their agricultural earnings.

From time to time, Pashas in Tripoli attempted to quell this warlike race, and, notwithstanding Chapelle's remarks, conflicts were hardly uncommon. In 1788, a severe defeat was inflicted on them, but in 1805 they bounced back and the army despatched by Pasha Yousef Karamanli (who would later welcome Lyon and Ritchie at the start of their own expedition) was completely routed by the Tubbu. The marauding tribesmen were partially brought to heel by both the Turks and the religious fraternity of the Sanusi in the later nineteenth century, when the latter replaced the Tubbu as the dominant group in the southern stronghold of Kufra, but the warmongering impulses remained, and Tubbu raiding continued deep into the twentieth century.

With European physical traits on black complexions, the Tubbu are perhaps the most enigmatic of the Saharan peoples, a 'prehistoric humanity' in the words of one French historian. 'Their characteristics are high nervous tension, impulsiveness, temperamental instability, unsociability and inveterate mistrust of their fellow-men,' wrote the historian John Wright, citing previous accounts. 'Personal status is judged by the number of a man's enemies, and the threshold of mortal offence is accordingly very low: sarcasm, innuendo, moral or material harm, the wounding of an animal, are enough to bring the daggers into play.' Neither of us had read this before engaging the services of Mohammed Othman. Would he be so ferocious?

If the Tubbu remain a shadowy historical phenomenon, with the advent of European explorers in the Sahara they began to receive closer attention. A unifying theme of these observations was the trait first remarked upon by Herodotus two-and-a-half millennia before. 'Their growth is slender; their limbs are well turned; their walk is light and swift,' wrote Horneman, the first European to travel in Tubbu country, in a letter of 1798 to the African Society in London. He judged them to have 'much natural capacity' but, surrounded on all sides by 'barbarous nations, or Mahometans', too little opportunity to develop it. 'Their intercourse with the Arabs, to whom they convey slaves, has probably corrupted them; they are accused of being mistrustful, treacherous and deceitful,' he reported. Their weapons were lances, six feet long, and knives up to twenty inches long carried in a sheath attached to the wrist. If he did not perish in his undertaking, Horneman wrote with a touch of prescience, he would provide more information on this nomadic race in five years. Two years later, he was dead, reportedly having succumbed to dysentery in the Niger region.

Lyon, too, was struck by their physical grace: 'The Tibboo men are slender and active in their form, and have intelligent countenances; their agility is proverbial; and they are frequently, by way of distinction, called "the Birds".' The Tubbu in the southern parts of Fezzan were relatively civilized, 'but those of the interior live chiefly by plunder, are constantly making inroads on their neighbours, and are not famed for fidelity to one another. They are not disposed to cruelty, but are most impudent thieves,' living in a state of nature in caves or grass huts clad only in animal hides. 'Their camels or maherries enable them to perform extraordinary journeys, from which circumstance they are constantly shifting their abode.' The youthful English traveller found the Tubbu women particularly compelling. 'These females are light and elegant in form, and their graceful costume, quite different from that of the Fezzaners, is well put on. They have aquiline noses, fine teeth, and lips formed like those of Europeans,' he commented approvingly. 'Their eyes are expressive, and their colour is of the brightest black: there is something in their walk, and erect manner of carrying themselves, which is very striking.'

It fell, perhaps inevitably, to the vitriolic pen of Richardson to paint the Tubbu in less than glowing colours. Having already witnessed the arrival of a Tubbu slave caravan in Murzuk, he was not well-disposed towards them. He considered them 'an immoral race of Africans', whose men were particularly worth-less creatures. 'The Tibboo ladies do not even allow a husband to enter his own home without sending word previously to announce himself,' he snorted. 'The Tibboo women, indeed, are everything, and their men nothing – idling and lounging away their time, and kicked about by their wives as so many useless drones of society. The women maintain the men as a race of stallions, and not from any love for them; but to preserve the Tibboo nation from extinction.'

Nachtigal was also much taken by the athleticism of the Tubbu he met south of Murzuk. He admired their leanness and slender limbs, their lively eyes and physical resilience, while noting their diminutive stature. 'The efficiency of their bodies in running and jumping is still now as proverbial as it was in antiquity, and . . . their capacity for resisting fatigue, hunger and thirst is unsur-passed.' On rations that would have been virtually a starvation diet for Europeans, Tubbu tribesmen would march with swinging ease for ten to twelve hours a day alongside their swift camels. Nachtigal recorded a local proverb that told how a Tubbu could survive on one date for three days. On the first day, he ate the skin, the next day the flesh, and on the last the pounded stone. The German traveller, usually an exemplar of Teutonic calm, could not resist a swipe at the Tubbu after one unpleasant encounter. 'My own journey had to be regarded as an extremely dangerous enterprise,' he wrote with a touch of vanity, 'for the Tubu were known to be faithless, treacherous, greedy, thievish and cruel.' Later, he called them, 'tedious, pre-sumptuous, arrogant beggars', but subsequently admitted that this verdict, heavily coloured by personal experience, was unreasonably harsh.

The affable Hassanein Bey provided a quite different, more innocent, account of the people:

> The Tebus are simple primitive fellows, with delightfully naïve habits of mind. Being poor, they take the best care of what possessions they have. They dress in a simple cotton shirt and pair of drawers, and devote much attention to making these garments last as long as possible. When a Tebu rides a camel, for example, he takes off his drawers to save wear and tear, and hangs them on his camel's back. When he sleeps also he removes his garments to protect them from friction from the sand, and wraps himself in his fur cloak.

At this early stage, Mohammed did not appear to exhibit any of the unhappy tendencies remarked upon by these eighteenth- and nineteenth-century explorers. He seemed, on the contrary, to be a man of great cheer, giggling as he mounted the dutiful but uninspiring Lebead for the first time. Watching him do so, it was difficult not to burst out laughing. He had piled his saddle, already raised to a great height above his plethora of belongings, higher still with a mass of rugs and blankets. He was not tall enough to swing a leg over the pommel of the saddle and his arms were proportionately short too, so he was unable to keep hold of the camel's upper lip while mounting. Instead, he had to control the animal with the head-rope in his left hand, before embarking on an ascent of the camel's flanks, levering himself up on both hands and knees with a mighty effort, like a struggling mountaineer on a steep incline. Eventually he would appear on the summit of the camel's back and peer around almost in disbelief as the camel lurched to his feet. Perched aloft, Mohammed cut an amusing figure with legs dangling hopelessly far above the animal's neck. Once ensconced in the saddle, he could only maintain discipline by hitting the camel with the rope rather than pressing his feet into its neck. The curious sight he presented gave the impression, false of course, of his being completely out of control.

For the rest of our first day travelling with our new guide, we moved across giant sloping slabs of hardened sand, passing away from the green life of date palms into more barren country. After about twenty miles, the dunes bounced back to life, heaving and rolling to greater heights, before crashing on to a plain coated with stones only slightly larger than grains of rice. Kicking through them, the caravan sounded like a light hail storm against a glass window. In the distance lay the scattered ranks of decapitated mountain ridges, through which we later ponderously filed before calling halt at a solitary acacia tree, a glowing skeleton in the dimming blur of sunset. This was the only fodder for the camels. Previous diners had already trimmed the lower branches, so they were forced to crane their necks to their full reach to pull down bristling mouthfuls of green thorns. While they chewed away on their uncomfortable dinner, we scurried around their ankles collecting wood for the fire. For the first time there was no sign of the dog. Perhaps she had had second thoughts and even now was returning home. We had not shown her great hospitality.

I set to work on our first post-Tmissah tuna fish pasta, but was quickly interrupted by Mohammed.

'What's that?' he asked urgently, spotting the tin I was opening.

'Tuna,' I replied innocently. He shook his head and waved his hand from side to side, as if admonishing me for some unforgivable culinary crime.

'I don't eat tuna,' he said emphatically.

His announcement came as something of a shock, particularly since we had just stocked up on thirty tins of the stuff. It would have been helpful to know Mohammed's dietary requirements before leaving Tmissah, but none of us had discussed, or even thought about, the subject of food for the journey. Abd al Wahab, Salek and Saleh had all, to varying degrees, been happy eating tuna fish pasta, so we had little reason to think Mohammed would be any different. But he came from another, more elderly, generation and owed his approach to food to the traditionalist school. The Royal Geographical Society notes frowned on us accusingly. 'It is accepted practice in the Sahara that the employer provide all food for his party,' they declared. This we had done. 'Since food is a notorious bone of contention on any trek, try to ascertain what your companion will and will not cat.' This wc had not. It was a little late to change our rations. The next shop was 350 miles away in Tizirbu.

We compromised with a desperately bland tomato, onion and garlic pasta, with Ned and I sharing a tin of tuna as an hors d'oeuvre. While we ate, we asked if there was anything else Mohammed did not like. Coffee and hot chocolate were strictly off limits, as were cheese, packet soups or anything else contained in a tin. It narrowed our already limited repertoire, but at least he was prepared to eat our chocolate bars, a large store of which we had laid on for this long leg. There were no difficulties, either, with tea, so the omens for life around the camp fire during the next few weeks were not too inauspicious.

I woke the next morning to what would become a familiar and chilling call from Mohammed. '*Heya, heya, soubha*!' (Come on, come on, it's morning), he barked. It was freezing and there was not the faintest hint of sunlight peeping into this still darkness. With one hand tentatively emerging into the vicious cold, I felt the outside of the sleeping bag. The overnight frost was starting to melt and the bag was sodden. Inside, it felt more comfortable than ever, but there was no time to indulge in any dawn reverie. '*Heya, heya,*' he hustled.

Clearly, there were to be no more lie-ins like those of the week in which we had travelled alone from Murzuk. Ned, a more astute camper than me, had taken his rollmat and sleeping bag much farther away from the camp the previous night. A heavy sleeper, he was immune to Mohammed's hectoring wake-up call and was, for the next quarter of an hour at least, blissfully unconscious. I rose reluctantly and, looking over enviously towards the recumbent Ned, cursed him silently for this extra lie-in. Some mornings I was unable to resist the temptation to wake him up as soon as Mohammed had disturbed my own sleep.

The greatest consolation for rising at this uncomfortable hour was the breakfast of *zamita* that Mohammed was lovingly preparing. Despite its unprepossessing appearance – half cowpat, half coffee cake – it tasted magnificent. He began by pouring a small quantity of ground barley into a metal bowl, stirring in warm water until it assumed the consistency of a stodgy brown dough. To this were added several glassfuls of sugar and a measure of *semin* (liquefied butter) that his daughter had made for him in Zuweila. The last ingredient gave the paste a curdled and slightly sour taste that was an agreeable counterpoint to the sweetness of the sugar. It was to be our breakfast for the next month.

*Zamita* is one of the desert's oldest and most basic dishes. Its popularity derives both from the little fuel and water required for its preparation and the solid nourishment it provides the traveller. Horneman called it '*simitée*'. On his camel trek, the barley was initially boiled until it swelled, then dried, first in the sun and later on the fire. Once ground into a powder, it was then mixed with salt, pepper and caraway seeds and stored in a leather bag until needed. 'I was often, for days together, without other food than this cold farinaceous pap, mixed with a few dates,' he recorded hungrily. En route to Ghadames, Richardson observed that '*zameetah*' was the food of choice for the Arabs and poorer merchants. Those who could afford it poured oil or fat over the barley, 'but many cannot afford this luxury, and must content themselves with a little water to make up the meal into paste'. Richardson, of course, was resolutely unimpressed, watching his companions tuck into a dinner of *zamita* and *bazeen* (dumplings). 'It is quite absurd to call this a supper for three persons; it is mocking European appetite,' he fulminated. 'How they live in this way I cannot comprehend.' *Zamita* failed to delight his demanding palate, but the three of us enjoyed it greatly.

Shuddering in the cold, I pottered about on a small hillock gathering wood while the sun roused itself and saw a small brown shape curled into a ball against the nip of the desert. The mongrel had decided to join our caravan and chance her luck in the desert, after all. As soon as he noticed the dog, Mohammed took exception to her and was incensed at Ned offering her a breakfast of a tin of tuna mixed with water. He was not an animal lover in the English sense and did not like to see our supplies being shared with a desert cur. '*Al kalb mish kwayis*' (The dog is not good), he muttered irritably, watching her lap up the dubious mixture with gusto.

Setting the pattern for the next few weeks, breakfast did not last long. Hassanein Bey (though for quite different reasons to our own reluctance to get started early) warned of the dangers of rushing this part of the day. 'The morning programme in camp is not one that can be safely hurried,' he advised. 'The Beduin dislikes intensely to be rushed over his meals, or to be deprived of those moments of leisure thereafter which are so essential to peaceful digestion and a contented spirit. The wise leader will see that these prejudices of his men are carefully observed.' This did not apply to our caravan. The only man hurrying our departure was Mohammed. A brisk man ruled by the simplicity of action, he just wanted to get on with the journey without delay and would not have understood the suggestion that he was being deprived of his leisure. We were the only ones who had such rueful thoughts in the piercing morning chill. Whether it was due to the confidence of empire or simply because they had more robust constitutions, the travellers of old loomed from the pages of their travelogues as far doughtier types. Rosita Forbes, the English desert explorer who had accompanied Hassanein Bey on his first journey to Kufra in 1921, was a woman of great mettle. 'The Bedawin hate the cold in the early mornings [as did we],' she complained, 'so it is rarely possible to get them to start before dawn or to walk much after sunset.' It barely occurred to us, weary as we invariably were, either to start so early or continue so late.

We pressed on across a gravel-swept plain, moving between isolated ridges for most of the day. Dusk saw us standing on the summit of a pass guarding a biblical wilderness of epic proportions. A solitary blob of shadow on the fading plain indicated another acacia tree or two that would make a suitable camp. There were no trails or tracks to follow and we descended precipitously between giant boulders – the camels halting frequently, in despair at such a challenging gradient – towards the vast expanse that spread for miles towards another distant smudge of a mountain range. We headed uncertainly towards the trees as the light fled into the horizon, losing our bearings as we continued into the thickening darkness. We realized we had no idea where the trees were and after thirty miles, our longest day yet, reluctantly halted without food for the camels. It was too early to start feeding them from our limited supply of dates. We needed to save as much as possible for the far bleaker leg from Wau al Kabir, our first oasis 100 miles from Tmissah, to Wau an Namus, an even more remote oasis where, according to everyone consulted except Mohammed, the water would be undrinkable for men and camels alike.

The next morning there was no sign of Mohammed when I woke. I looked at my watch. It was already much later than our usual starting time. Dozing in my bag, I had heard his light footsteps around the camp but guiltily had fallen asleep again. Ned was still lost to the world, his head poking out of his sleeping bag beneath a navy blue Los Angeles Raiders hat. I scanned the horizon for 360° across the gentle beige rolls of the plateau. There was not the slightest trace of our guide. I woke Ned and told him Mohammed had disappeared. 'God, you don't think he's died, do you?' I asked. 'Where can he have gone?' Ned was equally mystified by Mohammed's sudden evaporation.

We took turns looking though the binoculars. Nothing. I scanned the horizon again. In the distance, so far off it was barely perceptible, a tiny black figure was staggering desperately in the shimmering waves of heat, struggling to keep on moving. Suddenly the figure keeled over and fell to the ground. Disaster had struck. Had the old man succumbed? After all his exertions the previous day, it looked like he had fainted or, far worse, had had a heart attack. I remembered his sons' concern for their father when we had left Tmissah, their remarks that he was an old man, and began to contemplate the terrible prospect of two Christians performing a Muslim burial in the Sahara. Then, as despair was setting in, the figure disappeared from sight as quickly as it had flopped to the ground and I knew the light was playing tricks. Minutes later, Mohammed reappeared, churning busily across the plain.

'The *tholh* trees are over there,' he said calmly, pointing across the plain. 'We must take the camels there and stop for an hour or two to let them eat. Yesterday they had nothing.' The trees were hardly visible. He had walked more than two miles on a solitary sortie for camel food while we were still snoozing. I felt shamed by the resourcefulness of an elderly man that contrasted so killingly with our own inertia, a feeling sharpened by the total lack of reproach in his demeanour. A little less than an hour later, we trod into a meandering *wadi* and followed it to the welcome shapes of the acacia trees we had spotted the previous evening. The hungry camels, who still bore the scabs from past encounters on their muzzles, needed no incentive to start pulling at the branches ravenously.

It was not yet eleven o'clock, but the sun already bore down on us with an intensity that was unbearable now that we were sitting still. This was the first time we had stopped like this in the heat of the day. It was no time for great activity. Ned started to read Lawrence and was soon catnapping in the makeshift patch of shade cast by his upended saddle. We retreated into the deep silence of the desert, a throbbing stillness gently punctured by the light shuffle of cotton as Mohammed moved and teased away tirelessly at repairs to his saddle. Every noise that broke the all-pervasive quiet carried an exaggerated volume. The needle passing through the hessian cloth wrapped around the saddle pad: Mohammed's occasional heavy breathing as he tightened a knot; the rasping slurp as he drank tea; the soft pad of a camel moving from one shrub to another.

Tuna, as we had christened the mongrel after her first breakfast with us, had lost most of her bashfulness and, panting thirstily, trotted alongside the caravan throughout the day. This enabled her to travel in the shadows of the camels. In the full heat of the day, when the sun was highest, she was forced to come perilously close to their ankles to find a spot of shade, and more than once there was a yelp of pain as she overstepped the mark. Then, she would run off at a tangent to the caravan with a reproachful look towards the camels, before loping back out of the sun. The camels, who had grown used to this mild-mannered dog and were no longer afraid of her, were nevertheless always liable to kick out viciously if they felt someone or something was getting in their way. Dwarfed by their long legs, she had to maintain a brisk trot to keep up with the caravan. Every few minutes she would stop for the briefest of rests and survey her surroundings wearily before licking her lips and hurrying along to rejoin us. Seeing that we were beginning to grow fond of Tuna, a canine desert explorer of the highest order, Mohammed no longer opposed us giving her food or water and there was no more 'al kalb mish kwayis'.

'She is staying with us now because she knows we have food and water,' he said, almost affectionately. As we always tended to overdo the quantities of pasta at dinner, she usually ate well in the evenings. I forfeited his goodwill once, however, when I fed Tuna the pasta leftovers in our metal bowl. 'The dog must not eat from here,' he said brusquely, appalled at this lack of hygiene. 'She is dirty.' To show his kind intentions (and ensure the dog never shared our bowl again), he cut out a feeding bowl for her from a leaking *bidoun* and sometimes even served her breakfast in it himself.

We reached the mountains that had seemed so distant the previous day, climbing along well-worn camel tracks etched into the rough slopes, and smashing through brittle layers of flint that lay about in great fragmented shards. It was impossible to estimate the age of these tracks but it looked as though they had been there for ever. The camels marched prettily through this scene of desolation with minutely careful steps. We turned to look back across the plains we had crossed. Far beneath us, a

German Unimog was racing from left to right, dragging a lengthening tail of dust and sand behind it. The driver saw our caravan silhouetted on the ridge perhaps, for the vehicle slowed down for a minute, before continuing noiselessly on its way. A long spit of clouds pressed in on the declining sun, flared a rich orange before fading to a subdued pink, and slowly melted away. We camped next to the remains of a solitary tree, a blackened stump that emphasized the lifelessness of the place. Once more, there was no grazing for the camels. They were growing hungrier by the day. Worse still, there was little we could do about it.

As we rustled through bags unpacking everything we needed for dinner, they pricked up their ears and crowded around jealously until Mohammed shooed them away with rough grunts. 'Tomorrow we must give them some dates,' he said. 'It is better for their stomachs to feed them in the morning.' The camels seemed to disagree on this question of timing and looked ready for dinner, which was not forthcoming. We hobbled them a few yards away from the fire and commiserated with their expressions of fatigue and hunger. Later, I was woken several times in the middle of the night by a steady shuffling sound. It was The Big White trying to get into one of the food bags.

Pouring tea around the campfire, Mohammed fell into animated reminiscences of hunting expeditions he had made as a young man. He had spotted animal tracks shortly before we camped and they had recalled former times of sport. He had shot gazelle and *waddan* (wild sheep) with an Italian rifle on the Libyan border with Niger. We asked what he remembered of the Italian occupation of Libya, but he said he was too young to remember and had, besides, lived all of his life in the desert, first with his father's camels and later with his own. Mohammed was born in 1923, the same year Hassanein Bey made his groundbreaking camel trek in eastern Libya and the year in which Omar Mukhtar, then more than sixty, took command of the Jebel Akhdar, the north-eastern heartland of Sanusi resistance to Italian rule. Although the Italians had occupied the Libyan coastline as early as 1911, their 'pacification' of the interior proceeded only gradually, challenged at every step by Omar Mukhtar's resistance, and only completed with his public hanging in 1931 and final peace the following year.

Mohammed was at his most talkative around the campfire. For Lawrence, the hearth was the 'university' of Arabs. Around it they listened to 'the news of their tribe, its poems, histories, love tales, lawsuits and bargainings' and 'grew up masters of expression, dialecticians, orators, able to sit with dignity in any gathering and never at a loss for moving words'. The shepherds, however, missed out on all this.

> From infancy they followed their calling, which took them in all seasons and weathers, day and night, into the hills and condemned them to loneliness and brute company. In the wilderness, among the dry bones of nature, they grew up natural, knowing nothing of man and his affairs; hardly sane in ordinary talk; but very wise in plants, wild animals and the habits of their own goats and sheep, whose milk was their only sustenance. With manhood they became sullen, while a few turned dangerously savage, more animal than man.

Mohammed, who belonged to the last dwindling generation of Libya's nomads, had spent a lifetime immersed in the Sahara looking after his animals. But the great divide Lawrence stressed between tribal Arab and solitary shepherd, and the very remoteness of the desert itself, no longer applied. It had vanished with the advent of the motor car. The outside world, once so removed, had moved that much closer. Mohammed himself now owned a four-wheel drive, which helped him relieve the solitude of his calling. There was nothing harsh or savage about him. Instead, he was a man of natural grace, humour and steady charm. The hardships of the desert had toughened his physical aspect and he was strong and self-assured, but his manners were unfailingly soft and unthreatening. He retained the wisdom in plants, wild animals and their habits that had been handed down across generations, but was not lost in discussions of 'man and his affairs'.

The morning date feed became our newest ritual, eagerly awaited by the camels. The first time we fed them, Mohammed measured out enough dates for all five on a plastic bag, while Ned and I kept them at bay. Hobbled around their ankles, they lurched over as soon as their breakfast was served, burying their noses in the dark hillock of dates, which disappeared quickly, swallowed whole. Gobber, who was held in varying degrees of contempt by his colleagues, ate much more slowly than the other four and always came off worse in the race to down dates. His ponderous progress was further slowed by Bobbles, who would launch sniping and unprovoked attacks against him. From then on, he was fed individually, but he still had to keep his wits about him. Once their daily rations were nearing an end, the quickest of the four – usually The Big White and Asfar – would abandon their breakfasts and launch a raid on Gobber's meagre provisions. A stoic beast of burden, perhaps the strongest baggage camel of the caravan, he never put up a fight. Instead, he turned away sadly and looked towards Ghadames, where life had once been so much easier.

The plain ran its course for three miles or so the following morning. Another solitary acacia tree, a miracle of life in this burning wasteland, stood guard at the bottom of a pass that rose sharply – a narrow corridor of sliding sand. Dead or dying clumps of shrubs clung grimly to the rocky walls for what shade they offered. From the top, we looked across harsher country: the slopes that dipped into this new plateau were thick with boulders and cracked with deep crevasses that undid the camels' confidence. Behind another scattering of acacia trees in the middle distance, far-off ridges swam and glittered uncertainly in the shifting pools of boiling light. Descending gingerly as the ground fell away from us, Bobbles slipped awkwardly and eighty kilograms of water crashed forward on to his neck. He bellowed in distress and it took several minutes for us to rearrange his load, calming the whimpering creature all the time with handfuls of dates that had fallen from a split bag. The other camels looked on, indifferent to their friend's anguish and interested only in this impromptu brunch.

On reaching the acacia trees, we stopped to let the camels feed again and boiled up a packet soup improved with some pasta and spicy sauce. Mohammed, a tenaciously industrious man who only appeared happy when active, started repairing my collapsing saddle, despite the vice-like heat of late morning. To kill time while the camels fed, and because we were running out of supplies, I made some unleavened bread under Mohammed's watchful eye. First, I mixed up a paste of flour, salt and water, shaped it into a discus, and placed it in a hollow in the sand. Then, a layer of sand was raked over the bread to protect it as it baked beneath a pile of embers. After a quarter of an hour, it was turned over, already recognizable as a fizzing mass of soft bread among the embers, and after another fifteen minutes, it was ready. Beneath the coat of sand that stuck to the bread no matter how hard you tried to remove it, the consistency was all right, but there was a heavy tinge of kerosene. The fuel had leaked into one of our food bags and, as we discovered for the next month, seeped into everything. We passed the rest of the day fighting down kerosene burps.

By five o'clock we were approaching a denser mass of green. Although we were closing in on the oasis, it was still too early to be Wau al Kabir. 'It must be a government farm,' said Mohammed, as we caught sight of an abandoned truck. The word 'farm' should be used advisedly in the Libyan Sahara for those who take it to imply some form of agricultural activity. Nothing moved, and there were no fields or any other signs of cultivation. Instead, all we could see was a ragged line of trees, the squat mass of discarded machinery and several wrecked Portakabins. Although it was still early, Mohammed suggested we camp on the outskirts of the farm next to some acacia trees. It was unlikely we would come across more food for the camels if we continued farther today. He left us scouring for firewood and headed towards the shelter to check for signs of life.

Half an hour later, a tiny figure strode towards us, shouting something indistinct. At such a distance, and with an evening wind picking up, the prospect of making himself heard was less than minimal but this did not stop the man from trying. I walked towards him, and eventually made out the cry of 'Police! Come here.' Staggered by the ubiquity of the Libyan authorities, I carried on walking in his direction to see what he wanted. For a policeman, he appeared remarkably scruffy and unkempt. We met and he shook my hand heartily, repeating his entreaty. 'Please, come here,' he said, pointing to the Portakabin behind him that was fast becoming a shadow in the dying light. His name was Ahmed and he was one of three workers in this forlorn desert outpost. Mohammed was already inside, he said, and we were welcome to join the party for dinner.

Like Omar on the farm in Murzuk, Ahmed was a Sudanese immigrant who had come to Libya to make his fortune or at least earn enough to be able to return to his country and start a family. He led us to his accommodation, a filthy room reeking of fuel in which Mohammed and three colleagues from Chad were kneeling down in the middle of their evening prayers, their shadows bobbing about the walls in the dancing light of candle wicks dipped in jars of kerosene. When they had finished, we were invited to join them for dinner, an engrossing feast of fried beef cubes, aubergine slices, meat stew and dumplings. With the self-denying hospitality of the desert, Ahmed plied us with lemon squash and a quick succession of glasses of sweet tea. For pudding, we were served the shocking luxury of rice pudding, sweet with milk and sugar. We stretched out on the floor and sank into deep contentment, lighting cigarettes and chatting with Ahmed.

Wau al Kabir, he told us, was now closed to foreigners. The Libyan army had recently taken control of the oasis and we would not be allowed to pass by for supplies of dates, water or any other fodder for the camels. This was a serious blow. The camels needed plentiful grazing. Already they were showing signs of hunger and lethargy. A shopkeeper in Tmissah had shown me a photo of his recent trip to Wau al Kabir. In it, there was a comfortable looking lodge, complete with restaurant and swimming pool. It was one of the world's more remote hotels and would have made a pleasant, slightly surreal, stopover.

'It's no problem for you,' said Ahmed, seeing our reaction to this unexpected news. 'Five miles away, there is another farm where you can feed the camels. Tomorrow morning we will fill your water containers here and then you must go there.'

Mohammed said we would spend the next day at the farm to let the camels feed properly before moving on towards Wau an Namus a day later. Tonight, he would sleep inside, he added, looking more tired than usual. With these administrative details complete, he dropped off among the shadows, solicitously attended by Ahmed, who prepared a bed for him.

One of the other workers spoke to us with a touching frankness about his lot in Libya. His five years here had not been a happy experience. 'The Libyans treat us Chadians and Sudanese like animals,' he said sadly. He had not been paid for three months and was now resolved, as soon as this was settled (would it ever be?), to return home. There was no longer any work to do on the farm anyway. Libyan army officers had pillaged all the equipment in sight, and stripped bare the solitary four-wheel drive that had been provided for use about the farm and for trips to Tmissah and Murzuk. The four of them were now entirely dependent on their Libyan boss to bring them supplies. Sometimes he came, sometimes he did not. Crops were no longer planted, he went on, and the army was about to take over the whole area, for what reasons he did not know. There was a deep desperation about this place. If there was such a thing as a Sudanese or Chadian overseas agricultural placement scheme, this was its unrivalled booby prize. Faced with such grim prospects, this unfortunate trio sought a dreamy consolation in clouds of marijuana smoke. While waiting to be paid, there was little else to do.

Ned said goodnight and slipped out into the impenetrable dark to hobble the camels, with Ahmed expressing concern that he would not be able to find them without a torch. 'Don't worry, I'll be fine,' stated Ned confidently, and disappeared.

An hour later, Ahmed said he would escort me back to the camp because I would not be able to find it alone either. Outside, there was no sign of any fire, nor was there any evidence of Ned or the camels. Dropping his voice to a solemn whisper, Ahmed started telling me about the dangers of the magic *tholh* trees that spread thinly across this section of the plain. 'There are evil *jinn* (spirits) in the trees,' he warned. 'You must be very careful.'

I tried not to laugh, and we stumbled about fruitlessly in the thick night. After several more minutes, I recognized a tree and, embarrassed at having taken up so much of his time, thanked Ahmed for his help and bade him goodnight. As soon as he left, I realized I had no idea where I was, after all. Given his remarks about the magical malice of the *tholh* tree, the darkness of the night suddenly became eerie. Feeling like a frightened child, I called him back and confessed I was completely lost. We continued our search for the camp, and suddenly heard a distant shout from Ned.

'The camels wandered off,' he said sheepishly once we had regrouped. 'I couldn't find the camp.' He had recovered all five camels but like me had completely lost his bearings. We split into two groups and agreed to communicate our whereabouts every few minutes with the spark of cigarette lighters. The stumbling continued for another quarter of an hour, Ahmed all the time declaiming the mischievous powers of the *jinn*.

'You see, this is why we are lost,' he whispered, his features taut in an expression of great dread. 'The *jinn* are playing games with us. When we find the camp, you must not sleep near the *tholh* because it is too dangerous for you. You must sleep far away from the tree because then the spirits cannot reach you.' I looked at him doubtfully. 'Be very careful,' he implored me. 'I am serious.'

At last, we came across the mass of camel saddles and bags. The camp looked in greater disarray than before. Food bags had been torn into, our last supplies of bread had disappeared and mangled packets of soup and sauces lay in shreds across the ground. Stray dogs howled unpleasantly around us. Suddenly, the trees looked more sinister than ever. 'The *jinn* have been here,' said Ahmed, in a tone that combined a sense of awe with a strong dose of fatalism. 'You see, I told you they are acting against you tonight. Make sure you do not sleep near the trees and you will be safe. Do not worry.' I thanked him again for his kindness, compared notes with Ned on the nature of *jinn*, and slept sufficiently far from any tree to be beyond the reach of these malevolent spirits. The dogs kept up their ghoulish howls throughout the night.

In the morning, Ahmed showed us around the farm, though it was more a scrapyard on a grand scale, a wildly shambolic place sitting weirdly in the middle of the desert. Lorries with flat tyres sat on discarded metal containers. Their cabs had been plundered of anything that might be of value or use. A giant stack of rusting pipes lay outside a Portakabin that in happier times had been the farm mosque. Its roof had been adapted for devotional purposes: next to a dome perched aloft like an inverted egg cup, a makeshift wooden minaret rose crookedly, prevented from falling down by a couple of wire supports. The naked hulls of jeeps and more four-wheel drives crowded around in between vast piles of mechanical parts. Ruined axles, shafts, pipes, tyres, trailers, petrol pumps and tanks competed ferociously for space in this jumble of junk. It was a pathetic picture of failure. It would be pleasant to believe in Gaddafi's propaganda about greening the desert. In one of Tripoli's more picturesque portraits of the leader, he is superimposed over a picture of his pet project, billed as the Great Man Made River Builder. From a pipe of prodigious girth tumbles a torrent of foaming water, rolling back the golden slopes of sand and leaving in their place a pastoral idyll replete with dates, cereal crops and contented farmers busily cultivating fields. Out here in the desert, reality overcame such rose-tinted dreams.

The camels slurped down several oil barrels of water between them and waited patiently to be loaded with our full complement of 200 litres. Ominously, we had lost half of our water supplies from leakage on the journey from Tmissah. Had it not been for Ned's insistence on filling all the *bidoun*s before we left the town, we might have had serious problems. To stem the leaks we placed sheets of plastic over the top of the *bidoun*s and tightly screwed the caps down over them under Mohammed's unforgiving stare. Thus prepared, we thanked our hosts again, said goodbye, and set off to feed the hungry camels.

# CHAPTER X

# Wau an Namus

*Heaven! I stink like an old Poultice. I should mislead any Pack of
Foxhounds in Great Britain! Put a Trail of Rusty Bacon at a Furlong
Distance & me at a mile, and they would follow me . . . if I caught
only the Echo of a Tally Ho! I should climb into a Tree!*

SAMUEL TAYLOR COLERIDGE, *COLLECTED LETTERS*

The sun rose sharply, sweeping the colours off the landscape in
a brutal dazzle of light. For several hours we plodded over uneven
ground in the direction Ahmed had indicated without coming
across anything that suggested agricultural life of any kind. Our
progress was delayed every few minutes by the discovery of yet
another dripping *bidoun*. Some leaked sluggishly, others dripped
in a brisk *staccato*. It was the worst possible moment for leakages.
Now of all times, we could not afford to waste our precious
supplies. A dripping container could spell disaster. The nearest
water was eighty or so miles away at Wau an Namus and there
was no guarantee it would be fit for human consumption. Should
it prove undrinkable, the nearest source from Wau was another
220 miles as the crow flies to Tizirbu. We rearranged the plastic
covers beneath the caps as best we could, but the dripping continued, albeit at a reduced pace.

'*Mishkilla*,' said Mohammed in a tone of unusual earnestness.
'We must move the *bidoun*s so they do not touch the saddle.'
Among the ranks of dripping *bidoun*s, the worst offenders were

228

those carried by the riding camels. The wooden uprights of the saddles were pressing into their sides. Laboriously, the three of us fastened longer loops to the *bidoun*s so that they could hang free from the saddles against the camels' flank. This was the best we could do, and the dripping was reduced to a discreet dribble – but it was far from ideal.

We stopped again and scanned the horizon for signs of the farm to no avail. Mohammed suggested we give up the search and continue directly to Wau an Namus. Half-heartedly, however, we lingered and through the binoculars eventually made out a distant shelter next to the stretching giant spider legs of a portable irrigation unit. Another hour saw us arriving at a massive golden discus of a recently cut hay field, a kilometre in diameter, in the middle of which sat a single disconsolate Portakabin. A man rose to greet us, striding towards the caravan with a look of surprise. We made slow progress towards him, leading the camels through the field only with difficulty. With such plentiful grazing around them, they were in no rush to move on and at every step lowered their necks to feed.

The farm consisted of 250 sheep, grazing randomly on this surreal pasture. On all sides the arid desert pressed in on its fertile frontiers. A slate grey ridge, broken with sand, hemmed it in to the north-east. In the distance, on the rim of the field, twenty-five camels were also grazing. Two Chadians in their mid-twenties – Yousef and Abd al Ghani – presided over this wilderness, without a car or any other transport. Like Ahmed and crew on the neighbouring farm, they were cut off from the outside world, more completely so in fact, and were wholly at the mercy of their Libyan government boss for supplies of food and fuel. Unlike at the previous farm, there was no running water here. A former petrol trailer contained several hundred litres going stale beneath the sun. As if anything were needed to reduce their morale, these young shepherds had not been paid for months.

We hobbled the camels and let them graze. Listless and tired before, they now fed with glee, their crane-like necks bobbing rhythmically up and down like tireless oil derricks. Ned and I sat down in the field, leaning against our upended saddles, alternately dipping into books – Ned with Lawrence's translation of Homer's *Odyssey*, me starting Henry Fielding's *Tom Jones*, which I had picked up in Tripoli – and surveying this scene of afternoon stupor with pleasure. In the Portakabin, Yousef and Abd al Ghani were cutting strips of lamb to dry. Mohammed was squatting in the doorway chatting to them in his melodious Arabic.

Our reverie was suddenly shattered by the arrival of a monstrous visitor. It was a bull camel, the first Ned and I had ever seen. He was a stupendous animal. Everything about him was oversized, even down to his attitude, which exuded confidence to the point of contempt for all those around him, man or animal. Judging by his behaviour he was in full rut, ready to breed with anything that crossed his path. He was swaggering and hostile, his position as head of the herd unchallenged, since he was the sole male. 'Males in full rut grind their teeth, suck air, belch, draw the head back, lash the tail, crouch with jerky movements of the pelvis and generally look ridiculous,' wrote R. Trevor Wilson in *The Camel*. In this case, the bull camel looked less ridiculous than awe-inspiring.

For various reasons, it is not advisable to get too near a rutting bull camel. Apart from behaving aggressively, he is likely to urinate more often than normal, waving his tail as he does so, and is also liable to ejaculate vigorously. A study in 1927 recommended the male's tail be tied to one side while he is in rut, 'otherwise everything in the vicinity, including the load and the attendants, is liable to be covered with the urine, dung and semen which the animal splashes about at this time'.

Although he had a herd of twenty-four females to serve, this bull-camel was clearly ready for more (notwithstanding the fact that ours were geldings). According to Wilson, 'If the male is not allowed to tire himself out by overworking individual females he can be expected to serve up to 70 females in a rutting season at the rate of as many as three a day.' However, a bull can easily be distracted and spend an entire day copulating with a single cow until he falls off her, 'exhausted and unable to stand'.

This one made his way towards us ponderously, and the rolls of flesh on his flanks shuddered with each step. He had taken leave of his harem and appeared intent on having further sexual adventures with the new arrivals. He was well equipped to do so. Between his rear legs hung balls the size of squashed pumpkins. He was a terrifying mass of testosterone towering over our own caravan. Suddenly, Gobber seemed neither so large nor impressive. Without altering his pace – his steady walk made him all the more intimidating – he closed in on Gobber's rear and sniffed with the air of a connoisseur who intended to have his way, come what may. Gobber turned around smartly and delivered a well-timed bite to the intruder's neck. The bull camel did not flinch. Perhaps he had not even felt the attack. While the two beasts eyeballed each other muzzle to muzzle, the other four arranged themselves in a semicircle of solidarity, two on either side of their embattled colleague. All differences between them had been put aside in this hour of need. It was five against one. Standing in this neat formation, they formed a touching contrast to their rival. All were much smaller than the bull camel. His ankles were wider even than the thickest part of their legs. In height, too, there was no competition. Never had they seemed more effete, particularly the three whites and Asfar. One by one, however, they attacked him with effeminate snaps. Even Asfar, usually the daintiest of the five, attacked with aplomb. Tuna, who until this point had maintained a discreet profile, threw herself into the fray on the Ghadamsis' side, harrying the bull camel about his ankles and for the first time breaking into a menacing snarl. Gentle and unobtrusive by disposition, she had not barked once since leaving Tmissah.

The bull camel, overwhelmed for the moment, skulked off. We were forced to spend the rest of the afternoon fending him off as he made repeated return forays, invariably heading for Gobber's nether regions and disturbing our camels' valuable grazing time. In turns, we chased after him, whipping him hard across the rump with a length of hose pipe. He would snort off twenty metres or so, pause for a few minutes, and, resilient and persistent beast that he was, stride back with undiminished purpose to interfere with them.

In the late afternoon, a pick-up truck scythed through the stubble of hay towards the Portakabin. Out stepped a tall, slim man with a pert moustache and deep, dancing eyes whose intensity suggested many years smoking marijuana. The boss had arrived. After directing several questions to Mohammed, he treated us with great courtesy, putting himself entirely at our disposal and offering to procure anything we might need (looking knowingly at our cigarettes) for our onward journey. We thanked him and were on the point of declining when Ned made his most inspired suggestion yet.

'Could we buy a lamb from your herd?' he asked. The farm chief seemed to think this was the most commonplace and reasonable request in the world.

'Of course. I will bring one for you to look at. Yousef!' he barked. 'Come here.'

He disappeared into the herd with the hapless youth (he treated both Chadians brusquely), and re-emerged several minutes later with a well-formed lamb bleating pathetically. Mohammed cast approving eyes and hands over its most meaty parts and asked the man the price. He let us have it for the small sum of 40 dinars. At the official exchange rate, this translated into $120. At the black-market rate, the only one Libyans then used, and the most eloquent demonstration of the gulf between revolutionary orthodoxy and reality, the price was just $12.

Mohammed tied the lamb's front and rear legs together. It lay slumped on its side, its eyes, wide with terror, staring towards the flock, kicking convulsively and bleating for its mother. I told Mohammed I would slaughter the animal but he would not hear of it and started sharpening his knife carefully. 'You do not know how to do it properly,' he said with the wisdom of experience. There was no point arguing. As Richardson wrote 150 years earlier, 'All Mussulmans are instinctively butchers, and are familiar with the knife, and expert at killing animals; it is a sort of religious rite with them. What I have observed particularly, is there is none of that shrinking back and chilled-blood shudder at seeing a poor animal killed, which characterizes Europeans.' Instead, I was drafted in to secure both legs as he drew the blade firmly across the lamb's neck. Mohammed, Yousef and I bled, gutted and hacked the animal to pieces. After weeks of tuna, Ned and I could hardly wait to binge on red meat. The hide I hung up to dry, intending to use it as a saddle cover on top of the garish Libyan blankets that served us as cushions by day and mattresses by night.

The sun set as we finished preparing the meat. Pink clouds skidded across the bloody globe, hurrying it towards the horizon. Once it had retreated, the heavens fell quiet and a cool blue halo arose where the sky touched the sands. For the next quarter of an hour it glowed luminously and then faded, slipping softly into a light lilac before disappearing altogether into the darkening, liquid sky. A wind picked up, chasing through the golden pasture and scattering stray stalks of hay through the thickening air. And then, a marvellous electric storm broke out above the dark mass of grazing camels. The dying light roused itself in pulses as lightning cascaded down. As if responding to this unearthly call, the camels broke into a wild canter, their silhouettes dancing in the repeating bolts of light, blurred by a sudden drizzle from the clouds above. Dew we had seen, and felt, many times before. But this was the first time we had watched rain in the desert. It was a tantalizingly brief reaffirmation of life in this brazen wilderness.

We repaired to the Portakabin for dinner. It was thick with smoke. At the far end of the room a fire was raging in one half of an old oil barrel. The Chadians had made their home as snug as could be expected in such circumstances, but had evidently not given much thought to ventilation. Two open doorways – there were no doors – on the same side of the room provided a slight draught, but there was no escape hole in the roof, and the windows facing the doorways had both been boarded up against the cold. The modest food supplies – pasta, corn oil, tomatoes, onions, dried meat and milk – were neatly kept in one corner. Two single mattresses covered with rough blankets came next, and after that you were in the 'kitchen'. Here, half-obscured by swirling wreaths of smoke, Abd al Ghani was shovelling hot spices into a bowl of fried liver, kidney, assorted entrails and dripping cubes of slimy fat rich in meat juice. The lamb was tender and plentiful and we ate ravenously with streaming eyes. With two dozen she-camels on the farm, there was no shortage of milk, and we feasted on another rice pudding, followed by tea and cigarettes.

Outside, the rain started to fall again as night closed in. Oblivious to the drizzle, Ned opted to sleep beneath the stars. I slept next to Mohammed in the smoking chamber. Above me, in place of the Sword of Damocles, the swaying lines of drying meat were suspended from the roof on three lines of string. We ate more the next morning and the camels fed properly for the last time. There would be no more grazing for them until Wau an Namus.

For two days we headed south-east into a desert grey in clouds. With this cover the nights were less chilly, but the days were ferociously cold, outdoing anything the worst English January could throw at you. On the first morning, a freezing rain slashed into us shortly after we had said goodbye to our Chadian hosts, ripping through our thin cotton *jalabiya*s and tearing at us without letting up until the late afternoon. It was like the tempest stumbled into by Samuel Taylor Coleridge in the winter of 1803 while tramping across the Lake District from Glenridding to Grasmere. 'Such a storm as this was I never witnessed, combining the intensity of the Cold with the violence of the wind & rain,' he shivered. 'The rain-drops were pelted, or rather *slung*, against my face, by the Gusts, just like splinters of Flint . . . My hands were all shrivelled up . . . I was obliged to carry my stick under my arm. O it was a wild business!'

We were not alone in feeling the cold. Even the indefatigable Mohammed was moved to acknowledge the foul weather. '*Sugga wajid*' (It's very cold), he hissed, tucking his head into the hurling wind as we moved forward. The camels, too, looked put out by this unwelcome change in the weather, but soldiered on. Only Tuna was unperturbed. Her wagging tail suggested some contentment at this deliverance from the customary furnace of day. She and the camels had to make the entire journey by foot. We, at least, had the relief of the saddle and now spent almost half of each day riding.

We moved on through a sublime monotony of gravelled plains, where we sank through the cracking crust in patches of softer ground, before rising into brown-peppered hillocks from which sand streamed in the still-strong wind. This bleakness was something new and more exotic, perhaps akin to the high steppes of Central Asia. On our second day out of the farm, we notched up a record of thirty-three miles. Under the regime of this firm but benevolent taskmaster, our oldest guide by far, we were travelling more quickly than we had with any of his predecessors. Around the campfire Ned and I recalled our faltering performance under the hopeless Salek and dissolved into laughter.

At night, we consoled our weary feet and aching legs around a small fire – there was no fuel in this part of the desert but we were now carrying a supply of firewood – and luxuriated in lamb. I felt I had reached a plateau of fatigue from which there was no descent. A night's sleep did much to refresh my body, but marching long distances day in, day out, built up a cumulative level of aches, pains and general lethargy.

I asked Mohammed how long the meat would last.

'One week,' he replied.

'No way,' said Ned.

It soon became clear that what Mohammed meant was we had enough meat to last a week between the three of us, and that he would continue eating it until none remained. Ned was to last five days before he fell sick. The daytime temperatures returned to their full, burning force and the lamb sat sweating inside a plastic bag hanging from Lebead's side. It started smelling suspect. I ate on for another day and, not wanting to tempt fate any further, retired from lamb after one last dinner. By then the bag contained an indefinite mass of putrid blue flesh. You could smell the stench as soon as Mohammed opened the bag several yards away. He could not understand our reticence and ate on with undimmed relish. Ned and I returned without enthusiasm to the tuna of former days.

Black stones started to stud the plain on our third day from the farm, interspersed with occasional smooth lava fields of grey volcanic rock, increasing in number as the morning wore on, which indicated we were nearing Wau an Namus. Suddenly, clinging to the horizon and tiny in the unfathomable distance, the outlines of three separate mountains appeared. Mohammed halted and said he was not certain which of the three was the oasis. We held a brief conference, joined by the camels, who sensed a discussion of some importance and gathered around to share in it. 'Instinctively . . . the camel knows that he has a guide, and if you halt in the middle of the desert to debate some point in regard to the route, the camels crowd round the guide,' observed Hassanein Bey. 'The moment he moves, they follow him, ignoring the presence of every other member of the caravan, but never overtaking the guide.' Although formidable navigators when required to return to a place they already know, they were unfortunately of no use to us now. Nor was the combined genius of our GPS devices and tactical pilotage charts, which failed to shed much light on our position relative to Wau an Namus. Whoever had mapped this stretch of the Libyan Sahara had, unaccountably, omitted to include this huge landmark and oasis. Mohammed climbed a rocky outcrop for an improved perspective of the country ahead, but returned candidly confessing his ignorance and suggested we continue in the same direction until the outlines became clearer.

We pressed on past rocky ridges swept with sand and the mountainous silhouettes grew more distinct with each step. By mid-afternoon, the great crater of Wau an Namus appeared, first as a gentle grey bosom rising softly out of the plateau, unmistakably at last as a crouching cathedral of basalt, the southernmost eruptive outlet of Al Haruj al Aswad. This is the largest of four volcanic provinces in Libya and the greatest basalt plateau in North Africa, covering 45,000 square kilometres. Two episodes of basaltic volcanic activity are believed to have formed this otherworldly landscape, splashing a thick coat of grey across the vast, burnished canvas of the desert. The first produced an extensive lava field, the second a series of volcanic centres of which Wau an Namus was one. The majority of the lava flows are thought by geologists to be two million years old or younger, but because of the inaccessibility and extreme difficulty of the terrain, little is known about the geology and petrology of Al Haruj.

The ground underfoot started to change, the sand increasingly giving way to spatters of white and grey rock. Several miles from the crater itself, the land darkened dramatically to a thick carpet of black volcanic grit softened in places by light golden brushes of sand. The nearer we drew to this famous oasis, the more magnificently it loomed aloft from its ashy collar. We both felt a thrill to have reached one of the most remote and spectacular oases in the entire Sahara by camel. Although mentioned by the German explorer Gerhard Rohlfs in the late nineteenth century, there is no evidence that a European actually visited the volcano until 1916, when the Frenchman Lapierre was taken in captivity from Djanet in Algeria via Wau al Kabir and Wau an Namus to Kufra.

We advanced up its level grey slopes and stopped at the lip of the vast saucepan-grey basin. It was the most staggering prospect yet. Even the camels twitched in admiration and sniffed the air for signs of food. In the centre of the shallow bowl, which appeared to stretch several miles across, rose the furrowed slopes of the volcanic cone, brown against the dull grey of the amphitheatre around it.

It was a giant chocolate pudding dwarfed by the still larger bowl in which it had been served. Etched into its sides, rough ribbed scars trailed down several hundred metres from just beneath the summit to its base, the channels where many thousands of years ago hot streams of custard had been poured and

had eaten into the soft brown sponge. At the foot of this mountainous pudding, the lake of custard had almost entirely evaporated, sucked up by the gluttonous desert sun. All that remained
were a few isolated drops, girdled around the sponge like a
beautiful necklace of pearls. This shining circle was a series of
lakes of various sizes, some thin and long like glittering needles,
others tiny and round as bright jewels. All glowed in the sun.
After our eyes got used to the glare, we could make out their
different colours. One was a deep blue, the next a thick viscous
green and another the colour of rust. A vibrant emerald flourish
of date palms and waving bulrushes bordered every lake. There
was a wild grandeur about this place. A more breathtaking contrast to the lifeless monotony of the desert plains that stretched
for hundreds of miles around could not have been imagined.

'This place would make for fantastic tobogganing or skate-
boarding,' Ned said, casting an eye over the great downhill sweep
of the land. With the impatience born of excitement, he roped
his two animals to Asfar and plunged down the steep slope full
tilt with his *shish* unravelling spectacularly behind him in the
whispering breeze. High spirits prevailed on all sides. At last. We
had arrived. Here we could feed, rest and, with luck, water the
camels. The going from Wau an Namus would be even harder
for them.

Mohammed chuckled, watching Ned bound down towards
the nearest lake. 'We will stay here tomorrow and leave the
following morning to give the camels time to feed,' he said. There
would be no more food or water for them before Tizirbu, which
he still insisted was 440 miles away. On the map, it was 220
miles, still one week's travelling if we kept a decent pace.

In the basin, we were welcomed by a couple of crows wheeling
overhead and the wind singing through the swaying bulrushes
while we searched for a camp. It was a light, mesmerizing tune,
the only sound, with the soft padding of the camels, to break the
silence. In one of those rare moments when he was not dipping his
pen in vitriol to fire off diatribes against the barbarism of Islam
and the cruelty of slave-traders, or engaging in patriotic approval

of all things British, Richardson, too, was charmed by the sounds of the desert: 'The music of the wind in the date-palms is very agreeable, and tunes my soul to a quiet sadness.'

We unloaded the camels briskly, hobbled them and left them immersed in a thick clump of date palms whose leaves they started pulling off with unbridled delight. No sooner had they started their long-awaited dinner, than they suddenly paused with expressions of bafflement, then withdrew unexpectedly from the palms and started scratching themselves with their back legs, all the time looking distinctly uncomfortable. In the quiet of the oasis, we heard an unmistakable whine around our ears. We were all under attack from an advance squadron of the mosquitoes that give Wau an Namus (Mosquito Crater) its name. They came at us thick and fast. If they could give the camels, with their thick coat of hair and tough skin, such a hard time, what chance was there for us? It only took a minute to find out.

'Feel like a swim?' suggested Ned. 'I'm not hanging around here anymore.' It was an excellent idea. To escape more misery from the mosquitoes, we left for a reconnaissance trip around the basin, leaving Mohammed to supervise the camels. We walked across to a long, needle-like lake we had seen from the top of the basin. The glimmering blue waters were an invitation to swim that was impossible to refuse. None of us had washed since Tmissah and, like our sleeping bags, we now smelt like fetid, meaty casseroles. Under this desert sun, the clear waters would be heavenly. We hacked our way through a dense forest of bulrushes that guarded the fringes of the lake and dived in with our clothes and sandals on. It was a brutal shock to the system. The cold was paralysing. The waters had an Arctic chill that shot through your limbs and froze your bones. As we came to the surface spluttering, a flotilla of mosquitoes welcomed us with another full-blooded attack. It was a wretched experience and we scrambled out. The swimming expedition had lasted three minutes.

Not wanting to return to camp so soon, we split up to investigate the basin. After passing a small rusty lake of brackish water, bordered with a thick white scum, I came to the bottom of the chocolate-pudding volcano and decided on a quick ascent. The view alone would be worth the effort and the late afternoon sun would just about dry my soaking clothes before the evening cold fell upon us. Dripping and sweating, I clambered up one of the furrows. Although you could not fault it for its directness, this was the least sensible route to the summit. For each step you took, you slid back half a step in the light coating of gravel that covered the rearing slopes. Half-way up the channel, I noticed a more relaxed route in the form of a well-worn track gently winding up the sides of the cone, but it was too late to join it. After several false summits, I finally reached the rim of the crater and peered into the cavernous grey hollow of the volcano. From this overhanging ledge, sheets of compressed ash and cinders fell straight down for hundreds of feet, so steeply that you could not even make out the bottom. Deep inside, crows glided in the falling light. On all sides beyond the grey pudding bowl, loomed first the black volcanic ring and then, as far as the eye could see, the empty sands of the plains disappearing into the horizon. Inside the bowl, I made out the diminutive speck of Mohammed sitting to one side of the patch of date palms and, not far away from him, the five camels, tinier than ever, who should have been grazing. There was no sign of Ned. He was on the other side of the volcano.

'*Haj*!' I screamed to Mohammed. '*Kaif halek*?' The wind probably tore away the words and there was no reply. After a few minutes wandering around the crater rim, I reached an old, narrowly engraved track and descended gently to the foot of the volcano to rejoin Mohammed.

'Did you see me?' I asked him. 'I was waving and shouting to you from the top of the volcano.' There was no reply. His high spirits of an hour ago had clearly deserted him. 'Maybe you didn't hear me from down here?' I suggested.

'There are too many mosquitoes,' he muttered angrily, lashing out as another one found its target. This was an understatement. The air was now thick with them. Every few moments, they landed unerringly on any piece of exposed skin and stung sharply. Mohammed had battened down the hatches as much as possible against this onslaught and his face was hardly visible beneath his black *shish*. Nearby, the camels were under similar attack, a picture of discomfort. At intervals, they would lurch off towards the edge of the basin in a vain bid for relief. 'They don't want to stay here,' said Mohammed with a tone of reproach, shooing the camels back down the slopes. 'They keep trying to leave and I have to make them stay.'

He and the camels had been under constant siege since we had left on our volcano jolly.

There was no way we could sleep here. After Ned had reappeared from his solo ascent of the volcano, the three of us decided to camp on a small ridge a hundred feet above. Before we could relocate, however, Mohammed – perhaps in revenge – said we first had to strip off some palm leaves for the camels' dinner. It was hellish work, penetrating into the mosquito-infested trees with a penknife to cut off several dozen branches and then sitting down to strip off the leaves and put them into a sack, being bitten all the while. Finally, when the mosquitoes had decorated our faces with a pretty pattern that looked like a bad case of measles, Mohammed said we had collected enough. Gathering everything we needed for the night, we hotfooted it up the slopes, pursued by a dwindling band of mosquitoes. On this higher ground, open to the rushing wind, all but the hungriest and hardiest left us alone. We hobbled the camels for the night in front of individual piles of palm leaves – in the morning not a single leaf remained – and sat down to lamb ribs and pasta, our finest desert dinner ever.

Naively, I had imagined the next day would be a rest day for us as well as the camels. Mohammed had other ideas. After allowing us only the briefest hint of a lie-in, he was harrying us out of our sleeping bags with the customary cries of '*Heya*! *Heya*!' and telling us what needed to be done today. 'Come on, you must help water the camels,' he said. 'And then we must pick some more dates and leaves for them. Come on, get up.' While we were sleeping, he had already investigated the water situation and, remembering his last visit to Wau, had found a well containing sweet drinking water which he had given the camels. There was something especially impressive about this, considering that everyone else had told us there was only the undrinkable salt water of the lakes at Wau an Namus. If that had been correct, it would have made the journey infinitely more difficult, perhaps impossible, particularly with our collection of leaking *bidoun*s. As it was, we could now fill them with the full complement of 200 litres, more than enough, failing disaster, to see us to Tizirbu. Equally remarkable was the fact that Mohammed had managed to find this oasis at all. He had only been here once before, forty years ago, on a two-day date-gathering expedition by camel. His navigational skills were superb.

While we talked, the camels snaked mischievously towards freedom again, climbing up the grey pudding basin with tiny, hobbled steps. Comically, they marched in single file, following Gobber's stately lead. These persistent escape attempts were the only capacity in which he was the undisputed leader. In all other respects he was treated by his colleagues, rather unfairly, as the ugly duckling.

Before he departed to retrieve them, Mohammed set us the task of filling two more sacks with palm leaves for the onward journey. We spent a miserable couple of hours hunched beneath the mosquito-ridden trees stuffing the bags with this choice herbage. No sooner had Mohammed returned than he ordered us to relocate our camp next to the well where we could water the camels again and let them feed on the palms and bulrushes. We had to give them as much time to replenish themselves as possible. As Hassanein Bey wrote, 'Nothing is more important in trekking than the condition of your camels. Not only must they be fat and well nourished at the start, but they must be allowed to drink their fill with deliberation and permitted to rest after the drinking.'

With the camels grazing, I started preparing to wash myself and my foul-smelling clothes at the well. The relentless taskmaster shook his head. 'No, first you must think of the camels,' he said firmly. 'We must collect more dates for them. There is no more grazing after Wau an Namus. From here to Tizirbu it will be very difficult for them.'

For several hours we hurled rocks into the upper branches of the palms and collected the dates as they fell to the ground. Once the initial novelty of the job had faded (five minutes was more than enough), it was slow, hot and thankless work, made less comfortable still by the endless mosquito attacks. After we had filled all our bidouns, Mohammed was unable to think up any more tasks, so there was finally time for the luxury of a wash with soap and water.

Eschewing this last chance of a shower, Ned lay in a glade of palms, supervising the grazing camels from afar and stalking through the final pages of Homer. We read through the rest of the afternoon until the light was too poor to go on. The camels were then couched and hobbled for the night in front of five piles of palm leaves. We sat around another bowl of pasta in the deepening gloom, our thoughts turning to the next, most challenging, leg of our journey. Would this long, waterless stretch be asking too much of our camels?

# CHAPTER XI

# Hamlet in Tizirbu

---

*The desert can be beautiful and kindly, and the caravan fresh and cheerful, but it can also be cruel and overwhelming, and the wretched caravan, beaten down by misfortune, staggers desperately along. It is when your camels droop their heads from thirst and exhaustion, – when your water supply has run short and there is no sign of the next well, – when your men are listless and without hope, – when the map you carry is a blank, because the desert is uncharted, – when your guide, asked about the route, answers with a shrug of the shoulders that God knows best, – when you scan the horizon, and all around, wherever you look, it is always the same hazy line between the pale blue of the sky and the yellow of the sand, – when there is no landmark, no sign to give the slightest excuse for hope, – when that immense expanse looks like, feels like, a circle drawing tighter and tighter round your parched throat, – it is then that the Beduin feels the need of a Power bigger even than that ruthless desert. It is then that the Beduin, when he has offered his prayers to this Almighty Power for deliverance, when he has offered up his prayers and they have not been granted, it is then that he draws his jerd around him, and sinking down upon the sands awaits with astounding equanimity the decreed death. This is the faith in which the journey across the desert must be made.*

*The desert is terrible and merciless, but to the desert all those who once have known it must return.*

AHMED HASSANEIN BEY, *THE LOST OASES*

Like the camels, Tuna had drunk her fill during our stay at the volcano. When Mohammed was not looking, we had also fed her handsomely on lamb and she now trotted alongside the caravan with a new bounce in her step and a brisk wag in her tail. She was a leaner, fitter animal and, although she had already slogged 170 miles across the desert with us, enduring both the sapping heat of day and the numbing chill of night, she was still ready for more adventures. Her stamina was remarkable. We grew fonder of her by the day.

For the next week we made stubborn progress towards Tizirbu, averaging twenty-eight miles a day. The graceful outline of Wau an Namus retreated slowly behind us on the first day as we moved onwards across the plains, travelling into mixed country, where the hills were a soft beige at dawn, changing from a bleached colourlessness under the high sun into dark, brooding shadows as the light closed in on us. On the second day, we passed between pillars of brittle white gypsum that crumbled and collapsed at a touch. Countless years of erosion by sand and wind had sculpted them into strange shapes scored with layer after layer of protruding rims heaped up on top of each other like shattered dinner plates. Farther off, the golden ridges of rock, ragged with their coating of white icing, had all been decapitated to the same level, cropped by some unseen force.

Having spent the entire day scurrying behind dunes and hillocks, his stomach racked by fermenting lamb, Ned suggested we stop for the night at the top of a picturesque corridor of sand that rose gently from the ridge-strewn plain. There was a pathetic handful of dry scrub here that would last five minutes in a fire but it was better than nothing. Mohammed was fifty yards away in a slight depression, busy scrounging similarly meagre remnants of firewood.

'It's not a bad spot to camp for the night,' said Ned. 'What do you think?'

'Why not?' I replied. 'You've got the squits and I'm feeling pretty worn out. This is fine.'

We started unloading the camels as the sun set in front of us.

Overhead, brushed clouds of gold arranged themselves into a vast 'v' shape that framed the orb, slanting into the horizon like a path to heaven. On the ground two columns of sand reflected the picture in the skies, their fading golden flanks stretching like giant pincers into the distance. The clouds lingered long after the sun had departed, slowly sliding from glowing amber to the rich colour of claret. It was the flourish of nature at her most unearthly, the sort of heroic sunset that might have greeted Odysseus returning home from his epic wanderings.

Mohammed reappeared from the hollow and walked towards us. As soon as he saw we had stopped for the day, he was furious.

'What are you doing?' he shouted. 'We haven't stopped yet and we're not stopping here. We must go on.' We had already unloaded half the caravan and were continuing with the rest. The sun had set and both of us had had enough. It was too late to start again.

'Come on, we're going,' he repeated.

'That's enough for today, Mohammed,' I replied. I told him Ned was unwell and I was tired. Besides, we had walked almost thirty miles. He stood silently next to his camel for several minutes. You could tell he wanted to go on. It was a matter of honour. As our guide, it was his prerogative to decide where and when we stopped. The problem was that he knew we were resolved not to continue tonight. It was an embarrassing moment because we had usurped his role.

'It is the etiquette of the desert that no-one may interfere with the guide in any way,' wrote Hassanein Bey. 'The guide of a caravan is exactly like the captain of a ship. He is absolute master of the caravan so far as direction is concerned, and must also be consulted as to the starting and halting times.' It was the fact we had not consulted him first, before stopping, which so upset Mohammed. In his eyes, it insulted his pride and undermined his dignity as our guide. Disputes in the desert tend to have an intensity out of all proportion to their subject and this was no different. Gently, I tried to coax him back to his usual high spirits. He was not capable of sulking for long. 'I will stop whenever you want,' he said courteously. 'Just say when you want to finish for the day or I will ask you if you want to stop.'

We settled our differences and turned to the more important matter of refreshing ourselves after the day's march. With the prospect of hot tea and another lamb dinner before him, Mohammed's humour quickly returned. It was slim pickings again for the camels, however, finishing off the last palm leaves we had brought from the volcano. Since the date feed had been instituted as a morning ritual, they had begun to beg for other hand-outs too. Their ears always pricked up as we foraged through our own food bags and, if they were not hobbled a sufficient distance away, they would frequently try to break into our supplies while we slept. The grazing at Wau an Namus, if not exactly hearty, had been decent enough, but the animals' fatigue was cumulative. Each day they were getting weaker and they now needed a proper feed of barley. That would have to wait until we reached Tizirbu. Until we did, there would be no more grazing for them.

Leaking *bidoun*s continued to haunt us during the week and spotting drips from various containers became an irritatingly regular feature of our days across the plains. Even a pinprick-size hole in the plastic bags beneath the tops was enough to trigger a persistent flow which, once detected, required an immediate halt of the caravan. One afternoon, the two of us were travelling at some distance behind Mohammed, when we noticed another leak and dismounted to attend to it. After several minutes fiddling about with plastic bags, we rejoined Mohammed, who had stopped and wanted to know what was wrong. We explained and he cast an expert eye over the offending *bidoun*. With contempt for our recent efforts, it had resumed its steady trickle. Mohammed dismounted at once and started adjusting the ropes by which it was attached to the camel. Ned, racing through another book, remained on camelback. Engrossed in my own book, I stayed where I was, too. Mohammed found this display of Western indolence intolerable. 'Get down!' he barked with the wrath of a sergeant-major. Humbled, we jumped down and lent a hand. For the rest of the day, though, he remained unusually taciturn, with relations only thawing over our small campfire. After a week, he was still going strong on the rank blue lamb. He had a stomach of iron.

The wind slapped us with its freezing fingers as we moved on towards Tizirbu. There was no rain, as there had been on leaving the farm outside Wau al Kabir, but the daytime temperatures had fallen more sharply. I thought wryly of Anthony Cazalet insisting we would be 'bloody cold' in the desert, and re-membered Richardson's more evocative description of these bitter conditions as he traipsed from Ghadames to the southern oasis of Ghat. 'The north wind blows in these places with an intensity equalling the cold of hell; language fails me to express this rigorous temperature,' he shuddered. Climbing out of our sleeping bags in this raw weather, wearing only boxer shorts, was brutal. Our gaunt bodies shivered as we rushed to find shirts, socks and trousers, all glacial to the touch. With woolly hats pulled down half over the eyes and huddled in fleece jackets worn over our *jalabiya*s, we cut absurd figures.

Zipped and buttoned up against the cold as best we could, we left the plain and crossed a shoulder of sand, moving into dunes tidily piled into rounded summits from which the wind howled, scattering light plumes of sand far into the air. At times, they fell like a dry shower, finding their way into all of our clothes and many of our food bags. This, and the kerosene that already lingered over our baggage like a miasma – it had penetrated chocolate bars, flour, onions, sugar, nuts, biscuits and tea alike – ruined our meals. I took comfort from the fact that at least our tins of tuna were impregnable.

Our conversations had grown stale after two months in Libya together. Frequently, we were reduced to earnest discussions about what equipment or other personal belongings we would 'pare down' on arrival in Tizirbu, sometimes we told tedious explorers' jokes, and many evenings found us comparing notes on the consistency of our stools. To combat this ennui, Ned started retiring earlier after dinner to tune in to News Hour on the BBC World Service, updating me the following morning on moves to impeach President Clinton over the Monica Lewinsky affair, or the perilous state of global financial markets. Irritated by the babble of his radio, I took my sleeping bag and rollmat farther afield and lay beneath the silent stars, my amateurish survey of the constellations constantly interrupted by kerosene burps late into the night.

The country changed again two days before Tizirbu. Now we had to haul ourselves up, and sink uneasily down, steep rolling dunes, separated from each other by long corridors of sandy plains, some only a few hundred metres wide, others running several miles across. In the evening, traversing a featureless expanse of sand flats, clouds fell low upon us, obliterating a wan sunset and wrapping us in ghostly shrouds of white. The horizon disappeared and the sky and sand suddenly merged as one. The peering light of the half moon roused itself to penetrate this pale gloom, and then it, too, disappeared. We had never seen anything like this. Ahead, Mohammed seemed to tread on air and the camels walked through this mystical landscape, suspended in nothingness, like wandering spirits of the desert. We camped in mid-air and prepared a vegetarian pasta (gently flavoured with kerosene), Mohammed having consumed the final, putrefying remains of lamb and still adamant in his refusal to have anything to do with tuna. The camels looked on hungrily across this white wilderness. The kilogram of dates we were giving each of them every morning was not enough and all five were visibly weakening. You could see it as they rose to their feet more unsteadily in the mornings, and slumped heavily to the ground when we unloaded them for the night.

The following afternoon, tucked beneath light rolls of sand to our south, we made out distant black specks that Ned and I thought looked like *rassu*, one of the most versatile desert shrubs, combining excellent fodder for camels with solid fuel for fires.

'That's not *rassu*,' said Mohammed with a note of certainty that contrasted with his awkward squinting into the horizon. 'They're rocks.' He had hawk-like eyes and invariably detected things in the distance far sooner than we did. In this instance, however, we had an advantage over the old man. Through the binoculars, we could just make out clumps of the shrub with their wispy leaves stirring in the breeze.

'Have a look,' I said, passing him the binoculars. He looked through the wrong end. This confirmed his suspicions that the black marks were indeed rocks. Besides, he had already suggested they were not shrubs so he could not climb down too quickly. Like many men of the desert, Mohammed was a proud, autocratic fellow. I showed him how to use the binoculars and he had another look.

'No, no, no, they're just rocks,' he repeated, sounding less certain this time.

He wanted to continue in the same direction, bypassing the *rassu* altogether. As tactfully as possible, I told him he was already walking too far to the north. We needed to march just south of due east to reach Tizirbu, towards the black dots in fact, whatever they might be. Discussing our route, and the bearings we needed to follow, was always a delicate matter. Mohammed was a formidable navigator, who could march by the sun and stars. Very rarely did he ask to check our GPS. He did not need to. Often, and it was wonderful to watch, he navigated by the ripples blown across the dunes by the wind. In this stretch of the desert they ran from west to east. But however he was navigating now, we were still off course. He snorted in reply.

'I'm sorry, Mohammed, but we're going over there because they're not rocks and the camels need to eat,' I said finally, moving off in that direction with Ned. He became gruff and marched off on his previous bearing. For a quarter of an hour, our two caravans diverged. We walked on regardless, the camels craning their necks round regularly to keep tabs on where their real guide was going. They knew Ned and I were frauds and did not like being separated from Mohammed and their colleague Lebead. Eventually, seeing we were not going to alter our path and perhaps admitting to himself that he might (God forbid) have been wrong, Mohammed subtly altered his until he was following in our tracks at a suitably discreet distance. Any eagerness to catch up would have been unseemly. He would wait instead to see whether we were heading into a patch of rocks as he had foretold.

After half an hour, we reached the first clump of *rassu*, a fine-looking specimen with rich green leaves, the sort the camels loved best. They hurried around it, took several preliminary nibbles and then withdrew a few steps, looking awkward, like a guest at a dinner party sitting in front of a plate piled high with food he cannot stomach, not wanting to cause offence but uncertain how to proceed. We led them on to another shrub. The same reaction. Polite initial taste followed by an embarrassed silence. Mohammed caught up with us moments later. It did not matter that he had been wrong about the rocks. This was a situation in which his expertise was called for. He looked at the plant, pulled off a leaf, rubbed it between his fingers, and smelt it. '*Rassu*,' he said. 'I don't understand why the camels aren't eating it. They ate it in Tmissah.' I told him they had eaten it happily throughout our journey from Ghadames. It was their favourite food in the desert. He hand fed a piece to Lebead, who feigned interest, chewed half-heartedly on a fraction of the leaf he had been given and let the rest fall unceremoniously to the sand. Mohammed and the camels all looked baffled.

'Is it a different type of *rassu*?' I asked him.

'No, it's just the same,' he replied. 'I don't understand it, but it's very bad because they haven't eaten properly for several days. If they don't now, they'll just get even weaker.'

We continued walking through this semi-fertile stretch marked by regularly appearing beige hillocks flecked with dark clumps of *rassu* that rose out of the sandy floor. We stopped at each group of shrubs we came across with the same result. The camels abandoned their efforts to be polite and did not even venture to taste the leaves, standing to one side instead with expressions of profound boredom. '*Mishkilla*,' muttered Mohammed, still perplexed.

After several more attempts, we gave up on our fastidious diners and led them to the top of a small hillock dotted with *rassu*, both dead and alive, where we hobbled them for the night. They might not want to eat, but we did. Like Saleh before him (although never as morose by day), Mohammed was always greatly cheered by a roaring fire and glasses of sweet tea on putting up camp. Here, on our elevated perch, we were surrounded by endless heaps of dry wood and did not have to huddle around a mean fire. We exchanged further opinions on the properties of *rassu* and watched the camels sniff the air with a look of hunger. Closing in on Tizirbu, our spirits were high and Mohammed's face glowed in the firelight with a look of deep contentment. He asked us to send him photos of our journey once we returned to England.

'I will always keep them in my pocket,' he said, patting the front of his *jalabiya* affectionately. 'Then I will take them out and look at them and say these are the Englishmen I travelled with in the desert, *alhamdulillah*.' We warmed to him more by the day.

The next morning, we rose early, intending to camp just outside Tizirbu – still almost thirty miles away – that night. We marched on, picking our way through increasingly large hillocks studded with the ubiquitous clumps of *rassu* that still failed to interest the camels. Mohammed, at a loss to know why they were not eating, was amused by a recently discovered eccentricity of his mount Lebead. On spotting anything dark on the ground – such as a small black stone or a solitary leaf – this camel, for reasons known only to himself, would abruptly shy away from the offending item and skirt it at what he considered a safe distance. Each time he did this, there would come a high-pitched chuckle from Mohammed.

'Watch this,' he said to me, pointing to a black pebble twenty metres or so away, 'watch Lebead.' He steered the unwitting animal towards the stone until, suddenly catching sight of this terrifying object, the camel jerked away to one side. 'Did you see that?' Mohammed asked, with another chuckle. 'He's a very nervous camel. A little crazy.'

By evening we were moving among thickening masses of *rassu* towards lines of slender trees whose outlines were blurring in the dusk. Pinpricks of light twinkled among the dark shadows and the hum of farm work drifted over towards us. From farther afield came the mechanical noises of town life and the drone of cars, their headlights alternately blinking and hidden as they traversed a swathe of sand. For several minutes the three of us discussed where we should camp. I suggested a line of trees that bordered a farm. Perhaps this would have been bad form, but the camels were ravenous and no-one would see us in any case. Mohammed dismissed the idea at once. Ned proposed another spot, which was also summarily rejected. From time to time, Mohammed liked to throw his weight around and usually there was little to be gained opposing him. After all, he tended to know best. Tonight, however, I was not so sure as he led us to a mean-looking campsite consisting of a solitary date palm in a clearing of sand criss-crossed by deep waves of car tracks. It looked like the M25 of Tizirbu, as unsuitable a place to stop for the night as we could find among this plentiful grazing.

No sooner had we stopped and started to unload the camels than a great uproar of mad yelling and whooping started up. Seconds later, two Toyota Landcruisers swung round into the clearing and hurtled towards us, hooting. Their lights were on full beam and both cars were stacked with young men hanging onto cabs already stuffed to bursting point with their colleagues. Out they all jumped, more than a dozen of them, the noisy young studs of Tizirbu screaming a chorus of questions and greetings.

'Who are you?'

'Welcome to Tizirbu!'

'You can't stay here!'

'Where have you come from?'

'Which country?'

'You must come with us!'

'Are these your camels?'

'How much did they cost?'

'Crazy English on camels!'

Mohammed looked as baffled as we did and tried to sift through this unruly rabble to find its leader. It appeared there were two, both of whom were inviting us to stay the night at their home in Tizirbu.

An argument ensued between the two ringleaders and testosterone filled the air. After several more minutes of shouting and arguing, we were told we must accompany a young man called Faiz Mohammed to his house in town. We thanked him for his hospitality and said our most important consideration was the camels, who had to be fed and watered immediately. 'This is no problem,' Faiz replied breezily, 'you can keep your camels on the farm next to my house.'

At first sight he appeared an unlikely *capo di tutti capi*. He was the shortest and portliest of the group in a black leather jacket, jeans and flip-flops. He seemed positively mild-mannered, almost diffident. Perhaps the key to his authority lay in his facial hair, a trim but full-blooded beard and moustache which contrasted with the inferior wisps of hair that sprouted from his colleagues' faces. He looked several years older than them, too, perhaps in his early twenties. Most were in their late teens.

Everything appeared to have been settled when a rival faction made its last bid to host us. Before Mohammed or I knew what had happened, Ned was being spirited away on the back of one of the Toyotas, heading towards a large campfire several hundred metres away. For several minutes we heard the sounds of rhythmic clapping and strange singing as the light of the flames played across the surrounding trees. It was as though some sinister ritual or sacrifice was about to take place. And then, as quickly as they had left, they roared back across the clearing, still hooting and screaming wildly, and deposited Ned back with us. These boys needed girlfriends.

Determined to make a flamboyant entry into Tizirbu, Faiz insisted on riding Asfar to his house. I swallowed my reservations about imposing this fat creature on my treasured mount and let him ride, leading the camel by the rope. Within moments, two of his friends were also aloft on the remaining two riding camels. Those who had failed to get a ride kept pestering us to let them mount the two heavily loaded baggage camels, Gobber and Bobbles, requests we firmly refused. Delighted at their advantage, Faiz and his two colleagues crowed at their friends on the ground.

We threaded through groves of palms that Mohammed, recognizing a particular species, said the camels must not eat. It would make them sick and, if consumed in sufficient quantity, perhaps kill them even. It was difficult to enforce this new dining rule and the camels pulled vigorously at the leaves as they walked past, Gobber the gourmand devouring mouthfuls at great pace. Soon we came upon houses – one-storey buildings, some painted, most concrete grey – passed neat fences of palm fronds, and entered alleys so narrow they unnerved the camels. Children sat on their front steps, doors ajar in bright wedges of light that revealed tantalizing glimpses of family life. The evening air was heavy with the cool fragrance of tamarisk, which we breathed in and gulped down deeply, thankful to arrive in Tizirbu after a week's waterless traverse from Wau an Namus. As we penetrated deeper, the tamarisk was submerged beneath the competing smells of wood fires and cooking floating out into the darkness.

Tuna bounced alongside the caravan, a much thinner version of the bitch that had set out with us from Tmissah. Her tongue was hanging out, her ribs were beginning to press through her neat coat and her stomach had shrunk visibly. She looked beat, but was still going strong after almost 400 miles, a remarkable desert crossing. We intended to leave her in Tizirbu as the last leg to Kufra via Rabiana – 180 miles, of which the lion's share consisted of the formidable dunes of the Rabiana Sand Sea – would be even more punishing. Perhaps she had had enough of her odyssey by now and would decide this was to be her new home. We would see soon enough.

We reached another large open space, across which two rows of single-storey houses faced each other. Lamps glinted from within and threw pockets of white light onto the ground outside. Faiz pointed out his home and, leading us behind it, showed us the 'farm' he had mentioned. If it had been stretching the meaning of the word to call the settlement near Wau al Kabir a farm, here it was even more far-fetched. The farm consisted of a back garden, perhaps a hundred square metres of unkempt grass. He need not have exaggerated in any case. This was all the camels needed. Asfar threw himself on to the ground without waiting to be unloaded, and started cropping the grass with a look of delirious satisfaction. The other four followed his lead, and we unloaded them awkwardly, their necks rising and sinking repeatedly as they ate, their attentions focused solely on this long-awaited dinner.

The Tizirbu rogues looked on entranced, no longer shouting but contenting themselves by giving us unsolicited advice and arguing about what was best for the camels. One party advocated watering them immediately, the other said they should be fed first. Ignoring their well-meaning but interminable comments, we deferred to Mohammed, who said it was too cold to water them tonight. They should eat now – bales of hay and a sack of barley if we could find them – and we would water them first thing in the morning. An entrepreneurial-looking man in a shiny black bomber jacket presented himself and said he could bring both hay and barley in a few minutes. He named a price that suggested the capitalist spirit in Libya – whatever Gaddafi's *Green Book* might say to the contrary – was untamed. Too tired to haggle, we nodded resignedly. He smiled greedily and disappeared on his errand. Minutes later, he returned with the goods and we untied the bales of hay, heaping piles of it in front of the hobbled camels, who surged forward to devour it. Next, we poured the barley on to the plastic sheet and they appeared momentarily confused about what to eat first, faced with a choice of fresh grass, cut hay and a mountain of grain. We left them for the night and Faiz showed us inside his home, leading the growing entourage into a long rectangular room whose walls, lined with coloured cushions, were a two-tone colour scheme of brown and dirty cream. This was the family sitting room.

A roomful of eyes ogled us as we sat down. After weeks of seclusion in the desert, we wondered what the new company would be like. It did not take long to find out. Within moments, a scuffle broke out next to the exhausted Mohammed, who was reclining on the cushions. It was a text-book confrontation, beginning with the light-hearted provocation of one youth by another, escalating into an exchange of raised voices, some preliminary shoving and pushing, another furious barrage of insults, and then, finally, the inevitable flailing of fists and knees into heads and faces in all-out, hot-blooded conflict. The two young men tore into each other with venom, falling on top of the unfortunate Mohammed who was sitting ringside. After great exertions and with much difficulty, the pugilists were at last separated, and one was sent packing with a terrific kick to his behind. Inappropriately, this ruffian – who had certainly had the worst of the encounter – was called Omar Mukhtar, named after the fearless Sanusi guerrilla leader who had so harried the Italians in the 1920s. Ned nicknamed the man left behind 'The Contender'. His real name was Abd al Basset and he was Faiz's nineteen-year-old younger brother, which presumably explained why he had not been thrown out of the room, too. He was a smart fellow in a black bomber jacket with fur-lined collar, designer jeans, probably fake but well-fitting, and black leather boots. His hair was cropped short and his look was urban street chic. A well-groomed young boulevardier. The Contender would not have been out of place in a Paris nightclub, which ranked as some achievement for the inhabitant of a remote oasis in the Libyan Sahara. Now that the fight was over, he sat back with his handsome face bruised and cut from the flurry of fists and knees. He seemed acutely self-conscious and embarrassed. Mohammed, who had witnessed the bout at close quarters, looked tired and annoyed. He just wanted to have dinner before going to sleep.

It came at last, prefaced by a bowl of delicious moist dates and glasses of cool sheep's milk. Faiz brought in a steaming platter of saffron pasta heaped beneath large chunks of roast chicken, the first we had tasted since Germa. His companions remained rowdy throughout dinner, re-enacting the recent fight and teasing The Contender mercilessly. All of them were unfailingly courteous towards us, however, pushing far more than our fair share of chicken and fresh bread in front of us and insisting we finish the lot.

'*Koul*! *Koul*!' (Eat! Eat!), they urged us. 'You must eat more because you have been travelling in the desert. No, that's not enough. Here, have some more. You must be very hungry.' We were but, like Tuna, our stomachs had shrunk dramatically. We ate until I thought we would burst. No sooner had we finished what was in front of us than more chicken and rice was heaped on to our plates, to the same accompaniment of '*Koul*! *Koul*!' Faiz, an unstinting host, was disappointed that we had not made more of an impact on the immense platter and it took several minutes to convince him we had eaten our fill. When the chorus of '*Koul*! *Koul*!' had finally subsided, a tray of tea and soft drinks was brought in, which we rounded off with a volley of cigarettes.

Anything of ours that hinted at gadgetry aroused huge interest. Bizarrely, this even included our smoking paraphernalia, which consisted of packets of rolling tobacco and cigarette papers. None of them had ever seen roll-ups before, they explained, so could we put on a quick demonstration for them? Once the novelty of rolling cigarettes (and large quantities of tobacco) had been exhausted, they moved on to the contents of our bags. Another scuffle broke out over our desert sunglasses and it looked as though they would emerge from this encounter in pieces.

'Give them to me!' said one, pulling hard.

'Let go,' said his adversary.

'Get off, leave them alone,' said another.

Finally, one of the youths managed to get hold of them and, once he had put them on, started strutting up and down the room, striking absurd poses and breaking into exuberant disco moves for our benefit. Eventually, the glasses were grabbed by someone else and the same process was repeated several times until they were no longer considered interesting.

The next item to captivate them was Ned's Leatherman pocket tool, a more robust version of a Swiss Army knife. Everyone wanted to hold it and a dispute broke out again, this time more dangerous since it contained hideously sharp blades. Near Murzuk, one of them had sliced through my fingertip and I hardly dared use the tool anymore. Our new friends thought it a miracle of technology and several of them dearly wanted to keep it. We had not seen any of the shops in Tizirbu yet, but judging by those we had seen elsewhere in the country (with the exception of Tripoli), you would be lucky to find in them much more than Egyptian biscuits, washing powder, tins of tuna and soft drinks. It was little wonder they were so enthralled by these foreign gadgets.

'You give me,' one said to Ned, putting the Leatherman in his pocket confidently.

'Sorry, we need it,' Ned replied.

'No, I like it,' he went on, 'special present for me.'

It had to be prised from his fingers. By then, the group had discovered another gadget. They were fascinated by our GPS devices, less so by the compasses, and engrossed in our maps, walking boots and sleeping bags. These we had to pull away from them by force to prevent them climbing in.

Desperate for a break, I left the room to take Faiz up on his kind offer of a hot shower, the first since Tmissah. I lingered long under the luxurious stream of hot water, wondering how much thinner I would become and steaming the small shower room into a damp cloud. It was a joy to climb into fresh clothes again, although the austere regime of dates and pasta was having a visible effect. The clean pair of trousers seemed several sizes larger around the waist than the last time I had worn them. I tightened my belt a couple of notches and returned to our room, where the farcical scenes continued unabated. Besieged by admirers, Ned was relieved to see me reappear: 'Ah, you're back. Excellent, I'll leave you to it. I'm sure you'll be able to entertain them,' he said and promptly escaped to the shower.

Faiz sat in the middle of the group which arranged itself so that everyone was facing me. I felt as if I was meant to be giving an audience. 'You're the first tourists we have seen with camels,'

Faiz said, in explanation of the pillage of our equipment and the huge interest we were arousing. 'We do not get many tourists in Tizirbu and those who come here travel by car or motorbike.' By occupation, Faiz was a driver. His family owned a Toyota Landcruiser, which he used to transport people and goods, usually to the frontier town of Kufra in the south-east, but also to Jalo, Ajdabiya and Benghazi to the north. Sometimes, he took tourists into the desert, but only very occasionally because there were so few foreign visitors.

When Ned had returned, we asked about the best route to Kufra. There was a unanimity of opinion, surprising among such a hot-blooded assembly. No-one thought the oasis of Rabiana worth visiting, either for the sake of food and water for the camels, or even out of interest. 'You must go to Buzeima,' Faiz insisted. 'There are too many date palms for your camels to eat and there is also sweet water. Buzeima is very beautiful. You must see it. Everyone who comes to Tizirbu goes to Buzeima.' There was a murmur of approval. A man pressed up against me, watching me take notes with his nose almost in the pages of the book, and drew a picture of a palm tree in case I had not understood what Faiz was saying.

Buzeima was curiously absent from the Michelin map, although it did appear on the erratic pilotage charts. It seemed ideally placed for us, more so in fact than Rabiana, because it lay directly on our route, splitting the distance between Tizirbu and Kufra about seventy-five miles to the south-east. This was the oasis the English explorer Rosita Forbes had described as the most beautiful she had ever seen on her travels with Hassanein Bey in 1921. Apart from Buzeima, there was precious little grazing to be had before Kufra, Faiz continued. On our first day out of Tizirbu, we would reach a government farm about ten miles away where the camels could feed on the trees. After that, there was nothing but bleak, sandy wastes until Buzeima. And from there, the dunes of the Rabiana Sand Sea were piled higher still, all devoid of fodder. It would be severe going for the tiring camels.

Saleh Hassan Suleiman

Striking camp outside Murzuk.

Murzuk market. James Richardson, the English traveller who reached the great slave trade centre on 22 February 1846, was unimpressed by Murzuk, which he called 'a miserable dirty place' and 'a sink of vice and disease'.

More tuna? What a treat. Shopping in Murzuk (Ned is on the right.)

Murzuk Castle, drawn by Captain George Francis Lyon in 1819. When he and Joseph Ritchie arrived, the castle dominated the entire town. It was home to Mohammed al Mukni, the notorious slave-trader and Bey of Fezzan, his courtiers and his harem of fifty Negresses.

Mohammed Sherif (left) and his brother Ahmed in front of Murzuk Castle.

Mohammed Othman. Tubbus have long been admired for their extraordinary grace and stamina. According to Herodotus, who visited Libya around 450 BC, their ancestors were 'by far the swiftest of foot' of any nation.

Tuna joins the caravan.

Government 'farm' near Wau al Kabir.

Lebead refuses to budge.

Ned rests while the camels graze.

Wau an Namus, one of the most remote
oases in the Libyan Sahara.

Slim pickings for the camels.

Leaving Tizirbu: Faiz (right) and friend aboard The Big White and Lebead.

The author riding Asfar.

Buzeima, the oasis that so entranced the English traveller Rosita Forbes in 1921.

A desert sandstorm drawn by Captain George Francis Lyon in 1819. Historians estimate that between 10 million and 14 million slaves were transported across the Sahara between 650 and 1900, with a mortality rate of 20 per cent.

End of the road. The caravan arrives in the historic oasis and former slave market of Kufra, described by William Shaw in his history of the Long Range Desert Group as 'a story-book oasis, unattainable, remote, mysterious, the last goal of all African explorers'.

Half jokingly, Mohammed interrupted. 'You never mentioned Buzeima when we were in Tmissah,' he said to me with a smile, 'you said you wanted to go to Kufra by Rabiana.' I showed him the map, pencilling a line from Tizirbu to Kufra, which passed right next to Buzeima. Going to Rabiana would involve a signifi-cant diversion, I pointed out. Besides, back in Tmissah, none of us knew enough about this part of the desert to discuss the route in such detail. Mohammed made no opposition. He was not familiar with this region of the Libyan Sahara. Having listened to those around him who were, and cast a cursory glance at the map, he concluded the discussion with the words, '*Kaifa tibbi, nimshou li Buzeima*' (As you like, let's go to Buzeima). He was in a good mood now. He knew the end of our trek was in sight: if what Faiz and friends told us was correct, and the maps seemed to confirm it, we would be in Kufra within a week.

Just then, a small man appeared in the doorway. Faiz rose to greet him and introduced him to us. 'This is Abdallah, he is the tourist director of Tizirbu,' he said. He had already heard of our arrival, which was a little ominous. We exchanged greetings and he sat down next to us. A slightly nervous, twitchy man, Abdallah was nevertheless accorded a definite respect by all assembled by virtue of the official position he occupied. During his stay of half an hour he remained largely quiet, breaking his silence only to ask where we were going and from where we had come. Seeing me bite my nails, however, he was suddenly roused to more animated conversation, warning me in great earnest that this was extremely dangerous.

'My God, you must be careful!' he began, grabbing my forearm to rescue the fingernail I was in the process of biting. 'If you do this, you will go to hospital. You must not bite them like that.' He did not explain the disease I might contract, but was convinced I would finish my days in hospital unless I stopped at once. I told him I was sure I would be fine. In any case, I was only biting my nails because I did not have a pair of nailclippers with me. This he could scarcely believe.

'Messaoud,' he said, addressing Faiz's youngest brother, who was acting as gopher for anyone who required his services tonight, 'bring this man some nailclippers at once.' Messaoud looked slightly baffled by this unorthodox request but returned moments later armed with Chinese nailclippers. To assuage Abdallah's fears for my health, I began trimming what was left of my nails. 'Yes, that's good, much better,' he nodded approvingly as I snipped away, 'goodnight.' And with that he was gone.

With practical business finished for the night, the young men reverted to their loud male games, which consisted of joking, arguing and shoving each other about with hearty guffaws. Like Mohammed, both Ned and I were exhausted and wanted to sleep. Apparently impervious to the noise, our Tubbu guide had already retired for the night, shrouded from the world by his black *burnous*. In the other corner of the room, sat Ned, surrounded by a semicircle of tenacious gawkers. He had had enough.

'You know, I'd quite like to go to sleep, too,' he said, looking over at Mohammed.

'Me too, but I don't think this lot is about to leave anytime soon.'

'I think I know what to do,' he went on, looking unusually crafty, 'watch this.'

He reached into a bag and pulled out my copy of Shakespeare's complete works. He paused to survey his audience with a magisterial expression and waited for silence to fall. The young men looked mystified and completely engrossed by the prospect of this new and unexpected entertainment. He found his place, assumed an expression of profound anguish and launched himself into Hamlet's first soliloquy.

> O that this too too solid flesh would melt,
> Thaw, and resolve itself into a dew,
> Or that the Everlasting had not fixed
> His canon 'gainst self-slaughter! O God, God,
> How weary, stale, flat, and unprofitable,
> Seem to me all the uses of this world!

His audience was mesmerized. The novelty of Ned as English-desert-explorer-turned-thespian was irresistible. He raised his eyes to the heavens with a sorrowful gaze. This was the height of human misery and Tizirbu had never seen anything like it. He continued, warming to his theme.

> Fie on't, ah, fie! 'Tis an unweeded garden
> That grows to seed; things rank and gross in nature
> Possess it merely. That it should come to this!
> But two months dead. Nay, not so much, not two.
> So excellent a king, that was to this
> Hyperion to a satyr, so loving to my mother,
> That he might not beteem the winds of heaven
> Visit her face too roughly. Heaven and earth!
> Must I remember? Why, she would hang on him
> As if increase of appetite had grown
> By what it fed on; and yet within a month –
> Let me not think on't. Frailty, thy name is woman!'

None of them understood a word of it. From their expressions, it looked as though the novelty was fast wearing off. Undaunted, Ned showed no signs of stopping. In fact, he was just beginning.

> A little month, or ere those shoes were old
> With which she followed my poor father's body,
> Like Niobe, all tears – why she, even she –
> O God! a beast that wants discourse of reason
> Would have mourned longer – married with my uncle,
> My father's brother; but no more like my father
> Than I to Hercules. Within a month,
> Ere yet the salt of most unrighteous tears
> Had left the flushing in her galled eyes,
> She married. O most wicked speed, to post
> With such dexterity to incestuous sheets!
> It is not, nor it cannot come to good.
> But break, my heart, for I must hold my tongue.

His audience hardly knew what to do. They started looking about the room for someone or something else to occupy their attention and eventually settled on me. Ned continued reading aloud. Horatio, Marcellus and Bernardo had entered. I cringed inwardly as the group of young men relocated and took their places in front of me, patting me on the back, grinning, shouting, pushing and punching each other and delving into my bags to hunt for another gadget. I was too tired for this.

'Yes, I thought that would get rid of them,' said Ned, looking pleased with himself and stretching out on one of the long cushions. 'Nothing like a bit of Shakespeare to get them going.'

'Yes, but now I've got them,' I replied, cursing him.

'Goodnight,' he said, retreating into his sleeping bag with a smile. He looked horribly cosy and within minutes he was asleep. I could have strangled him.

'You bastard,' I said.

Finally, it dawned on Faiz that I was quite keen to sleep, too. To my relief, he herded out all the hangers-on, who left with loud bellows of 'Leila sayeedah' (Goodnight). After they had departed, he stood in the doorway and seemed about to say goodnight himself. Some sort of internal struggle followed, in which curiosity seemed to be the victor. He came back into the room and sheepishly asked if he could have a look at my sleeping bag. By all means, I replied, dreading this obsession with camping equipment. I just wanted to get inside the thing. He picked it up, stroked it lovingly, inside and out, then, before I could say anything, climbed inside, did the zip up around him and nestled snugly inside the hood, from where he waved both hands joyfully. None of this was ill-intentioned, he just wanted to get the most out of our visit. He knew we were only here for a day or two.

'Yes, yes, sleeping bag very nice,' he observed after this scientific test, 'good in desert.'

'Yes,' I replied, my patience wearing thin. 'Sleep would be good too.'

'How much it cost?' he persisted. 'Maybe you sell to me?'

'Sorry Faiz, out of the question. I need it. Anyway, I'm really tired and I'd like to go to sleep now.'

'Maybe you sell knife?' he suggested. He did not give up easily.

'Faiz, let's talk tomorrow.'

'GPS?' I had reached my limits. Mohammed and Ned were both asleep. I was exhausted.

'Goodnight, Faiz.'

'Goodnight,' he said, closing the door behind him.

At last. Silence. I replaced him in the bag and fell asleep instantly.

# CHAPTER XII

# Drama in the Dunes

*Curiously enough after a single day's rest, a fever of restlessness gets hold of one again and the luxury of abundance is left most eagerly for the privations of the road. No matter if it be a big well surrounded by a fertile oasis, full of the comforts of life, one returns with a sigh of contentment to the twelve hours' trek and the lunch of dried dates.*

AHMED HASSANEIN BEY, *THE LOST OASES*

*Buseima is the loveliest oasis I have ever seen, with its strange ruddy hills – jewels purple and crimson reflected in the silver salt mirage which girdles the bluest lake in the world. All this colour is clear cut against the soft, pale dunes. It is seen through a frame of drooping palm branches with perhaps a rose-hued figure, scarlet sashed, guarding a flock of goats by a dark pool among high green rushes.*

ROSITA FORBES, *THE SECRET OF THE SAHARA: KUFARA*

We awoke blissfully late. Even Mohammed was having a lie-in. Apart from watering the camels, procuring more food for them and buying additional supplies – we were running low on tuna again – we had nothing to do today other than rest. Or so we thought.

I looked across the road in front of the house. Faiz was squatting in the sunlight, still wearing his black leather jacket. It looked unbearably hot. He was playing with one of his younger brothers and at the same time keeping an eye on his house for signs of life. I crossed over and he told me he had already watered the camels this morning. They were couched in his back garden, still gorging themselves on their mammoth meal and catching up on all the bleak days behind them. The piles of hay were fast disappearing and the grass around them had been well cropped. All seemed perfectly content. There was no sign of Tuna. She had disappeared during our hectic arrival the night before and had probably decided, after her courageous 400-mile journey across the desert, that Tizirbu was as good a home as any. We never saw her again.

Mohammed joined us in the garden. 'We must take two bales of hay and some more barley with us,' he said. 'The camels are eating well now, but they will still be tired when we leave. They have made a long journey from Ghadames.' Faiz told us that we must register with Abdallah, the tourist director, before leaving. We were reluctant to have any further contact with the authorities but, as we did not want to compromise our host, agreed to see him. We drove off along a terrible piste, past rows of nondescript modern buildings, to a tidy Portakabin a couple of miles away. A large portrait of The Leader was mounted on the roof, slightly askew. Inside, along with various desert scenes, there were more. Abdallah, looking as twitchy and nervous as he had been the previous night, sat behind a desk. It was obvious he had nothing to do. We exchanged greetings.

'Please show me your passports,' he said in respectable English.

'Our passports are with a travel agent in Tripoli, but we have photocopies and a letter explaining why he kept them,' I replied.

He looked confused and rather unhappy. After reading our papers, however, like others before him, he came to the conclusion that if he made a fuss about this breach of protocol he would be in for a tedious spell of bureaucracy. At least Mohammed's papers were in order. As a man of Tizirbu, Abdallah appeared to regard himself as a cut above this nomadic Tubbu tribesman and treated Mohammed with some disdain. We signed a visitors' book and the interview continued.

'You must have a tent to travel in the desert,' Abdallah said abruptly. Whether he intended this as a friendly piece of advice or as a reminder of one of the government's lesser known statutes on tourist travel in the Sahara was not clear.

'Actually, we prefer to sleep in the open air beneath the stars,' I replied.

'I have seen other tourists here. They always have tents.'

'I'm very happy for them. Can we go now please?'

'Yes, a tent is very good in the desert.'

Mohammed winked at us. He did not think tents necessary either. The interview appeared to be over but Faiz had disappeared, leaving us without transport. Graciously, Abdallah offered to drive us into town so that we could finish our shopping. We climbed inside his ancient orange Range Rover, the only one in Tizirbu, the only one we had seen in Libya for that matter. Perhaps it was a mark of his distinction. Whatever it denoted, the vehicle was barely hanging on to life. Threadbare inside and throaty beneath the bonnet, it sputtered to life and we thundered along the dismal road. Outside, passersby watched us admiringly.

We made a round of the shops. Large, cavernous holes in the wall, they were replete with the usual basic supplies and we stocked up on tuna, pasta and a hundred bars of chocolate of various shapes and flavours, including Libyan milk chocolate, which tasted delicious. Smelling good business, the shopkeepers were an affable lot, planting various items in front of us with effusive recommendations of their quality.

'You must try this. This is *zamita*, very good for the desert.'

'Strawberry jam is very delicious.'

'Here, this is the best tuna for you.'

'You will need olive oil. You must buy this one.'

'Pasta is nice dinner for you.'

Oases had come a long way in the last fifty years. I thought of Thesiger's three-day ordeal without food in the Empty Quarter of Arabia. Not wanting to reveal himself as a Christian infidel travelling in the desert, he had waited for his companions to return from a nearby settlement to bring provisions. Miserable with hunger, he had dreamt of the masses of meat they would soon bring. 'Now all we had was this,' he wrote in disgust once they had returned. 'Some wizened dates, coated with sand, and a mess of boiled grain.' We were travelling in luxury.

After we had completed the shopping and rejoined Faiz, he said we must now go to the police station. Our hearts sank again. Was all of this really necessary? Had the authorities been having words with our host? What could the police want? We took leave of Abdallah and reluctantly clambered aboard the family Toyota. At the police station, three officers were playing cards – a favourite activity of Libyan law enforcement officials – while another was preparing tea. It was a pleasant picture of enforced idleness. Faiz and Mohammed explained our lack of passports and a bored policeman took down our details on a scrap of paper, dismissed us with a wave and returned to his game. Delighted with the brevity of the encounter, we drove back to the house.

The camels had been moved into a larger field nearby and were alternately grazing on withered bulrushes – the only vegetation in sight – and striking poses for the benefit of a gaggle of children admiring the animals with their fathers. I looked at them proudly. They seemed to enjoy being the centre of attention, while projecting a studied indifference to their audience. Standing next to each other, they made a handsome sight with their various shades – the thick cream of the three whites, the tousled beige of Asfar and the dark bulk of Gobber. Faiz asked to be photographed with the camels and started patting Bobbles affectionately. Then another of his friends appeared and soon there were more young men than small children, all clamouring for a photograph. Among the crowd, Mohammed had the air of a wise veteran of the desert. It was all very well ogling the camels like this and photographing them, but had anyone else here spent three score years and travelling tens of thousands of miles, perhaps much more, on them? He enjoyed these stops at oases. At the farm next to Wau al Kabir, at Wau an Namus and now here, he had carried himself as a dignified, no-nonsense tribal elder, affable but never vulgar, an elderly man of astounding physical fitness whipping two slack Englishmen into shape.

I asked him later to what he attributed his excellent health. 'My father brought me up on camels' milk and dates,' he replied. 'When he hunted, we had meat. Otherwise we lived only on milk and dates. This is what I have eaten all my life.' I thought of the rubbish we in the West ate and contrasted his simple approach to food – basically dictated by the rhythms of nature – with our elaborate diets. From his perspective, I could sympathize with the distrust of products from the outside world, packaged in tins and jars, whether tuna or coffee or packet soups. He had tried them all and disliked the lot. There was a certain loophole for chocolate, admittedly, and he never refused a bar, but he did insist that there was no contest between chocolate and dates.

During his stay in Ghadames, Richardson had been impressed by the great strength of the Touareg, putting it down to their simple diet, and studying their faecal deposits in wonder.

> These Touaricks are chiefly strong and powerful from drinking camels' milk. They drink it for months together ... not eating or drinking anything else. After they have drunk it for some time, they have no evacuations for four or five days, and these are as white as my bornouse. It is the camels' milk which makes the Touaricks like lions. A boy shoots up to manhood in few years; and there's nothing in the world so nourishing as camel's milk.

Certainly, it had had nothing but salutary effects on Mohammed. He had the frame of a gazelle and the strength of an ox. Almost fifty years older than us, and at an age when many elderly people are either dead, sitting in wheelchairs or clutching walking sticks, he could still walk our socks off without breaking into a sweat, churning across the plains with his wonderful, free-flowing gait. Abd al Wahab had been troubled by a swollen ankle, Salek had complained about his feet and Saleh had moaned about everything. Only Mohammed seemed impervious to discomfort. The moments of irritation or anger – invariably provoked by one of us – were exceptions. A strong, kindly man with dancing eyes, he was an inspirational figure.

The three of us sat outside in the shadow of the family Toyota and Faiz brought out a lunch of roast chicken, rice, tomatoes, tea and soft drinks. It was too hot to sit still and flies descended upon us in droves. Tizirbu was a furnace, just as it had been for the Long Range Desert Group patrol sent here after Allied Forces had captured Kufra in 1941. 'Life in Tazerbo was not pleasant,' remembered William Shaw, in his history of the LRDG. 'The thermometer climbed steadily towards 120 degrees F in the shade; from dawn to dusk the flies were beyond belief; every afternoon it blew a sandstorm; scorpions and snakes added to the hazards of existence.'

A few yards away our clothes lay stretched across a small date palm drying in the sun. The food bag, formerly Ned's overnight grip, latterly an unappetizing mess of sand, spicy sauce, olive oil, kerosene-flavoured melted chocolate, salt, sugar and loose pasta, now lay upside down, cleaned and emptied. Painstakingly, Ned had washed our modest collection of kitchen equipment: the army mess tins, the multi-purpose pot, three tea glasses, an enamel cup, his own crushed aluminium mug, three spoons and forks and the bowl in which Mohammed prepared the daily breakfasts of *zamita*. Even the kerosene stove, which had benefited from Muftah's attentions, was now working. The camels had been fed and watered. So had we. Now we felt the itch to get up and go, the restless urge to return to the desert for the last week to Kufra, the final, elusive oasis of our Libyan journey.

First we had to pass a final evening as chief curiosities in the two-tone sitting room where the familiar crowd had gathered for a farewell dinner and more entertainment. Together we sat with our legs tucked beneath us, eating a thick pea soup from the same bowl, dipping in fresh bread before racing through more roast chicken. The conversation began with a vigorous dispute between two men concerning the exact distance from

Tizirbu to Buzeima, moving on to a vivid re-enactment of the English striker Michael Owen's World Cup goal against Argentina. I spent the next quarter of an hour rolling cigarettes – still considered a mysterious Western luxury – for the crowd. The room was soon deep in swirls of smoke and Mohammed expressed his disapproval of cigarettes without managing to sound like an anti-smoking bore. The men bantered good-naturedly with him.

'Smoking is very excellent,' said one, drawing deeply on his roll-up.

'Ah! These cigarettes are too good, *alhamdullilah*!' agreed his neighbour, turning to me. 'You must show me how to roll one.'

'These things will kill you,' said Mohammed, and the crowd burst into laughter.

While Ned fended off more requests for his Leatherman pocket tool, another of Faiz's friends told tall stories, culminating in the solemn claim that the US Defence Secretary William Cohen had stayed in this house only several days ago. On the other side of the room, Mohammed was recounting tales of great desert journeys, and the younger men listened to him with evident respect. I opened my diary and was instantly surrounded by half a dozen inquisitors desperately keen to know what I was writing. At such times privacy evaporated, but this was only to be expected. Faiz had taken us under his roof for two nights. It was hardly unreasonable for him to want us to sing for our supper.

The next morning, he said he would ride out of town with us before saying farewell. He would not hear of accepting a single dinar for his hospitality, although we had eaten and drunk our way through his family's provisions. 'Maybe I will come to see you in England one day and then I can stay with you,' he said.

It was unlikely he would ever have enough money to make the journey and both of us knew it. The hospitality of the Arab is proverbial. Thesiger described how during his many years living and travelling with the Arabs – a term he understood to include only the inhabitants of Arabia and the tribesmen who had migrated elsewhere but still lived as nomads – he had never been lonely. Men he had only just met would invite him to drink tea with them and later offer lunch and dinner. 'I have wondered sadly what Arabs brought up in this tradition have thought when they visited England,' he wrote in *Arabian Sands*, 'and I have hoped that they realized that we are as unfriendly to each other as we must appear to be to them.' Much has changed, of course, since Thesiger's era and the processes of modernization he so deplored have made definite inroads into Arab culture. But the Libyans, Chadians and Sudanese we met in the Sahara still maintained this ancient tradition of hospitality to strangers. Everywhere we had been our impromptu hosts had welcomed us warmly, no matter how poor the family. In Tripoli, we had dined every night with one of my father's old friends. In Ghadames, Mohammed Ali and Othman had taken us under their wing, as had Salek in Idri, the Sherif family in Murzuk, Muftah in Tmissah and now Faiz in Tizirbu. All had been unstinting in their generosity towards us.

We brought the camels in front of the house for a last drink. They slurped down a little water and then we couched them to be loaded. A steady flow of onlookers started spilling into the road from neighbouring shops and houses and massed around the camels. They were of all ages. Most were small children, dressed in bright ragged clothes and caked in sand from their games. They looked on, mesmerized by these monstrous animals. Bobbles, like a showman playing to the audience, roared terribly when we heaped the heavy water *bidoun*s on to his back, half rising despite the knee hobble, pivoting about violently among the other loads and scattering the throng of momentarily terrified children. Mohammed grabbed his head-rope and tugged down on it with the soothing whisper 'Shh, shh', and the animal sank slowly to the ground with a look of resignation. Mohammed, too, played to the gallery, barking orders at the two of us, showing the crowd what he thought of our pathetic knots by redoing them in brisk businesslike fashion and rearranging loads that we had packed together.

Asfar roared, too, which was unusual for him, when I put on

his saddle. I had never been happy about exchanging saddles back in Tmissah but had done so to end the argument with Mohammed's son about which camel his father would ride. This saddle was of the same design, with a pair of wooden supports on each side shaped like a flattened 'x', but of a much narrower construction. When the rope around his chest was pulled tight, the saddle was now hurting where these supports met, the knobbly junction of the 'x' biting deeply into his hump. We tried the saddle on the other camels but it was too small for all of them. They had gained weight during their stay in Tizirbu. I tied it more loosely and stuffed some hessian cloth beneath the saddle to minimize the discomfort.

'Don't let him carry too much now,' advised Mohammed, who had always admired this camel. 'It will be painful for him and he is getting tired.' He rose to his feet slowly, roaring again. His eyes had lost their shine and he looked by far the weakest of the five.

We set off at last, like the Pied Pipers of Tizirbu with a crowd of perhaps 100 children trotting behind us, desperate not to fall behind, but frightened into keeping a safe distance from the cudgel-like legs that loomed over them. Faiz and another friend were mounted awkwardly on Lebead and The Big White. In black leather jacket and satin bomber jacket respectively, they made a curious picture – urban camel jockeys on an improbable joyride. Padding along the dusty road, we came across the grey concrete skeleton of an unfinished water tower that rose uselessly out of the ground, a familiarly ugly sight in a Libyan townscape.

'It's been like that for three or four years,' said Faiz, watching us stare at it. 'Never finished.' He said it in a tone that implied it never would be. Like Murzuk, Tizirbu needed a dose of urban regeneration.

Their sojourn in the saddle did not last long. Both were visibly uncomfortable and jumped off after less than a mile, wishing us well on our journey. We all shook hands, thanked them again and tramped on through the straggling oasis town with its thin lining of houses and shops that arose in scatters between long stretches of wasteland.

'They are good people, *alhamdulillah*,' murmured Mohammed, 'not like the people in big towns.'

Opposite the red and white radio mast in the town centre, we passed the police station. Two plainclothes men in a car pulled up alongside to intercept us.

'You must come to the police station,' said the driver brusquely.

'We've already been to the police station,' I replied. 'We came yesterday.'

He was not a man who brooked opposition.

'You must come to the police station,' he repeated.

We left the camels standing uneasily outside the building and went inside. One of the policemen went out as we came in. Treating the animals as though they were his property, he started yanking them by their head-ropes. They panicked, roaring with discomfort and kicking out in fear. He responded by jerking them around still more viciously. Ned rushed out and there was an exchange of raised voices. I was shown into an office in which a plain-clothes officer sat behind a desk, preening his resplendent moustache and baring a faded green skull and crossbones tattoo on his forearm. He was shouting orders to two shoddily uni-formed subordinates.

Ned rejoined me and we rehearsed the by now mind-numbing story of why we did not have our passports with us. The officer nodded solemnly. He treated us politely but firmly, and told us he had not been notified of our arrival. There was no reason why he should have been. Libya's dismal telecommunications system seemed to discount the possibility of an advance warning. Ubiquitous and suspicious the Libyan authorities undoubtedly were. Masters of modern technology they were not. He con-tinued, asking where we had come from and where we were headed. He had not come upon tourists on camels before, and was not sure how to proceed. When we mentioned Buzeima, his eyes lit up. 'Ah, Buzeima! I was born there,' he said fondly. 'But now there is no-one living there. Everyone left several years ago. But there is a donkey there,' he added as an afterthought. Think-ing it wisest to avoid politics, I refrained from asking whether this was another of Gaddafi's forced relocation programmes.

He said he would telephone Kufra to inform the authorities there of our imminent arrival. This he tried to do for a quarter of an hour but the office telephones were not up to this formidable task. Eventually, one of the subordinates went behind the desk, tweaked around the confusing spaghetti of telephone wires and tried putting them into different sockets. His juggling had a hit-and-miss aspect to it but seemed to work, for moments later the chief was connected to Kufra and was telling a doubtless bemused police officer at the other end of the line to expect two Englishmen, a Tubbu and five camels in a week. He was in full flow when he suddenly broke off into a volley of full-blooded curses. The line had broken off. I could see Ned's patience desperately close to its limits. He had taken an even more profound dislike to the Libyan authorities than I had, regarding their constant interference throughout our journey as an unacceptable infringement on his rights as a free Englishman and citizen of the world. I tried to calm him.

'We're travelling in their country and it's their law,' I said, sounding like a sententious schoolteacher. 'Anyway, we can't do anything about it.'

'It's totally ridiculous. We shouldn't stand for it.'

'If I were a Libyan policeman, I'd think two Englishmen travelling around the desert without passports were pretty suspicious.'

'It's a complete waste of time.'

'Oh, shut up. Let's just get on with it and get out of here.'

The officer had resumed barking at his subordinates who were now scurrying about behind his desk again trying to fix the telephone. Resigned to a long wait, I was beginning to enjoy this farcical scene. Ned had other, more practical, ideas. No longer able to restrain his English sense of fair play, he asked the officer whether we could leave now. 'We came to your police station yesterday and we've already answered your questions and given all our details, and Taher's contacts in Tripoli,' he said firmly. Taken aback, the chief considered the question for a few moments, and then said, yes we could leave. 'You see, you've got to take a more robust approach with them,' said Ned later, understandably pleased with his efforts. 'You've got to let them know we're not people they can mess around with.' I congratulated him on the success. There was much to be said for the 'more robust approach'.

Mohammed was waiting for us outside. 'Come on, come on, let's go now,' he urged us. 'We must leave. It's late.' We left Tizirbu at two o'clock on 30 January, and walked twelve miles across the blazing plain to the government farm Faiz had mentioned. It was much bigger than those we had seen so far, consisting of a long line of trees massed in a giant rectangle around green fields and several large Portakabins for the workers. We were heading for the south-eastern corner of the settlement when the camels suddenly pricked up their ears and swung round their necks in unison. A car was droning across the horizon. We stopped to watch whether it was going into the farm or approaching us. It grew steadily larger and louder, casting up thin veils of sand as it drew closer.

A smart blue Toyota Landcruiser pulled up next to us and three men got out. They were all Tripolines with tidy uniforms and matching black moustaches. On the doors a legend in Arabic announced them as 'Border Police'. I wondered again at the attention our small caravan was arousing. After a preliminary greeting of 'Salam a'leikum' (Peace be with you) – said with a distinct lack of warmth – they asked us the usual litany of questions, beginning with the request to see our passports. I felt like killing Taher. Blithely, he had told us we could travel around Libya without them. But to be fair to him, he had been in a difficult position, too. As our visas were valid for only a month, they needed to be renewed periodically, and this could only be done in Tripoli. Tourism being an embryonic industry in Libya, no-one had yet considered it worthwhile to issue longer visas.

The most senior of the three policemen spoke efficient English. Once we had settled the paperwork, his overriding objective appeared to be finding out how much our camels had cost. We pretended not to understand the question.

'Dollar, dollar, money, how much?' he insisted, pointing to The Big White.

'It's a secret,' I replied weakly.

He did not like the answer but saw we were in no mood to help him along this particular line of inquiry.

'Why are you travelling by camel?' he continued, as though this was the lowest crime known to mankind.

'Because it's the best way to travel in the desert,' I replied. 'We don't want to go by car.'

'Camels are too slow,' he said with a sneer. 'In one day we can patrol hundreds of kilometres in this,' he said, indicating the Toyota.

'I'm delighted for you, but you should give camels a go. You could patrol the desert on them.' He did not appreciate this last suggestion. They departed with gruff goodbyes and we were alone again.

'The people from the north are different from us southerners,' said Mohammed, who had been equally unimpressed by our latest visitors. A nomad who had spent his entire life in the desert enjoying unrestricted freedom of movement, he had nothing in common with these cold, arrogant urbanites.

We camped on the far corner of the farm and the camels moved into the trees to investigate their new grazing. None of the whites or Asfar appeared particularly excited about what was on offer and only Gobber attacked the foliage with his usual enthusiasm. There was no explaining their strange eating habits. Mohammed, too, said he did not understand why they were not grazing. The next morning, after the customary date feed, I emptied what was left of the previous night's pasta into their plastic bowl and they devoured the lot in moments. Mincing about with their forelegs hobbled, they looked hilarious. Tomato sauce was smeared across their muzzles like smudged lipstick. The three whites appeared particularly camp.

The end of our journey to Kufra was fast approaching, if not quite in sight. Perhaps sensing this, Mohammed kept an increasingly rigorous pace and we covered thirty-four miles across the plains the day after our meeting with the Border Police, another record. On the morning of 1 February, an hour after we had begun the day's march, pulsing dark patterns appeared on the horizon, massed together at one moment and then separating into smaller black fingers the next. This was it: Buzeima, the oasis which had so mesmerized Rosita Forbes, the extraordinary Englishwoman who arrived here with Hassanein Bey in 1921. Together, they had had to use all their powers of persuasion to get their entourage to escort them to Buzeima, and when they did arrive they almost lost their lives. Their guides were all in mortal fear of the inhabitants, who were known to be vicious to visitors.

'They assured me that Buseima was most dangerous, that a particularly savage portion of the Zouiya tribe dwelt there and attacked every strange caravan at sight,' she wrote. By this stage in her journey, she was used to her travelling companions' super-stitions and suspicions. Earlier, there had been problems when she showed too lively an interest in noting down place names in her journal and 'nearly a revolution' when she attached devices to the camels' legs to measure speed and distances. Her compass, too, was thought of as a 'dangerous weapon which might bewitch and destroy their beloved Jedi [pole star] . . . while once we nearly lost our lives by drawing a map in the sand'. To assuage their fears – she herself appeared fearless – the caravan took elaborate precautions on arrival in Buzeima. 'We posted sentinels at night, slept with our revolvers cocked beside us and by day went armed with such an array of weapons that the hostile Zouiya villagers decided we were better left alone,' she reported. It was probably as well they took such safety measures. On leaving Buzeima, she overheard a Zwaya tribesman mutter bitterly: 'You should not escape thus; we had men enough to kill you.'

We walked briskly at the dark shapes on the horizon, our tired limbs quickened by this far-flung goal. No matter how distant, it was a welcome contrast to the usual unbroken emptiness of the plains. As ever, it was impossible to judge distances across these vast flats and Mohammed was uncertain whether we would reach Buzeima that day. But the mere fact of having it there, unmistakably in front of us, was uplifting. 'It is so much easier to march with one's destination distinct before one than to be walking on that flat disc of a desert where every point of the compass looks like every other and the horizon keeps always at the same maddening distance,' wrote Hassanein Bey.

By mid-afternoon we were moving among huge rollercoaster dunes that lay on the plain like beached whales, lifeless but lovely with their gentle contours and subtle shades shifting as the winds played across them. This was the beginning of the wastes of the Rabiana Sand Sea, 350 miles across at its widest, and 250 miles from its northernmost slopes to its southern extremities.

Walking several hundred metres to the right of Ned, with Mohammed at some distance in front of us both, I was leading Asfar and Gobber when the *bidoun* containing kerosene fell to the ground, split, and started leaking into the sand. I couched and hobbled the two camels, poured the remnants of the kerosene into a spare water *bidoun* and rearranged the loads. It took time, and Asfar grew nervous as he watched his companions fade from sight among the dunes ahead. He began to roar and pivot, which only made matters worse for all of us by increasing the delay and transmitting his fright to the usually unflustered Gobber. Within moments I had two frantic, roaring camels on my hands. When I attended to one, the other would try to rise, tugging on the rope that kept them together. It was sheer panic.

I looked up to see where the others were. Mohammed was lost to sight completely. Ned was much nearer. Hearing the commotion behind him, he had stopped following Mohammed and was walking over towards me to see if everything was all right. As the camels had calmed down I waved to him to let him know the problem was over, finished repacking, and walked on bringing up the rear. Far ahead, Mohammed moved in and out of vision, depending upon the changing contours of the land. I kept an eye on his tracks to make sure I did not lose him. He would probably stop, as he usually did, to let us regroup. After another hour or so, Ned had caught up with him. Mohammed had indeed halted. I trailed in, several minutes behind, and arrived to see the two of them rowing furiously.

'*Mish kwayis, mish kwayis*' (Not good, not good), Ned was shouting at Mohammed. With even less Arabic than me, he was struggling to make himself understood to a man who spoke no word of English and for whom Arabic was his second language. He drew a diagram in the sand to show that Mohammed had been walking too far in front of us – which was arguably true – and that he considered this dangerous. Both men's tempers were flaring fast.

'What's not good? Are you saying I'm no good?' Mohammed stormed in Arabic, making neither head nor tail of the picture in the sand. I tried to pour cold water on the conflagration, but both merely looked to me to take their side and continued shouting at each other. For Ned, Mohammed had been guilty of leaving us behind in the desert, which as our guide he should never have done. For his part, Mohammed believed he had been unforgivably insulted by a younger man who should have shown him more respect. 'I always wait for you and your friend to catch up,' he said to me, highly aggrieved. 'I tell you we must go more quickly but you both read books while you ride and then you fall behind.' This was also true. Whoever we were travelling with, Ned and I usually brought up the rear while the guide went out in front.

Another round of '*Mish kwayis, mish kwayis*' followed from Ned. Sensing disaster if the row continued, Mohammed stepped to one side and departed from the fray. He rushed over to me.

'We can't understand each other because he cannot speak Arabic and I do not know English,' he said. 'It is better that I do not talk to him anymore.' He remained standing apart, still holding a camel rope in one hand and seething with the rage of wounded dignity. I tried to pacify Ned but he wanted to see the matter through now and walked over to continue the discussion. Mohammed turned away, determined to avoid having anything further to do with him.

'Come on, Ned,' I said, intervening, 'we can talk about this later when everyone's calmer. There's no point in making things worse.'

It was becoming an ugly scene, made more awful by the vast desolation around us.

'Mohammed!' barked Ned. There was no response. Suddenly, he grabbed at the camel rope in Mohammed's hand, to get his attention. Mohammed, initially startled, then with his anger rekindled, refused to let go of the rope and a tug-of-war began which would have been farcical if not so serious.

'Let go!' screamed Mohammed.

'Let go!' repeated Ned.

'Come on, this is ridiculous,' I said, moving between them. They separated, glowering as though they meant to strike each other. It had all escalated so quickly. Now, no-one spoke.

Seeing the fury on both men's faces, I doubted my powers of reconciliation. The situation called for a man like Lawrence, who, although hardly the consummate diplomat in his dealings with Englishmen, had mediated countless tribal disputes during his time in Arabia. First, I went over to Ned. I told him I was partly responsible for this disagreement, because I had held up the two of them after one of the *bidoun*s had fallen from Gobber's back. Mohammed had certainly been walking too far ahead of us, I agreed, but I understood why and did not hold it against him.

'I can't go on with him any more, Justin,' he said, still enraged, 'not after this. I'm sorry, but I'm going to Kufra alone now.'

'Listen, this is no time to do anything rash,' I pleaded. 'We're all in the desert together and it would be crazy to separate. We've got less than a week to go anyway. Everyone is fired up at the moment. We'll all cool down later. You don't have to talk to each other but please don't go off alone.'

I returned to Mohammed, who was still deeply upset by the confrontation.

'Look at me, I am an old man,' he said, touching his grey beard with his fingers. 'He is a young man and he attacked me. You cannot treat an old man like that.'

He was implacably angry and pathetically wounded. He would

not talk to Ned any more but insisted the three of us continue together. This was the only sensible thing to do. After several more minutes of this shuttle diplomacy, we set off, Ned moving far out to the west, Mohammed taking the eastern flank a hundred metres or so away. I marched in between them for the rest of the afternoon, alternating between both men and dismayed to find Ned still determined to separate from the caravan. I consoled myself with the thought that it was only mid-afternoon. By the time we halted for the night, at Buzeima if we could reach it, several miles before if we could not, passions might have subsided.

We pressed on uneasily. The dunes dipped and rose, and the country began to reflect the gloomy discord of our caravan. The wind picked up, and ponderous grey clouds the shape of funnels massed above, cloaking the jagged silhouette of Buzeima that loomed ahead and spitting flecks of rain into our faces. By the time the sun had fallen, fizzing weakly into the sand sea, Buzeima still appeared out of range for the day. Mohammed suggested to me we stop and the three of us gathered in a hollow at the foot of a giant dune from whose crest the wind – increasing with every minute that passed – was whipping off torrents of sand into our unhappy camp.

Ned came over to me. 'Listen, Justin, I'm really sorry for doing this and I hope you're not too angry with me, but I can't travel with Mohammed after what's happened,' he said. 'I'm still furious with him.'

I could hardly believe it. After going so far together, to split up so suddenly, over something like this, seemed pointless. Ned had been laid-back and good humoured throughout our journey, the best possible companion for a long desert expedition. We had both been irritable and irritating at times but had never had serious disagreements. This was different. The row with Mohammed had been furious. There was bad blood between them now and the pride of both men was at stake.

'Ned, I know you're upset with Mohammed, but we can still go on together,' I said.

He shook his head. I was getting nowhere. It was ridiculous to put his wounded pride above our safety, I continued. Mohammed was angry, too, but was still willing to remain with us. Solo treks across the Sahara were dangerous enough for those who had lived in the desert for years. For Ned, with barely two months' experience, it could be suicidal. Neither of us passed muster as a decent desert navigator, nor did we have enough maps to divide between us. Our passports were in Tripoli and there was only one letter from Taher explaining the lack of paper-work. Besides, we were already so near Kufra that there was no point in separating here. He and Mohammed could simply not talk to each other for the 100 or so miles that remained. It was only a matter of several days. The desert was a big enough place in which two people not talking to each other could travel without getting in one another's way. There was no persuading him.

'I'm really sorry to land you in it like this,' he said, 'but I'm not going on with him. I'm leaving now.' Then he smiled. 'Anyway, after all this time together, it will be good to have a break from each other for a few days.'

Sensing what was about to happen, Mohammed came over. 'If your friend leaves now, I'm going back to Zuweila,' he said solemnly.

I stared at him in disbelief and felt a sudden pit of fear in my stomach, picturing our small caravan breaking off into three separate groups only to be swallowed up by the desert. I looked at both Ned and Mohammed and wondered which of the two men was the more irritating.

Without talking to either of us, Ned started packing for his solo journey. He loaded some water *bidoun*s onto a bemused looking Big White, rummaged through the food bags and snatched a pack of chocolate bars and some tins of tuna. There was still some barley left that we were carrying for the camels and Ned picked it up, only to have Mohammed rise up in front of him and seize the other corner of the bag.

'Let go!' said Ned.

'Let go!' barked Mohammed.

'Stop it!' I shouted.

I had had enough of both of them. They continued tugging at the bag until Ned gave up and started looking for the bag of dates. Mohammed was sitting on it. Another scuffle ensued.

'Let go!' shouted Mohammed.

'He won't let me take the dates,' said Ned.

'You shouldn't be going,' I replied. 'Anyway, if you go now, we won't have a tin opener to get into our tuna. I think it's very mean of you.'

He ignored the remark. Another tug.

'Let go!'

'Get off!'

After giving up on the dates as well, Ned continued with his work. It was hasty packing – he had no stove, no wood and no food for the camels – just the sort of lack of preparation that could lead to disaster. If he pressed on tonight, how would he find where to feed and water the camels in this light? Buzeima was an important stop for them. All were tiring by the day and needed replenishment wherever and whenever available. Mohammed and I sat down, a disconsolate duo in the darkening desert, watching Ned pack his camel. After several more minutes, he came over to me, apologized again for going solo, and set off to leave.

'If you have to go, take two camels,' I said. 'What happens if The Big White dies or has an accident? You've got to have a reserve.'

He attached Bobbles to The Big White and left, climbing up the side of the dune in the thickening, sand-filled drizzle that filled me with dark thoughts. There was something profoundly reckless – and inescapably romantic – about what he was doing.

'See you in Kufra,' he boomed, and disappeared into the black night.

# CHAPTER XIII

# Buzeima

*I'll defy any traveller to write fairly and justly upon the late history of North Africa, without filling his pages with bona fide and well-founded abuse of the French and their works in this part of the world. They emphatically stink throughout Africa.*

JAMES RICHARDSON, *TRAVELS IN THE GREAT DESERT OF SAHARA IN THE YEARS OF 1845 AND 1846*

*There was a real need to know what the enemy was doing in the inner desert. Being Italian he was in fact doing nothing but we were not entitled to gamble on that.*

WILLIAM SHAW, *LONG RANGE DESERT GROUP*

The night was heavy with foreboding. The rain, which had been spitting down on us during the late afternoon, grew heavier. It hurled into our faces, borne by a wind that was now gusting between the dunes at full force. Deep drifts of sand streamed down from the heights into our beleaguered camp and shrouded everything in sight with a gritty blanket. Visibility fell rapidly. The air was a blur of stinging sand and rain. It was the worst storm we had encountered and Ned was out in it alone.

For half an hour Mohammed and I sat without talking, mulling over the sudden and inauspicious change that had befallen us. In the drama of the storm I wondered whether I would ever see

Ned alive again and started imagining the dreadful telephone call to his family informing them of the disaster. I had not stopped him setting out on his own. Although I had attempted to persuade him to stay, I had also stood by helplessly as he left. A better mediator might have prevented his departure. Reaching Buzeima, the last oasis before Kufra, was critical. The camels were deteriorating by the day and now needed fresh supplies of food and water to keep them going. In these conditions, Ned could easily miss the oasis.

The camels reflected the bad omens of the storm. Separated from his two fellow whites, Lebead was inconsolable. He swung around to see where they had gone and roared piteously, filling our camp with a terrible chorus of lament that continued deep into the night. Commiserating with him, Asfar added his own plaintive cries. Both were restless and kept trying to get up. Mohammed and I struggled to control them, tying an extra rope around each of their front knees to prevent them escaping. Only Gobber appeared unconcerned, tucking in to the tiny hillock of barley that Mohammed had put down to calm the distraught animals. He had never been greatly loved or well treated by the whites.

'The other camels never liked him,' Mohammed said quietly, looking at Gobber. 'He doesn't mind them leaving at all.' Wrapped against the storm in his black *burnous*, he looked a crumpled old man, dispirited and exhausted. I had never seen him like this. 'The desert is a dangerous place,' he said. 'It is never good to travel alone like that. You must always have a companion with you.'

At least Ned was a hardy man. If anyone could make it to Kufra alone, he could. He had taken some of the maps with him and still had his own GPS by which to navigate. As far as reaching Buzeima was concerned, if he did not get there tonight, surely he would find it tomorrow. Discovering the source of fresh water was another matter. From afar, Buzeima looked a large, sprawling oasis. The great lake, which had so entranced Rosita Forbes in 1921, contained only brackish water, which the camels would not drink. How would Ned find the solitary well?

The storm grew fiercer still, burying our bags and ruining a vegetarian pasta – the grittiest yet. We erected a barricade of bags, *bidouns*, and saddles, our only protection against the invading sand. As Richardson had advised long before, 'the first thing on encamping is to look for the direction of the wind, and so to arrange bales of goods, panniers, and camel-gear, as to protect the head from the wind. In this way one often lies very snug whilst the tempest howls through The Desert.'

I had a fitful night, with uneasy, dozing thoughts of Ned. Would he try to make Buzeima tonight, in these terrible conditions, or set up camp and hunt for the oasis the next morning? And what about his camels? If they had reacted like Lebead and Asfar, would he, alone, be able to control them in their blind panic? I drifted in and out of sleep, woken constantly by the roaring of the camels and the piles of sand that rushed through the barricade and swept in from all sides, pouring into my sleeping bag and streaming into my eyes, ears, nose and mouth.

We woke early. The wind had dropped and all was quiet. There was no rain, nor any signs of damp. Overhead, the sky was cool and cloudless. Apart from our submerged bags and the sand that caked our clothes and hair and faces, the storm might never have happened. Impatient to reach Buzeima, neither of us bothered with breakfast and we pressed on towards the stirring mass of rock that hung over us like a shadow. Morale was still low. I wondered how Ned had passed the night. Where was he now and was he all right? Would we be able to find him?

We walked for an hour or so and passed into a savage arena of dark mountain ridges. Towering cliffs of Nubian sandstone, dark despite the dazzle of the sun, lay in disorder for several miles around. There was something both awful and uplifting about these shattered cathedrals of rich purple rock, streaked black with iron and manganese, which rose so starkly from the sandy, flint-strewn plain. From such close quarters it was difficult to see how far they stretched. Rosita Forbes estimated the range as a little less than ten miles in length. Moved by the terrible beauty of the place, she described it as 'a veritable inferno of desolation ... it looked as if all the old slates in the world had been flung in careless piles in this dreary region'. There was not a trace of life here, but somewhere among this straggling waste-land of rock there was water and food for the camels. Dwarfed by these ragged cliffs – perhaps 500 feet at their highest – we filed along, pathetically insignificant, searching for the oasis that must be buried somewhere at their feet. Mohammed, who had never been to Buzeima, confessed he did not know where to go. I suggested we penetrate farther into the range. For a quarter of an hour we trod uncertainly over cracking slabs of flint and sank into drifts of sand. I looked around in vain for the tracks of Ned and his two camels. Nothing stirred.

'Over there, look, there it is!' said Mohammed suddenly. 'That's the oasis.' I followed the line of his outstretched finger. Perhaps a mile away on our right, at the most extreme edge of the mountains, was the unmistakable shadow, tinged with green, of a line of date palms. We changed our path and headed towards them, watching the oasis grow larger, opening up with each step we took until we could see a semicircle of trees and, beyond them, a disc of water, shining like a coin in the fury of the sun. As soon as the three camels saw the oasis, they roused themselves to a smarter pace and soon we were passing into its fringes.

Having heard from the tattooed policeman in Tizirbu that Buzeima was now deserted, we did not fear the sort of hostile reception Rosita Forbes's caravan had anticipated eighty years before us. The emptiness of the place, however, was discon-certing. We stopped next to a cluster of palms to pick some of these dates, which for at least a century have been considered the best in Libya. Unharvested, they lay on the ground in thick piles. Those on the trees were large and fleshy, slightly soft and pleasantly sweet. The camels joined in the impromptu fruit-picking, brushing them up from the floor rather than risking a confrontation with the sharp points of the leaves that guarded the dates and made picking them a bloody experience.

Signs of life increased as we went in. Through the layers of date palms we saw occasional wells that had once served small farmsteads. We checked each one, but all were empty and abandoned. At the north-eastern end of the lake, which stretched away on lower ground, was a collection of derelict houses, in much better condition than the deserted old city of Tmissah. Buzeima, it appeared, had been evacuated more recently. We picked our way around solid stone houses, looking for a water source. There were circular stone animal pens, more single-storey houses that would once have been handsome dwelling-places, and another disused well. I felt like a time-traveller walking through this forgotten village. The outlines were all here. Everything was ready, poised for action. It just lacked life. The screams of children, the babble of gossip and the chorus of animals had all passed away. All that remained were these solid testaments to times past. And soon, presumably, to judge by the deterioration we had seen everywhere else – from Ghadames to Idri, Germa, Murzuk, Zuweila, Tmissah, and now here – these too would crumble away and the village of Buzeima would disappear forever.

'What do you want to do?' asked Mohammed. 'I think we must keep looking for water for the camels and once we have found it, *inshallah*, they can feed later.' His plan was to feed and water them for several hours while we had lunch and then continue later in the day towards Kufra. After we had exhausted all possibilities of water in the empty village, we made our way around the lake, descending on to a rim of sand that bordered it. The water lay to our left, partially obscured by thick banks of bulrushes with their feathery caps shifting in the breeze. In one place, a path had been trodden between them and I followed it down to the lake, taking the plastic bowl with me to test the brackish water on the camels. 'I don't think the camels will drink it, but you can try,' said Mohammed doubtfully.

A thick white scum floated on the surface, bobbing about as I filled the container. The water itself was cool and clear. When I returned, Asfar was couched on the grass nibbling on some stems. I set the bowl in front of him. He sank his muzzle into the water and sucked down a deep draught. He rose instantly with a start, coughed and spat it out in disgust. It was no good. We would have to find the well. We continued without success for another hour, making our way around the lake and looking around the deserted farmsteads. In one, there was a well with a trace of water in it but heaps of rubbish had been thrown in and it looked rank. Eventually, with obvious dissatisfaction, Mohammed suggested we call off the search. 'I don't know where we can find water here,' he admitted, 'but we should let them feed now or they'll have no food either. You make lunch and I'll collect dates to take with us for the camels.'

It was not ideal but there was nothing else for it. We could carry on wandering around the oasis, with no guarantee of finding the well, or stop to let the camels graze properly before we pressed on. We halted at a patch of grass fifty yards from the edge of the lake, unloaded the camels and hobbled their forelegs. Taking a bucket with him, Mohammed disappeared up a hillock studded with date palms, while I scrounged for wood and lit a fire. Of the three camels, Gobber ate with obvious relish and Lebead with little interest. Asfar ignored the green grazing entirely and devoted himself instead to ridding the ground of dates. Down they went, swallowed whole and in great numbers.

Like Rosita Forbes's camels when they arrived in Buzeima after their long trek from the coastal town of Ajdabiya, ours were much thinner now. Not finding sweet water for them here was a blow. This was our fourth day out of Tizirbu and we were still a hundred miles or so north of Kufra. Since Tmissah, it had been slim pickings, and they had already had to travel eight waterless days from Wau an Namus to Tizirbu. They were still holding out, but as Mohammed Ali would have said, they were no longer in 'good condition'. Where was the famous Ain Nasrani (Christian Well), named after the probable camp spot of the pioneering German explorer Gerhard Rohlfs, who 'discovered' Buzeima in 1879? According to Rosita Forbes, there was only one fresh spring along the lake, but as this continued for several miles – she estimated it as five miles long, today it was much less – finding it was a thankless task. And what about Ned? Where was he now, and had he managed to find food and water for his camels? If Mohammed and I together had failed to find the spring, the chances of him doing it alone with two frightened camels was even more remote. What state would they all be in now? Had they got lost?

To distract ourselves from these grim thoughts, we turned to lunch, a spicy pasta soup and several glasses of tea. We sweated silently in the sun and beat off the hordes of flies that swarmed all over us. The camels finished their lunch and stood idly by. Behind them, the view was spectacularly beautiful. The lightly swaying bulrushes with their bright green stems and soft grey tufts jostled with the overhanging branches of dipping date palms. Behind them lay the cool blue flatness of the coin-bright lake, brilliantly reflecting in its waters the great ramparts of warm stone that rose beyond them in sweeping concaves. There was no sign of man here. Nothing disturbed the silence of the desert. There had been something ghostly about the village of Buzeima. Not here. On this side of the lake, all was serenity.

Lunch came to an end and we rounded up the camels. Asfar had returned to his deep-pile carpet of dates and was guzzling them down with a comic urgency. The sun was fierce and filled me with lassitude. Ned's departure and our failure to water the camels had dented our spirits. I took a south-easterly bearing and we set off into the dunes.

'Look! What's that?' asked Mohammed, as we made our way through the fringes of the oasis. He was pointing to something on our left. Several hundred metres away, I could barely make out a flicker of white in front of a cluster of date palms.

'I can't make it out. It's too far away,' I replied. We walked towards the bright shape. After a few more minutes, I could see it was a white camel feeding on palms, apparently alone. I thought nothing of it. Perhaps a farmer had brought his camels here to feed and water them.

'It's your friend,' said Mohammed suddenly. A *jalabiya*-clad figure was moving to and fro in front of the camel, poking the upper reaches of a palm tree with a branch to bring down the hanging parcels of dates. Whoever it was noticed us approaching but continued with his job. It was Ned.

'Please don't say anything to him,' I asked Mohammed, as we continued walking towards them. 'Let me do the talking.'

'I'm not going to say a single word,' he said calmly. 'But it is better for the three of us to travel together to Kufra from here.'

Diplomatically, he stopped twenty yards short of Ned, allowing me to go on alone. Ned had a studied air of independence. Once he had travelled in a small caravan with guide and companion. Those days were long gone. Now, he was the self-contained solitary desert explorer. I approached him and made some small talk about date-picking to break the ice of our estrangement. Mohammed and I had failed to find any water in the oasis, I told him.

'There's some over there,' he replied casually, pointing to the edge of the lake ten yards away, 'I've already watered the camels and had a swim.'

We compared notes on the eighteen hours we had spent apart. He had continued for about three miles last night, he said, and arrived in Buzeima shortly before us this morning. Here, he had been invited to a breakfast of tea and nougat by a couple of men he met, who had driven in from Kufra to collect dates. Perhaps they had pointed out the well to him.

'*Maya kwayis*' (Good water), he said pointedly to Mohammed, gesturing towards the elusive source of fresh water. Mohammed walked off down the slope of sand to investigate it, leaving me to embark upon a second round of diplomacy. Ned and I stumbled across several embarrassed silences until I asked him directly.

'Why don't you come with us? We may as well go on together, now that we've met here. It would be stupid to separate again. You and Mohammed don't even have to talk to each other.'

'You know, I'm really quite enjoying travelling on my own,' he replied.

'It's only for a few more days then we're in Kufra and Mohammed goes home.'

'I really think you should have a swim,' came the reply. 'The water's fantastic.' He recommended a good half-hour floating on the lake.

'I couldn't care less about swimming, Ned.'

Nor could he. He only wanted me to swim so he could then make his getaway alone.

'Listen, you and Mohammed can walk miles apart and you hardly have to see each other, let alone talk.'

He hesitated. It was in the balance. And then, after what felt like an age, he relented. 'Of course, I'll come with you,' he said. 'It would be silly not to. Anyway, now that I've pointed out the well to him, I feel much better.'

I walked over to Mohammed, who was watering all five camels from the plastic basin. 'We're going together,' I said.

'Come on then, let's go,' he replied, and we were off once again, Ned bringing up the rear at a discreet distance. He still felt angry about the argument with Mohammed and felt no great urge to speak to him for the time being. After the drama of the separation, I felt huge relief the caravan was back to its full complement. It did not matter that we had not spotted Buzeima's only inhabitant, the eccentric donkey mentioned by the policeman in Tizirbu.

The dunes here were the largest we had come across. Frequently, I arrived at the crest of one to see Mohammed several steps down from me on the steep face, trying to encourage Lebead down with a few words and then pulling him hard by the nosering when that failed. His camel, frightened by the severity of the gradient, would dig in for as long as possible until it seemed that surely his nose would give way. And then, the giant would lumber into action, roaring, sliding and skidding his way down in deep swathes of sand, making a path of sorts for the others to follow. From the summits of the highest dunes, we caught glimpses of two great stacks of black rock that rose from this milky white sand sea like floundering shipwrecks – apart from the retreating features of Buzeima the only landmarks to disturb this sun-bleached monotony. These were the outlying ridges of the Buzeima Gara. Their names, Rosita Forbes was told, were Gor Sibb al Abid and Saar al Khaddama.

Crossing these dunes was a tiring business. It was unsatisfactory to ride because the camels descended so painstakingly and the slopes were usually far too steep for them to carry a man without collapsing. Riding through this sort of terrain required repeated mounting and dismounting, which would only slow us down. Occasionally, the dunes subsided into less vertiginous stretches and then the three of us would clamber on to our tiring beasts. In the early evening, I swung on to Asfar and waited for him to lurch up on first two, then four legs. Usually, it was automatic. As soon as you hit the saddle, he would be up with a roar. Now, he did not move. Suddenly, with a pitiful whimper that was intended as a roar, he flopped heavily onto his side, still kneeling, trapping my leg underneath him for a few seconds until I wriggled free. After I had got up, I looked at him. The eyes were losing their lustre and he was the weakest I had ever seen him. He did not look in good sorts at all. The worst thing about it was that we could do nothing to help him, apart from remove his load and feed him a few dates. There was nothing else we could give him.

'He's very tired now,' said Mohammed. 'He needs a long rest. When we get to Kufra, *inshallah*, you must rest all of them for a week and feed them properly.'

'Do you think he'll die before we reach Kufra?' I asked.

'*Inshallah*, he will be all right, but now he has lost his strength.'

That night we had one of our quietest dinners. Ned and Mohammed maintained a civilized chilliness towards each other. Passing a bar of (kerosene-flavoured) chocolate or a glass of tea was allowed, perhaps a muttered '*shukran*' (thank you) in return, but no conversation of greater length. Instead, they competed persistently for my attention, not because I was more entertaining than usual, but to demonstrate they could manage quite happily without each other. Some of this was amusing, but it was also irritating. Neither of them was prepared to unload the same camel together, for example, since this required the exchange of a few words. Instead, they both insisted on working with me and me alone, which meant I did double the work and things took much longer than usual. I began to understand why middlemen get paid so well.

The next day was 4 February, two months to the day since we had left Ghadames. We woke to a strange milky landscape in which sky and dunes almost merged. The sun, usually so strong and naked, was a veiled disc, pale beneath a bed of cloud. It cast a wan, ethereal light over the sand sea and made the dunes, newly naked after another night of sweeping winds, appear softer still. Not a single car track or a camel trail disturbed this unearthly kingdom that stretched out in cream curves as far as the eye could see for 360°. In mid-morning, the dark silhouette of a ragged mountain range jutted out of the froth, and Mohammed said we were approaching the end of the Rabiana Sand Sea, which meant that Kufra was close. The range in front offered little clues as to its distance from us. It could have been a matter of several hours, or a day and a half away. It was impossible to tell, but it did not matter. We were almost there. I felt a deep thrill, mounting with every step we took, as we closed in on our longed-for goal: Kufra, the fabled oasis deep in the Libyan Sahara. Ghadames, where we had started the journey, felt a world away, both in time and space.

The sun roused itself from this misty stupor, frazzling the massed clouds around it and shining relentlessly once again. By mid-afternoon we passed into a rage of rocks, here crowded together haphazardly, there tapering off into the plain in layers like a neatly arranged row of giant's boots, each one a paler shade than the last. Rocks to the north-east and south-west framed our departure from the sand sea. Some rose to sharp points, others were decapitated to the same level, and were dappled in shadow. Others were blown a gritty gold with sand. Through this gravelly corridor we marched, filled with awe at the grandeur of this new scenery. Where water had once flowed, lazy 's' shapes etched into the plain meandered prettily around us. The dunes gathered themselves for a final assault on their old adversary, surging forward in waves, and then sputtered out into spitting dribbles of sand that faded first and finally disappeared altogether from the barren grey of the plain. We droned on through the plateau and came to the foot of a pass that slanted away from us towards Kufra. At the top, we turned and gazed back on the roiling rocks and dunes and said farewell to the sand sea for the last time. It was a picture I would never forget.

Here, too, on this higher ground, nature had decorated with abandon, carelessly strewing boulders the size of cars across the desolate plain. A *wadi* twisted uncomfortably between these obstacles and led us to a small patch of grazing, where we paused to let the camels feed without unloading them, although there was not enough foliage here to justify staying longer than a quarter of an hour. Methodically, they made their way through this frugal snack, moving from scrap to scrap and cropping whole mouthfuls of wizened herbage. We continued through the ranks of boulders for another half an hour until we came to another *wadi*, flanked by small hillocks, that stretched away from us to the south. Here the grazing was a little more plentiful and Mohammed suggested we stop for the day. It was only 4.30, but all the camels were moving slowly now. Asfar looked as though he was giving up the ghost. We hobbled their forelegs and turned them loose at the foot of the *wadi*, watching them wander off awkwardly into the distance – following the irrepressible Gobber as usual – and wondering why they did not stop to eat instead. After a preliminary tasting of the shrubs – exactly the same as those they had ripped at so hungrily only minutes before – they abandoned this early dinner and shuffled off towards freedom.

Asfar struggled to keep up with the caravan the next day as we wound our way through this rough playground of boulders. His legs were less steady now and he wobbled, tripping repeatedly on small rocks that before he would have carefully avoided. Several times he gashed the back of his forelegs with misplaced hoofs and both ankles were bleeding. When the three of us stopped to discuss the route to Kufra, as we did several times that day, he sank heavily to the ground while the other camels rested standing up. When it was time for us to move on, he rose only with difficulty, swaying uncertainly, punch-drunk with what I assumed to be exhaustion. His eyes were listless. It was just as well we were closing in on Kufra because he could not last long in this condition. I encouraged him forward with several flicks of the rope but his strength was fading fast. Nachtigal, the German traveller, had a similar problem south of Murzuk, when lack of food and water began to take its toll on his weary camel. 'Twice, despite my blows, my exhausted animal laid his weary limbs down under a tree, and twice, by redoubling the whipping, I succeeded in rousing the poor creature forward.' In this state, Asfar was not fit to carry me and we reduced his load to little more than the saddle. It was a sad sight to see this animal, so elegant and fleet-footed when well fed and watered, reduced to being dragged along by a taut rope at the back of the caravan. He was keeping up with his colleagues only with great difficulty and they themselves were in poor shape.

Having noticed Asfar's unusual refusal to join the morning date feed and watching his occasional loss of balance and apparent dizziness, Mohammed changed his diagnosis. 'He's sick from all those dates he ate in Buzeima,' he said expertly. 'Did you see, he didn't eat much of the grass or palm leaves there? All afternoon he was eating dates from the ground. He'll be all right once he has rested and eaten properly, *inshallah*, but it's not good for him to eat like that. Camels should never eat too many dates.'

Hassanein Bey had carried dried dates to feed his camels during his 350-mile trek from Jalo to Kufra in 1923, because there was no grazing en route. But before setting out, the camels were allowed to feed on green food for several days. Dates, said his camel men, were 'hot on the liver'. Marvellously versatile though camels are, there is no substitute for fresh grazing, particularly if they are travelling long distances each day. Asfar had binged on dates and was now suffering as a result.

We picked our way through patches of flint and gypsum and glimpsed the tiny outline of a radio mast erected on a prominent mountain, perhaps twenty miles away. In the afternoon, rounding a shoulder of rock, we caught sight of a distant smudge of green, supine on the slightly lower ground of the plain before us. 'That is Kufra,' said Mohammed, pausing with his three camels to study the prospect. He climbed a stout hillock behind us for an improved view, but returned saying he could not see anything more than the distant blur. We would camp outside Kufra tonight and make our entrance the following morning. The joy of reaching our long dreamt-of destination was offset by the fear that we were in a race against time to save Asfar. Mohammed, too, was looking forward to our arrival. He had only seen Kufra once, almost forty years ago, but still had some family here, including a nephew whom he was hoping to see. At dusk we came across a mini-oasis of date palms, the last chance of food, it appeared, before the town. The darkening mass of green, from which pinpricks of light were beginning to glisten, lay flat ahead of us, so close it seemed to be encircling us, though it was almost ten miles distant. The sounds of cars or lorries filtered out across the plain and the sky above glowed faintly with the orange neon of urban life.

The camels perked up on seeing the green fodder and, once unloaded, attended to it with gusto. Ned and I couched the still wobbly Asfar and were about to remove his saddle when he keeled over again. He kicked weakly at the air, trying to right himself in vain. The two of us had to lever him up into a sitting position, where he remained for several minutes with an expression of insurmountable weariness, as though he had lost the will to live. I asked Mohammed if I could give him most of our water as Kufra was now only several hours away. 'Yes, give it to him,' he replied, 'but keep the other camels away because they are also thirsty.'

I walked a few yards away to empty two ten-litre water *bidoun*s into the basin. Hearing the sloshing, the four more mobile camels tried to muscle in. Ned and Mohammed fended them off with a chorus of grunts. I led Asfar to the basin where he sank his muzzle into the water and swallowed twenty litres in a matter of seconds. It must have had some positive effect because he appeared to regain his appetite, and teetered over to join his colleagues grazing on the palms. He chewed thoughtfully for a while, turned round, slumped to his knees and promptly fell over again. Apart from righting him, there was nothing else we could do tonight. 'You should sleep next to him,' said Ned. 'He might fall over again in the middle of the night and he won't be able to get up on his own.'

The three of us, exhausted ourselves, lay on our backs while the teapot boiled on the fire, our heads tilted to the stars. We talked about the camels, about travelling in the desert, about Kufra and the famous religious Order of the Sanusiya that had once had its headquarters here, presiding over entire swathes of the desert from what is now Libya to Arabia and the Sudan. 'You mustn't talk about the Sanusi in Kufra,' Mohammed warned me. Once synonymous with resistance to Italian rule in the 1920s, the Sanusi today were associated with the reign of Sayed Amir Mohammed Idris as Sanusi. Libya's first king on independence in 1951, he was later deposed by Muammar al Gaddafi in the revolution of 1969. 'Today, there are not many Sanusi left in Kufra or the rest of Libya,' said Mohammed. 'Many of them went to Egypt or other countries.'

It was fascinating to enter Kufra – a city once ruled by the Tubbu – with our own Tubbu guide. The Tubbu had been defeated by the Zwaya tribe of Badawi in the early eighteenth century, which then used Kufra as the base for its notorious brigandage against caravans passing along this, the most easterly of modern Libya's three trade routes between Sudan and the Mediterranean coast. By the close of the nineteenth century, the Zwaya had in turn given way to the Sanusi and the pillaging and extortion came to an end.

The history of the Sanusi is one of the most romantic – ultimately tragic – stories of the Sahara. It pits the relentless march of 'progress' in the form of European conquest and colonialism on one side, and an austere religious confraternity, made up of proud desert dwellers, on the other. The story begins across the waters of the Red Sea in the Arabian desert, where in 1837

Sheikh Mohammed ibn Ali as Sanusi, known as the Grand Sanusi, established the Order. It was an Islamic revivalist movement, a fiercely orthodox order of Sufis, 'an ascetic confraternity, opposed to all forms of luxury or of ceremonial, intolerant of any intercourse with Jew, Christian or infidel', according to Hassanein Bey. Its objective was to 'remind the negligent, teach the ignorant and guide him who has gone astray'.

Born in Algeria in 1787, Mohammed ibn Ali was a Berber whose family claimed descent from the Prophet. A lengthy education took him to the celebrated Qairwan University in Fez in 1821 and later to Mecca and Medina on the Arabian peninsula. Here, his hatred of both Christian and Turk developed as he preached a return to a primitive, uncorrupted form of Islam to the Bedouin tribes of the Hijaz and Yemen. He dedicated his life to upholding Islam against the increasing encroachments of the European powers on North African soil. He regarded the Ottoman empire, flabby and decaying after 500 years, as a poor defence against these incursions by the infidel, and by 1841 he had alienated both the older sheikhs of Mecca, who suspected his orthodoxy, and the Turkish administration, which feared the firebrand's increasing appeal (in 1852 he excommunicated the Sultan). The renegade evangelist was obliged to relocate once more.

Beginning in Mecca, and spreading soon after to North Africa, the Grand Sanusi and his growing band of followers established a network of zawias, religious lodges in which travellers could rest, receive religious instruction and even trade. The first zawia in Libya was founded at Al Beda in 1844. More followed as the Grand Sanusi travelled farther west to Tripoli and Tunis. In 1856, he founded a zawia at Jaghbub in north-eastern Libya, around 150 miles south of Tobruk. This small settlement became the seat of the Order, out of reach of both Turkish and French interference. It commanded a strategic position, straddling a key Saharan trade route as well as sitting on the main pilgrimage road from north-west Africa to Mecca. Here, the Grand Sanusi and the ikhwan, the active 'brothers' of the new Order, embarked on their mission of civilizing the region and establishing peace between the warring tribes. From this unremarkable oasis, the Sanusi spread their influence far and wide. Their cultural contribution was impressive and the university in Jaghbub became the second most important in Africa, after Al Azhar in Cairo. The *ikhwan* set about the conversion of their fellow men with vigour and were ingenious at finding ways to propagate the Order's teachings. Henri Duveyrier, the nineteenth-century French explorer, recounted the curious story of the Grand Sanusi's purchase of an entire caravan of slaves en route from Wadai via Jaghbub to the coast. He subsequently freed them, gave them religious instruction and dispatched them back to Wadai as his missionaries.

The *ikhwan* in Jaghbub survived on an annual supply of goods sent from fellow *zawia*s in the eastern Libyan province of Cyrenaica, and revenues extracted from the regular flow of caravans. Ascetic they may have been, but the Sanusi were no fools when it came to business. Nor were they at all reticent about participating in the slave trade itself. Such was the Order's success in mediating age-old tribal disputes – particularly water and grazing rights – that the fearsome Zwaya tribe, which had so terrorized Rosita Forbes's party, sent a deputation from Kufra to Jaghbub offering allegiance. If the Grand Sanusi came to Kufra, said the Zwaya, the tribe would forego its raiding and pillaging activities and make over a third of its property – including palms and water rights – to the Order. A Sanusi deputation duly went south and the first *zawia* was established in the village of Al Jof.

Under the leadership of Sheikh Mohammed's eldest son, Mohammed al Mahdi (the position was hereditary), the Order grew impressively throughout the Sahara. *Zawia*s sprang up in the Libyan provinces of Cyrenaica, Sirte, Tripolitania and Fezzan, and further afield in Egypt, Algeria, Tunis, Morocco, present-day Chad and Niger, and as far south on the Atlantic coast as Senegal. These were in addition to the score that remained active on the Arabian peninsula.

In 1895, al Mahdi moved the headquarters of the Order south to Kufra. As a base from which to continue its religious teachings and earn revenues from the caravan traffic, the position of this small oasis was unsurpassed. By the late nineteenth century, the trade route running north from Wadai to Kufra to Benghazi on the Mediterranean coast was pre-eminent among Saharan trade links. Manufactured goods and smuggled arms – particularly muzzle-loading muskets – went south into the Sahara, slaves went north. As the historian John Wright wrote: 'If guns were used to acquire slaves (largely by inspiring terror in people wholly unused to them), slaves were used to acquire guns, by providing the most acceptable exchange for imported weapons. In 1907 one slave from Wadai was the exchange for an 1874-model French rifle in good condition, with forty cartridges included.' The Sanusi encouraged the arms trade both for commercial reasons and as a way of assisting their followers in the Sudan to resist the encroaching French in the 1890s and beyond.

Estimates suggest that around two million black slaves were exported to North Africa and the Middle East during the nineteenth century, of which one million came from the Upper Nile and Ethiopia and one-third of a million from East Africa. The remaining 650,000 were hauled across the Sahara from the Sudan. (These figures are dwarfed by the number of slaves exported to the United States from West Africa during that time.) Many of these unfortunate men, women and children died en route. Many passed through Kufra on the way to Benghazi. Few, if any, places in the desert could compete with Kufra in terms of its remoteness from European or Turkish interference and its great economic potential. By ending the Zwaya pillaging of caravans, by establishing peace and order throughout the region, by sinking wells and promoting agriculture, the Order brought a new civilization to the desert and helped the caravan trade grow from strength to strength.

The Order was originally resolutely apolitical. In 1884, the year in which General Gordon was killed in Khartoum by the forces of the Sudanese Mahdi, his conqueror sent a request for Sanusi help in ridding Egypt of its British masters. The Grand Sanusi would have nothing to do with it. While the Europeans pressed no farther into the African interior, there was room for the Sanusi to breathe. But it was clear that greater penetration constituted a profound threat to the Order, and indeed threatened to embroil the ascetic *ikhwan* in the secular world of international politics and possibly warfare. The French led the way. Extending their tentacles throughout the continent, they fast emerged as a direct challenge to the Sanusi monopoly of desert trade in the region, the bedrock of the Order's influence and power since it had no army of its own. By 1899, reversing the traditional Sanusi policy of neutrality, al Mahdi was organizing parties of the Aulad Suleiman, Touareg, Zwaya, Tubbu and Majabra tribes against the French. In 1902, al Mahdi died, leaving his successor Sayed Ahmed to lead the Sanusi into a bitter half century of decline. In the same year, the French captured Bir Alali, in 1906 Kawar and Bilma, and a year later occupied Ain Kalak, killing the sheikh of the Sanusi lodge, the Order's most senior Saharan missionary. All this, of course, was half a century after Richardson's time, but there is little reason to suppose he would have altered his conviction that the French 'emphatically' stank throughout Africa. One wonders what he would have made of the Italian Fascists, whose exploits in Libya left their own stench of cruelty.

The Sanusi were beginning to be hemmed in. In Europe, the great powers were carving up Africa. As the last country to join the scramble, there was little left for Italy with the exception of Turkish Libya. The Italians declared war in 1911, prompting the young Benito Mussolini, who would soon emerge as a delusional, bloodspilling Roman emperor *par excellence*, to observe that 'every honest socialist must disapprove of this Libyan adventure. It means only useless and stupid bloodshed.' Bloodshed there was, and much of it at Mussolini's behest. The Turks did not last long, but the Sanusi were another matter. Fighting for their homeland, their resistance under Omar Mukhtar was heroic and forced the Italians to spend twenty hard years bringing the country to heel. Ultimately, the Sanusi were doomed against the mightier Italian forces that had been instructed to fight a *'guerra senza quartiere'* (war without quarter). Rodolfo Graziani, Vice-governor of Cyrenaica, was bringing Mussolini's 'Western civilization' to Italy's 'Fourth Shore'. 'Butcher Graziani', as he was known, favoured such expedients as closing mosques and *zawia*s, rounding up the entire tribal and livestock population of Cyrenaica into mass concentration camps behind barbed wire and machine guns, conducting summary arrests, deportations and executions, poisoning wells, and sending men to die slow deaths in salt pans.

The Sanusi had already lost territory to the French and in Libya were seeing their sphere of action compressed into the provinces of Fezzan and Cyrenaica. Fezzan fell, and the Italians now looked to the final Sanusi stronghold of Kufra. Its capture embodied their genius for appalling brutality combined with moments of strategic brilliance. Attacking the remote oasis with camel convoys and mechanized columns, they routed the defensive garrison at al Hawari on 19 January, 1931. The following day the Italian flag was flying over Sanusi headquarters. Instructions were given to cut down the fleeing inhabitants without mercy. From Kufra, the hapless Bedouin had little chance of reaching safety. All four escape routes – to the Egyptian oases, to Siwa, Jebel Ouenat or Tibesti – required crossing vast distances of waterless desert. In times of peace, these were all dangerous journeys. In the midst of war, when the tribesmen had no time to prepare for such a hazardous expedition, they were suicidal. Bombed from the air and machine-gunned on the ground, Sanusi guerrillas and civilians alike went to their deaths.

Kufra had fallen. It remained only for the Italians to capture Omar Mukhtar, the sage-like leader of the Sanusi guerrillas. He was eventually taken, interrogated and, after a trial lasting thirty minutes, sentenced to death. On 16 September 1931, he was hanged in front of 20,000 prisoners of the Soluk concentration camp and the resistance was on its knees. The following year it was over.

The Italians only had a decade to enjoy the fruits of their success. The Second World War brought fighting back to Fascist Libya and, by 1941, Kufra was under attack again, this time by Free French forces operating alongside the British Long Range Desert Group. No longer important as a caravan centre, the town nevertheless retained its strategic importance in Allied thinking. Secure from attack to the north and east, and with good communications to the coast, it was only three days' drive from Wadi Halfa on the Nile. If the Italians could build up a sizeable force in Kufra, the Allies feared, they would be able to wreck the dockyard in Wadi Halfa, sink steamers and destroy the railway line connecting Egypt with Sudan.

Under French command, two LRDG patrols attacked from the northern Chadian base of Faya, 565 miles from Kufra. After repeated skirmishing, the Italians lost heart and on 1 March a white flag fluttered over the fort. In the signal room, Allied forces found a copy of the commander's last message: 'We are *in extremis*. Long live Italy. Long live the King Emperor. Long live the Duce. Rome I embrace you.' As Shaw dryly observed: 'Positions are not held on such stuff as this.' The Italian adventure in North Africa was over. Ten years later, on 24 December 1951, independence was proclaimed and Sayed Amir Mohammed Idris as Sanusi became King of Libya.

As we lay outside this celebrated oasis, I recalled Shaw's own excitement on entering Kufra victorious: 'For a desert enthusiast like myself the first sight of Kufra was a never-to-be-forgotten event. For Kufra, till the Italians took it, was a story-book oasis, unattainable, remote, mysterious, the last goal of all African explorers.'

Contemplating our own arrival, my thoughts were interrupted by the drone of an engine. It got progressively louder until we could see the beam of its headlights slicing through the night in front of our camp. After a while moving across the plain that separated us from Kufra, the car swung round, and the headlights caught us in their glare. As soon as we had been illuminated, the lights bore down on us steadily. The car circled the camp and came to a halt several yards away.

Two men in their early twenties descended and walked towards us, carrying Kalashnikovs and wafting a thick stream of hashish smoke into our camp. They stumbled and tripped their way through our scattered loads, giggling inanely. They were Libyan soldiers on desert patrol. Already stupefied by smoking joints, they looked completely staggered by the sight of two tourists camping in the desert with a caravan of five camels and an elderly Tubbu guide. One wore a natty skullcap and a dark corduroy jacket over army desert fatigues. His moustachioed colleague sported a black canvas bomber jacket over several layers of other coats, shirts and jumpers and khaki combat trousers. Both carried their guns nonchalantly, although you could see they were trying to appear as serious and businesslike as possible, a worthy endeavour for which their evening smoking binge had ill-prepared them.

'Can we see your passports?' grinned the man with the skullcap.

I rehearsed the usual story and noticed that within seconds he was no longer listening.

'What are you doing with camels in the desert?' asked the man with the moustache, not wanting to be left out.

'We're travelling to Kufra,' I replied.

He was no longer looking at me or listening, either. Instead, he was staring, with the same look of crazed wonderment in his eyes, at our camels, at Mohammed, and at our bags strewn across the ground.

'Please sit down and have some tea with us,' I said.

Both declined politely and promptly sat down around the fire.

'Is there anything you need?' asked the man with the skullcap, as he slowly found his bearings. 'I can bring you anything you want – bread, sugar, tea, pasta.'

'It's very kind of you,' I responded, 'but we have everything we need.'

'I can bring you anything,' he repeated. 'Maybe you want some whisky or hashish?'

'No thank you,' I replied, wondering at the entrepreneurial flare of this Libyan soldier-cum-drug-dealer-cum-bootleg-alcohol-salesman. He looked disappointed at this missed business opportunity and started inspecting our belongings.

'Can you give me this as a present?' he asked, lovingly fingering Ned's Leatherman pocket tool, the same piece of equipment that had been so admired in Tizirbu.

'Sorry, but we need that, it's our only one.'

'What about this? Can I have this?' he continued, lifting up the GPS.

'Sorry, we need that too.'

He made his way through various pieces of equipment, asking the same questions and receiving the same answers. Unfortunately, we had nothing to give him. I offered both of them chocolate bars, which they accepted without enthusiasm. Perhaps they had expected us to be dripping with riches, or certain customers for hard liquor and drugs. We had failed on both counts.

'Do you have dollars? Do you want to change money?' the man with the skullcap asked in a last effort to do business. As a Libyan soldier, he was nothing if not versatile. One minute he was a small-time drug-dealer, the next a foreign exchange trader. Our supply of Libyan dinars was almost exhausted, so we changed several hundred dollars with him at the black market rate, a transaction he celebrated by lighting a previously rolled joint and departing in high spirits, having first recommended we stay in the Hotel Sudan. With clean rooms, hot showers, cold drinks and television downstairs, it was, he assured us, the finest establishment in Kufra.

We stayed up late after they had left. Mohammed suggested we make a leisurely start at half past nine the next morning for the short walk-in to Kufra. I lay several yards from Asfar, lost in thoughts of reaching this evocative oasis by camel, and listened to the deep, volcanic gurgling coming from his stomach throughout the night. All the dates he had swallowed whole were churning around inside him uncomfortably. Twice I woke to see him lying helplessly on his side, not even making an effort to right himself. Silhouetted against the moon, I stood in the freezing night, clad only in boxer shorts, and pulled him upright with difficulty. He was on his last legs.

# CHAPTER XIV

# Hotel Arrest in Kufra

---

*I realised with a stab of regret that this was my last day in the real desert. I thought how I should miss my men and my camels, the desolateness and the beauty, the solitude and the companionship – in two words, the desert and its life. I thanked God for his guidance across this vast expanse of pathless sand, and found myself adding a prayer, half wistfully, that I might come back to it again.*

AHMED HASSANEIN BEY, *THE LOST OASES*

*One hundred friends is not enough and one enemy will vex you.*

LIBYAN PROVERB

After a lazy breakfast we left at the unheard-of hour of quarter to ten. Stretching across the plain in front of us lay a thick band of green: Kufra. We were exhilarated to have got this far, to have reached the famed oasis, one of the most isolated towns of the Sahara, by camel, and we walked in joyous, lengthening strides across this final furlong. There was a powerful sense of homecoming, the knowledge that at last, after 1,150 miles from Ghadames, the long trek across the Libyan desert was complete. It had been difficult at times, more so for the camels, who had been stretched to their limits during the bleakest traverses between oases. We were fortunate all five had survived. For Mohammed, too, there was the profound satisfaction of reaching our objective with the caravan intact. He had changed into a clean *jalabiya* and *shish* for our entry into Kufra, washed his face and hands, and was now a soigné Tubbu guide bringing his charges safely to their destination. It was a weary-looking caravan, with Asfar limping in at the end of his resources.

For me it had been a journey unlike any other. Willingly and completely, I had surrendered to the hold of the desert. I had grown used to its comforting rhythms: early rises; simple meals; hunger, thirst and exhaustion; long marches across rolling plains; freezing nights beneath the stars; the companionship of man and beast; the glory of the naked sand seas and the immense African sky. All this I had tasted and now had no wish to leave behind. But already, as we approached our endpoint, our return to civilization, I could feel the solitude of the desert slipping away from me and, although our journey had been neither as long nor as dramatic as Hassanein Bey's pioneering expedition of 1923, I felt the same sense of regret as we trod these last steps, and the same desire to return.

No European reached Kufra until the German explorer Gerhard Rohlfs arrived in 1879. He met with a hostile reception, was plundered of his scientific equipment and notes, and barely escaped with his life. Forty years later, captivated by thoughts of this mysterious desert stronghold, Rosita Forbes followed in his footsteps. 'For a year I had worked and plotted to reach Kufara,' she wrote, 'because the thought of this holy oasis, nucleus of the greatest Islamic confraternity rigidly guarded from every stranger, the centre of the mighty influence against which every European Power has battled in turn, stirred my imagination.'

Nor was she disappointed by the city. Just as Buzeima had aroused her poetic soul, so Kufra enchanted her: 'The Wadi of Kufara is always beautiful, but at sunset it is magical, for the girdle of strange hills glows with wonderful mauve and violet lights and the oasis lies half in shadow where blend the emerald and sapphire of palm and lake, half in flame, where the burning sands reflect the glory of the sky.' Hassanein Bey returned two years later en route to the 'lost' oases of Jebel Ouenat and Jebel Arkenu on what is now the border between Libya, Sudan and Egypt. Since then, few travellers have entered Kufra by camel.

With each step the city grew in front of us, like a caterpillar extending itself to its full length across the plain. Several antennae and radio masts nosed into the clear sky. Unsure which way to take, we tramped across another government farm, through piles of broken irrigation hose pipes that lay on the ground like demented black snakes. Several times we stopped next to clumps of shrubs into which the camels sank their muzzles, ripping away and chewing double time to catch up for all the missed grazing. Asfar, still shaky but just about hanging on, ate briskly and his eyes, which had been dull and listless, brightened a little. All looked much thinner now, with ribs showing where two months ago barrel chests and well-fed stomachs had hung.

We passed a small farmstead, a picturesque place tidily laid out with a makeshift table and chairs hammered together from scraps of wood. The mud floor of the outdoor area was swept clean beneath a roof that seemed to be made from everything from palm fronds to plastic, corrugated iron and concrete. On one side of the diminutive house was the kitchen garden, bordered by a mauve flourish of bougainvillea. In it, peppers grew in bright red clumps, dripping towards the ground from emerald green plants. Others lay in heaps drying on another table. Stacked next to them was a neat pile of firewood ready for cooking and heating. There was no-one at home.

Next we came across a filthy scattering of houses massed around a larger derelict building, the whole settlement squatting awkwardly on an open plain. Children ran out to inspect the new arrivals and promptly retreated in fear at the sight of the five loping camels. Mohammed asked a teenage boy the way to the Tubbu quarter – was there one, we wondered? – and we were given directions to the Hotel Sudan. After disappointments in Idri and Murzuk, we did not hold out any great hopes for food or comfort. But after two months walking and riding across the desert, anything resembling a bed would be welcome and any dinner that did not include tuna fish pasta would be a feast. We just wanted to get there.

We moved on to a road, passing Sudanese and Chadian farm workers resting under the shade of fruit trees, and reached a roundabout from where an Egyptian shopkeeper hailed us to have a round of cold drinks. He repeated what we had heard from the soldier the night before about the Hotel Sudan, but said that it was still about three miles away at the other end of town. He quizzed our guide about the camels, and while Mohammed revelled in travellers' tales, Ned and I binged on cold Cokes and Egyptian strawberry wafers.

Once we were on the road again, cars slowed down and pulled up alongside us, cyclists stopped pedalling and stared, and pedestrians rubbernecked as they passed us going in the opposite direction. By the standards of our previous arrivals at Libyan oases, this was a high-profile entry. Mohammed, enjoying the attention showered on our caravan, marched proudly, looking straight in front of him, stopping every twenty yards or so to answer the constant barrage of questions and acknowledge the greetings shouted at us.

'God bless you, where have you come from?'

'Peace be with you, welcome to Kufra!'

'Are these your camels? How much did they cost?'

'Where are you going now?'

'My God, I don't believe it!' said a lorry driver, stopping his huge vehicle in the middle of the road and jumping down from a driver's cabin decorated with a voluptuous Arab pin-up girl.

'I am very happy to see you,' he continued, shaking each one of us by the hand in turn. 'You have travelled too far, *alhamdulillah*,' he said in disbelief, when Mohammed told him we had come from Ghadames. 'By camel, really? Oh, my God! This is the first time I have seen anything like this.'

We made terminally slow progress through the streets of Kufra until we could hardly bear any more greetings. I asked Mohammed, who had stopped for another two-minute exchange, if we could press on more quickly, thinking of nothing other than finding our hotel and ensuring there was somewhere nearby for the camels. A distinguished-looking young man offered to guide us to the hotel and named an extortionate price. Mohammed dismissed him angrily and we continued through roads bursting with the usual medley of shops selling hardware, music, stationery and household goods. Unfinished construction work appeared to be the norm here, and thick wires sprouted from the roofs of many houses, whose owners were waiting until they could afford to add another storey. Cracks the size of small canyons ran across the disintegrating pavements. Along the middle of the road ran a battered concrete island on which urban planners had perhaps intended to plant a decorative line of trees. A few withered, knee-height specimens rose pathetically from the ground, contending with piles of litter – paper, plastic bags, tin cans, concrete blocks, pieces of carpet, anything that Kufrans felt like throwing out. There were plenty of butchers' stores with severed camels' heads hanging on the walls. Perhaps that was what would happen to our camels if we sold them here. We had to avoid that at all costs. Having them butchered for kebabs would be a cruel reward for their Herculean efforts. They deserved a more comfortable retirement. Best of all would be to return them to their home in Ghadames.

Through the city centre we marched, drawing stares as if we were moving magnets. Cars passed, hooting at us in welcome. Children waved at us in delight. Outside a petrol station whose forecourt was submerged under a black mire of oil and grease, perhaps fifty men squatted idly, waiting for work that would probably never come.

'These people are not Libyans,' said Mohammed. 'They have come from Sudan and Chad to find jobs.' We asked again for directions and a man pointed out Hotel Sudan several streets away, its three storeys looming over this unappetizing urban scene. A large modern building, it was notable only for the ugliness of its design and the shoddiness of its construction. The camels passed nervously into a narrow alley leading to the front of the hotel and at last, several hours after reaching the outskirts of Kufra, we had arrived. Our journey was over.

Within moments, a crowd of onlookers had gathered to look at our caravan. The five camels were hobbled in front of the reception and waited patiently for something to happen. Much to the crowd's delight, I fed Gobber half a dozen oranges, which he ate whole one by one as though each were the size of a pea. Only Gobber would eat them like this. The others only touched oranges if they had been peeled. 'This one is very sick,' said one man, pointing to Asfar who was drooping on his knees and looked terrible. He had no strength left.

The hotel manager arrived. He was a Sudanese man called Mustapha and wore a shiny two-tone white striped shirt over a pair of dark trousers. There was something irritating about his manner, a forced friendliness that did not inspire confidence. Nor did the way he looked at us, with dollar signs in his beady eyes. He gave the impression that we were about to be fleeced. By him. He had rooms for us, he said, but there was nowhere to keep the camels.

'You must take them to the camel market,' he said, 'it's not far from here.'

'Isn't there anywhere nearer we can keep them, behind the hotel or somewhere like that?' I asked, desperate to avoid more walking.

'No, there's nowhere else. The camel market is the best place for them.'

Now that we had reached the hotel, Mohammed excused himself and said he was going to find his nephew and family. He would return to see us either later in the evening or the following morning. Taking his cue from our guide, the manager was about to leave us and retire to the hotel.

'Please could you tell us where the camel market is?' I asked.

'It's not very far,' he replied unhelpfully.

'Can you find someone to take us there, please?'

He shouted something at the crowd, which had started to disperse now that Gobber had finished his party trick with the oranges. Several men stepped forward. 'My name is Issa,' said one, a timid-looking rake of a man. He was another of Kufra's Sudanese immigrants, keen to earn a few dinars, and said he would take us to the market. He was disconcertingly vague on how long it would take us to reach it. It appeared to be several miles out of town. We left our bags and saddles in a hotel store-room – Mustapha extorting a hefty fee for the privilege – and set off.

Within minutes of our departure the weather turned. It had been close, with a refreshing irregular breeze. Now the wind picked up, throwing itself against the town with increasing force until it was gusting at full throttle and a raging sandstorm was under way. The camels panicked, swerving in front of us on their head-ropes and roaring in discomfort. In this mood, they were extremely difficult to control. If you let them walk too close to you, you ran the risk of a pounding hoof on your foot. Twice Gobber lashed out, catching us glancing blows to our legs. If they had found their target, you felt there would not have been much of your knee left. All these antics and the constant efforts to calm the animals delayed us and we made miserably slow progress, dipping our heads into the swirling sand and dust-filled air, cursing Mustapha, the hotel manager, for sending us all the way out here. We staggered through the hurling wind, and sand streamed into our faces, stinging our eyes, and rushing into our ears and noses. We closed our mouths against the storm and our teeth crunched on grit.

'I suppose it's about time we ran into a proper sandstorm,' said Ned phlegmatically, as we walked along together. He looked like a madman. His face was layered with dirt, and his hair, streaked with dust, stuck out from his scalp as though he had received a massive electric shock. With the noise of the wind and our *jalabiya*s flapping against us like flags, we could hardly make ourselves heard. Cars on the road sped past us with head-lights peering weakly through the gloom. On the outskirts of town a smart Land Rover in British Racing Green pulled over in front of us. Without getting out of his vehicle, an officious police officer with hard eyes and an unfriendly moustache gestured us over.

There was little preamble. 'Show me your passports,' he said, fixing us with a hostile glare. He was probably a very senior officer to judge by his vehicle, suit and manner. For the umpteenth time I repeated the story of why our passports were in Tripoli. He looked at us as though we had committed high treason and took down our details in a notebook. Having finished with us, he turned to our guide.

'Where are your papers?' he barked. Issa came to the driver's window, bowed beneath the still raging wind. 'Take your hands off the car!' the officer shouted. Issa had no papers, either. He was probably one of Libya's untold numbers of African immigrants – from Sudan, Chad and Niger in particular – who had taken at face value one of Gaddafi's many declarations that Libya was an open country without borders. The officer looked at the three of us in disgust and drove off after we told him we were heading for the camel market and had already checked into our hotel in town. We pressed on into the sandstorm for what seemed like half a day but was, in fact just, a little over two hours.

There were no signs of activity in the camel market when at last we found it. Everyone was battening down the hatches in a concrete lodge at the entrance. In the near distance, shrouded by the storm, were the looming shapes and shadows of great numbers of camels in pens. Issa found one of the managers of the market, a man called Haj Shahat Sa'd Abubakr. He greeted us warmly, admiring our camels and complimenting us on their quality. Wrapped up in an old woollen overcoat and *shish*, he led us to a generous-sized pen protected on one side by a high concrete wall, bordered on the other three by a fence reinforced with lengths of pipe. Half a dozen mangy camels were pottering about inside. Our camels could be kept here for as long as we liked, he said, and they would be fed and watered daily. We could choose from straightforward bales of hay to more specialist cereal mixes such as barley and dates. This was the best possible place for the camels to recuperate after their gruelling journey.

We started discussing prices with him, at which point the green Land Rover reappeared.

There was even less preamble this time. 'Get in,' the police officer said. The combination of a long walk through a sand-storm, general fatigue and Libyan officialdom in its rudest form was too much. I lost my temper with the man.

'Be careful,' I said, wagging a finger at him furiously. 'We've already given you all our details, you know we're staying in the Hotel Sudan and now we're trying to arrange for our camels to be fed and watered here.'

'Forget the camels. You're coming with me.'

'What do you want us for?' I asked.

'Get in the car,' he repeated. I started to loathe the man. Perhaps sensing the worst, Issa meekly climbed into the back seat. Shahat joined the fray on our side and a shouting-match was soon in full flow. Hastily, we asked the manager to give food and water to the camels and said we would be back soon to pay him. All the time, the police officer fixed us with a look that seemed to blend contempt with indifference. You could imagine him disposing of cells full of political prisoners without batting an eyelid.

He did not speak a word to us once we were aboard the Land Rover. The vehicle was reassuringly British but the circumstances of the ride were not pleasant. Ten minutes later, we arrived at Kufra police station and were led upstairs, along a corridor containing rows of cells with heavy iron doors and no windows, into a large office with a view on to the front of the station. Now that we were out of the storm, we had a better look at our new host. He was a burly man, who made up for what he lacked in height with an excessive width. He looked like a pub brawler, only more dangerous because he commanded power and wore a suit. He took a seat behind a large wooden desk bereft of paperwork and gestured to us to sit down. On the wall behind him was a portrait of a youthful Gaddafi at his most benevolent, with a handsome smile and sunglasses that looked several sizes too large for him. Issa looked terrified. Ned and I were irritated and angry more than anything else. Exhausted after all the walking of the past two months, ragged and filthy from the sandstorm, and concerned that the camels might not be fed until Shahat had been paid, neither of us was in any mood for an interview. If this was to be one, the sooner it was over the better.

'Why are you travelling in Libya without passports?' the officer asked, collecting himself after the raised voices of several minutes ago.

'We aren't,' I replied.

'Why are your passports in Tripoli?' he continued.

'Because we were told to leave them there so the visas could be renewed while we were in the desert.'

'This is against the law. You have broken the law,' he said.

'We've travelled across Libya without the slightest problem up to now.'

'Now you have a problem,' he replied curtly. He barked an order and a uniformed subordinate trotted obediently to the door. The senior officer looked at us.

'You can tell your story to someone else,' he said ominously, as if he had done all he could to protect us from a much worse fate. Like Pontius Pilate, he was washing his hands of us.

Moments later, a man in plainclothes arrived. He wore a striped sports shirt and jeans and carried himself with a marked self-assurance. His lips, mean and thin, looked as though they had been designed for the express purpose of sneering. He had the air of a man who possessed more power than our present interviewer and was used to exercising it arbitrarily. His manner towards his colleague was supercilious, and to us he spoke with an affected bonhomie that grated on the ears. His English was fluent, by far the best we had heard during our time in Libya. We learnt later his name was Ali Ahmed. Beginning politely, he asked us to repeat our story. We did so and he listened carefully. More general questions about our journey followed.

'Where are you going now?' he asked.

'Nowhere. This is the end of our journey,' I replied.

'That is just as well, because the border with Sudan and Egypt is closed to foreigners.'

'Yes, we know that.'

'What are you going to do with your camels now?' he went on.

'We hope to sell them, but not to a butcher.'

There was a long pause.

'How much did your camels cost?' he asked abruptly.

We had heard the same question so many times before. Sometimes we had pretended not to understand it, at others we had simply changed the conversation. Coming from a policeman to whom it could scarcely matter whether we had purchased them for a dollar each or several thousand, it seemed especially pointless. I had had enough.

'It's none of your business,' I replied in Arabic, using the pithy expression my teacher in London had suggested.

Momentarily, he looked startled by this unexpected affront to his authority. Then his features contorted into an expression of fury. I had lit a fuse.

'No, my friend, you don't understand,' he said, his lips curling into an impressive sneer. 'YOU are my business. You are in Libya now. EVERYTHING about you is my business.'

'Gaddafi will be very interested to hear how you made us feel so welcome in Kufra,' I replied calmly. 'We have travelled across Libya by camel without any difficulties and this is the first time . . .'

Ned looked at me aghast. The officer interrupted me, rising purposefully from his seat and coming towards me with the same expression of self-righteous wrath. The word Gaddafi had lit another fuse. He was about to explode.

'NEVER mention Gaddafi in my country!' he shouted, trembling with rage. He waved his finger under my nose. 'He is my leader. How dare you talk of him in front of me. You are in Libya now, not Great Britain. You think we are still scared of Great Britain?' This last question was accompanied with a look of sneering disbelief. 'Those days are over. You British are nothing.

Britain is now just an island in the sea.' Britain had been an island for as long as anyone remembered, indeed owed much of her greatness to that very accident of geography, I thought, but the diatribe had not finished. 'You think you still rule the world and you can do what you like in Libya.'

'Not in the slightest. We would just like to leave now and return to our hotel. Have you quite finished?'

'I'm just beginning,' he retaliated, still shouting. 'You are guilty now. You are under the law.' Due process in Libya clearly had its limits. The concept of innocent until proven guilty would have been lost on Ali Ahmed. Besides, I had the sinking feeling that as far as we were concerned he was the law in Kufra.

'We're going to your hotel now to see your papers,' he said.

'And we're guilty before you even see our papers?' I asked.

'Come with me,' he stormed, moving to the doorway.

'What about our guide?'

'Never mind your guide. He has no papers. We're keeping him here.'

The interview was over. We had not even paid the hapless Issa and, even worse, had now got him into trouble with the police. Too angry to check myself, I had tried Ned's 'robust approach' with the authorities and got carried away. As a shouting match, it had proved a cathartic release. In all other more important respects, it had failed completely.

We climbed aboard the Land Rover and drove to the Hotel Sudan, Ali Ahmed reminding us all the way – with immense satisfaction – of Great Britain's fall from greatness. 'You think because we are a small country we are still frightened of Britain? Look what happened to Thatcher. She is finished but we are still here. You think you can finish us with a few bombs? Now you must hide behind America because you are nothing.'

Ned and I kept quiet. I wondered doubtfully what Ali Ahmed would make of our limited paperwork. We prepared for the inevitable. At the hotel, he wasted little time in looking through our papers. There was little to look at, after all. A letter from Muftah Kilani explaining that our passports were in Tripoli at

Taher's office and photocopies of our passports and Libyan visas. It had been enough for some of the authorities we had already encountered. But this was personal now.

'Yes, you are guilty. As I thought, you have broken the law,' he said, gloating, and pocketed the papers.

'You've seen we have passports and Libyan visas so how can we be guilty?' I asked.

'Do not leave this hotel and do not try to leave Kufra,' he replied. 'I'm going to investigate you.'

'I don't think you'll have much to investigate, but we would appreciate it if you did it as quickly as possible,' I told him as he departed. 'We've finished our journey and are ready to go home.'

He walked back to the hotel reception where I was standing and put a finger under my nose. It was an annoying habit of his.

'Don't you dare tell me how to do my job. You'll be hearing from me soon enough.'

He left us under hotel arrest ruminating on the day's events over an endless supply of cold soft drinks. We had completed our journey, but it was not clear what would happen next. Our hopes of exploring Kufra and the surrounding villages, to see what traces, if any, remained of the former seat of Sanusi power, were unlikely to be indulged now. Our biggest problem seemed to be Ali Ahmed's overt hostility towards us. A Libyan security officer in a desert frontier town, he probably had a lot of time on his hands. The arrival in his town of two British travellers without passports offered the tantalizing prospect of promotion and reward. We could be the break he was looking for. If only he could discover we had committed a crime more serious than misplacing our passports. There was little reason to assume that he would finish his investigation promptly for our convenience.

We dined handsomely on beef, pasta, cold omelette, fried chicken, salad, bread and soft drinks, harangued by the now jovial hotel manager, Mustapha, who had taken a keen interest in us on discovering that we were British. 'You are British gentlemen,' he said fawningly, 'you must get me British visa. I want to leave Libya. I can work in hotel.' The emigration from Sudan to Libya was not all it had been cracked up to be, but neither of us felt well-disposed towards Mustapha. He had not endeared himself to us after our latest brush with the authorities by telling us we should have kept the camels in the back 'garden' (i.e. car park) of the hotel. He had insisted we take them to the camel market in the first place.

After dinner, we adjourned to the lobby. A dozen avid television viewers were flicking between MBC's coverage of King Hussein of Jordan's death and something called Wonder Wrestling Disco Inferno, in which a musclebound redneck sporting a luminous orange jumpsuit with the legend 'Shake My Booty' on his rear was tangling with another long-haired giant.

We slept well in comfortable beds and woke the next morning to find another policeman waiting for us in the lobby. He was the third officer to involve himself in our case and was by far the most civil. A middle-aged man, he had perhaps watched too many detective movies and was wearing a heavy beige raincoat in flagrant disregard of the heat. It took a while for us to learn why he had been sent here because he spoke even less English than I did Arabic. Eventually, he managed to let us know that he would like Taher's telephone number in Tripoli. We wrote it down for him and he left us to our breakfast of tuna fish, hard-boiled egg, bread and coffee. Moments later, Ali Ahmed arrived, freshly groomed and dressed in sports shirt and dark trousers. He was smoking a Rothmans cigarette and smiling hatefully.

'I have the telephone numbers,' he said, waving the piece of paper in triumph, as if reminding us that nothing we did or said went unnoticed and that our fate was in his hands. He would call Taher to see if we were legal, bona fide travellers. If we were, we would be free to leave. He did not specify what he would do if we were not. Taking a seat in one of the fake leather armchairs that lined the hotel lobby, he then ordered a coffee from Mustapha and boasted he would not have to pay for it. No-one in the hotel wanted to get on the wrong side of Ali Ahmed. Unfortunately, we already had.

He turned to me. 'Yesterday you said things you should not have,' he said coolly. 'You must never mention Gaddafi in Libya. Even though he is my leader, I do not speak of him.' It was sacrilege for a mere mortal to let the word pass his lips. He paused for a moment, struggling to find the right words to express the greatness of his leader. Then it came to him. 'He is thinking and teaching things I have not even reached,' he said in a tone of awe. It reminded me of the drivel written on the back of Gaddafi's *Green Book* in which the reader is informed by some revolutionary party apparatchik that this great 'thinker' does not present his ideas for 'simple amusement or pleasure'. Worse, you could tell Ali Ahmed did not believe a word of it. 'I'm just a soldier doing my job,' he went on in nauseatingly humble mode. 'It's my business to implement the law and you have broken it.' It was difficult to keep up with his change of professions. Yesterday, he had been introduced by his grey-suited colleague as from Kufra 'immigration'. Someone else had told us he was from 'security'. Now he was a soldier.

'You are travelling by camel like Lawrence,' he said out of the blue. 'You are the first British people to travel like that since him.' For a provincial security officer, his range of literary and historical allusion was impressive, if not entirely accurate. 'Yes, I know all about Lawrence,' he continued, responding to our raised eyebrows. 'He pretended to help the Arabs but all the time he was betraying them. He was working for the British government. Now I must check your papers to see you are not another Lawrence.' The comparison was deeply flattering, if absurd.

Having disposed of this bee in his bonnet, he returned to his favourite gripe. 'You know, when Lawrence was working for the British, Great Britain was important in the world. It was the largest economy and it had the most powerful army. That is history. Yes, I know my history. But now Britain's time is finished,' he carried on, smiling and waving his hand dismissively, as if brushing away a fly. 'You have just returned Hong Kong to China. Next you will lose Australia. The world has had enough of British imperialism. And what about your monarchy? How long do you give it before it, too, is finished? I tell you, it will be over in fifty years. Yes, no more than fifty years,' he said, without waiting for us to answer. 'And anyway,' he added as an afterthought, 'it's German.'

This completed his insult of things British for the time being and he turned next to the glories of Libyan resistance to Italian rule. The day before, he told us, had been the anniversary of the 1931 skirmish against the Italians in which more than 200 *mujahidin* had lost their lives defending Kufra. 'Their bodies are still lying there in the desert, untouched,' he said. 'If you saw them, you would think they had died only yesterday. God and the desert have preserved them like that.' If we liked, he went on, in a tone of great magnanimity, we could visit the site. He called over a man standing by the hotel entrance.

'This is Younis,' he said. 'He will look after you while I am investigating what you are doing in my country. He can take you there.' A man in denim jacket and jeans came forward.

'First we must see our camels in the market,' I said.

'Must? What do you mean must? You will do only what I allow you to do,' Ali Ahmed replied curtly. 'Younis will take you to see your camels. Now goodbye. I will see you later.'

We drove to the camel market with our new government minder. Unlike his boss, he was a man of few words, which suited us perfectly. At the market, we were greeted kindly again by Shahat, the supervisor. As we had feared, the camels had neither been fed nor watered. He said he did not know what we wanted him to feed them. In their enclosure they looked settled but rather emaciated. He ran through the list of charges. Two dinars per head per day for lodging, five bales of hay at eight dinars a bale, twenty dinars for fifty kilograms of barley, two dinars each for water and ten dinars a day for the camel boy. Together it amounted to $30 a day (by the black market rate at which we had exchanged our dollars, or $270 at the official exchange rate), considerably more expensive than our own hotel. We sent for several bales of hay and asked Shahat to give them as much barley as they could eat every day. The camel boy then opened the gate and herded them several hundred metres away to a large cement trough where they joined half a dozen other camels being watered. All of them drank deeply. Younis, who owned several camels, said he had been told our animals were not good riding camels. As soon as he saw them, he changed his mind immediately. 'These are very fine, strong camels,' he said. 'You can see they are Touareg camels from their nose-rings. Once they have rested here, they will be all right.' He was not the only one admiring them. The three whites drew particular attention. There were thousands of camels in the market but most of them were unremarkable, small brown animals wasted by the long trek north from Chad, Niger and Sudan. Our handsome caravan, although battered, stood apart from the rest.

The Kufra camel market was a romantic dustbowl burning beneath the sun. Set over several square miles of desert, it was home to camels and camel-traders alike. A giant digger was scooping up dozens of the animals, one by one, into waiting trucks where they were tightly crammed for the journey north to Benghazi, Ajdabiya and Tripoli. There was so little space inside the back of the trucks that those camels who could do so hung their heads over the side. With pursed lips, they carried comical expressions of resignation to their fate. Those being loaded roared terribly, their legs tied beneath them by bright orange plastic ribbons that fluttered in the breeze. A man in the back of each lorry swung the pathetic animals into place as they were carefully lowered. Behind this small zone of activity there were more pens, increasingly makeshift as you went along, until it seemed there was little to prevent the camels escaping. Beyond the market, the ground rose and dark rocks lay in their bed of sand, naked beneath the gaze of the sun.

As government minders go, Younis was extremely relaxed. He had met a friend and was chatting to him next to his car. I walked off to a group of men standing outside a temporary shelter made from reinforced cardboard boxes with a roof of palm fronds held in place by a metal pipe. Led by a man called Izzadin, they had recently completed a twenty-day trek of about 600 miles from their home town in northern Chad, bringing 250 camels with them. They planned to stay in Kufra for as long as it took to sell the animals – probably ten days – then return to Chad by car. While I was talking to them, another group of men called me over.

This one was Sudanese and consisted of three fairly elderly men and one much younger. The head of the party was called Haj Abdallah, a dark handsome man with a penetrating stare beneath a pair of fertile black eyebrows. He had a broad face, a stubbly chin and an elegant black and white moustache that was slightly upturned at the sides. Despite the heat of the day, he wore an old woollen winter overcoat and a voluminous *shish* of crisp white cotton on his head. He invited me inside the shelter and pulled out a bottle of cold Coke from a refrigerator. Abdallah had been camel-trading for almost a quarter of a century, he told me. His father, a big livestock farmer who owned sheep, cows and camels, had taught his son how to travel in the desert, navigating by the sun by day, by night using the stars. The first time Abdallah had travelled from Sudan to sell camels was in 1975, when he stayed in Kufra for a year. Camels had been cheaper to buy in Sudan for as long as he could remember, as well as being bigger and more powerful than those bred in Libya. On the return journey, he took back cloth, canvas camel bags, or anything else that was in demand, and sometimes exchanged money. He had travelled between Sudan and Kufra many times, usually bringing a caravan of about 200 camels for sale. Sometimes he stayed several months in Kufra, but increasingly he sank roots for longer. The last time he had been in Sudan was in 1993. Although he tended to stay put now, his companions still moved regularly between Kufra and Hamra as Sheikh in northern Sudan, about 625 miles to the south. The journey took them twenty to twenty-five days.

It was gratifying, after reading all the nineteenth-century accounts of commerce in the Sahara, to discover there was still a thriving caravan trade in Kufra, Libya's most southern city.

Modern accounts of the desert tend to concentrate on the car and increasingly have taken for granted the demise of the camel as a means of transport, and by definition the caravan trade. Like the stretch of desert between Agadez and the oasis of Bilma in Niger, which salt caravans ply each year, Kufra is one of the last pockets of an ancient Saharan trade that has been all but extinguished. Certainly, there is nothing like it anywhere else in Libya. No-one travelled north from Kufra by camel, we were told. All of the animals destined for the north were loaded on to trucks and driven to the Mediterranean coast to be sold and butchered. Those men who had brought them up from Sudan, Chad and Niger all returned by car or truck.

There were three caravan routes from Kufra to Sudan, of which Abdallah used to take the most easterly. From Kufra, it was about a week travelling south-east to Jebel Ouenat, where the camels were fed and watered. South of Jebel Ouenat, he said, the temperature shot up. In the hot season, between April and December, the caravans were forced to move only between four o'clock in the afternoon and eight o'clock in the morning, when camp would be made for the day. At all other times it was too hot for man and beast alike. From Jebel Ouenat, it was six days to Bir Matass, five to Bir Rahib, another five to Wadi Sialtota where there was good grazing, three more to Bir Sawani and from there four days to Hamra as Sheikh. Many of the big trucks heading south from Kufra departed for this town, which until recently had been only a temporary settlement. It was now one of the biggest camel markets in Sudan, he told me. I thanked him for his time and said we hoped to travel by camel in Sudan one day. 'Inshallah,' he replied heartily. 'You are always welcome.'

I left him and rejoined Younis. Seeing our interest in the camel market, he suggested taking us to another, much bigger, section of it. It was nicknamed the 'Sudanese city'. This was where camels just arrived from the south were taken for veterinary inspection. If passed, they were then taken to the section from which we had just come. We drove a couple of miles up the main road and passed a caravan of 150–200 camels, a thick brown throng kicking up wreaths of dust as they moved in the opposite direction. Two riders rose aloft in the middle of the herd and two more prevented the camels straggling on to the busy road. It was a wonderful sight. How much longer would the caravan trade last?

We drew into a sprawling, makeshift town. The sun streamed down on us like liquid. In the distance, behind concrete walls, camels were walking about freely in a huge enclosure. Slightly nearer, half a dozen trucks were being loaded for the journey back to Sudan. Men moved between lofty piles of packaged goods stacked on dazzling tarpaulin sheets, shouting instructions at each other and swarming like ants around honey. In front of us, shacks and shelters made of the ubiquitous palm fronds and discarded cardboard boxes formed a long street. There were ramshackle restaurants serving camel meat and salad, tea and soft drinks, and small huts in which men sat sewing camel bags, making Sudanese horsehair slippers with leopard-skin prints and stitching girls' dresses. A mosque, less temporary looking than any other building insofar as it had a few blocks of cement at its base, sounded the afternoon call to prayer and men started filing in. A barber in a shelter the size of a cupboard scratched a razor across the chin of a stout man sitting on an upturned box. There were iron bedsteads for sale without mattresses, Chinese oil lamps from Shanghai, hair oil and muscular relief ointment from Nigeria, cigarettes, weird aftershaves called Dow Jones and Black Silk, toothpaste and soap. Here was everything you needed for a camel trek. Bundles of rope, twine, gaudy prayer rugs, plastic mats and bright blankets hung from stalls. Hundreds of 40-litre blue *bidoun*s were piled high, roped together in bundles of eight. In isolated patches of shade, in allotments demarcated by inverted tins of corn oil half-embedded in the sand, men lazed and lounged over games of dominoes. Black men in white skullcaps and *jalabiyas* squatted in the dust, rinsing their faces with water from terracotta jugs. Some sat in front of scattered piles of white cotton fragments, brilliant in the sun, others sold ornate Sudanese pocket knives with leather sheaths. Farther on, men squatted next to stacks of firewood for sale. Washing hung on lines, sizzling in the afternoon heat. Smoke curled into the sky from improvised chimneys. Women bustled from shop to shop bargaining shrilly with shopkeepers. With the exception of the market in Murzuk, it was unlike anything else we had seen in Libya. Arab North Africa was giving way to more primitive sub-Saharan Africa.

We returned to town and Younis deposited us at the Hotel Sudan, where Ned and I fended off more requests for British visas from Mustapha before seeking sanctuary in our room upstairs. Later, a neatly groomed and beaming Mohammed arrived with his nephew, Jumma Ahmed. He said he would stay in Kufra a little longer to finish the family rounds – several of them he had not seen for many years – and after saying a final farewell to us, would return to Zuweila by car. After he had collected his belongings, we paid him his money and he said goodbye for the time being. Moments later, Ali Ahmed came in.

'So you paid your guide $2,300?' he said with an unpleasant leer. 'You think I don't know that? I know *everything* you're doing in my town.' Mohammed had been hauled in as soon as he had left the hotel and forced to reveal the contents of his envelope. We were under close scrutiny. 'You have broken another law. You are not allowed to use dollars in Libya.' He was obviously a diligent man but his investigation of us was not having the dramatic results he so wished for. He warned us about the illegal use of dollars which, given the Libyan people's lack of faith in their own currency, was a national habit for those who could lay their hands on them. He had not been able to get a call through to Taher's office in Tripoli, he told us – had he really tried? – and we would have to remain in Kufra until he received more information on us.

We spent one last evening with Mohammed, who brought along his nephew again. Jumma, a government schools inspector who also taught classical Arabic, was a solidly built man with large intelligent eyes and a flourishing moustache. He wore immaculate clothes, drove a brand-new Toyota Landcruiser and was delighted to discover two British travellers in south-eastern

Libya. Tonight, he suggested we call on a good friend of his who ran a language school near to the hotel. After passing through a decrepit playground we arrived at the offices of the director, Hafiz Younis, a dark, smiling man who wore a sports jacket, blue V-necked jumper and a striped sports shirt. On the walls were various English proverbs, such as 'Blood is thicker than water', 'East or west, home is best', 'Knowledge is power', 'Manners make the man', 'Cleanliness is next to godliness', and, of least literal relevance to Kufra, 'It never rains but it pours'. On another piece of paper pasted to the wall, was a list of acronyms, from UN, USA and UK, to the more esoteric KPP (Kufra Production Project, another of Gaddafi's desert greening schemes), ESC (Egyptian Space Channel) and KSL (Kufra School of Languages). Every few minutes, the room was plunged into darkness by a brief power cut and Hafiz gave an embarrassed laugh. When the lights returned, he presented his teachers to us proudly. There were half a dozen of them, the majority either Sudanese or Iraqi. Hafiz had started the language school in 1995. It was an ingenious set-up for Gaddafi's Libya. By day, it was a normal Kufra state school, of which he was the headmaster. In the evenings, it was a private school teaching English at all levels from beginner to advanced. He showed me the teaching materials, which consisted of photocopied courses from the Bournemouth-based International English Language Centre. The Dorset connection had resurfaced yet again.

A tiny Iraqi man with a wispy moustache and beard, a floppy parting and a squeaky falsetto collared me as soon as we had been introduced. Deep in the Libyan Sahara, the opportunity to address questions about the English language to a native speaker was too good to miss. His earnestness took me by surprise. He began with a question concerning the correct usage of the glottal stop between the definite article and a word beginning with a vowel. I looked at him blankly. He explained tortuously until I thought I understood him.

'Ah, yes,' I replied, trying to be helpful but already regretting the conversation. 'The hotel . . .'

He looked at me in horror, scandalized by my error.

'The letter "h" is not a vowel,' he said primly, looking at me as though I was a complete blockhead.

'OK, what about "the astronaut, thee astronaut,"' I replied, varying the pronunciation to show him either usage was correct.

'But what is THE RULE?' he persisted shrilly. 'I want to get the correct intonation for the glottal stop.'

I looked at him in despair. There was no mistaking his seriousness.

'You speak excellent English,' I replied, in a weak attempt to side-step the issue. He looked flattered and flicked his floppy parting from his eyes with a look of great self-satisfaction.

'Now,' he continued mercilessly, 'I want you to tell me what is the correct way – to lower or raise the voice after a tag question?' I looked at him blankly again. 'Surely you know what a tag question is?' he asked in disbelief.

'I think you would be much better off talking to my friend, who is a noted grammarian of the English language,' I replied, interrupting what looked like a much more interesting conversation Ned was having with the others. I introduced him to Ned and turned towards Hafiz, Jumma and Mohammed. Jumma, too, was keen to ask me questions, but they were of an altogether different nature.

'Did you think the Sahara was a terrible and dangerous place before coming to Libya?' he began. He was fascinated by our decision, as British travellers, to visit an 'enemy' country. 'Were you not frightened that the Libyans would be hostile to you because you are British? I am very frightened of Great Britain.' He understood from the local press that Britain was a very dangerous country.

'I think you are very brave to come to Libya,' he added.

I told him I had visited the country several times before and had always been struck by the great hospitality of its people. Although relations between the two governments were not very friendly, this had little bearing on how British people regarded Libyans. He nodded.

'Here we are like the desert,' he said. 'The desert camouflages nothing. You can see everything around you. We talk sincerely.'

More questions followed. They spanned an eclectic range of subjects.

'Do you believe mankind came from a single source?' he asked.

'I like to think so, but science suggests otherwise,' I replied.

He admired the first part of my reply but looked at me disapprovingly because of the second. From the beginnings of mankind, we moved on to politics and history. 'Was colonialism a good thing?' he went on.

The Libyan experience of colonialism was rather different from that of Great Britain. Many British people believed the empire had been a source of much good for its colonies around the world, bringing such benefits as the rule of law, commerce and education to new populations, I answered. However, there were also many in Britain who argued that colonialism had been a great injustice. If I was Libyan, I went on, I would almost certainly have felt less positively about it. Libyan history, after all, had been dominated by a long line of foreign invaders, spanning 3,000 years from the Phoenicians to the Italians, British and French. He digested my reply for a few moments and continued.

'Does Tony Blair really hate all Libyans?' He was engagingly frank. His question said more about the nature of official state propaganda – in newspapers, on the radio and television – than Libyans' suspicion of the outside world.

'The British government has no quarrel with the Libyan people. I think relations with Libya are already improving. The only obstacle to full restoration of diplomatic relations is the surrender of the two Libyan Lockerbie suspects.'

Again, he was pleased with the first half of my reply. The second he liked less. After politics and history, it was time for religion. 'You are a Christian,' he observed. 'Do you believe all Muslims will go to hell?'

'Actually, I'm a very poor Christian,' I replied, 'and, no, I don't think all Muslims will go to hell any more than I think all Christians will. In fact, I'm not even sure if I believe in the idea of hell.' He approved of my comments about Muslims but found it impossible to credit my idea that hell might not exist. This was blasphemy.

After a while, Ned eventually managed to shake off the Iraqi teacher and joined us. With the help of Hafiz as translator, we wanted to ask Mohammed some questions before we said good-bye to him for the last time. I knew I would miss him once he left. He had been a marvellous teacher and companion through-out our crossing of the most difficult part of the Libyan Sahara. To begin with, did he regret the passing away of the old traditions of desert life?

He giggled self-consciously.

'All my life I have lived in the desert,' he replied. 'My first job was breeding sheep, cattle and camels in the Haruj al Aswad [east of the central Libyan city of Sebha]. I have never settled in one place for very long, which is why my home in Zuweila looks so temporary. I have always been a nomad. From time to time I come to town, but always rain and water takes me into the desert. I am very happy with my life. I have a car and if I wanted to build a modern house I have enough money to do so, but I don't want to. Other desert guides today do not like getting tired. They only travel by Toyota. Camels are like sport to me. They are a way of life, a tradition and an inheritance from our grand-fathers. After I die, my children have the choice to live this way or, if they like, sell my camels and have a more modern life. It's up to them.'

He spoke softly and a smile played across his lips. 'Travelling through the desert is not an easy thing,' he continued. 'You must have courage and patience to bear hardships otherwise you might feel a sense of hopelessness and consume all your food and water or get lost in a storm. There are many accidents that can happen. The longer the journey, the more problems there are for both men and camels.'

I asked him what he thought of us reading books while riding. He giggled again. 'Because you read books, you often fell far behind. One day, I got annoyed and just went on ahead and then you became angry and we shouted at each other.' He recalled the incident without bad feeling. 'You like reading,' he went on. 'From each book you get something new. Travelling is the same. From each journey you learn more things. The more you go, the more you know.'

I told him we had learnt many desert skills from him during our journey from Tmissah to Kufra. As a joke, I asked whether he had learnt anything at all from us. He immediately roared with laughter. Then, as it subsided, he answered with a touching sincerity. 'The benefits of life always bring men together. We did not know each other before we travelled together. We all benefited from each other. I realized you had patience and did not fear the desert though it is a dangerous place. I was very anxious to get us to Kufra as soon as possible but you did not mind and were very relaxed about delays.'

It was late and Hafiz was looking tired after all his translating. It was time to say goodnight. As he left, Mohammed delivered a few parting words. 'You are the age of my sons,' he said. 'If you want to continue travelling by camel, always remember he is an animal. He may get sick, become exhausted or die, which will be a big problem for you. Always take care of him for your own safety. Try to reach your destination as quickly as possible. As soon as I saw you had five camels, I knew you had acted wisely, instead of having just one each, and I knew this was a very good decision because we had a reserve. Remember this huge camel only has a small engine. Twice in my life in the desert my camel has died. And always, what kept me alive, after God's will, was having two camels.'

Outside the school, Mohammed shook hands with us and said farewell, giggling as he had done when we first met him in Tmissah. He climbed into Jumma's giant Toyota, the vehicle hummed to life and drove off, swallowed up by the night. Mohammed had been our most inspirational guide. We had been enormously fortunate. All our guides, to varying degrees, had been unforgettable companions, but we had spent the longest time with Mohammed, had covered more ground with him, and had been able to get to know him more intimately than his predecessors. He was one of the last of his breed. In a few more years, there would be no-one left with his level of experience to guide a long camel expedition across the desert.

We returned to the hotel, alternating between recollections of our travels with Mohammed and wondering when we would be free to leave. It depended on how long the stand-off with the Kufran authorities lasted. The next day we shuttled between the hotel and post office (where we were fast becoming regulars) to contact Taher in Tripoli. There was nowhere else in Kufra to make long-distance calls.

'Taher no come to office,' Hajer shouted down the line.

'Please tell Taher we need our passports immediately,' I shouted back. 'We can't leave Kufra until we have them.'

'Taher no come. Taher sick.'

'Well please tell anyone else in the office then.'

'No-one in office. Only Hajer.'

After several more attempts, we gave up. On our way out, we were accosted by a large man who asked us, first if we were British and then, whether we were travelling by camel. Yes we were, I replied, slightly suspicious. He said his name was Abd as Salam, a friend of Taher, who had mentioned to him several months ago that two British travellers were planning to reach Kufra by camel at some point in the future. He had thought nothing more of it until now, seeing two tourists trying to place a call to Tripoli. Gallantly, he offered us his services. The post office director was a friend of his, he said, and we could telephone Taher from his office. Moments later, after two Italian engineers working on a power plant had finished their own telephone call, Abd as Salam was talking to a recuperating Taher in Tripoli, asking him to send our passports on the next flight. If all went well, and Ali Ahmed was convinced we were legal, we would then be able to take the return flight to Tripoli ourselves.

At the Libyan Arab Airlines offices, the manager of the office was less obliging. I asked for two single tickets to Tripoli.

'Please show me your passports,' he replied.

'We don't have them here.'

'Then I cannot sell you a ticket,' he answered.

Abd as Salam intervened on our behalf and explained the situation. There was no persuading the man. Abd as Salam said he would resolve the problem with Ali Ahmed himself. In the meantime we should wait in the hotel for further news. It seemed there was little else to do for the time being.

'We may as well make ourselves as comfortable as possible,' said Ned. In practice, this consisted of orchestrating a daily programme of leisure. First, we had our beards trimmed by a marvellously fat Egyptian barber called Subhi. In the afternoons, we visited the camels, who were growing stronger and fatter by the day, and adjourned to a café run by Mahmoud, another portly Egyptian. Here we puffed away on Egyptian *shisha* pipes and watched Wesley Snipes and Jean-Claude van Damme action movies with an attentive crowd of Kufra's unemployed. We discovered a video rental shop nearby and one afternoon commandeered the television and video in another café to watch a James Bond film. When we started the film, the place was empty. By the time we left two hours later, you could hardly move. It was packed with Bond fans – from Libya, Sudan, Chad, Syria, Niger, Morocco, Tunisia, Somalia, Nigeria, Algeria and Iraq – cheering and wildly applauding Pierce Brosnan's every stunt.

Ali Ahmed arrived in the middle of the film and told us he knew we had been playing cards in a different café that afternoon. His investigation was not going well. Maliciously, he said he had received a fax from Taher's office explaining our situation, but that he was not satisfied by it.

'It is not official,' he said smiling unpleasantly. 'I need to have an official fax from immigration in Tripoli.'

'You said all you needed was notification from the travel agent,' I reminded him.

'No, that is not enough. You must stay in Kufra until I say you can leave. With Arab hospitality you must be very patient,' he added sarcastically. 'If your papers are regular, we will become very good friends and I will do everything I can for you. If they are not, there will be big problems between us.' You could tell which he would prefer.

Business over, he switched unexpectedly to discussing football. He praised Michael Owen generously and then checked himself, realizing perhaps that it would not do to give such unqualified approval of someone who, after all, was British. 'He must go to Spain or Italy,' he declared. 'There is no future in England.' We looked at him coldly. 'For football,' he added, condescendingly.

From football he moved to international relations. 'You British must make closer ties with Europe,' he said pompously. 'You must not follow the United States in everything. The British must remember their empire is finished now. You are just a small island in the North Sea.' A Libyan security official advocating closer integration with Europe was the best argument I had ever heard for Eurosceptics. This completed Ali Ahmed's latest instalment of Brit-bashing, and he departed.

The next day, one of the desert patrol soldiers we had met outside Kufra horrified us by reappearing in the hotel lobby to try to sell us hashish again. I thanked him for his offer and shooed him out quickly before someone like Ali Ahmed appeared. It was just the sort of thing that could lead to serious trouble and an extended stay in Kufra. We had already been forced to stay here almost a week.

Moments later, Younis, our phlegmatic minder, arrived to drive us to the memorial site of the 1931 skirmish between the Italians and the Sanusi guerrillas. We were filled with anticipation. This was where Ali Ahmed had told us the bodies of the Libyan *mujahidin* lay as they had fallen, preserved both by God and the desert climate. It was nonsense. There was little to look at apart from a solitary Italian tank. Painted white stones piled in untidy rectangles marked the presence of graves scattered over several hundred metres. There were no soldiers lying untouched on the ground. Many of the graves had been desecrated and a few bleached bones lay quietly under the sun. Empty bottles of Coke and mineral water were strewn all over the place. A broken building containing smashed urinals did little to improve the picture. Younis, embarrassed by the vandalism, said children must have desecrated the graves. The sixty-eighth anniversary commemoration of the fighting, celebrated several days before, was responsible for all the rubbish blowing across the site, he added. As a consolation to us, he presented us with an Italian army belt he had found lying on the ground. After all Ali Ahmed's comments, the expedition had not lived up to expectations.

A week after arriving in Kufra, and thanks almost entirely to the many selfless efforts of Abd as Salam, we were given permission to leave. Ali Ahmed's colleagues in Tripoli had at last confirmed our documents were in order. During our last interview with him, the change in Ali Ahmed was remarkable. He had ceased to be an aggressive Libyan security official. Perhaps sensing trouble if we were actually granted an interview with Gaddafi – he did not know I had made the whole thing up – he became wheedling and greasy.

'I am a human being,' he simpered. 'When I investigate, I investigate. When I discuss things with you, I do it in a civilized way. I have only been doing my job, so I hope you will not tell anyone I made problems for you in Kufra.' We shook hands quickly with him and left.

The next morning, we breakfasted with Abd as Salam and drove off to the camel market, where we told Shahat we would be in touch with him from Tripoli. Ned and I had an idea about what to do with the camels. After checking out of the Hotel Sudan (Mustapha reminding us of our 'promise' to get him a British visa) we drove to the airport, where the plane from Tripoli landed on time. The ever-helpful Abd as Salam had words with several officials in high places and moments later reappeared with our long-lost passports. We thanked him for all he had done for us, said goodbye and boarded the aircraft.

# CHAPTER XV

# 'Now You Are in Good Condition'

*My poor camel, for which, were I a poet, I would chant a plaintive strain of adieu! I was obliged to sell. The Bengazi Arab who bought her promised me, however, to treat her lightly, and only use her to ride upon.*

JAMES RICHARDSON, *TRAVELS IN THE GREAT DESERT OF SAHARA IN THE YEARS OF 1845 AND 1846*

The flight to Tripoli took two hours. It had taken us a little over two months to cover the same distance. On the motorway into town we passed the strangely comforting slogans from *The Green Book* printed on giant hoardings.

'No representation in lieu of the people. Representation is fraud'
'No democracy without popular congresses and committees everywhere'
'Unity is necessary for strength'
'The land is never the property of anyone'
'Arab unity'
'The Koran is the law of society'

Some were impenetrable – 'The tent destroyed the castle of the kingdom' – others sadly ironic – 'Struggle for democracy'. In the city centre, we came across a small mural outside a petrol station. One of Tripoli's more imaginative pieces of propaganda, it read 'CIA + FBI = CNN'. All that remained for us to do was to find a buyer for the camels. Ned and I were agreed not to sell them for slaughter. After all they had done for us, and the time we had spent with them, we had grown sentimental towards them. The thought of them being put to the knife was out of the question. Ideally, they should be returned to Ghadames, where they could enjoy a more peaceful existence. I telephoned Mohammed Ali to see if he could ask the Mehari Club whether it was interested in buying back the five camels. The voice at the other end of the line, awash with static, was unmistakable.

'Mr Justin? Ohhhhh, Mr Justin! Really, I am in good condition to hear you. Believe me, I am not expecting this, *alhamdulillah*. How are you? Fine? How is Mr Ned? Where are you? How is your journey? Oh my God, how are your camels? Fine?' After a minute or two of greetings, I outlined the idea to him. He sounded enthusiastic and grateful we had thought of returning the camels to Ghadames. 'This is very, very kind offer from you, believe me,' he replied. 'Thanks a lot for this, number one. Number two, really we are very glad to buy the camels from you.' I suggested a price to him and he said he would consult Abu Amama, the head of the Mehari Club, that afternoon. We could speak later that night.

While we waited for an answer, we visited the British Consul's residence, a building just off the corniche that still maintained a faded imperial grandeur. Overlooking the harbour, it had originally housed the Italian Admiral of the Fleet and for a period during the Second World War had been commandeered by Montgomery. In the long hall that stretched through the house we discovered a copy of the letter sent by the Foreign Secretary Lord Palmerston on 30 November 1849, requesting that James Richardson's second expedition into the African interior be given 'every assistance and protection'.

> Mr Richardson will be accompanied by two Prussian Gentlemen, Dr Barth, a distinguished African Traveller and a

member of the University of Berlin, and Dr Overweg, a Geologist and a member of the Geographical Society of Berlin. These Gentlemen have been selected by the Prussian Government to accompany Mr Richardson; but they are equally with Mr Richardson travelling on the Service and under the Protection of the British Government.

The Central African Expedition of 1849–55 brought back much new information, solved several geographical puzzles and confirmed Henry Barth as one of the great African explorers of the nineteenth century. In that sense it was a huge success. But the price was high. Six of the eight Europeans who took part in it never returned. Adolph Overweg died near Lake Chad and Richardson succumbed to fever and exhaustion on 4 March 1851 in Ungurutuwa, six days' march from Kukawa, west of Lake Chad. 'My way of looking at things was not quite the same as that of my late companion, and we had therefore often had little differences,' wrote Barth as he gazed sadly at the Englishman's grave beneath a fig tree, 'but I esteemed him highly for the deep sympathy which he felt for the sufferings of the native African, and deeply lamented his death.' Richardson's epitaph is best left to A. Adu Boahen, who in 1964 wrote a history of British exploration in the Sahara. 'He was tactless, impatient, irascible, and indeed too fanatical to succeed,' he argued. 'But he stood for a definite cause, and for this cause he died. His name is certainly worthy to stand beside those of Wilberforce, Clarkson, and Livingstone in the annals of the abolition of the slave trade and slavery in Africa.'

Back in the hotel, Mohammed Ali called on time. 'Abu Amama and the club, really they are in good condition and now they are glad with you because you remembered them,' he boomed. 'They are feeling excellent about this and they know you like the camels too much.'

He was in full flow. 'They say nobody finds a man like you. You want to help the camels and really they like this. Abu Amama is too afraid someone will kill the camels in Kufra. Maybe they will eat them also. The club is ready to buy them now. Small problem. They do not have any money. Now they have paid for new camels. But Abu Amama like your camels. Maybe we can reduce the price. Believe me, we are all glad and you are very welcome and now really we are shy with you.'

I tried to make sense of all this and told him I would consult Taher, to see if he might buy the animals instead. This would be another way of getting them back to Ghadames. 'Yes, this is good idea for the camels,' Mohammed agreed. 'Now they will go home, *inshallah*.' I went across to Taher's office and found him smartly turned out in a three-piece suit and recovered from a heavy flu. He was immediately interested in the proposition. Libya's fledgling tourist industry had been developing steadily for several years and Taher's business was expanding fast. He now wanted his own camels to hire out to tourists. We would be happy to sell them to him, I said, provided they would be used only for riding (as Richardson had specified on selling his). That was not a problem.

Negotiating a price was more difficult. Taher knew we had to leave Libya in the next couple of days because the visas he had renewed for us were about to expire. We had left the camels in Kufra and, since we wanted to sell them only for riding, rather than for meat – the camel's usual lot in Libya – there was little room for manoeuvre now we were in Tripoli. Once again, as we had been when we bought the animals, we were a captive market. Over several glasses of tea and late in the night, we negotiated who would pay the outstanding bill at the camel market (Ned and I), who would bear the transportation costs (Ned and I), and finally agreed a greatly reduced price (we are still waiting to be paid at the time of writing). Gobber, Bobbles, Asfar, Lebead and The Big White were destined for Ghadames.

I telephoned Mohammed Ali to thank him for all his help. He had been our most constant and supportive friend in Libya. Without his assistance in Ghadames we might never have started the journey. He had visited us after our first week in the desert, bringing supplies for the camels and new trainers for Abd al

Wahab and now we were back in Tripoli he was doing his best to help us again. I told him everything had been arranged with Taher. The five camels would be returning home. He was delighted. We said our goodbyes.

'Really, I am afraid and shy you are leaving,' he began. 'But now you are in good condition because you have made your journey and always you will be welcome in Ghadames. One day, *inshallah*, you will return.' I thanked him for the last time. 'Mr Justin,' he said, before we hung up, 'now we are not friends. We are brothers.'

I sat down in the hotel lobby, beneath a portrait of Gaddafi astride a handsome white stallion, and for the first time understood our journey was over. The final conversation with Mohammed brought it home to me. Already, the satisfaction of having completed a 1,150-mile trek across the Libyan Sahara was succumbing to regret at having to leave. Here in the capital we were a world away from that great, silent wilderness. The weary rhythm of days marching across plains and struggling up and down shifting mountains of sand had been broken for good. I missed the desert wind, fizzing over the dunes, the cushioned pad-padding of the camels, even the shivering nights beneath the glacial stars. Above all, I missed the space and silence, the vast landscapes undisturbed by man, the shroud of stillness over the barren earth. Throughout the journey we had complained about many things: the monotony of our food; the discomfort of riding a camel for several hours at a time; the misery of rising before the sun. None of that mattered now. I would have exchanged all the comforts of civilization willingly for the chance to remain in the Sahara. I had read enough about the desert to know how those who travelled in it became its captives and wondered how this could be. Now I understood.

Such is the spell the desert casts on all those who enter. Rosita Forbes experienced this powerful urge to return before she had even left the shores of North Africa. 'I lay on my back and looked at the stars, weighing the balance of success and failure and, suddenly, I felt that this was not really the end,' she wrote in

February 1921, after her daring journey to Kufra. 'Some time, somehow, I knew not where or when, but most assuredly when Allah willed, I should come back to the deserts and the strange, uncharted tracks would bear my camels south again.'

Even the robust Richardson was subdued by the knowledge his first, eight-and-a-half-month expedition was over. He tried consoling himself with the calculation that in eighty days' travelling he had covered 1,600 miles. Moreover, his expenses had totalled only £50, compared with the £3,000 spent by the British government on the Lyon and Ritchie expedition, 'whose journey did not extend further south than mine, nor did they, indeed, penetrate so completely into The Sahara as I have done'. But these reflections were little consolation now he had left the desert behind. Stretching out under a palm tree in a garden next to the British Consul's residence, he watched 'with a silent melancholy the last departing rays of the sun. I then thought all over my journey, beginning with the beginning and ending with the end, all the incidents of the route from first to last, and all the privations and sufferings I had undergone – praying to and thanking the Almighty for having delivered me from every ill and every danger.' Richardson was unable to resist the call of the desert for his second expedition. It cost him his life.

The great Wilfred Thesiger, hardly a man prone to sentimentalism, felt a stab of sorrow as he left Arabia. He considered his departure to be a form of exile. 'I knew that I had made my last journey in the Empty Quarter and that a phase in my life was ended,' he wrote in *Arabian Sands*. 'Here in the desert I had found all that I asked; I knew that I should never find it again.'

The ferry to Malta pulled out of Tripoli harbour the next afternoon. From the deck I stared back towards the murmuring city. To the forefront, reflecting their historical precedence, were the grand colonial buildings of the Turkish and Italian embassies, their flags flapping in the breeze. Behind them, half-hidden in the shimmering haze, were the overhanging palm trees that lined the old corniche. It was an elegant skyline in which Christian and Muslim alike had left their mark. The Italian cathedral with its

345

graceful dome presided over one small part of town. Slim minarets dominated the rest, tapering into the sky, from where the
*muaddin* called forth the faithful to prayer in measured, mournful
tones. On the other side of the city, the squat castle stared out
across the sea. Tripoli, Bride of the Sea and gateway to the desert,
steamed beneath the sun, a brilliant, dazzling white. The great
slave market was no more. Ships no longer plied the Mediterranean with their wretched cargoes. The caravan routes themselves had ceased to exist. Only the desert remained unchanged.
Somewhere out there, to the south of Tripoli, began the rolling
infinity of sand and rock we had crossed.

On the deck, heavily made-up matrons prowled up and down,
fretting over gangs of charging children. A solitary man smoked
a cigarette and stared into the fabric of the retreating city. Next
to me, a group of Filipinos chatted away in Tagalog. I stayed on
deck and watched and waited until the city, floating on the horizon, was finally lost to sight.

# Bibliography

Arnold, Guy, *The Maverick State: Gaddafi and the New World Order*, Cassell, 1996

Asher, Michael, 'Camels', a private article for the Royal Geographical Society

Awdi, Bibi, 'Southern Route to Kufra: From El Fasher to Senusi and back with Al Dinar's Caravan 1915–1916', *Sudan Notes and Records* (5), 1922

Badoglio, Pietro, *Italy in the Second World War*, trans. Muriel Currey, Oxford University Press, 1948

Bagnold, R. A., *Libyan Sands: Travel in a Dead World*, Immel, 1993

Barth, Henry, *Travels and Discoveries in North and Central Africa: being a journal of an expedition undertaken under the auspices of H.B.M.'s Government, in the years 1849–55*, Ward, Lock & Co., 1890

Bey, A. M. Hassanein, *The Lost Oases*, Thornton Butterworth, 1925

Bey, A. M. Hassanein, 'Through Kufra to Darfur', *Geographical Journal*, vol. LXIV, Royal Geographical Society, 1924

Boahen, Albert Adu, *Britain, the Sahara, and the Western Sudan, 1788–1861*, Clarendon Press, 1964

Bovill, E. W., *Caravans of the Old Sahara*, Oxford University Press, 1933

Bovill, E. W., *The Golden Trade of the Moors*, Oxford University Press, 1970

Briggs, Lloyd Cabot, *Tribes of the Sahara*, Harvard University Press, 1960

Burton, Captain Sir Richard Francis, *Personal Narrative of a Pilgrimage to Al-Madinah and Meccah*, Dover Publications, 1964

Chapelle, Jean, *Nomades noirs du Sahara*, Plon, 1957

Cooley, John K., *Libyan Sandstorm: The Complete Account of Qadafi's Revolution*, Sidgwick & Jackson, 1983

Denham, Dixon, *Narrative of Travels and Discoveries in Northern and Central Africa, in the years 1822, 1823, and 1824, by Major Denham, Captain Clapperton and the late Doctor Oudney*, London, 1828

Duveyrier, Henri, *Les Touareg du Nord*, Challamel aîné, 1864

Evans-Pritchard, E. E., *The Sanusi of Cyrenaica*, London, 1949

Féraud, L. Charles, *Annales Tripolitaines*, Vuibert, 1927

Fisher, Godfrey, *Barbary Legend: War, Trade and Piracy in North Africa 1415–1830*, Clarendon Press, 1957

Fleming, Fergus, *Barrow's Boys*, Granta, 1998

Forbes, Rosita, *The Secret of the Sahara: Kufara*, Cassell, 1921

Forbes, Rosita, 'Across the Libyan Desert to Kufara', *Geographical Journal*, vol. LVIII, No. 2, August, 1921

Furlong, Charles Wellington, *The Gateway to the Sahara*, Darf, 1985

Al Gaddafi, Muammar, *The Green Book*, 1976

Gemery, Henry A. and Hogendorn, Jan S. (eds), *The Uncommon Market: Essays in the Economic History of the Atlantic Slave Trade*, Academic Press, 1975

Herodotus, *The Histories of Herodotus*, trans. George Rawlinson, Dutton, 1964

Holmes, Richard, *Coleridge: Early Visions*, Hodder & Stoughton, 1989

Horneman, Frederick, *The Journal of Frederick Horneman's Travels from Cairo to Mourzouk, the Capital of the Kingdom of Fezzan in Africa, in the Years 1797–8*, Darf, 1985

Hufnagl, Ernst, *Libyan Mammals*, Oleander Press, 1972

Kirwan, L. P., 'Rome beyond the southern Egyptian frontier', *Geographical Journal*, Vol. 123, RGS, March 1957

Kirwan, L. P., 'Roman Expeditions to the Upper Nile and the Chad-Darfur Region', British Institute of History and Archaeology in East Africa

Lawrence, T. E., *Seven Pillars of Wisdom*, Jonathan Cape, 1935

Lyon, George Francis, *A Narrative of Travels in Northern Africa in the years 1818, 19 and 20*, accompanied by geographical notices of Soudan, and of the course of the Niger, with a chart of the routes, and a variety of coloured plates, illustrative of the costumes of the several natives of Northern Africa, Darf, 1985

Leo, Johannes, *A Geographical Historie of Africa*, London, 1600, Da Capo Press, 1969

University of Libya, Faculty of Arts, 'Libya in History', Historical Conference, March 16–23, 1968

Montgomery, James, Grahame, James, Benger, E., *Poems on the Abolition of the Slave Trade*, 1809

Nachtigal, Gustav, *Sahara and Sudan*, trans. Allan G. B. Fisher and Humphrey J. Fisher, C. Hurst & Company, 1974

Pesce, Angelo, *Gemini Space Photographs of Libya and Tibesti: A Geological and Geographical Analysis*, Petroleum Exploration Society of Libya, 1968

Pliny, *Natural History*, trans. H. Rackham, Heinemann, 1942

Public Records Office, Foreign Office papers on the slave trade and correspondence between London and Tripoli: FO 76 22, FO 78 5327, FO 84 1512, FO 101 16, FO 101 23, FO 101 26, FO 101 30, FO 101 34, FO 101 36, FO 101 45, FO 101 66, FO 160 33, FO 335 15, FO 335 40

Raven, Susan, *Rome in Africa*, Routledge, 1993

Richardson, James, *Travels in the Great Desert of Sahara in the Years of 1845 and 1846*, Frank Cass & Co. Ltd., 1970

Rodd, Francis Rennell, *People of the Veil*, Macmillan, 1926

Rohlfs, Gerhard, *Kufra: Reise von Tripolis nach der Oase Kufra*, F. A. Brockhaus, 1881

Rolls, S. C., *Steel Chariots in the Desert*, Jonathan Cape, 1937

Salem, M. J. and Busrewil, M. T. (eds), *The Geology of Libya*, Academic Press, 1980

Shaw, William Kennedy, *Long Range Desert Group: The Story of its Work in Libya 1940–1943*, Collins, 1945

Shakespeare, William, *Complete Works of William Shakespeare*, HarperCollins, 1994

Sheppard, Tom, *Desert Expeditions*, Royal Geographical Society Expedition Advisory Centre, 1988

Simons, Geoff, *Libya: The Struggle for Survival*, Macmillan, 1996

Strabo, *The Geography of Strabo*, trans. Horace Leonard Jones, William Heinemann, 1932

Strachey, Lytton, *Eminent Victorians*, Bloomsbury, 1988

Tacitus, *The Annals of Tacitus*, trans. G. G. Ramsay, John Murray, 1904

Thesiger, Wilfred, *Arabian Sands*, HarperCollins, 2000

Thomas, Hugh, *The Slave Trade: The History of the Atlantic Slave Trade 1440–1870*, Picador, 1997

Todd, Mabel Loomis, *Tripoli the Mysterious, Dar Al Fergiani*, Tripoli, 1994

Tully, Miss, *Narrative of a ten year's residence at Tripoli in Africa*, from the possession of the family of the late Richard Tully, Esq., the British consul, comprising authentic memoirs and anecdotes of the reigning Bashaw, his family, and other persons of distinction, also, an account of the domestic manner of the Moors, Arabs, and Turks, Darf, 1983

Vandewalle, Dirk, *Libya Since Independence: Oil and State-Building*, I. B. Tauris, 1998

Ward, Philip, *Sabratha: A Guide for Visitors*, Oleander Press, 1970

Ward, Philip, *Touring Libya: The Eastern Provinces*, Faber and Faber, 1969

Ward, Philip, *Touring Libya: The Southern Provinces*, Faber and Faber, 1968

Ward, Philip, *Touring Libya: The Western Provinces*, Faber and Faber, 1967

Ward, Philip, *Tripoli: Portrait of a City*, Oleander Press, 1969

Wilberforce, William, The Speeches of William Wilberforce Esq on the Abolition of the Slave Trade [House of Commons debate on a motion for abolition of slave trade, May 12, 1789], London 1789

Wilson, R. T., *The Camel*, Longman, 1984

Wright, H. C. Seppings, *Two Years under the Crescent*, Darf, 1985

Wright, John, *Libya*, Ernest Benn Ltd, 1969

Wright, John, *Libya: A Modern History*, Croom Helm, 1982

Wright, John, *Libya, Chad and the Central Sahara*, 1989

# Index

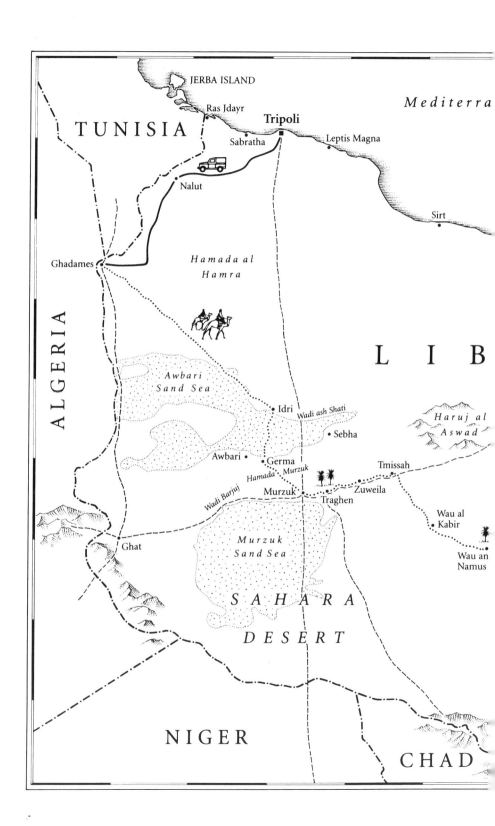